The International Struggle Over Iraq

A project supported by the
International Peace Academy

The International Struggle Over Iraq

Politics in the UN Security Council 1980–2005

David M. Malone

OXFORD
UNIVERSITY PRESS

OXFORD
UNIVERSITY PRESS

Great Clarendon Street, Oxford OX2 6DP

Oxford University Press is a department of the University of Oxford.
It furthers the University's objective of excellence in research, scholarship,
and education by publishing worldwide in

Oxford New York

Auckland Cape Town Dar es Salaam Hong Kong Karachi
Kuala Lumpur Madrid Melbourne Mexico City Nairobi
New Delhi Shanghai Taipei Toronto

With offices in

Argentina Austria Brazil Chile Czech Republic France Greece
Guatemala Hungary Italy Japan South Korea Poland Portugal
Singapore Switzerland Thailand Turkey Ukraine Vietnam

Oxford is a registered trade mark of Oxford University Press
in the UK and in certain other countries

Published in the United States
by Oxford University Press Inc., New York

First published 2006
First published in paperback 2007

A catalogue record for this title is available from the British Library

Library of Congress Cataloging in Publication Data

Malone, David, 1954–

The international struggle over Iraq: politics in the UN Security
Council 1980–2005/ David M. Malone.
p.cm.
Includes bibliographical references and index.
ISBN-13: 978-0-19-927857-2 (alk. paper)
ISBN-10: 0-19-927857-1 (alk. paper)
1. United Nations.–Peace-keeping forces. 2. United Nations–Iraq.
3. United Nations. Security Council–History. 4. Iraq–Foreign realtions–1979–1991.
5. Iraq–Foreign relations –1991– I. Title.
JZ4971.M32 2006
341.23′567–dc22

2006005532

Typeset by SPI Publisher Services, Pondicherry, India
Printed in Great Britain by Ashford Colour Press Ltd, Gosport, Hampshire

ISBN 978-0-19-927857-2 (Hbk.) 978-0-19-923868-2 (Pbk.)

10 9 8 7 6 5 4 3 2 1

Dedication

For the members of the Board of the International Peace Academy and my remarkable former colleagues there, with warm appreciation for their constant support and encouragement.

Foreword

Terje Rød-Larsen
President, International Peace Academy

The present monograph is an extraordinary book, both substantively and in terms of what it manifests: David M. Malone—diplomat, academic, journalist, and policy-maker—adds this latest work to his long list of outstanding contributions that have spanned the length of his tenure as President of the International Peace Academy (IPA) in New York. In it, David Malone investigates in great depth a two-fold story. On one level, this book is about Iraq and its complex and conflict-ridden history over the past quarter of a century. On another level, this is a book that sheds much light on the Security Council, its response to renewed or persistent crises, and the evolution of its approaches, interpretations, practices, and actions over the same period. In this sense, with its dual analysis, this book makes an important and timely contribution to our understanding of present-day international relations.

As I write this foreword, Iraq remains as high as ever on the international agenda, continuing to be a critical and complex issue. In spite of the ongoing transition from US-led occupation to Iraqi sovereignty and self-rule, the country witnessed continued spasms of extreme violence and prolonged difficulties with the formation of a new government in the aftermath of the December 2005 elections. This is not a good omen for the future. It is a reminder of how difficult it is to establish a democratic political order and state structures and institutions in a society as alienated from the rule of law as Iraq.

The crisis of confidence that gripped the United Nations in 2004–2005 and that is described in chapter 8 also very much remains. The Organization has not yet fully recovered from the divisive debates and tensions that characterized the period preceding the invasion of Iraq and the months following it. Organizational confidence was, as David Malone describes in this book, severely shaken by the tragic bombing of UN headquarters in Baghdad on 19 August 2003, which affected many of us. The following year, after what was widely considered an outstanding tenure at the organization's helm, Secretary-General Kofi Annan would confront his *annus horribilis*. Even though there was some recovery, a broad crisis of confidence and of deadlocked reform efforts continued to prevail in and around the United Nations.

As both Iraq and the United Nations remain in crisis, the present book is a highly relevant and timely contribution. I would hope that its analysis and critique will be closely studied by the members of the Security Council and help to inform the next phase of Security Council involvement vis-à-vis Iraq. A "Middle Easterner" myself (by profession, not by origin), I am delighted that we publish this volume in what will perhaps turn out to be the most crucial year for Iraq over the past twenty-five years. At the same time, as David Malone reminds us on the first page of the following manuscript, while the current ferment in the Middle East and in Iraq specifically may strike us as particularly acute, conditions there have been at least as lethal and geo-strategically threatening in other eras gone by. In consequence, I should stress that this book's longer-term approach, distanced and yet so close to its subject matter, is what makes it so outstanding and so valuable.

The fact that David Malone's academic and conceptual work has not stopped since he has left IPA to re-join the Canadian diplomatic service as Assistant Deputy Minister dealing with Global Issues is perhaps the best testimony to his outstanding personal qualities and academic talents. I would therefore like to seize the opportunity to pay tribute to the author of this volume: outstanding diplomat, respected academic, brilliant writer. David has all of these qualities.

IPA's work would not be possible without the support of our donors. Academic work of policy relevance can only blossom if it is cherished, sustained and buttressed by those who believe in it, and who should believe in it, because they ultimately benefit from it. I should therefore like to express our deep gratitude to the governments of Denmark, Switzerland, Sweden, Norway, the Ford Foundation, the Hewlett Foundation, our board members and other individual donors supporting our work. These governments, departments, and foundations have persistently provided their support and assistance, and thus make possible the publication of books as outstanding and important as the present study.

Preface to the Paperback Edition

As I write these lines in mid-2007, eighteen months after the events documented in the volume were drawn to an arbitrary close, all too little has changed for the good in Iraq. Indeed, intercommunal and other tensions have now crystallized into what many see as an embryonic civil war that could lead to a split-up of the country.

On the international level, however, a number of developments suggest a return to more consultative, mutually accommodating approaches by major countries to the management of international crises, not least because the unilateral route has proved one fraught with risk, and those risks have involved very significant costs. Nevertheless, on several questions addressed in part through UN Security Council decision-making, notably on Kosovo, differences among the Permanent Five (P-5) members have flared up anew, with the Russian Federation more assertive in the promotion of its perspectives. (China, on the other hand, was exhibiting a greater degree of sensitivity to the perspectives of others, notably on Darfur.)

This volume aims to shed light on the policy and actions of key countries in the sphere of international security as refracted through decisions of the Security Council. The Council's significance needs to be assessed not in isolation—from that perspective, it would be adjudged by most as fairly modest—but rather as a nodal forum in the conduct of international diplomacy that is constantly shifting from one set of bilateral discussions to another, one multilateral forum to another. While policy is set nationally (influenced by a multiplicity of factors), the frequent need or preference for mandating (and legitimizing) Security Council resolutions often encourages efforts at conciliation of national approaches in the absence of which, as the countries forming the international Coalition in Iraq as of 2003 were to discover, the costs of intervention and the risks associated with it can rise precipitously.

But it is important to emphasize—as the subsequent account makes clear—that domestic politics and national interests (where present) play the central role in determining the international posture of states. If only for that reason, this volume refers often to the domestic drivers of the foreign and defence policy of key states in relation to Iraq.

This preface discusses some recent developments relevant to Iraq and to the Security Council. It also touches on some notable recent contributions to the literature. The views expressed here, as in the main body of this volume, are my own alone and not those of my employer, the Government of Canada.

Iraq

At the time of this volume's publication in June 2006, immediate prospects for Iraq looked grim. Today this is more the case than ever, with the added dimension that differences have hardened among and within two of the principal contending communities: the Shi'a and the Sunnis. While a number of Kurdish politicians, not least Iraqi President Jalal Talabani, have sought to reconcile Kurdish interests with those of other Iraqis, a trend towards greater autonomy (perhaps one-day independence) for the Kurdish provinces has set in, not least because they have been at relative peace while elsewhere violence has continued to flare—even in areas earlier thought to have been largely pacified, such as Basra.

As the patience of the US electorate with an unsatisfactory situation on the ground in Iraq eroded, a trend towards blaming Iraqis and their leadership(s) for these unhappy circumstances took root in the USA.[1] The frustration was justified to the extent that the Iraqi government, under Prime Minister Nouri al-Maliki, remained weak and unable to extend its writ very far, challenged as it was by militias of all sorts, notably those of the Shi'a.[2] However, it was increasingly questionable whether a strong Iraqi government capable of uniting Iraqis could emerge as long as the Coalition, under US leadership, continued to call many of the shots, notably on security strategy.

The toll in casualties continued to be frightening, regardless of the security strategy of the day. While the 'surge' in US military numbers deployed in Iraq initiated in late 2006 seemed for a time capable of making a difference, by mid-2007 violence was continuing to claim large numbers of Iraqi lives and an undiminished number of American ones, as fighters on the ground adjusted to new strategies, constraints, and opportunities.[3]

The lack of domestic traction of the Maliki government in Iraq was disappointing, not least its seeming incapacity to challenge effectively the excessive influence of militias of all sorts. Civilian Iraq deaths in 2006 were estimated by the UN at 34,452, while Coalition combat deaths see-sawed in early 2007 at a higher rate than in 2006.[4] Oil production remained well below its pre-2003 levels at roughly 2 million barrels per day with the sharing of oil wealth emerging as a flashpoint in relations among Iraqi communities.[5]

Coalition policy on Iraq continued to favour a united country constitutionally organized along a federal model, with a democratic form of government, but influential voices in Washington frequently called for greater Kurdish autonomy—some indeed for independence—creating the impression that should circumstances on the ground so dictate, the USA might contemplate withdrawing militarily into the Kurdish provinces, concentrating its regional military presence in one or several bases there and a continued strong presence in the Gulf. *Faute de mieux*, calls for a 'soft partition' in Iraq, however risky, were increasingly heard.[6]

The UK, which had earlier hoped to leave Basra pacified, announced a draw-down of troops in 2006 amidst continuing, probably growing, violence there as local politics diverged sharply from Coalition objectives. Continued shrinkage of the allied portion of the Coalition, with a few striking exceptions such as significant Australian re-engagement on the ground, accelerated.

The Region

Neighbours of Iraq, and the broader Middle East, continued to be greatly affected by, and anxious about, the country's turmoil.[7]

Although the extent of Iran's involvement in the internal affairs of Iraq was disputed, and the degree of its influence over Iraq's disparate Shi'a actors was particularly so, Iran's growing regional salience unsettled many at a time when its nuclear energy programmes and its resistance to international monitoring thereof had led to the imposition of (modest) Security Council-mandated sanctions against it. Heightened fears arose elsewhere in the region that Iran was asserting a threatening (or potentially threatening) capacity to dominate its subregion, including the politically and economically hypersensitive Gulf. Further, Iran's role as a patron of Hizbollah in Lebanon, widely seen to have wrestled Israel to a draw in the conflict between the two that unfolded in July and August

2006, gave its position added weight. But the internationally isolated position in which its nuclear policies had placed it by mid-2007 gave rise to apprehension within the country, fearful of further sanctions and even of military attack.[8]

The 2006 conflict between Israel and Hizbollah in Lebanon seemed also to strengthen the hand of Syria, previously under much international pressure in relation to the assassination of former Lebanese Prime Minister Rafiq Hariri in 2005. The deadlocked Palestinian political situation (as between a Hamas majority in the Palestinian parliament and Fatah) left Palestinians in deep economic and social distress and Israel with no broadly based Palestinian political partner it was willing to engage. Further, a sense of political drift developed in some traditionally moderate Arab countries, notably Egypt, and a more assertive Saudi role emerged in crafting regional strategies with which its traditional Western friends were not always comfortable, introducing new elements of uncertainty in the region.[9]

The Iraq Study Group, led by Washington grandees James Baker and Lee Hamilton across party lines, reported in October 2006, inter alia, recommending that Washington establish a dialogue with Syria and Iran, at first seemed destined to be ignored by the US Administration.[10] But, over time, several regional meetings were held, involving the Iraqi and American governments and those of Iran and Syria. They yielded little of substance, with a large-scale international conference involving sixty countries convened in Sharm el Sheikh in May 2007 viewed by observers as particularly vapid. More meaningfully perhaps, bilateral discussions on the situation in Iraq were initiated by Iran and the USA at senior levels in Baghdad on 28 May 2007.

Thus the international and regional calculus on Iraq had reached a perilous equilibrium: fear of a sudden or at least arbitrary Coalition withdrawal from Iraq was increasingly balanced by a realization that Iraqis could and would only take their affairs decisively in hand once free of outside involvement. Former UN Special Envoy in Iraq, Lakhdar Brahimi, made clear in May 2006 that serious engagement by regional actors

> simply will not happen as long as Washington seeks to determine what roles international actors should play and how. Active engagement on Iraq will only become attractive to non-coalition countries and multilateral organizations if they can chart their own path freely, alongside Iraqis and the coalition. There is little sign yet that the US is prepared to promote such an overtly freewheeling process.[11]

From a different perspective, Richard Perle seemed to agree, arguing on CNN that: 'The biggest mistake was not turning political authority over to the Iraqis immediately when Baghdad fell.'[12]

But as time moves on, casualties mount, and political realities evolve in Washington as elsewhere, a shift away from American dominance in Iraq is inevitably drawing closer.[13] Discussion of a more meaningful role of the UN in the run-up to that contingency intensified in early 2007, stimulated in part by the worrying large refugee outflows from Iraq with which the UN High Commissioner for Refugees was increasingly being asked to deal.[14] But, despite energetic posturing in Congress and elsewhere, a lack of real urgency marked the Washington debate. Philip Stephens describes

> [a] broader, unspoken consensus within the foreign policy establishment that it will be for the next occupant of the White House to extricate the US from the sectarian fighting. For now, just as the president refuses to admit that the war is lost, so his political opponents decline to contemplate the consequences of admitting defeat.[15]

International Relations in mid-2007

In some respects, the balance of international relations in mid-2007 had changed little, but a number of developments were significant. Congressional elections in the USA brought the Democratic Party to majority both in the Senate and in the House of Representatives, a strong showing owing a great deal to dissatisfaction among Americans with the situation in Iraq. The Democratic leadership was soon engaged in efforts to constrain the President's Iraq policy and to embarrass the Republican administration over past political and administrative decisions.

Several architects of (or more modestly, contributors to) the Bush Administration's stance on Iraq in 2002 and 2003 turned on the Administration, excoriating its incompetence in implementing their ideas. A number of them also turned on each other. Although its military might continued to far outstrip that of any potential conventional adversary or grouping of adversaries, US standing internationally was much affected by the situation in Iraq.

Indeed, some commentators saw in the US failure to prevail there a possible turning point in its international fortunes, for example, equating it with the long-term consequences of rash UK and French policies over the control of the Suez Canal in 1956.[16] Other respected voices saw Iraq as only one element in the broader flow of history, perhaps ultimately a blip on the screen.[17]

In the UK, Prime Minister Blair, whose strong domestic policy legacy was seen as hobbled by the Iraq war, resigned on 28 June 2007. In France, a

President sympathetic to the USA (if critical of its Iraq venture), Nicolas Sarkozy, was elected in May 2007 and appointed as Foreign Minister Bernard Kouchner, one of the few French political figures, and a socialist at that, who had been supportive on humanitarian grounds of Saddam Hussein's overthrow. German Chancellor Angela Merkel, a tough critic of the Russian Federation's approach to human rights, sought to develop better relations with Washington. As President Putin's second term drew to an end, Moscow's rhetoric grew rougher, particularly with respect to European issues, while China moderated its unquestioning support for the government of Sudan accused of complicity with warm crimes in Darfur.

Thus, while the situation in Iraq itself remained profoundly discouraging, the exit of several of the leaders centrally involved in the corrosive 2003 international debate over Iraq, outlined in Chapter 7 of this book, may introduce an element of fluidity into international relations that could prove helpful to securing happier outcomes in Iraq and its anxious region.[18]

The Security Council

On Iraq, the Security Council continued to maintain a low profile, 'at the request of the Government of Iraq', extending its cover for Coalition operations there until December 2007.[19] The Council continued to comment extensively on other crisis situations and to issue myriad resolutions. Its zeal for cross-cutting thematic discussions continued to diminish and it reverted increasingly to its traditional methods of work, situation by situation, crisis by crisis—although the UK's controversial decision to champion Council consideration of climate change in April 2007 might suggest otherwise.[20]

To cover the withdrawal of combatants from the wreckage of the Israeli–Hizbollah fighting in 2006, the Council reconfigured and significantly expanded the presence of its previously ineffective peacekeeping operation in Southern Lebanon. And, after much negotiation and in a divided vote on 30 May 2007, the Council imposed under Chapter VII of the UN Charter (as it had the International Criminal Tribunals for the Former Yugoslavia and Rwanda in the mid-1990s) the establishment of an international tribunal (with Lebanese participation) to address the Hariri assassination.

In the face of continuing North Korean provocations, the Council in October 2006 adopted a unanimous resolution of exceptional severity calling upon North Korea to rejoin the Six-Party talks to defuse the crisis surrounding its nuclear weapons programme, which doubtless contributed to Pyongyang's decision to do so and to a de-escalation of the crisis in early 2007.[21] And the Council, not least through a process of intensive consultation in capitals, managed to retain unity on Iran's nuclear programme.

In 2005, a UN Summit had endorsed the concept of the Responsibility to Protect, as did, subsequently, the Council. By early 2007, the Council seemed eager to salvage its own credibility with respect to implementation of this principle on the Darfur crisis.[22] It had decided in 2006 that the UN should take over responsibility for international monitoring in Darfur from the African Union and in May 2007 considered a plan to make this happen.[23] The most high-profile of the four cases on the docket of the International Criminal Court in 2007 related to Darfur further to a decision in 2005 by both China and the USA, to swallow their hostility to the Court and to allow referral to it of the findings of a Security Council-mandated expert panel on serious crimes committed in relation to Darfur.[24]

For some years, a number of countries, most consistently the USA, had been pressing for improved human rights performance in Myanmar (formerly Burma) and had sought to involve the Council in discussing the matter. While the human rights situation in Myanmar is indisputably bad, several Council members were highly resistant to the Council's involvement. As a procedural matter, the USA was able (by a vote of 10 to 4, with one abstention) to have the issue placed on the Council's agenda.[25] But an effort to secure passage of a resolution upbraiding Myanmar was met by two vetoes on 13 January 2007. That China and Russia should vote against this resolution was less of a surprise than that they were joined by South Africa, a traditional ally of the USA at the UN, perhaps influenced by the divisive debate on UN Reform dating back to 2005, in which South Africa and the USA had often come to be opposed.[26] The result was widely seen as counterproductive for the resolution's sponsors.

The permanent status of Kosovo, a delicate diplomatic challenge deferred in 1999, came to a head in early 2007 with publication of a report by UN Special Envoy Martii Ahtisaari.[27] He recommended that after a period of international supervision, Kosovo should become substantively independent. Moscow soon threatened to veto a decision by the Council along these lines, but did not deter Western powers from circulating just such a draft resolution on 12 May 2007. Moscow's resolve seems unshaken for now.

The Council's dynamics evolved somewhat. China emerged as the 'swing' player, powered by substantive flexibility and the skill of the new wave of its diplomatic representatives. Its key role in the Six-Party talks on

North Korea boosted its profile, and its willingness to pressure the government of Sudan on Darfur added somewhat to its lustre. As noted above, Russia affected a growing sourness and abrasiveness in debate but often quietly proved quite collegial on issues such as Iran and Lebanon. The appointment of the emollient (if tough-minded) Zalmay Khalilzad to succeed the combative John Bolton as US Ambassador in early 2007 was widely welcomed.[28]

The Secretary-General

Kofi Annan's tenure as UN Secretary-General adversely affected in his second term by great power disagreements over Iraq, the results of the Oil for Food inquiry, and perhaps quite simply by exhaustion after an exceptionally accomplished first term crowned by the Nobel Peace Prize, ended on a subdued note.[29] Those contending for his succession were not widely seen as an exciting group, although Shashi Tharoor of India lent it personal panache as did Zeid bin Raad, Jordan's candidate who entered the race too late to establish his credentials. Ban Ki-Moon, Foreign Minister of South Korea, emerged as the winner, having run an effective campaign. Worries soon surfaced that he might prove oversensitive to the bidding of China and the USA, whose support he acknowledged as critical to his election. His early months in the job were widely criticized as listless. But it is much too early to make confident predictions about his ideas or ultimate success.[30]

Wide-ranging UN reform, which Kofi Annan had seen as the antidote to the UN's slough of despond in 2004/5, continued to elude the membership. Changes in the composition of the Security Council and in the workings of the veto seemed as far off as ever, with the cohesiveness of the group of four countries aspiring to permanent seats (Brazil, India, Germany, and Japan) appearing to fray. Administrative reform, always much resisted by vested interests, evinced little real progress. The new Secretary-General even experienced difficulty in securing agreement to his modest early proposals for restructuring of the secretariat.

The Literature

A number of very fine books relating to this story have appeared in English since late 2005. The one most satisfyingly combining scholarly rigour with narrative drive and sharp judgement is, to my mind, Thomas Ricks' *Fiasco: The American Military Adventure in Iraq*, which focuses largely on the tale of how Iraq policy in Washington developed after March 2003.[31] The backdrop to the USA's Iraq policy is discussed with great acuity in *Looming Tower: Al-Qaeda and the Road to 9/11* by Lawrence Wright.[32] A notable Iraqi contribution has been Ali A. Alawi's *The Occupation of Iraq: Winning the War, Losing the Peace*.[33]

On the UN, James Traub's terrific inquiry into Kofi Annan's leadership and the forces with which he contended for better and worse, *The Best Intentions: Kofi Annan in the Era of American World Power*, stands out.[34] More scholarly volumes that can be strongly recommended include *Making War & Building Peace* by Michael Doyle and Nicholas Sambanis; *The UN Security Council: Practice and Promise* by Edward C. Luck; *After Anarchy: Legitimacy & Power in the United Nations Security Council* by Ian Hurd;[35] and *Secretary or General: The UN Secretary-General in World Politics* edited by Simon Chesterman. The most thought-provoking book published of late on the UN is *UN Voices: The Struggle for Development and Social Justice* by Thomas Weiss, Tatiana Carayannis, Louis Emmerej, and Richard Jolly.[36] And a new book, *The Oxford Handbook on the United Nations* edited by Thomas Weiss and Sam Daws, features thoughtful contributions by many of the leading UN scholars of the decade.[37]

Envoi

The melancholy tale unfolded in the ensuing pages has no happy ending, not yet and perhaps never. Iraq was much oppressed by Saddam Hussein before 2003 and it is wracked by horrendous violence today that may portend an even more murderous civil war. The UN, at grips for many decades now with Iraq's often malign influence over security in the Middle East, suffered sharply in international opinion from its inability to avert war there in 2003 and from growing questions about its legitimacy as arbiter in international law and relations of the use of force.[38] (However, polling continued to suggest widespread support, including within the USA, for a central role of the UN in regulating war and peace.[39]) Weighed down by Iraq, the USA in 2007 was pursuing regional and international strategies once again rooted in greater cooperation and consultation with allies and other international partners, but often with limited results.

The optimistic calls of President George H. W. Bush in 1991 for a 'New World Order' seem distant indeed in 2007, with the Middle East in turmoil and relations among the permanent members of the Security Council often testy. That said, as outlined by the University of British Columbia's comprehensive 'Human Security Report' in 2005, conflict deaths globally had been much reduced since their cold war peaks, and economic growth was significantly reducing poverty in many parts of the globe, including large swathes of Asia (albeit at the cost of growing economic inequalities within societies and worrying changes to climate trends).[40]

Progress is rarely a linear phenomenon.

David M. Malone
New Delhi, July 2007

Notes

1. See Fareed Zakaria, 'What the Warriors Cannot Do', *Newsweek*, 5 March 2007. For a sharper attack on Iraq's body politic, see Charles Krauthammer, 'Past the Apogee: American Under Pressure', Foreign Policy Research Institute, 14 November 2006, available at www.fpri.org.
2. See 'Moktada al-Sadr's Gambit', *New York Times* editorial, 18 April 2007.
3. The military 'surge' tactic was reportedly complemented later by a US political strategy for Iraq. See Ann Scott Tyson, 'New Strategy for War Stresses Iraqi Politics: US Aims to Oust Sectarians from Key Roles', *Washington Post*, 23 May 2007.
4. On Iraqi deaths, see "Human Rights Report", January 2007, at www.uniraq.org. On US fatalities, see http://www.cnn.com. The US death rate in May 2007 was higher than for any month since November 2004, following on a very high rate also for April 2007.
5. See Javier Blas, 'Iraq to Pump First New Oil since Saddam's Fall', *Financial Times*, 16 May 2007. See also www.iraqupdates.com/p_articles.php/article/17603.
6. See, for example, Edward P. Joseph and Michael E. O'Hanlon, 'The Case for Soft Partition in Iraq', Saban Center Analysis, Washington, DC: Brookings Institution, Number 12, June 2007, available at http://www.brook.edu/fp/saban/analysis/june2007iraq_partition.htm.
7. See Egyptian Foreign Minister Ahmed Aboul Gheit's article 'In Iraq, the Stakes Are High on all Sides', *International Herald Tribune*, 18 May 2007.
8. See 'The Iran Plans: Would President Bush Go to War to Stop Iran from Getting the Bomb?', *New Yorker*, 17 April 2006. See also Michael Eisenstadt, 'Iran: The Complex Calculus of Preventive Military Action', The Washington Institute for Near East Policy, Policy Watch No. 1152, 25 September 2006 at www.washingtoninstitute.org; and 'Olmert Declines to Rule Out Military Action Against Iran', Haaretz, 9 December 2006.

9. A growing tension between Americans and Arabs over the distressed condition of the Middle East was perceptible in early 2007. For an illustration of the analytical divide, see David Brooks, 'A War of Narratives', *International Herald Tribune*, 10 April 2007 and Rami G. Khoury, 'Where Columnist David Brooks Went Wrong', *Daily Star* (Beirut), 12 April 2007.
10. The report, supported and published by the US Institute of Peace, can be drawn from www.usip.org/isg/iraq study group report (also available from Vintage Books).
11. Conclusions, *Iraq: Preventing a New Generation of Conflict*, Markus E. Bouillion, Ben Rowswell, and David M. Malone, Eds., Boulder, CO: Lynne Rienner, 2007, p. 310.
12. Quoted in Roger Cohen, 'The Failure of Iraq Captured in one Sentence', *International Herald Tribune*, 28–29 April. See also Simon Jenkins, 'Poor Iraq. First the Lies, Now Even Worse: More Help', *The Guardian*, 21 March 2007.
13. The International Crisis Group advocated a thoughtful multidimensional strategy to involve a broad range of actors, including the UN Security Council, in developing a design for Iraq's future. See, 'After Baker-Hamilton: What to Do in Iraq?', Middle East Report No. 60, 19 December 2006, available at http://www.crisisgroup.org.
14. Refugee outflows from Iraq were widely estimated as at least 2 million with nearly 2 million more displaced within Iraq itself. See, www.unhcr.org/iraq. See also, Barbara Crossette, 'Step by Step, the UN Expands in Iraq', UN Wire, 15 May 2007. See, Warren Hoge, 'UN Chief Isn't Discouraged by His Close Call in Iraq'; *International Herald Tribune*, 24 March 2007. (Ban Ki-Moon visited Iraq in March 2007 under mortar fire, reportedly with the purpose of establishing himself as a 'player' on the file. See UN Document SC/8974 Of 22 March 2007.)
15. Philip Stephens. 'America's Dismal Debate Brings Little Hope of Peace in Iraq', *Financial Times*, 20 April 2007.
16. Brian Urquhart, 'Disaster from Suez to Iraq', *New York Review of Books*, 54 (5), 29 March 2007.
17. Edward C. Luck, 'Iraq and the Future of the United Nations', *Literary Review of Canada*, 15 (3), April 2007.
18. Several secondary but important American figures in the Iraq story met with unhappy circumstances. Paul Wolfowitz, was pressured out of the World Bank presidency in May 2007 over ethical concerns but very much against a backdrop of resentment over his earlier role on Iraq. On the flight from personal responsibility and professional accountability of others, see Gideon Rachman 'Simplify, then Exaggerate: the Neo-cons' Route to Disaster', *Financial Times*, 16 January 2007. See also 'Sidelined by Reality: The Neocons Are Suffering One Humiliation after Another', Lexington, *The Economist*, 21 April 2007.

19. Security Council Resolution (SCR) 1723 of 28 November 2006. For a recent comprehensive UN report on Iraq, see UN Document S/2007/330 of 5 June 2007.
20. See 'UN Council Is Criticized for Debate of Climate', Associated Press dispatch in the *International Herald Tribune*, 19 April 2007.
21. SCR 1718 of 14 October 2006.
22. The Sudanese Government's decision in October 2006 to expel outspoken UN envoy in Khartoum Jan Pronk excited particular outrage, although the deaths in Darfur represent the strongest indictment of the government.
23. See SCR 1679 of 16 May 2006, adopted explicitly under Chapter VII of the UN Charter.
24. On 31 March 2005, the Security Council adopted SCR 1593, with 11 votes in favour, 0 against, and 4 abstentions, with the USA and China abstaining. On the first indictments, announced 27 February 2007 by the ICC Prosecutor, see, Press Release ICC-OTP-206 at http://www.icc-cpi.int.
25. See Security Council Report Update No. 4 of 27 September 2006, at http://www.securitycouncilreport.org.
26. See Peter Henlein, 'Russia, China Veto UN Resolution on Myanmar', *Voice of America*, 13 January 2007. See also Associated Press dispatch, 'Desmond Tutu "deeply disappointed" with South Africa's vote against UN Security Council Resolution on Myanmar', *International Herald Tribune*, 21 January 2007.
27. See UN Document S/2007/168.Add.1 of 27 March 2007.
28. Khalilzad's immediately previous tenure as US Ambassador in Iraq had been widely judged a uniquely successful one by many Iraqis to whom I have spoken.
29. Corporate fallout from the Oil for Food and related inquiries continued to claim casualties. See 'Admission by Chevron on Saddam kickbacks', *International Herald Tribune*, 9 May 2007. See also Claudia Rosett, 'UNder the Law: A Chance at a Bit of Justice in the Oil-for-Food Scandal', *National Review*, 17 January 2007.
30. Some were not so cautious. A *Newsweek* cover story dated 5 March 2007 confidently blared 'Bound to Fail: Secretary-General Ban Ki-Moon Has Taken on 'Mission Impossible' '.
31. New York: Penguin, 2006.
32. New York: Knopf, 2006.
33. New Haven, CT: Yale University Press, 2007.
34. New York: Farrar, Straus & Giroux, 2006.
35. Princeton, NJ: Princeton University Press, 2007.
36. Bloomington, IN: Indiana University Press, 2005.
37. Oxford: Oxford University Press, 2007. Several other fine volumes provide broader context: *Leashing the Dogs of War: Conflict Management in a Divided World*, Chester A. Crocker, Fen Osler Hampson, and Pamela All (eds.), Washington, DC: US Institute of Peace, 2007; and *Can Might Make Right: Building the Rule*

of Law After Military Interventions by Jane Stromseth, David Wippmann, and Rosa Brooks, Cambridge: Cambridge University Press, 2006;

38. See Ramesh Thakur, 'Law Versus Legitimacy at the UN: The UN Is Respected Today More for What It Represents and Symbolizes than for What It Actually Accomplishes', *The Hindu*, 11 May 2007.
39. See 'World Publics Favour New Powers for the UN', 26 May 2007, www.world publicopinion.org
40. www.humansecurityreport.info. The decline in conflict deaths continued through 2005 as documented in the Human Security Brief 2006 available at www.humansecuritycentre.org. On economic growth and development trends, see the IBRD's report 'Global Economic Prospects 2007: Managing the Next Wave of Globalization' available at http://econ.worldbank.org.

Contents

Acknowledgments

This writing project was launched during my last year at the helm of the International Peace Academy (IPA) in New York. I am tremendously indebted to the IPA Board, particularly its chair, Rita E. Hauser, for allowing me to undertake work that necessarily distracted me from the tasks for which I was primarily paid relating to the management of this terrific institution. My colleagues at IPA, notably its Vice President, Dr Necla Tschirgi, backfilled heroically, for which I shall always be grateful.

In order to get myself started—as many writers will recognize, often the single greatest challenge—I repaired to Nuffield College, Oxford, in April 2004 for five weeks of reading and developing a skeleton of this book. To the Warden and Fellows of this relaxed, civilized, and welcoming community, my heartfelt thanks. Professor Andrew Hurrell made this possible, and to him, as always, I am very grateful. My doctoral supervisor, Adam Roberts, the head of my own house at Oxford (Magdalen College), Tony Smith, and many others made this brief sojourn a highly productive and agreeable one.

In parallel to this writing project, I undertook for another publication a much shorter review of the UN's involvement in Iraq, writing with James D. Cockayne, a brilliant former student of mine at the New York University School of Law. That joint effort proved sufficiently happy and substantively rewarding that we have continued to publish together frequently. What started with my quest for research assistance has turned into an unusually fruitful research partnership. I am very grateful to him, above all else for challenging constantly my own view of events and for offering much better ones of his own, many of them reflected here. Relevant to this volume, and greatly enriching it, he prompted and then shaped my interest in the Council's drift into decision-making in a regulatory mode.

I am also greatly in debt of Maciek Hawrylak who has tirelessly checked my facts, tracked down others, suggested ideas, and prepared this manuscript for publication—no small task. Claudia Comeau and Françoise Paris, managing my office in Ottawa, were tremendously supportive throughout, as had been, earlier, Jilla Moazami in New York. Anna Pollock also helped greatly in reviewing proofs.

Simon Chesterman, Sebastian von Einsiedel, Tom Franck, Peter Hobbs, Nahid Mozaffari, and Ann Phillips all provided me with strong encouragement, and this has meant a great deal to me.

I completed this project after my return to the Canadian Foreign Service, and am grateful to many colleagues within it for their forbearance in accommodating my partiality to all developments Iraqi and UN-related as the writing progressed. I greatly admire the Deputy Minister of Foreign Affairs, Peter Harder, and our Associate Deputy Minister, Marie-Lucie Morin, for fostering an atmosphere within the Foreign Service in which scholarly inquiry and policy debate are actively encouraged.

A number of colleagues and friends have greatly influenced my thinking about the UN over the years and some of them are quoted in these pages. I always look forward to learning from Simon Chesterman, Elizabeth Cousens, Sam Daws, Michael Doyle, Gareth Evans, Tom Farer, Shepard Forman, Thomas M. Franck, Jeremy Greenstock, David Hannay, Paul Heinbecker, Michael Ignatieff, Jean-David Levitte, Edward Luck, Adam Roberts, John Ruggie, James Traub, Brian Urquhart, and Tom Weiss. I owe them a great deal.

A number of journalists, some of them quoted in these pages, have covered the UN with genuine distinction: Afsané Bassir Pour, Barbara Crossette, Raghida Dergham, Maggie Farley, Carola Hoyos, Edie Lederer, Evelyn Leopold, Corinne Lesnes, all impressive women, have shaped my understanding of events at the UN. From the male gender, Warren Hoge chronicles the UN with patrician discernment, Colum Lynch with a sharp mind and pen, Mark Turner with entrepreneurial flair. Successive BBC correspondents lavish the UN with much intelligent attention.

In Terje Roed Larsen, IPA has attracted a particularly distinguished and dynamic President. I am very grateful for his encouragement of this project.

In Ottawa, Margaret and Jim Mitchell have been endlessly supportive. Lucie and David Johnston in Montreal, and Cristina and Gyuri Karady in London, helped me maintain a modicum of perspective on the matters chronicled here, as they have for many years. I am very fortunate in their friendship.

I am also grateful to Dominic Byatt, who responded to the idea of this book with enthusiasm and who, with his colleagues at Oxford University Press, has seen it through to publication with the dynamism and care for which they are widely known and admired.

Finally, I should record that the views expressed in this volume are my own alone, and most definitely not those of the Canadian government.

Abbreviations

BMENA	Broader Middle East and Near Africa Initiative (US)
CEIP	Carnegie Endowment for International Peace
CIA	Central Intelligence Agency
CPA	Coalition Provisional Authority
CTC	Counterterrorism Committee
DFI	Development Fund for Iraq
DMZ	Demilitarized Zone
ECOWAS	Economic Community of West African States
EU	European Union
FLN	Front de libération nationale (Algeria)
G-8	Group of Eight
GCC	Gulf Cooperation Council
GRL	Goods Review List
HLP	High-level Panel on Threats, Challenges and Change
IAEA	International Atomic Energy Agency
ICC	International Criminal Court
ICJ	International Court of Justice
ICRC	International Committee of the Red Cross
ICTR	International Criminal Tribunal for Rwanda
ICTY	International Criminal Tribunal for the Former Yugoslavia
IECI	Independent Electoral Commission of Iraq
IFOR	Implementation Force (NATO in Bosnia)
IGC	Interim Governing Council (Iraq)
IIC	Independent Inquiry Committee into the United Nations Oil-for-Food Program
IMF	International Monetary Fund
INC	Iraqi National Congress
ISAF	International Security Assistance Force (NATO in Afghanistan)
KDP	Kurdish Democratic Party

KFOR	Kosovo Force
MINUSTAH	United Nations Stabilization Mission in Haiti
MINUCI	United Nations Mission in Côte d'Ivoire
MNF	Multinational Force
MONUC	United Nations Mission in the Democratic Republic of Congo
MOU	Memorandum of Understanding
NAM	Non-Aligned Movement
NATO	North Atlantic Treaty Organization
NGO	Nongovernmental organization
NSC	National Security Council
OAS	Organization of American States
OFF	Oil-for-Food program
OIC	Organization of the Islamic Conference
OIOS	Office of Internal Oversight Services (UN)
OIP	Office of the Iraq Programme (UN)
OMV	Ongoing Monitoring and Verification regime
ORHA	Office for Reconstruction and Humanitarian Assistance (US)
P-3	Permanent Three (Western members of the Security Council: France, UK, US)
P-5	Permanent Five (Members of the Security Council)
PKK	Kurdish Workers' Party
PLO	Palestinian Liberation Organization
POW	Prisoner of War
PUK	Patriotic Union of Kurdistan
SIPRI	Stockholm International Peace Research Institute
SC	UN Security Council
SCIRI	Supreme Council for Islamic Revolution in Iraq
SCR	Security Council Resolution
SOMO	State Oil Marketing Organization (Iraq)
SRSG	Special Representative of the Secretary-General
SWAPO	South West Africa People's Organization
TAL	Transitional Administrative Law (for Iraq)
UAE	United Arab Emirates
UK	United Kingdom of Great Britain and Northern Ireland
UN	United Nations
UNAMI	United Nations Assistance Mission for Iraq
UNCC	United Nations Compensation Commission
UNDP	United Nations Development Program

UNHCR	United Nations High Commissioner for Refugees
UNHUC	United Nations Humanitarian Urgency Council
UNICEF	United Nations Children's Fund
UNIIMOG	United Nations Iran-Iraq Military Observer Group
UNIKOM	United Nations Iraq-Kuwait Observation Mission
UNMOVIC	United Nations Monitoring, Verification, and Inspection Commission
UNOCI	United Nations Operation in Côte d'Ivoire
UNOHCI	United Nations Office of the Humanitarian Coordinator in Iraq
UNSCOM	United Nations Special Commission
UNSSS	United Nations Security and Safety Section
UNTAET	United Nations Transitional Administration in East Timor
UNTSO	United Nations Truce Supervision Organization
US	United States of America
USSR	Union of Soviet Socialist Republics
WMD	Weapons of mass destruction

1

Introduction

Since the establishment of the United Nations over sixty years ago, some situations have remained almost permanently of concern to the Security Council—most obviously the Israeli–Palestinian conflict, Kashmir and, since 1964, Cyprus. In the last twenty-five years, it has been Iraq which—even more than the splintering conflicts in the Balkans—has provided a staple item of the Security Council agenda.

At the time of writing, memory of the international involvement in Iraq tends to dwell on the recent coalition military intervention there in 2003 and its unhappy fallout. Some memories stretch back to events of 1990–1 when the Security Council authorized a less controversial coalition to expel Iraqi forces from Kuwait, and the innovative, far-reaching measures to contain Iraqi arms procurement (and to protect Iraqi minorities) that followed. But the earlier murderous Iran–Iraq conflict and its lessons for the Security Council are largely forgotten.

The current ferment in the larger Middle East, stretching into Central and South Asia, strikes us today as particularly acute. But, in another era, conditions there were not just more lethal but also geostrategically more threatening than today. Talk of an 'arc of instability' was perhaps even more pertinent twenty-five years ago, with the Soviet Union's invasion of Afghanistan in 1979 unfolding just as the fervor of Iran's Islamic revolution was peaking and with relations within the Arab World already unsettled by Egypt's decision earlier that year to conclude a peace treaty with Israel. It was against this backdrop that Saddam Hussein opportunistically launched a sanguinary war with Iran in 1980, placing world oil supply at significant risk. He did so only a year after consolidating his position as Ba'ath Party leader and President of Iraq. The Security Council's efforts to induce a settlement initially reflected the superpower jockeying and lack of trust among the major powers that characterized the years 1948–1986 at the UN. Later, the Council pursued a more assertive approach offering an early signal of the end of the Cold War. The UN has had a presence on the ground in Iraq since 1984, when it dispatched an investigatory team to the area, and more continuously since 1988, when it stepped in to monitor a cease-fire between Iran and Iraq. The form of that presence has changed significantly, from a truce-monitoring group, to a coalition of states assembled to repel Iraq's invasion of Kuwait, to weapons inspections, sanctions enforcement, humanitarian relief and most recently political brokerage, electoral assistance, and support in state-building.

The Security Council's involvement in and with Iraq since 1980 has both reflected and defined broader patterns of international relations, disproportionately affected by the Middle East since World War II. It is the broader significance of the Security Council's approach to Iraq at various points over the last quarter-century that initially drew me to the topic of this volume. Secondarily, I became increasingly interested in how the Council's dealings with Iraq shaped the Council's methods of work, the substance of its decisions, and the drivers of decision-making in the Council on many other cases.

Twenty-five years of dealings with Iraq had serious consequences for the Security Council. That quarter-century of Council activity serves as a remarkable portrait of political developments at the global level, and of their effect on the practice and prospects of the Security Council. The volume traces four major trends, which I reflect upon further in Chapter 9: (*a*) the instrumental multilateralism of all five permanent members on the Council; (*b*) the emergence of new threats, and questions of legality and legitimacy, representation and democracy; (*c*) the underlying evolutionary trajectory of Council practice, away from a politico-military mode in which it mediated between warring states, to a mode in which it sits at the apex of a global legal-regulatory architecture; and (*d*) the emergence of a comprehensive approach to peace, justice, security, and development.

1.1 Telling a Story

In a volume such as this one, aiming at concision, much, including on the United Nations, must be neglected. With the onset of Security Council activism, signaled by its authorization of Operations Desert Shield and Desert Storm in 1990 and 1991, so large a number of events have taken place within that body, and so much has been written thereon, that this book cannot seek to reflect it fully. For a clear understanding of the role the Security Council has played in all of this, for good and ill, I warmly recommend *The Procedure of the UN Security Council* by Sydney D. Bailey and Sam Daws—an encyclopedic work substantively richer than its title suggests.[1]

My aim here is to tell a story, profiting from the benefit of hindsight, highlighting elements that in my view merit particular attention as they relate to each other and to the tale overall. Many of these individual incidents look rather different, and their significance greater, within the broader sweep of time.

No effort is made to impose a theoretical straitjacket on this narrative. To force the events chronicled here into such a framework would not best serve either the capacities of the author or the attention of the reader, particularly given the very limited space available. Nor is the story told from the single vantage point of the academic disciplines of international relations, international law or history. If adherents and champions of each of these academic fields find some aspects of this account of value in constructing their own accounts of events detailed here, I shall judge myself modestly successful.

My varied employment—diplomatic, academic, journalistic, and in policy development—over the past fifteen years, much of it in New York, has provided me with the opportunity to meet many of the protagonists of this tale. In discussing their roles therein and views thereon, I have only rarely heard anything that could not be linked to a published source.

During the writing of my previous monograph, on a topic (Security Council decision-making, drawing on the case of Haiti) not exhaustively covered by the media and in academic writing, I relied to a great extent on interviews, often confidential ones. While necessary in the absence of published sources, this was far from ideal. I have also interviewed extensively for this book, speaking with over 200 individuals of many nationalities, backgrounds, and affiliations, some of them many times. The main benefit of these discussions has been to influence my thinking on Iraq and the Security Council, rather than to establish new facts. The conclusions at the end of some chapters and at the volume's close have been tremendously enriched by these many conversations. But they have not required much reference to confidential sources.

Tales as complex as the one recounted here always occur against an important historical backdrop. This volume assumes a reasonable level of knowledge (involving international relations, law, history, and economics) among readers that will inform their interpretation of the tale. But certain elements of context are too important to leave to chance and it is to the introduction of those elements that I now turn.

1.1.1 *Iraq*

Writing in 1958, in the florid style sometimes still invoked then, Stephen Longrigg and Frank Stoakes thus described Iraq's significance:

> Iraq's claim to consideration as the scene of the earliest human civilization, of the great empires of conquering dynasties, at and soon after the dawn of history, with their legacy of famous names, and of a medieval Islamic pre-eminence such as to make Baghdad, for five centuries, almost or quite the leading city of the world, cannot well be contested. From earliest antiquity until the end of the middle ages, Iraq's place in the world was one justly eminent in the eyes of civilized man. In no country of the world are archaeological remains richer, or more keenly studied. The place of the territory today in the tradition of three great religions—Islam, Christianity, Judaism—is considerable, and it contains famous shrines of both the dominant branches (but most notably the Shi'i branch) of the first named of these.[2]

The most revealing volume I have encountered on Iraq's transformation into both a modern society and a totalitarian nightmare, is Hanna Batatu's magisterial and massive *The Old Social Classes and Revolutionary Movements of Iraq: A Study of Iraq's Old Landed and Commercial Classes and of its Communists, Baathists and Free Officers*, material for which was culled in part from the Iraqi Communist Party Archives.[3] It charts the clashes and accommodations, confrontations and alliances among Iraq's many communities in the colonial and postcolonial eras and helps explain why many Iraqis accepted Saddam Hussein's terror as, in their eyes, the lesser of several evils that could have overtaken the country.

The history of government instability between 1932 and 1958, with numerous cabinet changes, many unconstitutional, and the violent upheavals of Iraqi politics between 1958 and 1968, may go some way to explaining an acquiescence by the population in the brutal stability of Saddam Hussein's regime.[4] Knowing what we do now about the development of the Ba'ath regime over thirty-five years, not least the costs of Saddam Hussein's international military adventurism, it is easy to overlook early hopes that the Ba'ath government could not only remove the military from Iraq's political equation, but also institute a degree of inclusiveness under principles of social democracy.[5] Such hopes were gradually dispelled not merely by the regime's homicidal response to actual or apprehended dissent, but also by its emphasis on economic development as its platform for seeking popular consent. As Phebe Marr has pointed out, economic modernization offered the Ba'ath party the means to centralize state control, particularly through building up its 'military sinews', including through a nascent nuclear program. By 1979, she assesses, 'the edifice of the monolithic, one-party state, in control of not only the instruments of political and military power but of society as well, was complete.'[6]

While Saddam Hussein's authoritarianism was extreme even by Middle Eastern standards, it reflected to some degree a political culture ingrained in Iraq since its emergence as an independent state in October 1932. As Charles Tripp has argued in more detail than I can in these pages, '[m]arking ... Iraq's history has been a powerful tendency for politics to be seen mainly as a way of disciplining the population to ensure conformity with the rulers' vision of social order. Even those who have challenged established order have been equally authoritarian.'[7] In Tripp's analysis, the 'idea of politics as civility, advocating a framework of laws and shared space for political activity' has been 'overwhelmed by people organized according to very different notions of trust, where the community is not one of citizens, but of family and clan members, fellow tribesmen or conspirators'.[8] Toby Dodge echoes this assessment, arguing that Iraqi politics since 1921 has been dominated by

> the deployment of extreme levels of organized violence by the state to dominate and shape society; second, the use of state resources ... to buy the loyalty of sections of society; third, the use of oil revenue by the state to increase its autonomy from society; and, finally, the exacerbation and re-creation by the state of communal and ethnic divisions as a strategy of rule.

But Dodge's analysis goes further, suggesting that these interlinked characteristics of the Iraqi state provide structural causes for not only the illegitimacy of the state, but also

> its tendency to embark on military adventurism beyond its borders, and even the Baathist regime's drive to acquire weapons of mass destruction. Seen in this perspective, Saddam Hussein must be understood less as the cause of Iraq's violent political culture—or even of Iraq's role as a source of regional instability—and more as a symptom, albeit an extremely consequential one, of deeper long-term dynamics within Iraq's political sociology.[9]

That analysis is lent support by Samir al-Khalil, who argues that in the late 1970s, the 'time was ripe for the Ba'th to take externally the kind of decisive action they had already taken internally, to signify to the outside the rising pre-eminence of Iraqi Ba'thism in regional and Arab affairs'. Of course, he recognizes, there were 'economic, material and strategic benefits (the oil-rich province of Khuzistan, territory and better access to the Gulf)' to be won; but ultimately, the 'Ba'athist motives were singularly political, derivative ultimately from deeply held ideological tenets to which they had given ample proof of their commitment.'[10]

1.1.2 *Saddam Hussein*

One of the lessons of this volume is that while history's pages may unfold with a certain retrospective inevitability, personalities matter. Without the force of personality, history's opportunities remain just that. The Iraqi Ba'ath Party stood poised, in the late 1970s, to translate its growing domestic military power into external adventurism; but that translation in fact owes a great deal to the unique personality that is Saddam Hussein.

Delusions of grandeur (reminiscent of those of the Shah of Iran which led to his downfall in 1979) were embedded in the personality cult Saddam Hussein encouraged from the time of his own accession to ultimate power in 1979, but his pursuit of absolute control for himself and primacy for Iraq was deadly earnest and purposeful. His early and aggressive interest in a nuclear weapons program, thrust into the spotlight by the Israeli bombing on June 7, 1981 of Iraq's nuclear reactor at Osiraq, has now been fully documented. But a number of experts and governments proved mistaken in their assessments of his intentions and policies, because neither his ambitions nor his capabilities were easy to grasp.[11] After 1991, he never seriously resumed Iraq's quest for nuclear weapons and his interest in developing biological and chemical weapons systems, beyond those found and destroyed by UN inspectors, 1991–8, seems to have waned. By then, the viper had largely been defanged—though few believed this, due to his tireless posturing designed in part to keep Iraq's neighbors, potentially keen to eliminate the threat he represented, off balance.[12]

Saddam Hussein was born near Tikrit in 1937, in the heart of the Sunni-dominated center of Iraq, in conditions of poverty. Accounts of his early life are not authoritative. His father disappeared early on, whereupon he acquired a brutal stepfather. A more overt influence in his life was an uncle, a former military officer, cashiered after a coup attempt. By 1956, Saddam Hussein was himself participating in an unsuccessful coup against the monarchy. Having joined the fledgling Iraqi Ba'ath party (an offshoot of the original Syrian Ba'ath movement) a year later, he participated in 1959 in an assassination attempt on strongman Abdul Karim Qassem, fleeing first to Syria, then to Egypt, when the operation failed. In 1964, he plotted again, against President Aref, leading to a crackdown on the party and two years in prison.[13]

His involvement in the Ba'ath party is replete with intrigue. When the party split in 1963, Michel Aflaq, the Ba'ath's leading ideologue and cofounder, sponsored him for a position on the party's 'Regional Command'. He was further helped by the prominent position within Ba'ath circles of his cousin, General Ahmed Hassan al-Bakr, who, in 1965, became the party's Secretary-General. From then until 1979, when Saddam Hussein would supplant al-Bakr as President of Iraq, he figured in official Ba'ath iconography as the latter's loyal deputy. In fact, soon after the successful Ba'ath takeover of 1968, he started operating as the regime strongman, managing the state security apparatus and the party machinery so as to place elements loyal to him in key positions. Vicious outbursts of violence were to mark his career, such as the 1969 public hanging of fourteen alleged participants in a Zionist spy ring, eleven of them Jewish.

Most murderous of all was the purge that followed his appointment as President in July 1979, when up to five hundred individuals he judged to be disloyal or treacherous were eliminated. From that point on, the cult of his personality in Iraq was unconstrained.[14] Soon, Saddam Hussein saw himself not just as the leader of Iraq, but also of the Arab World (the Ba'ath styled itself a pan-Arab movement even though it never took hold beyond Syria and Iraq). If anything, his leadership pretensions were boosted by Israel's attack on the Osiraq nuclear facility.

Early appraisals of Saddam Hussein within the Arab World (and beyond, sad to say) tended toward the hagiographic. Not atypical is the claim that, against the backdrop of the Iran–Iraq war, Saddam Hussein displayed 'exceptional ability to direct a war'.[15] Apologists from within the Arab world were not the only ones pointing to Saddam Hussein's genius and Iraq's potential. Due in large part to hostility toward revolutionary Iran, Iraq and its ambassador, Nizar Hamdoon, were the toasts of much of Washington during the 1980s, and a number of US scholars and security experts burned their reputations in the heat of their enthusiasm. Not all were taken in or prepared to be bought off, as Samir al-Khalil noted:

> Saddam Hussein exercised a very special kind of power. He had become an institution unto himself, one virtually without checks. His leadership was related to sentiments of the broad mass of Iraqis in a complicated and yet resilient way as proven by the later course of the war once the initial self-confidence had ebbed away. He presided over a regime that had gradually, but nonetheless inexorably, changed all the parameters affecting societal and state-organized violence. Eventually, expansion of the means of violence—army, police, security apparatuses, networks of informers, party militia, party and state bureaucracies—underwent the classic inversion: from being a means to an end, the elimination of opponents and exercise of raw power, they became horrific ends in themselves, spilling mindlessly across borders that had once contained them.[16]

The ties between family, clan and politics being what they are in Iraq, much speculation over the years has been devoted to the roles and loyalties of various family members. Particular attention has been paid to his hapless son-in-law (who fled Iraq in 1995 only to meet with summary execution when he returned voluntarily), and to his two sons, Uday and Qusay, the former pathologically violent and inept, the latter more cautious but no less ruthless, who died together in a hail of Coalition bullets in late 2003. But the sadly colorful family were relevant only in relation to Saddam Hussein himself and, with his fall, are no longer of significant interest.[17]

Much has been made of Saddam Hussein's messianic personality. Writing in 1991, in wake his invasion of Kuwait, Bishara A. Bahbah nevertheless detected a degree of pragmatism:

> Saddam Hussein's personality, compounded by the fact that he exercised absolute control in Iraq, played a key role in the unfolding of events in the Gulf. He views himself as one of the great leaders of history, ranking himself with Nasser, Castro, Tito, Ho Chi Minh and Mao Zedong. He has been consumed by dreams of glory, and he identifies himself with Nebuchadnezzar, the King of Babylonia who conquered Jerusalem in 586 BC, and Salah ad-Din, who reigned in Jerusalem in 1187 by defeating the Crusaders. He believed ... that there could be only one supreme Arab nationalist leader, and he was the one. He was driven by what he perceived as his mission to lead the Arab world. Nevertheless, based on his actions and statements, Saddam Hussein is a pragmatic man. When he deemed certain 'unthinkable' actions ... better than the existing alternatives, he carried out the 'unthinkable'.[18]

One such instance of the 'unthinkable' was his agreement under the 1975 Algiers Treaty to share sovereignty of the Shat al Arab with Iran, 'in return for Iran ceasing to supply aid to the Kurdish rebellion'.[19]

Thus, Saddam Hussein's multiple and outsized miscalculations and delusions were balanced, to a degree, by shrewd tactical calculations. Never knowing what to expect from him, his international interlocutors—in the region, from the United Nations or among the major powers—never really knew on what foot to dance with him, greatly complicating for them the design of diplomatic strategies aiming to contain or cow him. This remained true until his capture by American troops in late 2003.

It is not the purpose of this volume to analyze Iraq's system of governance prior to the Ba'ath regime, under Saddam Hussein, or following his overthrow by a US-led coalition in early 2003. However, Saddam Hussein's conduct of Iraq's international relations is virtually incomprehensible without grasping the absolute control he sought to exert on all aspects of Iraqi political, military, and economic life, even going so far as to virtually eviscerate the Ba'ath party, of which he had himself named 'imperative leader' in 1982. No ideology was to interfere with his command of every aspect of society. As Jan Eliasson, one of the UN's senior envoys to Iran and Iraq, comments, 'Nobody [in Baghdad] interfered with his ideas, his thoughts. He was completely isolated.'[20]

War served Hussein's purposes at home and abroad. At home, the fractious nature of the Iraqi state—where the minority Sunni community dominated government absolutely, at the expense of the majority Shi'a and the Kurds in the country's north (with whom confrontation and accommodation alternated)—to a degree invited totalitarian control from Hussein. Keeping Iraq on a war footing greatly facilitated this approach. This may help explain his resort to unprovoked war against Kuwait, so soon after clutching victory of sorts from the jaws of defeat at the conclusion of the Iran–Iraq war. Indeed, other would-be rulers of Iraq have long recognized the challenge posed by the fissiparous tendency of 'Iraqi' society: President George H. W. Bush resisted toppling Saddam Hussein in the 1991 Gulf War in part to avoid the splintering of Iraq. National cohesion proved a significant challenge for Ambassador Paul Bremer and his colleagues of the Coalition Provisional Authority in 2003 and 2004, and for the fledgling Iraqi government since, as Iraq's three main communities have vied for power and for other forms of influence or autonomy.

Abroad, Hussein appears to have calculated that war would buttress his Arab leadership credentials and produce an expanded pool of national wealth through the appropriation of neighboring oil-fields. Nevertheless, the help offered Iraq by the superpowers during the Iran–Iraq war, together with Hussein's preoccupation with domestic developments, may have obscured for him the profound changes taking place in international relations during the 1980s. As we shall see, the Soviet Union and the United States were drawing closer, at the United Nations and elsewhere, with the logic of superpower confrontation being overtaken by Gorbachev's *de facto* withdrawal from the Cold War. This was to have profound implications for their willingness to tolerate Hussein's regionally destabilizing style of government in Iraq, and his propensity to export that rule by coercion beyond Iraq's borders. As Elaine Sciolino points out in her perceptive and lively volume on the Iran–Iraq war, Hussein made major mistakes of appreciation and strategy in the run-up to and during his invasion of Kuwait:

> The first was poor timing, invading in the year of the new international order, when the world's greatest powers were uninterested in capitalizing on what once might have been regarded as a local dispute. His second mistake is that he swallowed Kuwait whole rather than just nibbling at its edges. If it had remained a border dispute, there would never have been an international coalition and

> a US-led war. Saddam's third mistake was to move troops toward the Saudi border, an action that gave the impression that his aggression was unbounded. Saddam's most serious mistake was that he miscalculated the world's response. He gambled—incorrectly—the Arab states would never allow foreign forces into the region or fight on the side of the United States. He further assumed that when put to the test, the coalition would crumble.... But Saddam was blind to the fact that despite its enormous weapons arsenal, Iraq remained a small player on the world stage.[21]

Other mistakes compounded these. Saddam Hussein's decision not just to invade Kuwait but to attempt its annexation proved much more threatening to small states the world over than he might have imagined. Most countries, not just Gulf emirates, border on more powerful neighbors, and if the full annexation of a UN Member State could be allowed to stand, how many states could consider themselves truly safe from a similar fate?

As well, Hussein's relentless pan-Arab leadership pretensions (honed during the Iran–Iraq war) grated on other Arab leaders, not least because it pointed to their own limited legitimacy in living up to the ambitious content of Arab political rhetoric, particularly after the 1973 Israeli–Arab war put paid to any prospect of actually punishing the Zionist enemy in any effective way. Thus, while the Palestinian leadership generally followed Yassir Arafat's disastrous lead in supporting Saddam Hussein, and while King Hussein of Jordan seemed to panic at the prospect of the Jordanian masses rising up in support of Saddam Hussein, most Arab regimes viewed Saddam Hussein's bold gamble as a reckless, dangerous initiative threatening their own stability and future. Hussein may have counted on Arab resentment of Kuwaiti wealth and arrogance to sway both public opinion and governments to his side, and while Kuwait enjoyed little support among many Arab publics, he was dead wrong about Arab governments.

Writing in the late 1970s, Hanna Batatu, the most prudent of historians, ventured to predict:

> Whether the regime will stand out historically hinges, in the long run, upon its ability to contribute, in a creative manner, to the process of nation-state building that the 1920 Revolt had set afoot. This will involve, sooner or later, the necessity of binding the peasants to the townsmen and the Shi'is and the Sunnis; and creating mutually advantageous relations between the Kurds and Arabs.[22]

This is of course precisely what did not happen. Saddam Hussein enforced national unity through terror and focused his attention on territorial expansion and other forms of aggression rather than constructive state-building. On these choices hinged his absolute failure.

1.1.3 *The Mood in the UN Security Council*

This story spans the Cold War and post-Cold War periods. During the former, the Security Council maneuvered at the margins of conflict (and not all major conflicts at that), often, as in the Israeli–Arab theatre of conflict, first encouraging, then monitoring cease-fires after fighting had broken out. Ingenious techniques were worked out in the UN's first two decades to permit the UN to protect cease-fires through various types of monitoring and eventually through larger-scale peacekeeping operations. But these efforts, with occasional exceptions (such as authorization of force by UN Member States against North Korean aggression; and the more qualified authorization of a degree of force by UN peacekeepers in the Congo in the early 1960s), were prudent and respected the 'red lines' of the superpowers.

With the end of the Cold War, and early successes attending the UN's newly bold conflict resolution strategies, a period of euphoria overtook UN headquarters, particularly after the August 1990 Iraqi invasion (and subsequent annexation) of Kuwait was reversed by the Security Council-mandated Operation Desert Storm. Soon after, large-scale UN peace operations, featuring complex mandates executed by civilian as well as military components, had been launched in Cambodia, the former Yugoslavia and Somalia. Smaller UN missions were launched to support the end of civil turmoil in such places as Angola, Mozambique, Rwanda, El Salvador, and Haiti.

After serious peacekeeping setbacks in Somalia and Bosnia, UN Secretary-General Boutros Boutros-Ghali concluded that the UN itself could not successfully engage in enforcement operations. The UN's failure to halt genocide in Rwanda in the spring of 1994 reinforced the perception that the UN's own capacity effectively to manage risky peace operations was limited. A pattern then emerged of the Security Council authorizing operations by coalitions of Member States to enforce its decisions, with Operation Uphold Democracy deploying in Haiti as of September 1994 and the launch of IFOR in December 1995 to implement provisions of the Dayton Agreement in Bosnia.[23] As of early 1995, the deployment of 'Blue Helmets', which had reached a peak in July 1993 with 78,444 troops, began to decline, dropping to 14,374 in November 1998.[24]

The period of relative harmony between the Council's five Permanent Members (P-5), ushered in at the end of the Cold War and marked by genuine P-5 cooperation in addressing challenges to international peace and security, drew to a close in 1998 with France, Russia, and China objecting furiously to US and UK bombing of Iraq, and Russia resisting a lead role for NATO in addressing the crisis in Kosovo. By late 1998, the Council was effectively deadlocked on these two key issues. It seemed, instead, increasingly focused on crises of geostrategically marginal (if real) importance, as in Sierra Leone.

By 1998, the Russian Federation was so enfeebled that few contested the emergence of the United States not so much as the sole remaining superpower but, in the words of the Egyptian jurist and diplomat Nabil Elaraby, 'the supreme power'.[25] Although at the time the European Union (EU) was making strides toward both expansion and further integration, its common foreign policy remained amorphous and unconvincing on international security issues, nowhere more so than at the UN, where the United Kingdom and France not only acted independently of their EU partners but also of each other on certain key issues—such as Iraq. China, while essentially passive on most Council agenda items, responded to Taiwan's diplomatic maneuvers by vetoing Security Council Resolutions (SCRs) relating to Guatemala (1997) and Macedonia (1999). (Ironically, these displays of Chinese self-interest were very much in line with Washington's contention that all Security Council decisions must somehow serve its own interests.) Russia navigated cautiously at the UN, seeming to agree with Western powers on many crises, perhaps acutely aware of the extent of its reliance on Western financial largesse (which was interrupted at the time of a financial crisis in Russia in mid-1998). With the rise to power of the assertive Vladimir Putin, and the cancer of the Chechnyan rebellion gnawing at the Russian Federation, Moscow was increasingly prone to defecting from the Western consensus (not least on issues in its own backyard, such as Ukraine's Orange revolution in late 2004).

1.1.4 *Civil Society*

The Iraq case is interesting not least because it reveals international civil society organizations interacting with states and their agendas, particularly through their lobbying, starting with the humanitarian crisis in Northern Iraq in early 1991 and, with striking vigor, later in highlighting the humanitarian costs of comprehensive economic sanctions. This forced the Security Council to devise the narrowly effective but mismanaged Oil-for-Food (OFF) Program. Andrew Hurrell writes:

> Understanding the nature of foreign policy on many issues often involves understanding the links between states and actors within transnational civil society. State action may be shaped by NGO lobbying, but it is often crucial in fostering

the emergence of civil society to begin with and in providing the political framework that enables civil society to flourish. More important, state power is increasingly determined by the ability of governments to work successfully with civil society and to exploit transnational and transgovernmental coalitions for their own purposes.[26]

The United States and its allies were initially able to galvanize transnational civil society to support their policy and actions relating to Operation Provide Comfort. Over time, their inability to do more than cave in reluctantly to insistent NGO demands refracted through a receptive international media on subsequent challenges in and around Iraq, lost them this critical set of international voices. This divergence was most stark in Iraq in 2003–4 when deteriorating security conditions conspired to chase away even the most determined humanitarian organizations not directly contracted by the Coalition.

1.1.5 *Post-Cold War US Multilateralism*

The most striking trait in US approaches to its international relations in the post-Cold War era, following the transitional Administration of George H. W. Bush from 1989 to 1993, was not so much the risk of imperial overreach—although this impulse brought the United States low in Iraq in 2003–4—or the equally decried threat of isolationism, but rather its growing reliance on unilateralism and exceptionalism. Thus Madeleine Albright initially advocated 'assertive multilateralism' as the basis of US foreign policy, but later characterized the United States as the 'indispensable nation' and explained the short shrift sometimes given by Washington to the views of its partners by claiming that '[w]e stand tall and we see further than other countries into the future.'[27] This self-identification fed tendencies toward exceptionalism, most clearly on display during negotiations toward a treaty banning the use of antipersonnel land mines (which, in spite of the US opposition, entered into force for its State Parties in March 1999) and during those which led to the adoption of the Statute for an International Criminal Court in Rome in July 1998.

If the Presidential inauguration of George W. Bush in January 2001 signaled an even greater antipathy in Washington to treaties, the events of September 11, 2001 (hereafter referred to as 9/11) seemed—as I shall explore in later chapters—to induce a testosterone rush and a wish for powerful deterrent 'demonstration effects' to intimidate potential and real enemies of the United States. This seems to have produced agreement within the Administration that force needed to be deployed against a sizable target (certainly a more convincing one than the Taliban in Afghanistan, easily defeated in 2001). The target selected was the weakest element of the 'Axis of Evil' identified in President Bush's 2002 State of the Union address, Iraq. After the events of 9/11, views of allies were generally brushed aside (although Prime Minister Blair of the United Kingdom and some of his supporters claimed otherwise) with serious consequences not so much for the military campaign against Saddam Hussein in 2003 as for the subsequent Coalition occupation of Iraq.

As of the mid-1990s, with no remaining alternative centers of power, the United States developed a marked and growing impatience with the constraints of multilateral diplomacy. The give-and-take required within the UN Security Council in order to secure support for US policy initiatives came to be perceived in Washington increasingly as an unnecessary tyranny. There was also a decreasing disposition to convince allies and others of the wisdom of Washington's views: it was deemed sufficient that they be stated. Any disagreement with the US policy was viewed by many in Washington as driven by irrational anti-American sentiment or as posturing.

These attitudes predominated in the US approach to Iraq within the Security Council in 1998 and 1999, causing it, through a combination of absentmindedness and bloody-mindedness, to allow the Desert Storm Coalition to fray beyond repair. As I explore in later chapters, other Great Powers, particularly France and Russia, played their parts in the erosion of this coalition; but though the latitude always remained with the United States to work to accommodate their—and others'—concerns, it failed to do so. This disposition also contributed to diplomatic stalemate in the Council over Iraq in 2003 and subsequently to distress on the ground in Iraq for the Coalition Provisional Authority (and for Iraqis). American realists—both among practitioners and international relations theorists—have always appreciated that 'good company' and multilateral endorsement of its policies are of value to Washington. But particularly after 9/11, policymakers there lost the habit of genuine consultation and compromise with allies initially cultivated following the end of the Cold War. The contradictions in Washington's policy toward Iraq seemed to be apparent everywhere but in Washington: 'The problem . . . is that we can't demand compliance with Security Council resolutions while simultaneously shunning the Security Council by pursuing a unilateral campaign to remove Saddam from power.'[28]

1.1.6 *The P-5 Split*

After their impressive cooperation further to Saddam Hussein's invasion of Kuwait in 1990–1, the falling out among the P-5 in the latter half of the 1990s produced a pattern of spectacular flare-ups (for example, at the time of the December 1998 bombing campaign of the United States and the United Kingdom against Iraq), followed by heroic but pyrrhic efforts to paper over serious policy differences, often through compromises at the UN that convinced neither Baghdad nor others of any seriousness of common purpose.

The bitterness of the split between the P-5 in early 2003 stood out as quite extraordinary in the post-Cold War era, with nationalism in some countries leading to defamatory caricatures of others. Perhaps the most famous sound-bite in this vein was the description of the French as 'cheese-eating surrender monkeys' by Jonah Goldberg of the *National Review.*[29] Descriptions of President Bush in the European media returned the favor (although with less venom). He was depicted as a mindless warmonger bent on imposing American civilization on the world. In this atmosphere, serious mistakes were made, not least President Chirac's comment that the candidate members of the EU had lost a good opportunity to shut up rather than support the UK view on Iraq, a remark still resonating within the enlarged EU.[30] That nationalism so raw, caricatures so gross, widely supported ventures so inane as re-styling 'French fries' as 'freedom fries', could gain currency is to remind us that nationalism remains a strong instinct within most societies and that the self-righteousness of leaders can rapidly contaminate supposedly objective media coverage and, through the latter, public opinion. This volume traces the growing tensions among the P-5, after the period of euphoria in the early 1990s referred to above, resulting in this outbreak of high pettiness.

1.2 The Story in Brief

The Table of Contents summarizes the tale as recounted here. It is told largely in chronological fashion, in the interests of clarity. From 1980 to 2005, five phases of UN Security Council involvement in Iraq can be discerned. Chapters are arranged to address each of these five phases in succession, though the third, covering the period 1991–2001, requires three full chapters to introduce its different aspects.

Each chapter ends with conclusions, a number aiming for policy relevance, pertinent to the events detailed therein. The volume's final chapter seeks to impart cross-cutting conclusions centered on the Security Council and its principal members.

Chapter 2 addresses the first phase, in which the UN acted as a **Cold War Peacemaker** and peacekeeper, using its neutral position eventually to broker a settlement between Iran and Iraq in 1987–8 and then to monitor the agreement it had brokered. The chapter focuses on several critical moments during the Iran–Iraq war, the significance of which was overlooked at the time: first, the Security Council's inadequate, indeed misguided, reaction to Iraq's attack on Iran in 1980 that doubtless contributed to Saddam Hussein's contempt for the UN—with fateful consequences ten years later and resulting in Iran's conviction ever since that UN objectivity cannot be trusted. The UN's involvement over the next decade provides a catalog of the measures available to it as a peace-broker in the Cold War years. And it introduces a new phase, in which, with Cold War tensions subsiding, the P-5 working together could be more creative (and quietly assertive) than previously, as of 1987. A new era in P-5 relations and in the capacity of the UN to address hitherto intractable conflicts, had dawned.

Chapter 3 addresses the second phase of UN involvement in Iraq, which seemed to herald the emergence of the Security Council as a **New World Order Policeman**. The Security Council's capacity to legitimize the use of force provided a legal basis for international action to expel Iraqi forces from Kuwait in 1991. The chapter recounts the diplomatic and military success of Operations Desert Shield and Desert Storm, mandated to compel the withdrawal of Iraq from Kuwait and conducted by a coalition of states (a so-called 'coalition of the willing') drawing legitimacy from Security Council decisions under Chapter VII of the UN Charter. Chapter VII also provided a newly assertive basis for traditional activities such as ceasefire implementation and border-monitoring, tasks the Council gave to a new mission, UNIKOM, deployed along the border between Iraq and Kuwait. This new police role for UN peace operations was part of a larger 'New World Order' heralded by President George H. W. Bush,[31] which seemed to hold the promise of an international rule of law, enforced by a united P-5 operating through the Security Council.

Chapter 4 commences a three-chapter examination of the third phase of UN involvement, characterized by **Creeping Unilateralism**, occurring in the context of a more multidisciplinary approach to peace operations. That approach often incorporated humanitarian objectives into peace operations, as reflected in the deployment of UN 'Guards' to northern Iraq; but it was also characterized by the early resort (or reversion) by several

Security Council members to unilateral action. The chapter specifically examines the imposition by France, the United Kingdom, and the United States of no-fly zones over Iraq in 1991 and 1992, and the launch of Operation Provide Comfort to protect Kurdish refugees in northern Iraq. This creeping unilateralism was a harbinger of further unilateral enforcement measures to come that would, by 1998, sunder the unity of the Security Council's purpose on Iraq. Operation Provide Comfort also suggested a drift away from politico-military solutions administered by the parties to the conflict, toward regulatory approaches to conflict prevention and postconflict peace-building implemented through the UN (of interest not least in relation to a growing focus on administrative law). The UN system increasingly took on the role of proxy administration in areas not under sovereign control, and administered supranational controls on Iraq and other conflict protagonists. These developments foreshadowed much greater UN involvement in essentially internal conflicts and in complex humanitarian situations.[32] Some of the related challenges were discussed in Secretary-General Boutros Boutros-Ghali's *An Agenda for Peace*, calling for the UN to take a stronger lead in preventive diplomacy, peacemaking, peacekeeping, and peace-building.[33]

Chapters 5 and 6 examine the inspections-plus-sanctions approach to Iraqi disarmament which characterized the enforcement aspects of this third phase of UN involvement in Iraq. These two chapters address the two pillars of a comprehensive disarmament regime, giving the Security Council and its agents the dual role of **Sanctions Enforcer** and **Weapons Inspector**. With these two roles, the Security Council increasingly acted as a global regulator containing Iraq's military capacity, moving away from its traditional politico-military approach. Ultimately, this regulatory approach met with mixed success: Iraq was effectively deprived of weapons of mass destruction (WMD), and the UN agencies kept millions of Iraqis alive. The OFF Program, as Kofi Annan noted, was 'one of the largest, most complex and most unusual tasks [the Security Council] has ever entrusted to the Secretariat—the only humanitarian program ever to have been funded entirely from resources belonging to the nation it was designed to help'.[34] At the same time, the approach came at a heavy cost: massively depressed Iraqi living-standards, a failure to satisfy Washington and some others of Iraqi disarmament—eventually producing a second Western invasion in 2003, and massive corruption of the sanctions regime that severely damaged UN credibility after 2003. Ultimately, this third phase may stand as a warning against the Security Council adopting the complex role of global regulator in the field of peace and security, without creating adequate administrative apparatus to discharge that regulatory role—a lesson of signal importance given the proliferation of Security Council regulatory machinery charged with overseeing the implementation of specific administrative standards or regimes, not least on WMD, counter-terrorism measures, and sanctions enforcement.

Chapter 7 addresses the fourth phase of UN involvement in Iraq, in which it was largely **Sidelined**. Negotiations within the Security Council in late 2002 and early 2003 resulted in deadlock, and the decision of a US and UK-led Coalition to overthrow Saddam Hussein forcibly without a Council mandate. This outcome in the Security Council in March 2003 was in many respects surprising, given the pattern of mutual accommodation among the P-5 that had so often prevailed since 1990.[35] But expectations of compromise in the Council may have given too little weight to new dynamics unleashed after 9/11, particularly in the United States, and to the creeping pattern of unilateralism that had earlier been established in Iraq. The chapter also addresses the early Coalition occupation of Iraq; subsequent decisions by the Security Council to lend this international action a patina of legal cover (without providing *post facto* authorization of the use of force against Saddam Hussein); the nascent Sunni-dominated insurgency against Coalition forces and their local allies; and the bombing of UN headquarters in Baghdad in August 2003 that was to traumatize UN staff and inhibit significant UN post-conflict roles on the ground.

Chapter 8 examines events in Iraq during the most recent fifth phase of involvement of the UN. Having been largely sidelined on Iraq in the fourth phase, the UN underwent a **Crisis of Confidence** in 2004–5, searching hard for means to address its demotion. This narrative suggests that the deadlock in the Council over Iraq in 2003 had critically undermined the UN's credibility globally, which no amount of activity elsewhere, notably in Africa, could recover. During this period, under Council resolutions, the UN was meant to be playing a 'vital' role in Iraq, but its margin for maneuver was circumscribed on the one hand by the continuing strong guiding hand of the United States in Iraqi affairs and on the other by the dreadful security situation in Iraq, precluding deployment of a large UN international staff. During these years, various aspects of the UN's earlier activities in Iraq, notably the OFF Program, returned to haunt it, making 2004 Kofi Annan's *Annus Horribilis*. In that atmosphere, the UN was confronted with a reform imperative: attempt reform or perish.

However, serious efforts to promote comprehensive and meaningful UN reform during the organization's September 2005 Summit convened to review implementation of the Millennial Development Goals floundered in an atmosphere of distrust aggravated by disagreements over Security Council composition and by the penchant of UN delegates for the narcissism of ideological differences.

Chapter 9 offers the volume's **Conclusions**. It focuses on the instrumental approach of all five permanent members to the Council as a resource for their own purposes, in effect their instrumental multilateralism. Different members of the P-5 need, and use, the Council for different purposes, as a comparison of the French approach to Côte d'Ivoire and the US approach to Iraq makes clear. While the interventionist impulses of these protagonists were perhaps not so different from each other (each of these P-5 members acting in what they considered their geostrategic backyard, or 'sphere of influence'), the perceived need of Paris and Washington for political and legal legitimacy and consequently their diplomatic tactics at the UN and elsewhere diverged. The chapter also addresses conceptions of legality, legitimacy, representation, and democracy in the Council. More broadly, it seeks to draw lessons from the Council's drift into decision-making in a legal-regulatory (rather than politico-military) mode, not least with respect to accountability. And, finally, it examines some of the challenges the UN and its Member States face when attempting peace-building, perhaps better thought of as (responsible) state-building.

Notes

1. Sydney D. Bailey and Sam Daws, *The Procedure of the Security Council*, 3rd edn. (Oxford: Clarendon, 1998). A more recent and rather different account of the Security Council, sliced, diced, and edited in various ways can be found in David M. Malone (ed.), *The UN Security Council: From the Cold War to the 21st Century* (Boulder, CO: Lynne Rienner, 2004).
2. Stephen Helmsley Longrigg and Frank Stoakes, *Iraq* (London: Ernest Benn Ltd., 1958), 14.
3. Hanna Batatu, *The Old Social Classes and the Revolutionary Movements of Iraq: A Study of Iraq's Old Landed and Commercial Classes and of its Communists, Ba'thists, and Free Officers* (Princeton, NJ: Princeton University Press, 1978).
4. See Majid Khadduri, *Independent Iraq, 1932–58: A Study in Iraqi Politics*, 2nd edn. (Oxford: OUP, 1960), 364–7. See also Sandra Mackey, *The Reckoning: Iraq and the Legacy of Saddam Hussein* (New York: Norton, 2002), 156–97.
5. See Majid Khadduri, *Socialist Iraq: A Study in Iraqi Politics Since 1968* (Washington, DC: Middle East Institute, 1978), 179–80.
6. Phebe Marr, *The Modern History of Iraq*, 2nd edn. (Boulder, CO: Westview, 2004), 176.

7. Charles Tripp, *A History of Iraq*, 2nd edn. (Cambridge: Cambridge University Press, 2002), 2.
8. Tripp, *A History of Iraq*, 2.
9. Toby Dodge, *Inventing Iraq: The Failure of Nation Building and a History Denied* (New York, NY: Columbia University Press, 2003), 169–70.
10. Samir al-Khalil, *Republic of Fear: The Politics of Modern Iraq* (Berkeley, CA: University of California Press, 1989), 270–1.
11. An interesting first-hand account of Iraq's nuclear weapons program has been provided by one of Saddam Hussein's leading scientists, Mahdi Obeidi, in *The Bomb in My Garden: the Secret of Saddam's Nuclear Mastermind* (Hoboken, NJ: John Wiley & Sons, 2004).
12. A useful account of the successes of UN weapons inspectors in Iraq is to be found in Jean E. Krasno and James S. Sutterlin, *The United Nations and Iraq: Defanging the Viper* (London: Praeger, 2003).
13. On this episode, see Efraim Karsh and Inari Rautsi, *Saddam Hussein: A Political Biography* (New York: The Free Press, 1991), 27–8.
14. The cult-related bureaucracy in Iraq was extensive. On this, see Simon Henderson, *Instant Empire: Saddam Hussein's Ambition for Iraq* (San Francisco, CA: Mercury House, 1991), 78–9.
15. Fuad Matar, *Saddam Hussein: The Man, The Cause and the Future* (London: Third World Centre, 1981), 15.
16. al-Khalil, *Republic of Fear*, 271.
17. See Henderson, *Instant Empire*, 80–91.
18. Bishara A. Bahbah, 'The Crisis in the Gulf: Why Iraq Invaded Kuwait', in Phyllis Bennis and Michel Moushabeck (eds.), *Beyond the Storm: A Gulf Crisis Reader* (New York: Olive Branch Press, 1991), 53. Among Saddam Hussein's most consistent miscalculations was the degree to which Arab populations were inclined toward his politics and policies. He also, clearly, understood little about the United States and possibly about much of the non-Iraqi world with which he dealt so extensively and on which he had such significant impact during his 24-year presidency.
19. Bahbah, 'The Crisis in the Gulf', 53.
20. Jan Eliasson, interview with the author, June 23, 2005.
21. Elaine Sciolino, *The Outlaw State: Saddam Hussein's Quest for Power and the Gulf Crisis* (New York: John Wiley & Sons, 1991), 16.
22. Batatu, *The Old Social Classes*, 1133.
23. Subsequent coalition authorizations included the Italian-led Operation Alba (authorized by SCR 1101, March 28, 1997), the Australian-led INTERFET (SCR 1264, September 15, 1999), ISAF in Afghanistan (SCR 1386, December 20, 2001), and the AU mission in Darfur (SCR 1556, July 30, 2004), among others.
24. These figures have since recovered to peak again at nearly 68,000 peacekeepers (as of August 2005), with the potential of 80,000 peacekeepers within the near

future. For more on figures, see the UN Department of Peacekeeping Operation's website, www.un.org/depts/dpko.

25. Elaraby interview with the author January 10, 1996. Complaining about the conception and execution of US foreign policy insensitive to the views of its allies and others, French Foreign Minister Hubert Védrine in February 1999 described the United States as a 'hyperpower', dominating the world economically, militarily and culturally. See 'To Paris, U.S. Looks Like a "Hyperpower" ', *International Herald Tribune*, February 5, 1999, 5; and Hubert Védrine, *France in an Age of Globalization*, trans. Philip H. Gordon (Washington, DC: Brookings Institution Press, 2001).
26. Andrew Hurrell, 'America and the World: Issues in the Teaching of U.S. Foreign Policy', *Perspectives on Politics* 2/1 (2004), 108.
27. From an interview with Secretary of State Madeleine Albright by Matt Lauer, *The Today Show* (NBC), February 19, 1998.
28. Scott Ritter, 'Policies at War', *New York Times*, Editorial, August 16, 1999, A19.
29. Gary Younge and Jon Henley, 'Wimps, weasels and monkeys—The US media view of "perfidious France" ', *The Guardian*, February 11, 2003, 3.
30. See 'Can the EU Rift be Healed?', *BBC News*, February 20, 2003, www.news.bbc.co.uk/2/hi/talking_point/2771713.stm.
31. Chapter VII of the UN Charter addresses both the coercive measures the Security Council can invoke and their binding nature for all states.
32. In describing certain conflicts as internal or civil, the prior qualifier 'essentially' is added because these conflicts rarely remain strictly internal for long, with neighboring countries often spilling in (as in the Democratic Republic of the Congo) or the conflict spilling over (as with Colombia's turmoil affecting border areas of Ecuador and Peru and the domestic politics of Venezuela).
33. *An Agenda for Peace, Preventive diplomacy, peacemaking and peace-keeping* (UN Doc. A/47/277—S/24111), June 17, 1992.
34. 'On eve of its expiry, Annan hails "unprecedented" Iraq Oil-for-Food programme', *UN News Center*, November 20, 2003.
35. I, for one, overestimated the inclination of the P-5 to accommodate each other's priorities, believing that a confrontation would ultimately be avoided. See David M. Malone, 'The UN will come around to the Bush-Blair view', *International Herald Tribune*, February 1, 2003, 4.

2

Cold War Peacemaker: Brokering Peace in the Iran–Iraq War

The often overlooked conflict between Iran and Iraq in the 1980s was one of the most murderous of its era. With deaths on each side of at least 100,000 and much larger numbers of casualties, it proved a harbinger of further troubles for the region originating in Iraq. There, a young, determined, and brutal dictator, Saddam Hussein, had newly supplanted the figurehead leader of the Ba'ath regime only a year before the outbreak of the conflict with Iran. As Dilip Hiro, the most prolific English language historian of this war and its aftermath, commented in 1989:

> The 1980–88 Iran Iraq conflict [was] the longest conventional warfare of [the last] century ....[1] With more than a million casualties, the Gulf War [was] also one of the bloodiest. The cost of conducting it, and direct and indirect damage caused by it, is put at an astronomical $1,190 billion.[2]

These statements translate only inadequately the trauma visited on both societies by warfare involving 'human wave' techniques leading to wholescale slaughter and maiming on the front lines, chemical gas attacks by Iraq, bombing by both parties, and military leadership on both sides that might best be described as blinkered. Indeed, it is the gentle but incisive films emanating from Iran since the mid-1980s, often centrally or tangentially concerned with the social and human wreckage of the war, that best convey the breadth and depth of damage to Iranian society. The effect was akin to the virtual elimination of a generation of young men sustained by several European countries during World War I.

Into this murderous mix stepped the UN. Chapter 2 focuses on several critical moments during the Iran–Iraq war, the significance of which was overlooked at the time, beginning with the Security Council's inadequate, indeed misguided, reaction to Iraq's attack on Iran in 1980, that doubtless contributed to Saddam Hussein's contempt for the UN—with fateful consequences ten years later. The UN's involvement over the next decade provides a catalog of the measures available to it as a Cold War Peacemaker. This was the first phase of UN involvement in Iraq, in which the UN used its neutral position eventually to broker a settlement between Iran and Iraq in 1987–8 and then to monitor the agreement it had brokered. With Cold War tensions subsiding, the P-5 began as of 1987 quietly to work together in more creative (and assertive) ways. With the apparent success in brokering a compromise between Iran and Iraq, a new era in P-5 relations and in the capacity of the UN to address hitherto intractable conflicts appeared to have dawned.

2.1 Root Causes of the Iran–Iraq War

Hostility between Iran and Iraq has long been a staple of regional politics. The border demarcating these two countries separates not only nation-states but also different histories, ethnicities, cultures, and religions. The Persian border marked the end of the Arab World. The mighty empires of the Persians had historically aggressed or defended against Arab and earlier Mesopotamian powers centered in Baghdad, Nimrud, and many other Iraqi cities, the names of which spell archeological import and glamor. Both countries were swept at regular intervals by continental-scale conquests such as those of Alexander the Great, Genghis Khan, and Timur Lang, but their strong respective national identities rapidly reasserted themselves. Culturally and politically, Baghdad, along with Cairo and Damascus, has long been one of the Arab World's three great capitals, serving as the capital of the Islamic World for a period with the movement of the Abbasid Caliphate from Damascus to Baghdad in 748 AD. Political and cultural tensions between these neighbors continued to surface during the uneasy centuries of cohabitation between the Ottoman Turkish empire (1517–1918), then controlling the three provinces that were to become Iraq after the World War I, and successive Persian dynasties.

Division lines were cemented by divergent religious beliefs. The Safavid dynasty (1501–1722) in Persia systematized the imposition of Shi'a theology in Iran, which became a unifying factor for Iranians, largely surrounded by Islam's Sunni majority. It also provided an additional source of tension with the Ottoman Empire and with subsequent Iraqi governments that feared Iranian attempts to undermine the loyalty of Iraq's Shi'a communities, whose members actually constitute a majority in the Iraqi religious landscape as well. Access by Iranians to the Shi'a holy sites of

Najaf and Karbala (and some other lesser pilgrimage destinations) added a further dimension to the complex relationship between the two countries. Religious antagonism was a critical *casus belli* according to Jan Eliasson, the Personal Representative of the Secretary-General on Iran–Iraq in 1988, as Iraq's greatest fear was that 'Iran's threat to "export revolution" would wreak havoc among Iraq's Shi'a population.'[3]

The final major source of alternating tension and cooperation related to the Kurdish territories and populations, fiercely independent and wishing to fashion as much autonomy as possible for their politically fractious but militarily adept community. Kurdish tribes have traditionally sought to ignore the national borders of Iran, Iraq, Turkey, and Syria in pursuit of their lives. A variety of international treaties, such as that of Zuhab in 1639, between the Ottomans and the Persians, several involving external major powers, such as Russia and Great Britain, failed lastingly to settle either the issue of borders or of population flows driven by autonomous traditions or religious pilgrimage. Intrigues surrounding and involving the Kurdish communities continued to bedevil relations between first the Ottoman and Persian Empires, then Iraq and Persia, and finally Iraq and Iran, until the Iran–Iraq war broke out in 1980.

Other strategic and balance of power concerns soon appeared. The early twentieth century added further sources of tension with the discovery of oil in the southern regions of both countries, most readily accessed, to a large extent, through the Shat al Arab waterway through which both the Euphrates and the Tigris rivers flow into the Persian Gulf.[4] The boundary of the two countries relative to the Shat al Arab and navigation rights thereon would prove a rich vein of disputation between Baghdad and Tehran, particularly following the collapse of the Ottoman Empire and the emergence of modern Iraq. Relations became so fraught that in 1934 Iraq took its grievances to the League of Nations, but the League, with much else on its mind, encouraged further bilateral negotiations leading to an unstable accord, the Iran–Iraq Border Treaty of 1937. That Treaty opened the Shat al Arab to navigation by all, responding primarily to the influence and interests in the area of Britain, the period's regional hegemon.

2.1.1 *The Modern Period*

Post-World War II decolonization raised the specter of Iranian regional domination, though initially all energies were directed inward toward state-building. The feebleness of Britain's attempt to manage security in the area via the Baghdad Pact of 1951, encompassing Britain, Pakistan, Iran, Iraq, and Turkey, was revealed in 1958. In that year, the superficial amity within this group was torn asunder by revolution in Iraq, ploughing under the ersatz monarchy the British had imported to Baghdad from Saudi Arabia. The revolution spawned a nationalist—initially military—regime hostile to the British. The 1960s proved a period of great instability in Baghdad, with several coups culminating in a consolidation of power in 1968 by the Arab Ba'ath Socialist Party.[5] Turbid Ba'ath revolutionary ideology conjoined with intense nationalism to dictate absolute rejection of the new cast of the Western-inspired balance of power in the Gulf. During this period, Iraq's integrity was threatened by Kurdish uprisings covertly supported by Iran, Israel, and the United States to varying degrees. It was also threatened by numerous Shi'a insurrections, put down by Hussein through a mix of savage repression of ring-leading organizations (mainly Al Dawaa al Islamiyah and later Al Mujahiddin) and a degree of accommodation with religious leaders.[6] Finally, the 1973 Israeli–Arab war added another ideological and military enemy to the long list Baghdad had been compiling since 1958.

In the midst of these overlapping intrigues in Iraq's north, in 1971 Britain confirmed its withdrawal from the Gulf as a protector power, and acted to strengthen the hand of the Shah of Iran as the new guarantor of security for the smaller Gulf emirates and for the free flow of oil. The Shah's regional pretensions soon generated disputes between Iraq and Iran, which led to skirmishes that grew sufficiently worrying in early 1974 to draw in the Security Council, eventually resulting in a Council resolution urging more amicable behavior on both parties.[7] Iran subsequently used the threat of its preponderant military power to force Hussein, then serving as Iraq's Foreign Minister, to sign the 1975 Algiers Agreement, reaffirming the 1937 Treaty recognizing joint sovereignty of the Shat al Arab, as well as several other border clarifications in Iran's favor. This was a humiliation that Hussein would not soon forget and for which he vowed retribution. In July 1979, Hussein replaced his erstwhile patron Ahmed Hassan al-Bakr as President, marking his ascent with a bloody purge addressed to foiling an allegedly Syrian-inspired plot. The stage was now set for a dramatic denouement.

2.1.2 *Proximate Causes*

Ultimately, however, it was the Iranian Revolution of 1979 that simultaneously infused the relationship with new venom while offering Hussein the opportunity to address Iraqi grievances and achieve his lofty visions of Iraq's place within the region. First, Hussein and Iran's new spiritual leader, Ayatollah Ruhollah Khomeini, shared an intense dislike for each other. The Shi'a Iranian religious icon had been exiled to Najaf in Iraq in 1964 by the Pahlavi regime, but had in turn run afoul of Hussein who expelled him in 1978. The sharply personal nature of the feud was inescapable. Khomeini referred to Hussein as a 'deviant', 'completely uninformed about Islam, and, among other things ... an Arab'.[8] Hussein's retort was to highlight what he saw as a battle of wills between individuals: 'He [Khomeini] has wagered to bend us and we have wagered to bend him. We will see who will bend the other.'[9]

Second, tensions between the two countries were exacerbated by mutual meddling in the other's affairs. Khomeini's accession to the leadership of Iran was enthusiastically but imprudently greeted by Iraqi Shi'a leader Ayatollah Muhammad Bakr al-Sadr in the following terms: 'Other tyrants have yet to see their day of reckoning.'[10] (He was soon executed.) However, the nadir of this interference, from Hussein's perspective, was the attempt on the life of the deputy premier of Iraq, Tariq Aziz, by Iranian agents in April 1980. Alongside Khomeini's exhortations later that month to all Shi'a within the Iraqi army to desert, the formation of the 'Revolutionary Islamic Army for the Liberation of Baghdad', and the Ayatollah's plea to Iraqis to '[w]ake up and topple this corrupt regime in your Islamic country before it is too late', this was too much for Hussein to ignore.[11]

Third, Khomeini's rise to political power in Iran proved highly threatening to Iraq at a time when Hussein was strategically seeking to capitalize on Egypt's abdication of Arab preeminence in light of its peace treaty with Israel in 1979. Hussein soon emerged as the champion of collective Arab rights, officially demanding in a letter to the UN Secretary-General in April 1980 that Iran withdraw from three islands in the Straits of Hormuz—which controlled access to the Persian Gulf—it had seized from the United Arab Emirates (UAE) in 1971, and agitating for greater autonomy in the Arab-dominated state of Khuzistan, which Iran had swallowed in 1924.[12]

If the Iranian Revolution directly threatened Hussein and Iraq's position in the Middle East, it also gifted him the opportunity to revisit the humiliation of the 1975 Algiers Agreement. Saddam Hussein appears to have calculated that the turmoil produced by the Iranian Revolution, particularly the ideologically driven thinning of Iran's officer ranks, would undermine Iran's fighting capacity. As well, he must have concluded that his geostrategic position was far superior to that of Khomeini, given Iraq's long-standing trading partnership with Moscow and Washington's overriding enmity for a regime in Iran that was still holding US hostages (and this in a Presidential election year, when President Carter's failure to secure release or effect the rescue of the hostages was gradually alienating the American public). Tehran had few obvious sources of high-tech military hardware. As Charles Tripp has noted, '[t]he [Iraqi] armed forces had been massively reinforced and rearmed as a result of the great increase in the military budget since the mid-1970s' and were now superior in virtually every statistical category to the Iranians.[13]

2.1.3 *Saddam Hussein's Strategic Objectives*

These now institutionalized, overt, and strategic tensions soon gave rise to sporadic but persistent violence in the form of border clashes, which throughout 1980 portended the outbreak of war. While responsibility for the earlier border clashes was clearly shared, the outbreak of full-scale hostilities was equally clearly initiated by Iraq—a fact acknowledged twenty-five years later by the first post-Saddam government, itself Shi'a dominated.[14] On September 17, 1980, after some preliminary skirmishing, Saddam Hussein renounced the Algiers Agreement. On September 22, he launched a full ground invasion of Iran, officially starting this devastating war, described by his ambassador at the UN at the time as an exercise in self-defense.[15]

If Hussein reasons for pursuing war with Iran are relatively clear, his strategic objectives were slightly less so. On September 28, Iraq publicized its war goals: full control over the Shat al Arab, freedom from external interference in Iraq's domestic politics, adherence to good neighborly relations, and the return of the UAE islands.[16] In addition, Hussein probably hoped to regain Khuzistan, destabilize the Iranian regime, and possibly even topple Khomeini's theocracy.[17] Iranian defectors filled Hussein's head with images of a tottering regime, whose gutted army would quickly collapse. Hussein, having learned from Israel's preemptive air strikes against Arab targets in the 1973 war, ordered his pilots to destroy Iran's air capabilities, and envisioned an Iraqi blitzkrieg that would swiftly bring Tehran to its knees. Unfortunately for Iraq, Iranians rallied to defend their revolution, and the woeful Iraqi military could not unfetter itself from an overly centralized and cautious military strategy. Indeed, military analyst Kenneth Pollack notes that the Iraqi air-strikes were so poorly planned and executed that 'in many cases bombs fell so far from any nearby military facility that the Iranians could not determine what the Iraqis had been trying to hit.'[18] The war would not end quickly.

2.2 Enter the UN?

The UN response was immediate—but ultimately vacuous. UN Secretary-General Kurt Waldheim swiftly called for Security Council consultations. Meanwhile, Waldheim himself implored both parties to settle their differences by peaceful means and offered his own good offices to facilitate any discussions to this end. The Security Council, briefed by Waldheim, issued only a weak statement endorsing the Secretary-General's position, a Council stance qualified by Cameron Hume, the most thorough historian of the UN's involvement in the Iran–Iraq war, and himself then a serving senior member of the US Foreign Service, as 'exceptionally limp'.[19] In spite of Mexican calls for a binding UN Security Council decision seeking to force a halt to the fighting, the Council on September 28 adopted SCR 479 (1980) calling for a cease-fire (but no withdrawal of troops behind recognized borders). This stock UN response generated little resonance. Again, Hume is withering, noting the view of a then senior US National Security Council Adviser: 'Gary Sick ... criticized the resolution for its "lackadaisical approach", because it referred to the war as merely a "situation", not even a "dispute", when surely there was already a breach of the peace.'[20] For Brian Urquhart, the matter should have been straightforward: 'Iraqi action was a clear and massive violation of the sovereignty of another state which should, if only as a matter of principle, have immediately been denounced as such.' 'The Security Council', Urquhart continues, denouncing the pusillanimity of the world's premiere international security organ, 'had seldom seemed less worthy of respect.'[21] From this date onward, until 1987, Iran mostly boycotted the Security Council in protest against its perceived anti-Iranian bias, which weighed heavily on the Council's ability to mediate and manage the situation.[22]

The Security Council's muted response to an act of aggression (by Iraq) against a Member State (Iran), which on its face warranted a proactive approach under relevant provisions of the UN Charter, probably bore out Saddam's initial calculations of Great Power disinterest. Iran's revolution and the incandescence of its Islamist zeal threatened most of the major powers in one way or another. The United States (and to a lesser extent, the United Kingdom) had lost footing in Iran—earlier seen as the principal local agent of stability in the Gulf region—as a result of the revolution and the dramatic seizure of its embassy in November 1979. Although the realignment of alliances in the Gulf region that would later move Washington closer to Baghdad had not yet occurred, any alternative to regional military dominance by the revolutionary regime in Tehran must have appeared at least mildly attractive. The prospect of Khomeini's Iran being brought low, even by Iraq's thuggish regime, can only have made for rejoicing among officials in Washington. At the same time, initial policy in Washington was to profess neutrality, in order to work out a 'spares-for-hostages' deal in which the United States would ship desperately needed spare parts to Iran in exchange for the American hostages held by Tehran.[23] Indeed, the United States attempted to decouple the issues of the war and hostages, in order to ensure that the door to the hostage crisis resolution remained open just as the American election was drawing to a close.[24]

The United Kingdom, France, and the Soviet Union had extensive dealings with Iraq, especially in terms of arms. Moscow was additionally nervous about the intentions of an Islamist state on its southern border—one which had recently outlawed its Communist Party at that.[25] Nevertheless, none of these powers were eager to associate themselves with Baghdad's aggressive and brutal regime. With China functionally neutral, the unique constellation of interests of the P-5 at the point of the outbreak of the war produced an attitude in the Council, which might be most accurately summed up as hoping both belligerents would lose—but that Iran must not win.[26] The idea of an active UN role to stop the fighting, lacking a geostrategic payoff in the Cold War framework, generated little support. The Council, still characterized by this Cold War calculus, was not yet, as it would later become, much moved by the idea of large-scale casualties, including among civilians, and was seen mainly by Washington and Moscow as an inconvenience at a time when they were wrestling with the Iran hostage crisis and the troubled Soviet invasion of Afghanistan, respectively. There was no champion yet for a settlement, and there would not be one at the UN until 1986 when Secretary-General Javier Pérez de Cuéllar articulated a strong case for bringing the hostilities to a close. In the meanwhile, Security Council members largely trod water while recording 'pious' wishes for a cease-fire at the UN.[27]

2.2.1 *Stalemate*

Early Iraqi gains on the ground against disorganized Iranian forces soon yielded to unproductive but murderous trench warfare, and a massive and largely successful Iranian counterstrike. Initially, most Arab countries evinced a degree of indifference toward Iraq's initiative, possibly because Saddam Hussein had failed to consult them before attacking Iran, perhaps because the extent of Iran's interference in Iraq's domestic politics through the latter's Shi'a community was not widely appreciated, and largely because the Iraqi media presented the war primarily as the crusade of one man (Hussein) against another (Khomeini).[28] Arab attitudes were to shift from a lack of commitment to Iraq's cause to fear of Iranian victory after battlefield developments in 1982.

By then, most Iraqi gains on the ground had been reversed. Baghdad's military advantage had been eliminated. This shift, in many ways surprising, in turn brought about a warming in relations between Baghdad and Washington (which, under President Carter, had been highly critical of Iraqi domestic human rights abuses). Washington removed Iraq from the list of countries sponsoring terrorism (while adding Iran) and in 1984 restored full diplomatic relations with Baghdad, soon sharing with it vital intelligence on Iran's capabilities. While oil markets were affected by the fighting in a number of ways, with prices oscillating up and down in the short term, Washington simply could not afford to allow the balance of power in the Persian Gulf to shift decisively in the long run toward a country sworn to enmity with the United States. This explains why, as the fighting eventually spread to shipping in the Gulf, the United States intervened to protect its Arab allies in the area and their navigation rights. While Moscow attempted to project a degree of neutrality toward the combatants, it viewed the militancy of the Islamic revolution as anathema, particularly as Tehran made every effort to export its ideology to the Soviet Republics of Central Asia. Moscow disapproved of Iraq's unprovoked attack on Iran, but strong preexisting ties between the two countries soon overcame this impediment to active Soviet support for Iraq's war effort.

The Security Council evinced disinterest. Despite issuing regular, repetitious and ultimately bland resolutions, it seemed preoccupied with more pressing concerns such as Israeli activities in Lebanon and the eruption of the Falklands War.[29] Nonetheless, without seeking or obtaining any explicit support from the Security Council, the new UN Secretary-General, Javier Pérez de Cuéllar, reappointed a Personal Representative, former Swedish Prime Minister Olof Palme, to help nudge Iran and Iraq toward compromise. Such high-level mediators operating under the authority and control of the Secretary-General were not an innovation, and sometimes created no more than the illusion of diplomatic movement. But Palme, an energetic and acute operator, later assassinated in his own country when again Prime Minister, engaged actively with both parties. Sweden's continuing commitment to resolving the crisis, later through the involvement of Jan Eliasson, one of Palme's closest associates and Sweden's ambassador to the UN, was widely welcomed. More significantly, it was evidence that in conflicts essentially paralysing or leaving indifferent the permanent members of the Security Council, mid-sized countries can make significant contributions to conflict resolution even in the least promising circumstances.[30] Nevertheless, after several rounds of talks in Tehran and Baghdad, and faced with Iranian insistence that Iraq would have to relinquish all captured territory before any matters of substance could be discussed, Palme reached the conclusion that the situation was not 'ripe' for settlement.[31]

Iraq's battlefield reversals persuaded it to seek out, through allies in the Non-Aligned Movement (NAM), a basis for negotiations under the aegis of the UN. By July 1982, Security Council President Guyana overcame the hesitancy of the other Council members and forged SCR 514, which called for a cease-fire, withdrawal to internationally recognized borders, and even a dispatch of UN observers to monitor the cease-fire. A similar resolution was adopted in October in the form of SCR 522.[32] But, Iran's military good fortune, coupled with the fact that it doubted 'the impartiality and objectivity of this distinguished body [the Security Council] which had remained silent for more than 22 months of Iraqi occupation of our territories', compelled it to reject SCRs 514 and 522.[33] The ensuing three years would be terrible, indeed terrorizing ones, for both countries, whose regimes cloaked themselves in self-righteousness, committed to ill-conceived field tactics and advanced extreme negotiating positions when they advanced any at all.

2.2.2 *An Early Glimpse of Humanitarianism*

The year 1983 saw steps toward the eventual establishment of the first resident UN presence in the area, resulting from international revulsion over attacks on civilian sites, including the cities of both countries, as well as some concern over the use of chemical weapons. This was the first glimpse of a new form of UN involvement in Iraq, as a neutral protector of humanitarian interests, which was to come increasingly to the fore in years beyond.

The UN response to the use of chemical weapons by the Iraqis as early as August 1983 was tempered by P-5 reticence to acknowledge and deal with the problem. Iran's repeated letters to the Security Council eventually forced the dispatch of an investigatory team to the area in March 1984. However, the guarded report that followed from the investigation studiously avoided assigning blame and contended that Iran may also have resorted to gas attacks in reprisal.[34] The moral and geopolitical ramifications of this abdication of responsibilities were clear to Sweden's Eliasson who felt that 'reacting weakly and meekly to the use of chemical weapons may have been the single most objectionable feature of the international community's response to Saddam Hussein's aggression and foreshadowed his further depredations through chemical weapons in 1988.'[35]

There was greater but still mixed progress on the conventional warfare front. Both Iraq and Iran appealed to the Secretary-General to authorize a team to investigate claims of abuse. Pérez de Cuéllar agreed, both on the grounds of humanitarian concern, as well as the fact that with such teams in place 'it might be feasible to construct a basis for dialog between the two countries and, possibly, to persuade Iran to restore contact with the Security Council.'[36] Attacks continued, however, and on June 9, 1984, Pérez de Cuéllar appealed to both sides to refrain from deliberate military attacks on purely civilian centers of population. When both Iran and Iraq agreed to this, the Secretary-General informed the Security Council of his decision to deploy inspection teams in the region. Their task would be to investigate alleged attacks on civilian areas. This produced a short-lived truce in the 'war of the cities'. By the end of June, two teams were installed in Baghdad and Tehran, each composed of three officers seconded from the United Nations Truce Supervision Organization (UNTSO) operating in Israel/Palestine, and one senior official of the United Nations Secretariat. (Their presence in the capitals four years later facilitated the establishment of UNIIMOG, which oversaw implementation of the UN-brokered Iran–Iraq cease-fire.)

Only nine months later, fresh Iranian offensives in the south were again accompanied by air raids by each side on urban centers. The fighting had also migrated to new fronts, taking hostage the shipping lanes of the Gulf, increasingly the theater for attacks on oil tankers—the so-called 'tanker war'. These attacks failed to halt the flow of oil to international markets but did create significant anxiety and increased greatly both risks and costs related to oil transportation in the region. In 1984, fifty-four tankers were struck, most by Iraq. In response to a plea from the Gulf Cooperation Council (GCC—essentially allied with Iraq), made up of Arab oil-producing States on the southern shores of the Gulf, the Security Council adopted SCR 552 condemning and demanding an end to such attacks on shipping to and from nonbelligerent states.[37] But the resolution had little impact. On the other hand, arms sales to the region, particularly to Iraq and Saudi Arabia, were booming. (While Russia and the United States focused mostly on sales to Iraq, China was an equal opportunity supplier.) Escalation of the war had increasing international repercussions. Several countries dispatched minesweeping and escort craft in an attempt to facilitate safe commercial passage through international waters. The fragile emirates of the GCC, long opposed to an internationalization of the Iran–Iraq conflict, now became afraid that one or the other belligerent might cut off their economic lifeblood and even threaten their sovereignty. The GCC countries had originally been leery of overtly alienating Iran, but as the latter's military edge in the conflict increased in 1982–3, they increasingly called on the major powers to guarantee freedom of navigation in the Gulf.

2.3 Winds of Change

The stagnating situation between Iran and Iraq was ruffled by the winds of change in 1986, a year that was both tumultuous and sobering. P-5 interests aligned fortuitously, presaging expanded cooperation within the Council on Iran and Iraq—and perhaps beyond.

The key to the increased assertiveness of the Council on the issue was the changed position of the Soviet Union. Under its new leader, Gorbachev, the USSR began to edge away from the logic of superpower confrontation and increasingly turning to 'new thinking'. On February 25, 1986, at the 27th Communist Party Congress, Gorbachev launched his policy of perestroika—restructuring—by admitting frankly that '[f]or a number of years, the deeds and actions of party and government bodies tailed behind the needs of the times and life—not only because of objective factors, but also for reasons above all of a subjective order'. In the international arena, Chairman Gorbachev hinted at rapprochement in declaring that '[m]ilitarism is gorging itself on the arms race' between the United States and USSR.[38]

2.3.1 *A 'Meeting of the Minds'*

Moscow's position, however tentative, was a positive step. But again, personalities mattered. Prince Saud al-Faisal, the Saudi Foreign Minister, suggested in late summer 1986 that the Security Council consider a more balanced position on the conflict in an effort to encourage the Iranians to join negotiations, perhaps reflecting a recognition by major Arab states that the war had degenerated into a protracted stalemate.[39] Sensing an opportunity not only in this proposal, but in the winds of change from

Moscow, Pérez de Cuéllar, hardly a bold Secretary-General during his first term, stepped in.

In January 1987, the newly reelected Pérez de Cuéllar challenged the permanent members of the Council to cooperate with each other to promote a settlement of this deadlocked but spreading crisis. With Iran boycotting the body at that time, his initiative may have seemed quixotic, but Pérez de Cuéllar knew better than most the reach of the UN Charter, if political will were available to resort to its provisions. What was needed, he argued, was a 'meeting of the minds'.[40]

The timing of Pérez de Cuéllar's suggestion was propitious, as 1987 witnessed a constellation of interests on the part of the P-5, particularly in the United States. In Washington, scandal and shipping problems in the Gulf combined to encourage the White House to give the Secretary-General's vision a try. The embarrassing revelations regarding the Iran/Contra affair, which broke in November 1986, 'dramatically weakened Washington's credibility in the Middle East'.[41] The scandal involved several senior contemporaneous and former members of the Administration, and featured illicit covert transfer of missiles to Iran, as a sweetener for improved relations. A chastened Administration was also increasingly disturbed by the rising frequency of attacks on shipping in the Gulf. By December 1986, it had reached agreement with the Kuwait Tanker company to place its ships under American flag, and later redeployed its naval assets in the Gulf to escort more aggressively the reflagged ships.[42] Iraq's missile attack on May 17, 1987 on the *USS Stark*, which killed thirty-seven, highlighted the growing external dangers of the war.[43] Though Iraq quickly apologized and the United States displayed tremendous retributive restraint, it was glaringly apparent to Washington that the expansion of the conflict to the Gulf sea-lanes threatened stable oil supply and the world economy. The United States responded by persevering with the reflagging of Kuwaiti vessels under US colors, thus 'internationalizing' the conflict to a degree,[44] but the upshot of these two events was a willingness in Washington to seek a negotiated end to the conflict.[45]

France and Britain were similarly enticed to the table during this period as a result of scandal and grievances. Allegations in the French media that Defense Minister Charles Hernu had personally benefited from the secret export of arms to Iran between 1983 and 1986 may have stimulated French support for a negotiated reduction of the conflict, especially as the Iraqi attack on the *USS Stark* used French-manufactured Exocet missiles. France's enthusiasm for negotiations was also fuelled by its desire for access to the Iranian diplomat, Wahid Gorji, in connection with a series of bombings in France. The United Kingdom similarly sought a negotiated solution to the detention of a British diplomat by the Iranian government. As Hume points out, France and Britain were doubtless delighted to explore new potential for an underused forum in which their permanent seats gave them leverage out of all proportion to their actual international weight.[46]

Finally, signals from Moscow continued to indicate a cautious willingness to seek diplomatic resolution. In January 1987, just weeks after Pérez de Cuéllar's call for a 'meeting of the minds', Gorbachev complemented perestroika with glasnost—openness—declaring that '[w]e want more openness about public affairs in every sphere of life.... Truth is the main thing.... We need glasnost as we need air.'[47] This 'openness' to new ideas was put to the test by an Iranian Revolutionary Guards attack on a Soviet vessel in the Persian Gulf on May 7, which added visible urgency to the situation. Gorbachev responded positively, and operationalized the new spirit in the Kremlin by arguing that the world's 'regional conflicts'—the wreckage of the Cold War—should be resolved through the intermediation and under the guidance of the UN Security Council. In a famous article published in *Pravda* and *Izvestia* on September 17, 1987, Gorbachev called for

> wider use of ... the institution of UN military observers and UN peace-keeping forces in disengaging the troops of warring sides, observing ceasefires and armistice agreements.[48]

Thus, the USSR opened the door to robust Security Council involvement in international peace and security. Moscow certainly feared an outright defeat of its ally, Iraq, but more than this genuinely wished to move toward less tense international relations, using the Security Council as a key forum for consensus-building. Robert S. Litwak wrote:

> During the Iran–Iraq war, the United States and the Soviet Union shared certain common interests and goals. Both emphasized the dangers of escalation and inadvertent involvement; neither Washington nor Moscow desired to see a decisive victory by either combatant. True, each superpower ... continued to pursue essentially a zero-sum approach in pursuit of unilateral advantage at the other's expense; however, through words and actions, Gorbachev ... made clear that he strongly wishe[d] to avoid the repetition of the experience of the late 1970s during which Soviet activism in the Third World was a major factor underlying the demise of détente.[49]

2.3.2 *Breaking Through: Resolution 598*

The circumstances were right for a denouement. The permanent members initiated consultations among themselves in private, away from the UN, at both senior and technical levels, to establish whether a common approach might be possible.[50] Potential stumbling-blocks included Iranian insistence that responsibility for the war be clearly assigned to Iraq, the specifics of protection for shipping in the Gulf, the documented use of chemical weapons in the conflict (contrary to the provisions of the 1925 Geneva Convention), the continuing wholesale (and highly lucrative) supply of arms to the belligerents—not least by the P-5—and issues of reparations and reconstruction. Each of these issues would need to be addressed, if a cease-fire and a return to the *status quo ante* borders were to be seriously promoted by the UN. Several of the elements (notably the security of shipping in the Gulf) had been addressed directly or indirectly by the Council in the set of incantatory resolutions adopted since 1980, but little political energy could be detected behind these texts.[51]

Newly liberated (from the strict Cold War mindset), invigorated (by a sense of cautious optimism generated by this sea change), and motivated (by the growing costs on shipping), the P-5 rose to the Secretary-General's challenge. This turning point was reflected in new working methods. The P-5, and eventually the Council as a whole, largely left behind their public wrangling in the iconic Security Council chamber for quieter and more productive discussions behind closed doors in so-called 'informal consultations' of various kinds.[52] The positive and constructive energy generated by these informal sessions even led the Secretary-General to later declare that '[o]nly at this point in 1987, 45 years after the founding of the United Nations, did such cooperation become—tentatively at first—a reality'.[53] While infinitely more fruitful an approach than the set-piece confrontations that characterized the Security Council during the Cold War, these 'informals' were soon to arouse the resentment and ire of UN members not included. The ability and willingness of the P-5 at last to work closely with each other reinforced the second-class status of the Council's elected members. As to the UN members not sitting on the Council at any given time, they were consigned to an outer circle of the hell of the excluded. P-5 delegations meanwhile developed a new *modus operandi* among themselves, akin to how friendly nations negotiate with one another: 'no unambiguous lies, no breaking of explicit promises, no invective or threats, and no blatant backtracking on agreements in principle and mutual understandings.'[54]

The series of events to May 1987 precipitated the 'meeting of the minds' that Pérez de Cuéllar had sought. The first question was the extent to which the provisions of Chapter VII of the Charter should feature in a meaningful Security Council initiative. During the Cold War years,

Chapter VII had been mostly ignored due to the absence of trust between the permanent members, but with the P-5 gaining greater confidence in each other's good faith and better understanding each other's interests and positions, aspects of Chapter VII were seen as potentially useful in impressing on the belligerents the seriousness of the Council's intent to curb and bring major hostilities to an end.[55] Thus, in what was to become Resolution 598, the P-5 agreed among themselves informally to include references to Articles 39 and 40 of the Charter, formally establishing a threat to or breach of the peace and authorizing provisional measures, for now leaving out any reference to Articles 41 and 42, which could have authorized enforcement measures. Today, in an age when a broad range of Chapter VII provisions is routinely invoked by the Council, the delicacy of this diplomatic minuet may seem odd, but it is historically significant in pointing to a new and profound shift in perspective among the P-5 in early 1987. The P-5 were now suggesting that the Council 'demand' a cease-fire and a withdrawal of forces behind internationally recognized boundaries, an escalation in tone and legal nuance pregnant with significance for the UN community (and perhaps to a limited extent also for the self-involved belligerents).

By June 23, 1987, the Council as a whole was seized of the P-5 ideas. Elected Council members offered some suggestions of their own, notably Ghana, a long-standing participant in UN peacekeeping, which advocated the provision of UN peacekeeping to help consolidate the proposed cease-fire, an idea the P-5 were to accept. On July 20, 1987, the Council adopted Resolution 598, establishing a new high-water mark of Council assertiveness in interstate conflicts. The key demands were that Iran and Iraq observe an immediate ceasefire, discontinue all military actions on land, at sea and in the air, and withdraw all forces to the internationally recognized boundaries without delay. Significantly, the resolution gave the UN Secretariat key roles: dispatching a team of observers to verify, confirm and supervise the cease-fire, and withdrawal; mediation to achieve a comprehensive, just and honorable settlement, acceptable to both sides, of all outstanding issues; exploring the idea of entrusting an impartial body with inquiring into responsibility for the conflict (a key demand by Iran); assigning a team of experts to study the question of reconstruction; and, in consultation with Iran and Iraq and with other States of the region, examining measures to enhance the stability of the region.

The US Secretary of State, George Shultz, was ebullient—and rightly so—in recognizing this turning point for the Security Council, remarking that 'nothing like this unanimous vote on an issue of real importance and difficulty had ever happened before in the history of the United Nations.... Constructive action through the United Nations was now possible.'[56] This praise was echoed by US President Ronald Reagan, who in a letter to Pérez de Cuéllar opined that '[b]y this action, the United Nations is living up to the highest purposes set for it by its founders so many years ago.' The President did, however, note that without a commitment to enforcement if necessary—a concerted effort which was still mostly taboo for the Council—this historic pronouncement would be rendered meaningless.[57] Washington had attempted to link the notion that noncompliance with the Council's demands—anticipated mainly by Iran, now in the ascendant militarily—could lead to mandatory, UN Security Council-imposed sanctions, agreed to only twice before (against Southern Rhodesia and South Africa). Washington saw this approach as giving the cease-fire demand teeth, building up Security Council credibility, and serving to intimidate its arch-enemy in the region, Iran. Eventually, Washington attempted to combine adoption of Resolution 598 with a private agreement among the P-5 to move on to adoption of sanctions should compliance not ensue. Other permanent members were not keen, and when Shultz, on the occasion of the resolution's unanimous adoption on July 20 advocated the adoption of enforcement measures should the parties fail to comply, the United States threat fell flat. Already, here were signs of the problem of enforcement that was to plague the Council over Iraq for many years to come.

2.4 UN at the Helm

Unfortunately, while the Council was demonstrating newfound unity, events on the ground continued to be dictated by the gains or losses of the respective militaries. Iran had recently gained the upper hand militarily, and to such a degree that Iraq agreed to the investigation proposed by SCR 598, designed to identify the party culpable for the start of the war.[58] 'This was an open concession to Teheran,' according to UN veteran Giandomenico Picco, 'which had always insisted that the war had been started by Saddam Hussein.'[59] With Iran able to extract concessions on the battlefield, it emphatically rejected SCR 598, denouncing 'fundamental defects and incongruities' and criticizing it as an American diplomatic maneuver.[60] Iraq was understandably more forthcoming, welcoming the resolution, but continuing to place more faith in its fighting forces.

Pérez de Cuéllar adjusted his own diplomatic stance. Drawing on the momentum SCR 598 generated, he invited Council guidance (and thus support) for his own mediation efforts (a departure from Olof Palme's mediation in 1982 under the Secretary-General's sole authority). This support he received. Thus empowered, in his own contacts in the belligerent capitals he pointed to the terms of SCR 598 as a straitjacket constraining his own flexibility. For the Iranians, a prime objective remained Iraq's identification as the aggressor, in light of the ongoing investigation. Iraq was able to shelter behind Iranian obduracy, claiming to accept the resolution's terms. Iran, acutely aware that its uncompromising stance could play into the hands of Washington on the sanctions question, redoubled efforts to engage Moscow and Beijing on its side.

In September 1987, the Secretary-General travelled to Tehran and Baghdad, and a period of intense diplomatic activity ensued, with negotiations in the region and at United Nations Headquarters in New York. In October, the Secretary-General tabled the implementation plan of a resolution, which he had originally presented to the Council in September. In the spring of 1988, he met repeatedly with representatives of both countries in an attempt to reach accord on the implementation of SCR 598, inviting both sides to send special emissaries to New York for consultations, which took place in April 1988.

2.4.1 *Iran Comes to Terms*

Ultimately, however, it was the combination of Iraqi gains in the field and increasing US military intervention that forced Iran to concede and turn to SCR 598 as a viable option. A failed attempt to take Basra, together with a series of sallies by the Iraqis exhausted the Iranian forces. 'The destruction', wrote Kenneth Pollack, 'at the hands of the Iraqi army was the most important factor that compelled Iran to accept a cease-fire, but it was certainly not the only one.'[61]

The Iraqi victory was made possible by American exasperation with the Iranians and an increasing desire to force them to the table. First, Operation Staunch ensured that no American military supplies reached Tehran (with the embarrassing but brief exception of the Iran/Contra scandal). Second, the United States moved to protect its vital interest—oil—in the region. Throughout 1987, a number of vessels of multiple nationalities were struck by Iranian fire, inducing the United States to signal its intent to police the region.[62] Thus in September, the US Navy intercepted Iranian attempts to mine international shipping channels, scuttling several ships in the process. In October American helicopters sank three Iranian patrol boats, and on October 19 the United States destroyed two offshore oil platforms equipped with radar in response to an Iranian missile, which had hit a US-reflagged tanker, blinding its American captain. By April 1988, the US Navy escalated the naval war by conducting Operation Praying Mantis, sinking numerous other speedboats and even frigates, decimating Iran's navy and thus removing it from the military equation.[63] (Some of these incidents ultimately found their way into the UN's principal judicial organ, the International Court of Justice. It did not render a judgment until 2003, a delay indicative of the generous opportunities for stalling tactics afforded litigants by the ICJ's rules of procedure, and the resulting irrelevance of the ICJ to active conflict resolution, as opposed to norm development on conflict.[64] Ultimately, the Solomonic judgment denied reparations to both.[65])

The Iranians promised a crushing response, but national exhaustion prevented this. At the time, the Iranian regime's truculent tone may have contributed to new momentum behind the American idea of an arms embargo (as opposed to broader sanctions) against it. In bilateral negotiations, the Russians agreed to support this approach, but insisted on two caveats: (*a*) a delay in the coming into effect of the resolution, to allow for a last-ditch diplomatic effort to bring Iran into compliance with SCR 598; and (*b*) the appointment, to this end, of a special emissary of the Secretary-General.[66] But events on the ground, specifically the aforementioned Iraqi counteroffensive, sidelined this strand of diplomacy in the war. Renewed Iraqi use of chemical weapons and its indiscriminate attacks on Iranian cities made sanctions against Iran seem less appropriate to many in the UN community.

However, it was an American action on July 3, 1988 that produced the war's final major convulsion. While the remnants of the Iranian navy skirmished with two US warships in the Strait of Hormuz, the *USS Vincennes* mistakenly shot down an Iranian civilian airliner en route from Bandar Abbas to Dubai.[67] Tehran viewed both Operation Praying Mantis and the airliner incident as evidence that the United States was moving from tacit support of Iraq to full-blown engagement with Iran, and that 'America could be expected to use its full military might against Iran if the fighting continued—which even Ayatollah Khomeini was eventually persuaded would be disastrous.'[68] Having already quietly disclosed that it would 'co-operate with the Secretary-General for the implementation of all substantive provisions of the resolution as a continuous process and within as short a total time-frame as practicable', while stopping short of formal acceptance of SCR 598,[69] Iran finally began again to deal with the Security Council on July 5 and accepted SCR 598 on July 18.[70] Dilip Hiro comments, 'Iran was no longer able to overcome its inferiority in arms, financial strength and diplomatic power with manpower and high motivation.'[71] Iraq having accepted SCR 598 (with several reservations), the endgame was now in sight, a very bloody year after the Council's approach was first adopted.

2.5 Implementing Peace

As noted above, SCR 598 addressed the need both for verification and supervision of a cease-fire and for mediation to resolve all outstanding issues between the two countries. With formal agreement to a cease-fire in sight, the Secretary-General sent a technical mission, led by the Chief of Staff of UNTSO, to Iran and Iraq in July 1988 to work out the modalities for the dispatch of the UN observer group. The mission held detailed discussions with the authorities in both capitals about the method of operation of the observer group, its deployment in each of the two countries, and the cooperation and facilities it would require from both parties.

As for Baghdad, despite its military advantage, exhaustion, ballooning debt, and Great Power pressure compelled Hussein to agree to the cease-fire, with the result that the Security Council was able to announce a critical path for the implementation of SCR 598.[72] The Secretary-General then set August 20 as the date for the cease-fire and announced the dispatch of 350 UN observers from 25 countries to be in place to verify compliance by both sides.[73]

This small force, authorized in SCR 619 of August 11, 1988, the United Nations Iran-Iraq Military Observer Group (UNIIMOG), under the Secretary-General's command and with a limited mandate (to establish a cease-fire line, verify compliance, investigate violations, and confirm the withdrawal of forces), proved one of the UN's most successful ventures in the 'classic' peacekeeping of interposition. Overall, compliance was remarkable.[74]

Initially, implementation stalled, as the Shat al Arab boundary became a major issue. With the possibility of reopening the waterway now in play, Iraq insisted on gains relative to the Algiers Agreement (which Saddam Hussein had so dramatically discarded at the outset of hostilities) as its bottom-line. Pérez de Cuéllar, having launched the talks, left Eliasson in charge, perhaps sensing that Iran would not soon yield on the Algiers formula as its own bottom-line. They remained deadlocked for a year, with Iraq insisting on direct talks and Iran insisting on the troop withdrawals that SCR 598 mandated. But on July 3, 1990, Pérez de Cuéllar finally engineered a face-to-face meeting of the two chief negotiators (Ali Akbar Velayati for Iran, Tariq Aziz for Iraq) in Geneva, improving the atmospherics. With both sides respecting the cease-fire agreement, a (limited) exchange of prisoners having taken place, and the sense of threat to global order receding fast, the permanent members and the rest of the Council had long since bowed out of active involvement.

On July 30, 1990, just hours before his unprovoked invasion of Kuwait, Saddam Hussein wrote to his Iranian counterpart in a show of conciliation, although reiterating hard-line negotiating positions. This gesture of *détente* unblocked negotiations between Iran and Iraq. On August 8, Iranian President Rafsanjani responded, rejecting Iraq's various proposals, laconically noting: 'No doubt, while peace talks are in process between the two countries, unexpected aggression against a neighbour country without the slightest notice, and accompanied by all its grave consequences for us, could weaken our trust and create serious doubt on the motives of the past few months' talks.'[75] Less than a week later, on August 14, in the spirit of occasional pragmatism he was wont to display and having found opposition to his Kuwait venture stronger than he had anticipated, Saddam Hussein abruptly abandoned his position on the Shat al Arab boundary, signaling to Iran that the Algiers Agreement could serve as the basis for settling the dispute. He initiated release and repatriation of prisoners of war on August 17, and Iraqi withdrawal of troops was completed four days later.

Thus ended one of the late Cold War's most violent and intractable of conflicts, overtaken by Saddam Hussein's expansionist drive (and need for financial resources) in another direction—one he presumably hoped would prove more successful. Iran played no major role in Iraq–Kuwait hostilities, although its relevance to Iraq was brought sharply into relief by Iranian involvement in the Shi'a uprising in Iraq's south in March 1991, and resurfaced again during and following US-led action against Saddam Hussein in early 2003.[76]

In the difficult circumstances surrounding Iraq's invasion of Kuwait, the Secretary-General recommended that the Security Council extend the mandate of a downsized UNIIMOG for a limited period of only two months, instead of six months as it had done on three previous occasions. That approach was effected by the Council in SCR 676. Over the two months which followed, both sides continued the process of withdrawal of their forces to the internationally recognized boundaries, without serious incident.

The Secretary-General undertook consultations with the two parties about the future of UNIIMOG. His position was that after the withdrawal of the forces had been completed, UNIIMOG should have a continuing role to play in facilitating the early solution of residual problems arising from the withdrawal and in helping the parties to negotiate and implement agreements on an area of separation and an area of limitation of armaments. This foreshadowed the administratively intense regulatory approach to implementing peace that the UN would adopt in the region in subsequent years. Partially as a result of these efforts, in January 1991 the two parties agreed to convene a technical meeting of military experts to discuss and resolve outstanding issues, with boundary, mining, and separation agreements reached shortly thereafter.

Despite the extreme difficulties posed by the commencement of Coalition military operations in mid-January 1991, implementation of SCR 598 as related to UNIIMOG continued to inch toward completion. On January 31, 1991 the Security Council unanimously adopted SCR 685, extending the mandate of UNIIMOG one last time. On February 20, the Group reported that the last of the disputed positions along the internationally recognized boundaries had been withdrawn. UNIIMOG had thus completed verification and confirmation of the withdrawal of all forces. On February 26, the Secretary-General reported that the forces of the two sides had withdrawn fully to the internationally recognized boundaries. He recommended replacing UNIIMOG with small civilian offices in Baghdad and Tehran. These offices included a few military officers to allow the UN to continue to respond to requests for help in resolving matters for which military expertise was required. By the end of 1992, the offices in Baghdad and Tehran were phased out, and the Permanent Missions of Iran and Iraq became the channels of communication between those countries and the United Nations for matters related to SCR 598.

2.6 Conclusions

In retrospect, the trends of UN involvement in the Iran–Iraq war reveal patterns that have shaped not only developments in that region, and the UN's role therein, but also the subsequent development of the UN's role as guardian of international peace and security. The patterns of UN involvement in this first phase, recurring throughout subsequent phases, include:

P-5 use of the Security Council as a geostrategic resource, a growing role for the UN as independent guardian of humanitarian interests, management of tensions between senior UN officials and the Security Council, and the challenge of maintaining UN legitimacy.

2.6.1 *Security Council as Geostrategic Resource*

The international backdrop to the conflict was critical both to its outcome, and to the role the UN played in brokering that outcome. Although neither Iran nor Iraq achieved its basic objectives, the antipathy Shi'a Iran's Islamic revolution had attracted, not least within the Sunni-ruled Muslim countries, greatly constrained Iran's options, both militarily (in terms of the weaponry available to it) and diplomatically. Conversely, Iraq, not previously close to Washington, was greatly helped by growing American concern (leading to diplomatic and other help) over the possibility of an outright Iranian victory. It also received continuing support from Moscow in the form of a steady stream of Russian weaponry. Thus, Saddam Hussein was able to recover from his disastrous initial calculation of Iranian weakness. For Washington, the scorecard was less satisfactory.[77] Reflecting on war and peace in the Middle East, Avi Shlaim notes:

> America's policy towards Iran left a legacy of suspicion and hostility. Its policy toward Iraq, although inconsistent, ended up by accepting Saddam Hussein as a junior partner in preserving the status quo in the Gulf, a ... remarkable irony in light of America's subsequent war with Saddam in early 1991.... The war solved nothing. The hostility between Iran and Iraq, and Iran and America, was as great, if not greater at the end of this eight year war as it had been at the beginning.[78]

Writing in 1989, Charles Tripp described perceptively the challenges facing Saddam Hussein at that point:

> The war with Iran has had the effect of reinforcing Saddam Hussein's autocracy in Iraq, by allowing him to demand complete submission to his will, as the means of ensuring effective mass mobilization to prevent an Iranian invasion.... His major problem is how to maintain such a degree of control in the absence of so pressing, immediate and relatively uncontroversial a task as the defense of Iraq against Iranian armed forces. This is, to some extent, the problem facing all autocrats.... In terms of Saddam Hussein's political survival, the war may have ended, but the battle may have only just begun.[79]

Saddam Hussein, in looking forward, apparently failed to comprehend the extent to which he was saved from disaster by both superpowers, the USSR by providing arms and a degree of political support, and the United States mostly by withholding the same from its new arch-enemy in the region, Iran. In contemplating an attack on Kuwait, it is not clear that Hussein fully appreciated the extent to which the loss of such support would cripple his military potential and effectiveness.

The UN had had little opportunity to influence the course of the Iran–Iraq war until 1986, constrained by the Cold War standoff in the Security Council and the limited independent capacity of the Secretary-General. But with the changes in Moscow, a consensus developed among the P-5 that the time had come to give the Council a greater role, rooted in a greater confluence of their perceptions of self-interest. This might have signaled to Hussein that a threat to the interests of some of the P-5 would no longer be met with Council indifference, but with a meaningful response.

More significantly, from the perspective of the Council's development, the shift that occurred in its approach to the Iran–Iraq war after 1986 reveals the extent to which the P-5 treated the Council as a geostrategic resource, to be called on when its binding resolutions offered value-added in the pursuit of their strategic objectives. This conception of the Council as a resource to be used when convenient rather than as the indispensable hub of collective security, was obscured for a time by the euphoria and climate of cooperation that developed after the success of the Iran–Iraq experiment and even more so the ejection of Iraq from Kuwait under a Security Council mandate, both influenced by alarming threats to global oil supply.

2.6.2 *Independent Humanitarian Guardian*

The costs of the Iran–Iraq war in human lives, injuries, property and environmental damage (not least through the lingering effects of land-mines), and resources were horrendous. Dilip Hiro advances figures of 367,000 war dead (262,000 Iranians and 105,000 Iraqis), citing conservative Western sources.[80] Iran's Minister of Islamic Guidance admitted to nearly 185,000 dead and missing.[81] The Stockholm International Peace Research Institute (SIPRI) estimates that Iran spent in excess of $74 billion, and Iraq in excess of $94 billion, to prosecute the hostilities.[82] While Iran funded its expenditures from current revenues, Iraq borrowed massively to underwrite its military effort—perhaps explaining in part why it remained so important for Saddam Hussein to access additional oil revenues, from Kuwaiti wells, if Iranian ones were not to be available for plunder.[83]

Alongside geostrategic considerations, international consternation over the humanitarian impact of the war played an increasingly important part in motivating P-5 involvement in the resolution of the conflict. Pérez de Cuéllar used that sentiment as a mandate for his efforts to mediate, in the process carving out a beachhead for independent action by the Secretariat as a guardian of humanitarian considerations. Here were the seeds of potential tension between Secretariat attention to humanitarianism, and Security Council attention to geostrategic concerns, which played out throughout the subsequent years in Iraq.

2.6.3 *Flexible Institutional Architecture and Strategies?*

At times, the separation of roles between the Secretary-General and the Security Council can be extremely fruitful. This was made clear on a number of occasions throughout the Iraq saga, including following Kofi Annan's trip to Baghdad in 1998 (discussed in Chapter 6), but also in Pérez de Cuéllar's creative intervention in the Iran–Iraq war. Lead responsibility for initiation, implementation, and completion of the UN measures called for in SCR 598 increasingly shifted to the Secretary-General and the Secretariat. The Council's role became one of supporting the Secretary-General (and formally endorsing through resolutions his recommendations for UN action). Of note was Iraq's willingness to cooperate intensively with the Secretary-General on disengagement along the Iran–Iraq boundary at a time when Saddam Hussein was engaged in a serious clash with the Security Council (including at least four of the permanent members) over his Kuwaiti policy. The Secretary-General was successful in segregating the issues. That this suited Saddam Hussein's purposes takes nothing away from the value of UN's ability to conduct negotiations at different levels with different players on related issues at any given time.

The flexibility UN structures and practices provide in calibrating diplomacy is one of the organization's great strengths. At the same time these events imply that when the Council is itself divided, the Secretary-General may easily be hamstrung. Any CEO requires clear direction—and a measure of independent management discretion—from the Board. As subsequent events in Iraq also show, too often, the Secretary-General and his staff did not receive that kind of support. As the Security Council increasingly mandated hands-on, administratively demanding regulatory operations for the enforcement of its resolutions (moving from border monitoring to weapons inspection, from military embargoes to the OFF Program), the consequences of actual and potential differences over strategy and tactics became increasingly dire.

2.6.4 *The Legitimacy Challenge*

Another aspect of the UN's involvement in the Iran–Iraq war that has been somewhat overlooked is what it tells us about the constraints and contradictions the UN confronts in maintaining its legitimacy as ultimate arbiter of international peace and security. The universalist claims of the UN Charter, not least those relating to human rights, raise objections in some quarters, notably among Islamist social movements, of which Iran remains the primary state-sponsor. For these and other reasons the legitimacy of the Security Council's authority was called into question by Iran as early as 1980, marked by its boycott of the Council because of its perceived (indeed real) anti-Iranian bias. The Council's preoccupation with Iraq in the 1990s has drawn attention away from the anxiety Iran created and still generates for several of the P-5, as the leading exponent and exporter of Islamist theocracy. This has resurfaced with concern over Iran's nuclear program, but Iran's success in establishing its influence over the young Iraqi state post-Hussein has been much overlooked, at least in Western media. The difficulties the UN confronts in reconciling theocratic Islamism (now more prevalent in insurgencies and terrorist movements) and the system of secular sovereignty and universalist international law which underpins the UN remain undiminished.[84]

What the Iranian boycott highlights is that the Council's legitimacy is limited for some by prevailing social norms. Where norms develop rejecting the international rule of law and the Council's centrality to that rule, the UN's effectiveness may be seriously constrained. Importantly, this can be as much the case in Washington and London, when the Security Council is perceived as an obstacle to legitimate humanitarian intervention or preemptive military action against WMD proliferation, as it is in Tehran.

Notes

1. In order to back up this sweeping claim, Hiro dismisses the Vietnam wars and the fighting between China and Japan over Manchuria as insufficiently conventional or sustained over extended periods of time.
2. Dilip Hiro, *The Longest War: The Iran-Iraq Military Conflict* (New York, NY: Paladin, 1990), 1, 250–1. As noted in the quote, the astronomical figure of $1.19 trillion includes war conduct, military imports, direct damage from warfare, and indirect damage (to oil, agriculture, etc.).
3. Jan Eliasson, interview with the author, June 23, 2005.

4. Exploration for oil on the offshore continental shelf was to become a further source of contention between the two countries in the 1960s.
5. The Iraqi Ba'ath Party, which originally seized power in 1963, was, in effect, an offshoot of the pan-Arab, anticolonialist and broadly humanistic Ba'ath Party founded in Damascus in 1947 by Michel Aflaq, Zaki Arsuzi, and Salah al din Bitar. Eventually, the Iraqi and Syrian Ba'athist regimes, the latter having consolidated its power in 1966, would feud viciously (so much so that Damascus sided with Tehran during the Iran–Iraq war—shades of the multi-decade Moscow–Beijing rivalry as of the 1950s in part rooted in conflicting interpretations of Marxist-Leninist orthodoxy).
6. It is too often assumed, nevertheless, that the Iraqi Shi'a community makes common cause with Iran (where the Shi'a are dominant in society and government). On this, see Yitzhak Nakash, *The Shi'is of Iraq* (Princeton, NJ: Princeton University Press, 1994), 271–2. Conversely, some Iraqi-Iranian Shi'a collusion has occurred since the 2003 Iraq war.
7. UN Security Council SCR 348, May 28, 1974.
8. Tareq Y. Ismael, *Iraq and Iran: Roots of Conflict* (Syracuse, NY: Syracuse University Press, 1982), 24.
9. Shahram Chubin and Charles Tripp, *Iran and Iraq at War* (London: L.B. Tauris, 1988), 32.
10. *The Guardian*, February 28, 1979, quoted in Hiro, *The Longest War*, 26.
11. Edgar O'Ballance, *The Gulf War* (London: Brassey's Defence Publishers, 1988), 11–12. See also Daniel Pipes, 'A Border Adrift: Origins of the Conflict', in Shirin Tahir-Kheli and Shaheen Ayubi (eds.), *The Iran-Iraq War: New Weapons, Old Conflicts* (New York, NY: Praeger, 1983), 11.
12. Pipes, 'A Border Adrift', 22–3.
13. Tripp, *A History of Iraq*, 232.
14. Sabrina Tavernise, 'Iraqi Government, in Statement with Iran, Admits Fault for 1980's War', *New York Times*, May 20, 2005.
15. *Letter dated 22 September 1980 from the Chargé d'affaires a.i. of the Permanent Mission of Iraq to the United Nations addressed to the Secretary-General* (UN Security Council Doc. S/14191), September 22, 1980, 113–14.
16. Stephen R. Grummon, *The Iran-Iraq War: Islam Embattled* (New York, NY: Praeger, 1982), 15.
17. O'Ballance, *The Gulf War*, 30.
18. Kenneth M. Pollack, *Arabs at War: Military Effectiveness, 1948–1991* (Lincoln, NE: University of Nebraska Press, 2002), 185.
19. Cameron R. Hume, *The United Nations, Iran and Iraq: How Peacemaking Changed* (Bloomington, IN: Indiana University Press, 1994), 38. See also, generally, Gordon M. Goldstein, *Leadership, Multilateral Security, and Coercive Cooperation: The Role of the UN Security Council in the Persian Gulf War* (New York, NY: G. M. Goldstein, 1998).
20. Hume, *The United Nations, Iran and Iraq*, 40.

21. Brian Urquhart, *A Life in Peace and War* (New York, NY: Harper and Row, 1987), 324–5.
22. Javier Pérez de Cuéllar, *Pilgrimage for Peace: A Secretary-General's Memoir* (New York, NY: St. Martin's Press, 1997), 132.
23. Hiro, *The Longest War*, 71–2.
24. Grummon, *The Iran-Iraq War*, 59–60.
25. Giandomenico Picco, *Man Without a Gun: One Diplomat's Secret Struggle to Free the Hostages, Fight Terrorism, and End a War* (New York, NY: Random House, 1999), 53.
26. See Pérez de Cuéllar, *Pilgrimage for Peace*, 134, in discussions with US Secretary of State Alexander Haig.
27. Hume, *The United Nations, Iran and Iraq*, 41.
28. See G. H. Hansen, 'The Attitudes of the Arab Governments' in M. S. El Azhary (ed.), *The Iran-Iraq War: an Historical, Economic and Political Analysis* (London: Croom Helm, 1984), 82–3.
29. See Urquhart, *A Life in Peace and War*, 334–48.
30. This has also been the case in Norway's active promotion of efforts to resolve Sri Lanka's civil war, the peace process in southern Sudan, and the Oslo Accords between Israel and the PLO.
31. Warren Christopher et al., *American Hostages in Iran: The Conduct of a Crisis* (New Haven, CT: Yale University Press, 1985), 98.
32. Pérez de Cuéllar, *Pilgrimage for Peace*, 135.
33. Pérez de Cuéllar, *Pilgrimage for Peace*, 136.
34. *Report of the specialists appointed by the Secretary-General to investigate allegations by the Islamic Republic of Iran concerning the use of chemical weapons* (UN Security Council Document S/16433), March 26, 1984.
35. Jan Eliasson, interview with the author, June 23, 2005.
36. Pérez de Cuéllar, *Pilgrimage for Peace*, 137.
37. This resolution followed up on the equally ineffective SCR 540 (1983) advocating safety of navigation in the Gulf.
38. 'Highlights of Gorbachev Talk to 27th Congress', *Los Angeles Times*, February 26, 1986, 11.
39. Picco, *Man Without a Gun*, 73.
40. *Transcript of Press Conference by Secretary-General Javier Pérez de Cuéllar at Headquarters* (UN Secretariat Document SG/SM/3956), January 13, 1987, 4.
41. Picco, *Man Without a Gun*, 75.
42. Kuwait had earlier sought naval escort from both superpowers for its commercial shipping. Both complied, although the United States came to dominate this field of endeavor.
43. Marrack Goulding, *Peacemonger* (Baltimore, MD: Johns Hopkins University Press, 2003), 123.

44. Joint military action by Moscow and Washington to protect shipping in the Gulf was also discussed bilaterally in 1987, while the idea of reflagging commercial vessels in the Gulf under UN colors was seriously explored in 1988. The notion of a UN naval force, pressed by Moscow, was never fully fleshed out, and, through the ebb and flow of diplomatic exchange, lost steam in early 1988, as support increased for an arms embargo against Iran.
45. Revelation of these near-farcical antics was not greeted with levity by GCC countries, who knew that Iran would likely use some of the missiles at least to attack shipping to and from their countries.
46. See Hume, *The United Nations, Iran and Iraq*, 91.
47. Andrei Melville and Gail W. Lapidus (eds.), *The Glasnost Papers: Voices on Reform from Moscow* (Boulder, CO: Westview, 1990), 27–8.
48. Mikhail S. Gorbachev, 'Reality and Safeguards for a Secure World', *Pravda*, September 17, 1987. Reprint in English: *Letter dated 87/09/18 from the deputy head of the delegation of the Union of Soviet Socialist Republics to the 42nd session addressed to the Secretary-General* (UN General Assembly-Security Council Document A/42/574-S/19143), September 18, 1987.
49. Robert S. Litwak, 'The Soviet Union and the Iran-Iraq War', in Efraim Karsh (ed.), *The Iran-Iraq War: Impact and Implications* (London: MacMillan, 1989), 212.
50. See Hume, *The United Nations, Iran and Iraq*, 71–2, 90–102 and David M. Malone, *Decision-Making in the Security Council: The Case of Haiti, 1990–1997* (Oxford: Clarendon Press, 1998), 7–8, 32–3.
51. See Security Council Resolutions 514 (1982), 522 (1982), 540 (1983), 552 (1984), 582 (1986), and 588 (1986).
52. See Bailey and Daws, *The Procedure of the UN Security Council*, 60–8.
53. See Pérez de Cuéllar, *Pilgrimage for Peace*, 152.
54. See Hume, *The United Nations, Iran and Iraq*, 101 [citing Fred C. Iklé, *How Nations Negotiate* (New York, NY: Harper and Row, 1965), 87].
55. On the gradual metamorphosis of the Council during this period, see Philippe Kirsch, *The Changing Role of the Security Council* (New York, NY: Ralph Bunche Institute on the United Nations, 1990).
56. See Pérez de Cuéllar, *Pilgrimage for Peace*, 159.
57. See Pérez de Cuéllar, *Pilgrimage for Peace*, 160.
58. In relation to Iran's demand that responsibility for the conflict be established, the Secretary-General in 1991 came as close as he would to venturing an opinion by stating that the attack of September 22, 1980 against Iran could not be justified under any recognized rules and principles of international law, but went on to assert that no useful purpose would be served in pursuing the matter further. Rather, in the interest of peace, he suggested it was imperative to move on with the settlement process. See *Further report of the Secretary-*

General on the implementation of Security Council resolution 598 (1987) (UN Secretariat Document S/23273), December 9, 1991.

59. See Picco, *Man Without a Gun*, 76–7.
60. See *Letter dated 87/08/11 from the Permanent Representative of the Islamic Republic of Iran to the United Nations addressed to the Secretary-General* (UN Document S/19031), August 11, 1987, 2.
61. Pollack, *Arabs at War*, 228.
62. It is instructive to contrast the American responses to Iran's actions in the Gulf (bellicose) to its responses to Iraqi actions in the Gulf (more pacific, as its response to the *Stark* incident demonstrated).
63. For a detailed account of the naval war, see Marr, *The Modern History of Iraq*, 190, Chubin and Tripp, *Iran and Iraq at War*, 217–18, and Pollack, *Arabs at War*, 228–9.
64. The February 1994 ICJ decision on a territorial dispute between Libya and Chad, which led within months to a peaceful Libyan withdrawal from the Aouzou Strip monitored by a small UN observer team, UNASOG, is an exception to this general proposition. See *Territorial Dispute* (*Libyan Arab Jamahiriya v Republic of Chad*), International Court of Justice, February 13, 1994.
65. See *Case Concerning Oil Platforms (Islamic Republic of Iran v United States of America)*, International Court of Justice, November 6, 2003, 45, 54–5.
66. See Hume, *The United Nations, Iran and Iraq*, 143. The practice of building delays in application of Security Council resolutions was to become more routine in the future, notably with SCR 678 (1990), particularly where sanctions were in play. As argued by David Cortright and George Lopez in *The Sanctions Decade: Assessing UN Strategies in the 1990s* (Boulder, CO: Lynne Rienner, 2000), 27–9, the threat of sanctions are widely seen as most effective when deployed as leverage in negotiation, rather than in their implementation phase.
67. This incident was also litigated in the International Court of Justice. See *Aerial Incident of 3 July 1988 (Islamic Republic of Iran v United States of America)*, International Court of Justice, February 22, 1996, 9.
68. See Pollack, *Arabs at War*, 229.
69. Pérez de Cuéllar, *Pilgrimage for Peace*, 169.
70. See Pérez de Cuéllar, *Pilgrimage for Peace*, 170.
71. See Hiro, *The Longest War*, 245.
72. Giandomenico Picco writes that posturing and bluffing was one element used by Pérez de Cuéllar to convince the Iraqis and their Saudi intermediaries to accept the text, rather than press for more advantageous terms, as they were wont to do. After one such request in a meeting on August 8, Picco and Pérez de Cuéllar conferred in Spanish, with Picco advising that he did not want to risk alienating the Iranians with yet more modifications. Pérez de Cuéllar coolly turned to the Saudis and replied, only half in jest, 'Unfortunately, I cannot accept that change because Mr. Picco tells me we cannot. Please do not ask me to do what I cannot do.' After much discussion, Iraq agreed to the deal an hour later. See Picco, *Man Without a Gun*, 94–5.

73. Detailed planning for this observer force can be found in *Report of the Secretary-General on the implementation of operative paragraph 2 of Security Council resolution 598 (1987)* (UN Secretariat Document S/20093), August 7, 1988.
74. Much of the information herein on UNIIMOG is drawn from a UN document summarizing the group's mandate and activities throughout its history which can be found at United Nations, 'Iran-Iraq—UNIIMOG Background', www.un.org/Depts/dpko/dpko/co_mission/uniimogbackgr.html. See also UN SCR 685, January 31, 1991, on UNIIMOG's conclusion. There were thousands of complaints of alleged cease-fire violations, though they declined steadily. The most serious violations recorded involved the capture of several hundred Iranian soldiers by Iraqi forces in a serious incident near Eyn-e-Khowsh, and the Iranian flooding of an area of no man's land in the Khusk region. See *Interim report of the Secretary-General on the United Nations Iran-Iraq Military Observer Group* (UN Secretariat Document S/20242), October 25, 1988, and *Report of the Secretary-General on the United Nations Iran-Iraq Military Observer Group* (UN Secretariat Document S/20442), February 2, 1989 for further details.
75. See *Letter dated 90/08/17 from the Permanent Representative of the Islamic Republic of Iran to the United Nations addressed to the Secretary-General* (UN Document S/21556), 17 August 1990, 4.
76. This volume does not directly address the 1991 Shi'a insurgency, whose fighters were shunned by international actors for fear that their success could fracture Iraq. A number of accounts appear in the literature, including in Anthony H. Cordesman and Ahmed S. Hashim, *Iraq: Sanctions and Beyond* (Boulder, CO: Westview Press, 1987), 101–2 and in various volumes by Dilip Hiro dealing with this phase of Iraqi history.
77. Indeed, after Saddam Hussein attacked Kuwait in 1990, Washington became the theater of a 'blame game' centered on the question of 'who lost Kuwait?' due to excessively cosy relations with Iraq. On this, see Judith Miller and Laurie Mylroie, *Saddam Hussein and the Crisis in the Gulf* (New York, NY: Times Books, 1990), 222–3.
78. Avi Shlaim, *War and Peace in the Middle East: A Concise History* (London: Penguin Books, 1995), 87–8.
79. Charles Tripp, 'The Iran-Iraq War and Iraqi Politics', in Efraim Karsh (ed.), *The Iran-Iraq War: Impact and Implications* (London: MacMillan, 1989), 72, 73, 76.
80. See Hiro, *The Longest War*, 250.
81. Tehran Radio, September 19, 1988, cited in Hiro, *The Longest War*, 285 s. v. 15.
82. *SIPRI Yearbook 1988* (Stockholm: Almquist & Wiksell, 1988), 178. These figures only include the cost of conducting the war, as opposed to Hiro's inclusive estimate from the beginning of the chapter.
83. According to Marr, Iraqi debt had mushroomed from about $2.5 billion at the start of the war to about $50 billion at its termination. A further $30–40 billion was technically owed to Gulf states such as Kuwait and Saudi Arabia, but which Baghdad considered as 'contributions' to the war effort.

This characterization and the potential for non-repayment, coupled with the decline in oil prices in the late 1980s, 'caused hardships' within these states and contributed to tensions in the immediate postwar period. See Marr, *The Modern History of Iraq*, 205.

84. Those tensions were revealed at times in the Iranian conduct of hostilities in the Iran–Iraq war, which drew heavily on Islamic teachings, starting the trend toward Islamist justifications of attacks on civilians and suicide operations, which has now been exported throughout the Middle East: see James Cockayne, 'Islam and International Humanitarian Law: From a clash to a conversation between civilizations', *International Review of the Red Cross*, 847 (2002), 616–19.

3

New World Order Policeman: Responding to Iraqi Aggression Against Kuwait

Partly because of Saddam Hussein's continuing preoccupation with Iran, partly because it was widely assumed that the Iran–Iraq war would have produced a sobering effect on his designs, his attack on Kuwait on August 2, 1990 came as a major surprise.

There had, of course, been early warning signals, easily detectible in retrospect. Although Iraq and Kuwait had increasingly been seen as linked in interests and strategy during the Iran–Iraq war, Kuwait took advantage of the war's end to press Iraq to settle its long-standing border dispute with Kuwait. To do so, it used the crude but effective means of exceeding its Organization of Petroleum Exporting Countries (OPEC) oil production and export quota, flooding the market and depressing prices for Iraq's oil. This exacerbated Iraq's desperate need for cash to fund its debt servicing obligations and its reconstruction aims, creating a strong incentive to settle the dispute with Kuwait. Indeed, after forcing on his population the hardships of the seemingly endless war with Iran, Iraq's leader now needed to deliver rewards. Grandiose plans for new infrastructure (a Baghdad subway system, expanded road networks, new airports) were discussed, but Iraq was by now deeply in hock not only to its Arab brethren (whose claims could be safely ignored by challenging their inability to do more than pay for Iraq's sacrifices) but also to Europe, the Soviet Union, China, Japan, and the United States. And there was a further priority: rebuilding, and particularly rearming, Iraq's military with the best high-tech weaponry he could access. Declining oil prices as of 1988 had canceled the benefits of greater Iraqi oil production, and with it produced declining Iraqi credit, particularly with powerful Western banks, companies, and governments.

One of Hussein's responses to the adverse developments was to cloak himself in the Palestinian cause. He also took on the rival Ba'athist regime in Damascus over its hegemonic and heavy-handed role in Lebanon, urging the Arab Summit in Casablanca in May 1989 to confront the Assad regime over its contempt for Lebanese sovereignty. While Hussein doubtless viewed perestroika in Gorbachev's Soviet Union with puzzlement, he does not seem to have registered that this major shift in Moscow's approach to domestic politics might have international ramifications and implications for the relationship between the USSR and Iraq. Moscow's new interest in restoring relations with Israel might have been a tip-off.

Oblivious, Hussein resorted to invasion, occupation, and annexation to win his dispute with Kuwait. He had not anticipated the unified response this provoked from the Security Council, the product of perestroika, and an increasingly cooperative working relationship among the P-5. In response, the Council authorized a coalition of states to undertake the largest police action since that in Korea four decades earlier.[1]

Chapter 3 addresses this second phase of UN involvement in Iraq, which seemed to herald the emergence of the Security Council as a New World Order Policeman. The Council's capacity to legitimize the use of force provided a legal basis for international action to expel Iraqi forces from Kuwait in 1991. The chapter recounts the diplomatic and military success of Operations Desert Shield and Desert Storm, mandated to compel the withdrawal of Iraq from Kuwait and conducted by a coalition of states (a so-called 'coalition of the willing') drawing legitimacy from Security Council decisions under Chapter VII of the UN Charter. Chapter VII also provided a newly assertive basis for traditional activities, such as cease-fire implementation and border-monitoring tasks, the Council gave to a new mission—the United Nations Iraq-Kuwait Observer Mission (UNIKOM).[2] This new police role for UN peace operations was part of a larger 'New World Order' heralded by President George H. W. Bush, which seemed—all too fleetingly, as things turned out—to hold the promise of an international rule of law, enforced by a united P-5 operating through the Security Council.

3.1 Origins of the Iraq–Kuwait War

Iraq's border dispute with Kuwait had roots in the European colonial period, deriving from British preferences and tribal patterns, including extensive nomadism, in the Gulf region. Iraq, although enjoying Gulf access through the Shat al Arab, possessed no significant Gulf port and only 26 miles of

Gulf shoreline. With the Shat al Arab remaining closed, in spite of the cease-fire with Iran, Iraq's window on the trading world must have seemed too narrow for a man of Saddam Hussein's ambitions. Kuwait's real estate, including several ports and naval bases, can only have tantalized him.

Kuwait came late to its geostrategic significance. The importance of Iran, Iraq, and Saudi Arabia in supplying the economic lifeblood for Western economic growth was recognized early in the century and factored into both post-World War I and (particularly) World War II Western strategies. In contrast, Kuwait remained a small nomadic community revolving around a capital resembling an overgrown village as late as the mid-1960s.

Kuwait had escaped Ottoman invasion and control and was organized socially and politically around the Sabah clan. Nevertheless, Turkish sovereignty over Kuwait was recognized by the major Western powers, notably the British, who accepted the 'Sabahs as Ottoman vassals'.[3] Early in the twentieth century, the Sabahs developed close ties with the British and fought with them against the Turks in World War I. The border between Kuwait and Iraq (by then also a British protectorate) was set in 1922 by Sir Percy Cox.[4] At the time of Iraqi independence in 1932, this border was recognized by both countries, but not demarcated. As early as 1937, the Iraqi King called for Kuwait's annexation. A more serious challenge arose in 1961 at the time of Kuwait's independence from Great Britain, when then Iraqi leader Abdul Karim Qassem laid claim to the country (which he described as an oil well). British reinforcements in Kuwait were joined by troops from Saudi Arabia, Syria, Egypt, and Jordan, forcing Qassem to back off (and perhaps causing Saddam Hussein to place more of a premium on surprise in 1990). Subsequently, Iraqi relations with Kuwait varied between grudging recognition of its independence to truculent claims and incursions against it, generally reversed by Kuwaiti financial largesse.

After the Iran–Iraq cease-fire, border differences between Iraq and Kuwait reemerged, centering on two strategically located islands off Kuwait's shore that Saddam Hussein had long coveted. Iraq rejected a Kuwaiti suggestion of taking the border demarcation dispute to the World Court in The Hague.[5] Meanwhile, his rhetoric on Israel reached new fever pitch. On April 2, 1990, Hussein threatened the use of chemical weapons against Israel—a troubling means of mobilizing Arab support. Israel, which had preemptively destroyed the Iraqi Osiraq nuclear installations in 1981, and which had always feared Iraqi military capacities, belligerence, and ideological fervor, had good reasons to worry, as Saddam Hussein was to target it during the days of the Desert Storm campaign, although not with chemical weapons. (The debate over whether Israel's strike at Osiraq was a legitimate instance of 'anticipatory self-defense' not only continues to echo in the academic literature but also clearly remains in the forefront of those contemplating Iran's burgeoning nuclear capacity.[6]) The United States, on the other hand, beyond ritual condemnation of Iraqi rhetorical excess seemed to be focusing more on improving relations with Iraq than deterring its threats. In an interview with Saddam Hussein only days before his invasion of Kuwait, US ambassador April Glaspie was quoted (in a transcript of the conversation released by Iraq) echoing Washington's own press lines, emphasizing on the one hand that the United States had 'no opinion' on the Kuwait–Iraq border dispute and on the other that it was seeking improved relations with Iraq.[7]

By this stage, Iraq's financial plight was serious. Due to overproduction by Kuwait and the United Arab Emirates, the price of oil had plummeted from $20 to $14 between January and June 1990. If Saddam Hussein had seriously expected assistance with reconstruction following the Iran–Iraq war (much discussed in UN resolutions but like so much evoked in SCRs, a dead letter—particularly for this oil-rich aggressor country), he had been sadly disappointed. Now an assertive Kuwaiti strategy apparently designed to force Iraq into concessions on the border issue risked humiliating him in the eyes of the Iraqi population and the Arab World. By July 17, he was publicly accusing Arab countries of trying to do in the Iraqi economy, claiming that Iraq had sacrificed heavily for the Arab World in order to contain the Iranian threat and that it had been treacherously rewarded. On July 18, in a memorandum to the Arab League, Iraqi Deputy Prime Minister and Foreign Minister Tariq Aziz accused Kuwait of attempting to weaken Iraq, encroaching on its territory, draining oil from the Rumaila field, which straddles the two countries' border, and conspiring to undermine oil prices. This, it concluded, was tantamount to military aggression. With rhetoric escalating between Kuwait and Iraq, Saudi King Fahd invited senior Iraqi and Kuwaiti representatives to Jeddah, only to find Izzat Ibrahim, Saddam Hussein's envoy (and Ba'ath regime number two), unyielding in his demands. Nevertheless, the Saudis thought they had initiated a meaningful dialog.

3.2 A Rude Wake-up Call

A rude wake-up call was delivered on August 2, 1990 with Iraq's invasion of Kuwait in the predawn hours. By 6 a.m., Iraqi forces had advanced to the heart of Kuwait City, besieging the Emir's palace. The well equipped but poorly managed and deployed Kuwaiti military was able to muster little resistance to overwhelming Iraqi numbers buttressed by the key element of surprise. (So much for the high-tech weapons that had cost Kuwait so dearly.) Although there had been Iraqi troop movements, indeed, a significant buildup near the border, Kuwait had not reciprocated for fear of escalating the military dimension of the border dispute. It appears to have believed Iraqi assurances relayed through various Arab leaders that it would not attack. The Emir's guard put up just enough resistance to allow for much of the royal family to escape (many others were abroad for the hot summer months). At first, the Iraqi propaganda machine broadcast claims that Iraq's forces were supporting a coup d'état by Kuwaiti revolutionaries, who, it was claimed, favored free elections. The emirate was essentially subdued within 24 hours.

Sympathy for the plight of Kuwaitis has generally muted criticism of the fecklessness and incompetence of the royal regime in the run-up to the invasion, but, in retrospect, the Sabahs and also Saddam Hussein allies, such as Yassir Arafat and King Hussein of Jordan (a particular darling of the Western media and many Western governments), appear to have been singularly naïve and self-serving in downplaying the threat Iraq posed, all the more so as Iraqi military movements in July clearly threatened Kuwait. Had the American cavalry not appeared over the horizon, Saddam Hussein was right to have believed that his plans would result in a Kuwaiti rout, and, beyond Kuwait, possibly the demise of the more powerful Saudi regime.

News of events in Kuwait filtered through to UN actors in New York nearly immediately. Indeed, it was still August 1 in New York when US ambassador to the UN Thomas Pickering was contacted during a dinner party by Washington with word of the invasion and asked to alert his Security Council colleagues with a request that the Council meet immediately to condemn the invasion.[8] Working through the ambassador of Kuwait, the United Kingdom and the United States soon mobilized other Council members to this end. They were aiming for a Chapter VII finding of a breach of the peace, with hints of enforcement to come. As Cameron Hume points out, it had taken six months to negotiate such a finding with respect to the Iran–Iraq war in 1987, culminating in SCR 598; this time around, it was achieved in a matter of hours.[9]

3.2.1 *A Different Council*

Much had changed in the Security Council, building on the degree of tentative mutual trust the P-5 created in working toward SCR 598 and its implementation. The increasingly productive working relationship was evident in the Council's new seriousness on knotty problems from Namibia to Cambodia and Central America.

Implementation of SCR 435 of 1978 on international support and guidance for Namibia's independence had been held up by Cold War tensions, most clearly manifest through the presence of Cuban troops in neighboring Angola, which encouraged the Western bloc to stall South African withdrawal from neighboring Namibia. On December 22, 1988, agreement was consecrated in New York by the Foreign Ministers of Angola, Cuba, and South Africa on interlocking arrangements and understandings to govern Cuban withdrawal from Angola and South African withdrawal from Namibia. This latter process, and implementation of SCR 435 leading to Namibian independence in 1990, required the UN to organize and field one of its largest and most ambitious peacekeeping operations to date. That mission in turn encountered early challenges in the field, which the UN could not have met successfully without significant cooperation on the part of the Permanent Members. Both the USSR and the US were forced in ensuing months to reassure and cajole into full compliance the Front-Line States and South Africa, respectively, helping the UN to stare down a military challenge from unruly SWAPO forces out of Angola. In the process, the UN controversially (but with excellent results) condoned a South African counterattack—all of this requiring a high degree of management coordination and confidence between the UN Secretary-General, his representative on the ground Martti Ahtisaari, and relevant P-5 members.[10]

At roughly the same time, Moscow and Washington were coming to terms with their confrontation in Central America through local proxies in Nicaragua (first) and El Salvador. The superpowers looked to the UN—and the Organization of American States (OAS) in the case of Nicaragua—to play key negotiating and implementation roles, resting on confidence-building discussions between, and measures agreed by, the superpowers with diplomatic support from a 'Group of Friends' of the Secretary-General involving several other interested countries, mainly from the region.[11]

Elsewhere, Cambodia represented the largest challenge to date for multilateral diplomacy in the early post-Cold War era. In part influenced by broader international trends, it became clear in 1988 that the civil war in Cambodia, characterized by extensive external involvement, in terms of military support, weapons supply, and diplomatic assistance, might be amenable to resolution. In February 1989, the Security Council first formally tackled this situation. After preliminary discussions at the UN, the action shifted to a high-profile conference hosted by the French Government in Paris, June–August 1989, at which Vietnamese military withdrawal from Cambodia, international auspices and arrangements for power-sharing there, elections, international recognition, and many other sensitive issues were discussed (without resolution being reached on several key matters). It would take several more years before full agreement was reached on these various points, but the process of meaningful dialog was launched and a beginning of momentum toward success had been initiated. Of significance for future dynamics in the Security Council, China played a crucial role in the Cambodian equation, one of influence over the Khmer Rouge, which would prove decisive not only in reaching agreement eventually but also in delivering a degree of Khmer Rouge compliance with the UN implementation process further to SCR 745.[12]

3.3 A Swift Response

With this cooperation behind them, the Council members sprang swiftly into action upon receiving the unexpected news of Iraq's invasion of Kuwait. With Pickering and his Kuwaiti counterpart working the phones and meeting with colleagues into the night, early signs of Saddam Hussein's diplomatic isolation emerged.[13] Both Malaysia and Ethiopia—stalwarts of the Non-Aligned Movement (NAM) to which Iraq also belonged—agreed to cosponsor a resolution condemning the invasion and calling for Iraq's unconditional withdrawal, in turn bringing aboard other NAM members Côte d'Ivoire and Colombia. When the Council met formally, Iraq's representative, seeking to rebut Kuwait's arguments that the Council needed to defend Kuwaiti sovereignty, claimed that with new Kuwaiti authorities in place, the Kuwaiti ambassador no longer represented his country. Yemen did not participate in the vote, indicating it had been unable to secure instructions from its capital. All other delegations supported SCR 660, which, adopting the formula settled on in SCR 598, first established the existence of a breach of international peace and security in relation to the conflict in question, and then, acting 'under Articles 39 and 40' of the Charter, laid the foundations for the subsequent strategy in the Security Council to reverse Iraq's aggression by demanding an immediate and unconditional withdrawal of Iraqi troops.

Importantly, on August 2, the Soviet Union announced an arms embargo against Iraq. The same day, President Bush issued an executive order banning trade with Iraq and freezing Iraqi and Kuwaiti assets in the United States. Others, including the European Community countries, Canada, and Japan followed suit.

This spirit of newfound superpower cooperation manifested itself most clearly on August 3 with the issuance of a joint statement by the two countries' foreign ministers, the US' James Baker and the USSR's Eduard Shevardnadze. The statement denounced Iraq's invasion as a 'blatant transgression of basic norms of civilized conduct' and called for a global arms embargo. The momentousness of this joint statement was not lost upon Baker. Whereas the fall of the Berlin Wall had heralded a paradigm shift in East–West relations, for Baker '[t]hat August night, a half-century after it began in mutual suspicion and ideological fervor, the Cold War breathed its last'.[14]

Washington quickly sought to capitalize on this bilateral cooperation. On August 5, President Bush asserted that Iraqi aggression 'will not stand'. He began seeking Council approval for the institution of mandatory comprehensive economic sanctions against Iraq, excluding medicine and food. In another sign of how the times had changed, this—only the third authorization of sanctions by the Security Council in its history—was swiftly agreed in SCR 661 on August 6, 1990, by thirteen affirmative votes, with two countries recording abstentions: Yemen and Cuba.[15] This resolution signaled an important decision by Moscow—to value its relationship with the United States above that with its erstwhile client state Iraq. All of this was facilitated significantly (and often invisibly to the media's eye) by the telephone diplomacy President Bush initiated with many of his counterparts around the globe.[16]

SCR 661 also set into motion a new logic of coercion against recalcitrant states by the Security Council, practice of which grew greatly during the 1990s and beyond. This shift was signaled in the reference in SCR 661 not to Articles 39 and 40 of the Charter, but to action 'under Chapter VII'. The SCR established a committee to oversee implementation of the sanctions, which was to play a central role in many of the dramas between Iraq and the Security Council in the years to come, as I will explore in Chapter 5. It represented an important step by the Council away from its classical politico-military approach, interposing peacekeeping forces between warring parties, toward a more legal-regulatory approach, imposing standards of conduct on a Member State, which it then monitored and implemented through a regulatory agent—on this occasion the 661 Committee.

3.3.1 *Arab Reactions*

Arab regimes had reacted with shock to Iraq's moves, none more so than Saudi Arabia, now sheltering the Kuwaiti Emir. Other Arab leaders duped by Saddam Hussein's assurances that he would not attack, such as Egyptian President Hosni Mubarak, were more inclined to search for 'face-saving' solutions than to recognize that Saddam Hussein was determined to hold on to all of his conquest, and possibly press his military advantage beyond Kuwait. In the Arab media and among Arab decision-makers the talk was of an 'Arab solution'—one that would obviously need to give Saddam Hussein something significant in exchange for a complete, or more likely, partial withdrawal. The Saudis, now most threatened by Iraq's stance, were prepared to confront Saddam Hussein diplomatically within the Arab League, but other capitals preferred to focus more on the dangers of foreign intervention than on the patent threat in their midst. The Arab League did meet, but could agree only on a declaration of concern. According to Elaine Sciolino, Clovis Maksoud, the widely respected Arab League representative at the UN, indicated that his 'Member States do not believe it is advisable ... to render moral judgment'.[17]

However, Saudi Arabia was taking no chances: on August 6 it invited friendly forces to reinforce its defenses, rapidly accepting US troops from 'Operation Desert Shield'. On the same day, Iraq announced that its takeover of Kuwait was irreversible, and on August 7 announced its annexation of Kuwait, making a mockery of its earlier claim that the ouster of Kuwait's government had been driven primarily by Kuwaiti politics. This attempted annexation of Kuwait, a major and unnecessary self-inflicted wound, compounded Saddam Hussein's inept diplomacy to date. Border disputes leading to military action have not been uncommon in the UN's history, but the annexation of an entire Member State of the UN by another had never been attempted.[18] Acquiescence would have implied a profound threat to the sovereignty of many a small country—many of which, located in the Gulf and poorly armed, must have felt the threat of Saddam Hussein quite acutely. Hussein also erred by targeting Western nationals in Kuwait. On August 8, his troops moved against foreign diplomatic missions in Kuwait, demanding they be removed to Baghdad. Within a week, he ordered 4,000 Britons and 2,500 Americans in Kuwait to assemble in hotels, announcing that he would use them as 'human shields' against attack by any international coalition. If Hussein thought that these 'human shields' would provide him with useful bargaining chips, rather than reinforcing public support in Western countries for military action against him, he was sorely mistaken.

3.3.2 *Building a Coalition*

Thanks in large part to these Iraqi missteps, it was not difficult for Iraq's opponents at the UN on August 9 to secure unanimous passage of SCR 662 rejecting the annexation, which had clearly exceeded the tolerance even of Cuba and Yemen, the latter caught up in the maelstrom of Arab consultations and indecision on the crisis. Washington had never viewed the Kuwaiti government with great regard, seeing it largely as a backward family-run conglomerate, although an important one for the stability of oil markets and the source of rich military contracts for American companies. Saudi Arabia, on the other hand, was critical to America's geostrategic calculations. From the outset of the crisis, Washington had focused more on Saudi Arabia's security than on the restoration of the Sabahs to power in Kuwait.

Although opinion was divided in Washington over whether Saddam Hussein would move quickly to challenge Saudi Arabia, President Bush ultimately decided that he, like King Fahd, would take no chances. However, the deployment of American troops to Saudi Arabia was a delicate matter for King Fahd vis-à-vis Saudi and Arab opinion. Consultations were held on August 6 in Jeddah between the Saudi government, US Defense Secretary Dick Cheney and General Norman Schwarzkopf. The next day, President Bush ordered to the Gulf region an initial contingent of the 200,000 troops that were to form the vanguard of Operation Desert Shield.

While some Arab countries viewed this development as driven by the Saudi need for self-defense, others were predictably and deeply perturbed by foreign, particularly the United States, massive military intervention within the Arab World, even by invitation of the Arab governments involved. The fact that Saudi Arabia was the site of Islam's two holiest shrines made the American presence all the more problematic for some. At the Arab League Summit of August 9, President Mubarak of Egypt was able to rally only twelve of the twenty-one members to support explicitly the UN sanctions and to provide troops for an all-Arab force in Saudi Arabia.[19] Nevertheless, this decision paved the way for a number of Arab governments later to join in Operation Desert Storm to expel Iraq from Kuwait.

3.4 Incremental Enforcement

The preference for a diplomatic solution, bordering at times on an unwillingness to resort to military action, of the administration of President George H. W. Bush stands in stark contrast to the often bellicose rhetoric of his son's administration a decade later. In response to a pointed question from journalist Helen Thomas on the morning of August 2, 1990 as to whether he was considering intervention as one of his options, the elder Bush replied negatively, though the response was diplomatically couched and qualified. This response, taken by some as a sign of indecision and passivity, was not well received by Britain's Margaret Thatcher, who met later that day with Bush and 'put some stiffening in his spine'.[20] Later that month the steely Prime Minister famously counseled the President that '[t]his is no time to go wobbly.'[21]

Bush also emphasized the value of the UN, noting in his memoirs that

> [w]hile I was prepared to deal with this crisis unilaterally if necessary, I wanted the United Nations involved as part of our first response, starting with a strong condemnation of Iraq's attack on a fellow member. Decisive UN action would be important in rallying international opposition to the invasion and reversing it.[22]

The administration continued to build upon the blossoming US–Soviet relationship to generate constructive and substantive positions with respect to UN involvement. Following a meeting in Helsinki on September 9, Presidents Gorbachev and Bush reiterated their determination to act jointly on Iraq and hinted at further measures under the UN Charter in order to secure Iraqi compliance with existing resolutions.[23] At no point until the outbreak of military action against Iraq in January 1991 did Saddam Hussein evince the slightest interest in a negotiated settlement involving any climbdown by him. Whether this represented his bottom-line or simply a negotiating posture in a dangerous game of brinkmanship we may never know. However, his stance dictated both the substance and pace of a steady escalation of UN decisions against Iraq culminating in SCR 678 authorizing military action.

Meanwhile, measures were being taken to impose the embargo against Iraq, enforcement having been explicitly authorized in SCR 665 of August 25, in the Persian Gulf and also in the Gulf of Aqaba (exacerbating Jordanian resentment of the position adopted by opponents of Iraq). At a meeting in Bahrain on September 9, twenty-eight countries, including several Arab ones, agreed to share the task of enforcement in the Persian Gulf. Keeping up the pressure on Iraq, the Security Council on September 13 in

SCR 666 established guidelines for the passage of medicines and humanitarian assistance through the blockade, and reminded Iraq of its responsibility for the safety of foreign nationals.

Compounding problems for Iraq at the UN, a day later Iraqi forces entered the French ambassador's residence in Kuwait, detaining the French military attaché. Such incidents were part of a much broader pattern of lawlessness and looting that characterized the Iraqi occupation of Kuwait, during which the emirate was stripped of virtually every movable asset. On August 18, SCR 664 unanimously demanded the release of all 'hostages'. The next day, Hussein offered to exchange foreign nationals for an American withdrawal from Saudi Arabia supervised by the UN, and a US pledge not to attack Iraq. Understandably, the United States refused. Instead, on September 16, in SCR 667, the Council unanimously condemned Iraqi violation of diplomatic premises and aggression against diplomatic personnel in Kuwait. In SCR 670 of September 25, the embargo was extended to air cargo. Meanwhile, a complication had developed in the smooth march toward sanctions enforcement. A number of Iraqi trading partners had complained to the Security Council about the losses incurred due to the embargo, seeking compensation. While the Charter does not specifically foresee compensation, under Article 50 the Council is obligated to consider such complaints. In SCR 669, it set out procedures for the Iraq Sanctions Committee established by SCR 661, co-chaired by Council elected members Canada and Finland, to do so.[24]

Opposing policy impulses soon came to the fore among Security Council members, challenging what seemed an inexorable march toward the use of force. Many believed that allowing sanctions time to induce flexibility in Iraqi positions was the prudent course. Some in the United States, including the former National Security Adviser to President Carter, Zbigniew Brzezinski, believed that patience should prevail as the law of unforeseen consequences could well affect options requiring the use of force.[25]

3.4.1 *Non-Aligned Movement Tactics*

Coincidentally, the Security Council in 1990 included among its elected members several committed members of the NAM—Colombia, Cuba, Malaysia, and Yemen—less charitably designated among Western delegations as the 'Gang of Four'. Each had foreign policy reasons of their own for reservations over the use of force. Colombia shared in the Latin American foreign policy tradition of viewing the use of force to settle disputes as a legacy of colonialism, and often as an echo of US hegemonic tactics in the Western hemisphere. Fidel Castro's Cuba, violently opposed to virtually any American foreign policy priority, had experienced US aggression, repelled at the Bay of Pigs, and suffered the reminder of its proximity to the United States in the form of the US military base at Guantánamo Bay on Cuban soil. Malaysia, a Muslim state hostile to the US policy of near-automatic support for Israel in its confrontation with Arab states, frequently complained about 'double standards' at the UN, and, in particular, in the Security Council. Yemen was in some respects in the most difficult position of all. At the time, it was ideologically closer to Saddam Hussein than to his opponents within the Arab World, including Saudi Arabia, Yemen's powerful neighbor with which it entertained complex, often strained, relations. Yemeni officials were conscious of representing a deeply split Arab World on the Council, and thus tactically were often drawn to seeking refuge behind the NAM shield as a first line of defense.

Non-aligned activism on the Council in the fall of 1990 took two forms, neither of which ultimately succeeded in arresting the steady drive toward enforcement. Unusually violent clashes on Jerusalem's Temple Mount on October 8 provided Iraq and its PLO allies with an opportunity both to agitate for a more energetic Council position on protection of Palestinians and to draw attention to the Council's purported double standards in pressing Iraq to comply fully with Council decisions while Israel was perceived by many to be flouting them. This first tactic of attempting to link enforcement against Iraq with enforcement against Israel largely failed, because Egypt and some other powerful and relevant voices outside the Council refused to provide full backing. Still, it was not without significant support: on September 24, French President François Mitterand, speaking at the UN General Assembly, proposed a four-phase peace plan, including dealing with the Arab–Israeli problem. Perhaps decisive was the US display of flexibility, voting for a Security Council resolution on October 24 deploring Israeli failure to cooperate with the Secretary-General in an investigation of the October 8 violence.[26]

More narrowly pertinent to Iraq's invasion of Kuwait was a non-aligned effort to head off any authorization of the use of force against Iraq by seeking to mandate the UN Secretary-General to play a mediating role in the crisis. While the permanent members accommodated this initiative in SCR 674 of October 29 (which focused on Kuwaiti financial losses, the rights of foreign nationals in Kuwait and Iraqi human rights violations in Kuwait), the United States seemed to perceive this NAM effort as a direct challenge to the leadership of the P-5 within the Council, particularly when Colombia, sensing itself in a minority position in the Council, took its ideas on the specifics of a negotiating track to the General Assembly for endorsement.[27] The latter tactic ultimately collapsed. This was in part because of the Charter strictures against General Assembly action on issues still on the Security Council agenda. It was perhaps also a result of a sense among many Member States that playing off the General Assembly against the Security Council in so grave and urgent a crisis—as opposed to the long-running Israeli–Arab conflict, on which the General Assembly frequently endorsed Palestinian or Arab initiatives blocked in the Security Council by vetoes, veto threats, or a lack of majority support—could only undermine the UN as a whole.

3.4.2 *Toward Military Confrontation*

The failure of opposition to this ratcheting toward military confrontation, the continued intransigence of Saddam, and the lack of success of sanctions and their enforcement measures to generate any 'give' in Iraq's diplomacy compelled the Council to inch toward the use of force as a means of last resort. In the United States, several voices, including that of respected former judge and State Department Legal Adviser Abraham Sofaer, argued against seeking Security Council authorization for such use of force (a breach to the peace having already been established by the Council) on the grounds that Kuwait and its allies possessed an inherent right of self-defense, obviating any need for further explicit authorization.[28] (Variations on this theme were to be heard again in 2002–3 among those who argued against the second Bush administration's inclination—under United Kingdom pressure—to return to the Security Council for a 'second' resolution following the determination of a 'material breach' in SCR 1441.) However, President Bush, his talented, tough and energetic Secretary of State, James Baker III, and the spectacularly effective US ambassador to the UN, Thomas Pickering, had been so successful in securing diplomatic support from a broad cross-section of countries that continued engagement with the UN on an issue as potentially volatile as the use of force seemed the more prudent course.

By the beginning of October, when Bush addressed the UN General Assembly, the talk was of 'a new partnership of nations that transcends the Cold War: a partnership based on consultation, cooperation, and collective action, especially through international and regional organizations; a partnership united by principle and the rule of law'. Like Baker,

Bush recognized the seminal importance of Soviet–US cooperation on Iraq: 'when the Soviet Union agreed with so many of us here in the UN to condemn the aggression of Iraq, there could be no doubt ... that we had, indeed, put four decades of history behind us.' Consequently, it was now feasible to envisage the UN bringing 'about a new day ... to cap a historic movement toward a new world order and a long era of peace'.[29] Bush would return to this theme of a 'New World Order' based on the UN enforcing a global rule of law time and again over the next year. Former US ambassador to the UN, Jeane Kirkpatrick, took up the theme, stating categorically that the United States could no longer play 'global policeman'.[30] That role, it seemed, now fell to the Security Council.

3.4.3 *A Historic Ultimatum*

The month of November was largely given over by the Permanent Members to discussing the form any authorization of the use of force would take. Presidents Bush and Gorbachev met in Paris on November 19 with the Soviet Union mainly focused on building in a grace period so that the leverage provided by an authorization for the use of force could be fully exploited in diplomacy before any trigger was actually pulled.[31] Secretary of State Baker, after joining in these discussions, visited both Yemen and Colombia to make the strongest case he could for a united Council authorization of force. (Baker had wanted to register the US determination and arguments directly with these key Security Council member governments, having become concerned that their ambassadors might be promoting personal rather than national views in New York. This turned out to be at least somewhat the case for Colombia, as became clear in its vote on the use of force.[32])

With Moscow's cooperation, Washington was successful in telescoping the time necessary for the consultation process over this important resolution, and Moscow also supported Washington in its effort to secure participation of foreign ministers at the Security Council session adopting the required resolution, on November 29.[33] The previous day, the UN General Assembly voted 148–1 to condemn the acts of violence by Iraqi occupiers in Kuwait against diplomatic and consular missions, and called for an immediate end to its violations of earlier Security Council resolutions, sending a signal of unwavering support to the Security Council.[34] Invoking Chapter VII as a whole, the draft SCR authorized 'Member States cooperating with the government of Kuwait to use all necessary means to uphold and implement resolution 660 ... and to restore international peace and security in that region' if Iraq did not comply with earlier SCRs. In deference to Soviet wishes, the resolution allowed for a grace period until January 15, 1991.

SCR 678, almost certainly the most important text agreed by the Security Council in the immediate post-Cold War period, was adopted by twelve affirmative votes, one abstention (China), and two votes against (Cuba and Yemen). Yemen criticized the Council for leaving the means up to the US-led coalition of the willing, operating beyond Council control. Cuba, in stark evidence of how far its foreign policy had now diverged from that of its former superpower patron in Moscow, described the resolution as providing the US carte blanche and as contrary to procedures envisaged by the Charter. China rather blandly repeated its attachment to the peaceful resolution of disputes and mildly argued that more time should have been devoted to diplomatic efforts—apparently eager to avoid antagonizing P-5 partners after the diplomatic setbacks following the Tiananmen Square massacre.

Moscow's vote for the resolution signaled more clearly than any other single act by the Soviet Union how far its foreign policy had evolved since President Gorbachev's rise to power. Indeed, it seemed determined to move from a superpower confrontation to a superpower condominium over major international security decisions. This shift left Saddam Hussein (and many other former Moscow allies, not least Cuba) in the lurch and, incidentally, has posed a challenge to the concepts underpinning non-alignment ever since. The shift engineered by Gorbachev did not go without challenge and resistance in the USSR. The Soviet military (and the Russian weapons production sector) were attached to their Arab clients, and viewed the abandonment of a key Arab ally with alarm, especially as it brought no immediate strategic benefits for Moscow. The military's attitude helps explain why, although Moscow provided valuable diplomatic support for Washington's strategy, the USSR did not participate in either operations Desert Shield or Desert Storm. Even though Moscow has since adopted a more independent, often resentful, international stance, beset as the Russian Federation has been by the Chechnyan insurgency, other domestic and economic problems and the mutation of Central and Eastern Europe into zones of Western influence, Moscow today remains truer to Gorbachev's vision than to that of previous communist leaders.

Votes in the Security Council on critical geostrategic issues can carry heavy costs for unwary delegations. In 1990, Yemen was in the unenviable position of having to vote, as an elected Council member, on several resolutions it substantively opposed. After bobbing and weaving with some success, it was cornered on the Council's most important decision of the crisis, embodied in SCR 678, authorizing the use of force against Iraq. After it voted against the text, hundreds of thousands of Yemeni workers were expelled from several Arab countries friendly with Kuwait, the United States suspended its sizable aid program and other disastrous fallout overtook it. (Pickering commented to the late Yemeni ambassador Abdallah al-Ashtal that this was the 'most expensive' vote he would ever register.) Al-Ashtal later recognized that the vote was a mistake (an abstention would have been more politic), reporting that his head of state did not know what position to adopt and had left the vote to him.[35]

Although the United States had been reserved about a leading role for the UN Secretary-General in conducting negotiations with Saddam Hussein, Washington recognized that the adoption of SCR 678 placed the United States and its allies in a strong position to settle the conflict peacefully, if Iraq proved open to reason. On November 30, President Bush invited Iraqi Foreign Minister Tariq Aziz to Washington and offered to have his own Secretary of State visit Baghdad.[36] This move was, in part, dictated by internal American political considerations as the President wished to secure Congressional support for the use of force and needed to do what he could to reassure the American public that he remained keen on a peaceful outcome if possible. Ultimately, Tariq Aziz and James Baker met in Geneva on January 9, 1991 for civil but unproductive talks after considerable tactical skirmishing between their capitals, including Hussein's mediagenic decision to release 2,000 or so foreign nationals detained by Iraq. In these discussions, Aziz attempted to cast the key issue as one of differences between the United States and Iraq (reciting various Iraqi grievances against Washington), largely unrelated to Iraqi actions affecting Kuwait. He displayed no negotiating flexibility.

3.5 A New World Pecking Order

On October 3, 1990, three signal events occurred. First, Germany reunified, signaling a true end to the Cold War. Second, the USSR launched a diplomatic campaign to resolve the Iraq crisis. The ultimate failure of that campaign—even as Gorbachev was awarded the Nobel Peace Prize on October 15—served only to re-emphasize the diminished role that the Soviet Union could now play in world affairs, and marked a shift from bipolarity to unipolarity. The Soviet push culminated with a proposal of a peace plan in February 1991, at the height of the military conflict. The plan was rejected by the Western powers when it was brought to the Security Council, led by the Americans, making clear where power ultimately lay in the emerging world order. Third, the foreign ministers of the Organization of the Islamic Conference (OIC), meeting in the margins at the UN, demanded Iraqi adherence with UN resolutions and expressed support for those Gulf states seeking foreign military assistance. The stance of the OIC was crucial: it signaled a universal legitimacy for UN peace enforcement, transcending religious and civilizational divides, giving the United States the green light to use the moral authority of the UN to lead a drive to push Hussein from Kuwait.

The place of the other P-5 members in this new order remained somewhat unclear. Despite or perhaps due to the productive cooperation between Moscow and Washington, the crisis catalyzed a shake-up in the USSR, with Foreign Minister Shevardnadze being forced to resign because of his support for military action against Iraq. The deployment of forty-two aircraft by NATO to Turkey on January 2 also spoke volumes, showing just how far strategic thinking had moved on from considering the USSR as the only real threat to the North Atlantic alliance. China was largely confined to the sidelines, still recovering from the Tiananmen Square fiasco. It had not yet attained the aura of an awakening giant, to paraphrase Napoleon, which it has now assumed. The United Kingdom was closely aligned in its 'special relationship' with the United States. But where did France fit in?

Never to be outdone by the United States, the French attempted to intercede in the crisis on a number of occasions, first through Mitterand's September 24 proposal of a four-stage peace plan, linking Iraq to the Israeli-Palestinian crisis, and then again on December 19, when the French indicated that if the United States had not held talks with Iraq by January 3, France would arrange its own. When US-Iraqi talks were not set until January 9, the French sent a delegation to Baghdad, without much success. As all eyes turned to the Security Council on January 15, with the deadline for Iraqi compliance imminent, France unexpectedly took center-stage, as it did again a dozen years later. The French suggested a simple trade: if Iraq withdrew from Kuwait, the Security Council would agree to an international conference on Palestine. The United States and the United Kingdom strongly opposed the suggestion, perhaps annoyed at what they perceived—as their successors would perceive French tactics in the Security Council in 2003—as grandstanding. The French withdrew the proposal and then bizarrely threatened to veto a British resolution making a last-minute appeal to Iraq to withdraw unconditionally from Kuwait, perhaps as a reminder that whatever the new informal pecking order, formally, they wielded the same veto power as the British and the Americans.[37]

3.5.1 *To War*

On January 12, 1991, the US Congress endorsed SCR 678, mandating Bush to use force against Iraq. The Senate approved the resolution by only five votes. The UN Secretary-General Javier Pérez de Cuéllar made a last-minute dash to Baghdad to attempt to impress on Saddam Hussein the imminence of military action and the strength of Coalition determination, but was kept waiting by Saddam Hussein, who then failed to show any flexibility.

On January 15, as events unfolded in the Security Council, Pérez de Cuéllar made one last appeal to Hussein to avoid a catastrophe. It went unheeded, and at midnight, the deadline passed. At 3 a.m. local time, the Coalition air campaign, labeled 'Operation Desert Storm', began. American, British, Saudi, and Kuwaiti aircraft bombed targets in Iraq and Kuwait, as the United States formally notified the UN Security Council of the commencement of hostilities. Planning for the operation, which had been personally named by General Schwarzkopf,[38] had begun just days after the launching of Operation Desert Shield, on August 10, 1990. American war-planners initially considered a draft plan for strategic air strikes inside Iraq named 'Operation Instant Thunder'.[39] Within a week, the plan had been revised to include ground, naval, and other military elements.[40]

Desert Storm began with extensive bombing aimed at degrading Iraqi defensive infrastructure, with special priority given to command and control centers, government buildings, bridges, power stations, and other strategically significant sites. Iraq's nuclear installations, later assessed by the International Atomic Energy Agency (IAEA) to have been much more advanced in terms of weaponization than had earlier been thought, were pulverized during the bombing. Much military hardware was also destroyed, not only to inhibit the Iraqi military machine's capacity for action but also in order to demoralize its troops. In the early days of the war, Iraqi attempts to escalate the conflict by firing Scud missiles at Israel failed, the Israeli government declining to respond with force, under strong pressure from Washington. The Coalition's own sorties produced significant 'collateral damage', most notoriously when

US bombers destroyed an air raid shelter in Baghdad on February 13, killing at least 400 civilians. Spain's argument in the Security Council for a pause in hostilities and an international inquiry was disregarded.

Two days later, having endured four weeks of steady pounding from the skies, the Iraqi Revolutionary Command Council invoked the possibility of withdrawal from Kuwait, but leadened this trial balloon with a variety of conditions unacceptable to the Coalition, notably a simultaneous end to other regional occupations—a reference to Israel. Bush rejected the proposal as a cruel hoax and called on the Iraqi people to force Saddam Hussein to step aside. However, President Gorbachev sought to tease out Saddam Hussein's intentions, and perhaps to assert his diplomatic independence. Seizing this opening, Tariq Aziz engaged in frenzied shuttle diplomacy to and from Moscow, culminating in an Iraqi offer of full and unconditional withdrawal, but ostensibly because the offer did not meet all of the Security Council's terms in the flood of resolutions initiated with SCR 660, this was rejected by President Bush.[41] Presumably, having traveled this far down the path of active military engagement, Bush was fearful of dilatory diplomatic tactics that might save Saddam Hussein from outright defeat and preserve for him a measure of credibility internationally, particularly in the Arab World. Nevertheless, in recognition of the fact of the Iraqi offer, on February 22, President Bush delivered an ultimatum: unless Iraq began its withdrawal within 24 hours, the ground war would start. President Gorbachev increased his diplomatic efforts, but to no avail. The deadline passed without an Iraqi move.

The ground campaign, launched on February 24, featured 200,000 Coalition troops, rapidly overwhelming Iraqi defensive tactics. Command of the skies, the ability to insert troops behind enemy lines, the effectiveness of the bombing campaign, and the demoralization of Iraqi troops all counted for more than Iraq's dug-in positions around and within Kuwait. Iraqi front lines rapidly disintegrated, with large numbers of defectors surrendering to the Coalition, which took between 60,000 and 85,000 prisoners. During the entire war (both air and ground phases), Iraq's only major successes were scored by its Scud missiles aimed at US military installations and at Israel, the latter hit several times, first on January 22, killing three, injuring many others. Chemical weapons, such a vital element of Saddam Hussein's arsenal against Iran, were never used, perhaps for fear of the Coalition reprisals this risked entailing.[42] After 48 hours of fighting, Baghdad Radio announced that Iraqi troops had been ordered to withdraw from Kuwait in accordance with SCR 660. The United States responded by reiterating that Iraq must abide by all twelve relevant SCRs.

By February 27, the Iraqi forces were routed and Kuwait liberated (with Arab Coalition troops liberating the capital city). Hammering home the scale of Iraqi defeat, a long retreating column of Iraqi troops was pursued and essentially incinerated from the air, probably killing thousands (and raising questions about vengeful American tactics at this late stage of the fighting). Tariq Aziz sent to the Council a letter accepting SCRs 660, 662, and 674. The P-5 demanded the unconditional acceptance of all resolutions relevant to the crisis, and when this followed, President Bush declared a cessation of hostilities as of midnight on February 27, with Coalition troops occupying roughly 15 percent of Iraqi territory. Saddam Hussein declared his own cease-fire on February 28. On March 2, a formal framework for a permanent cease-fire was set out in SCR 686, which required Iraq to rescind its purported annexation of Kuwait, accept liability under international law for war damages, release all Kuwaiti and third-state nationals, return all seized property, cease hostile and provocative actions, and release POWs.

President Bush indicates in his memoirs that he did not press on to Baghdad in order to overthrow Saddam Hussein because, on the one hand, such an objective had not been authorized by the Security Council and, on the other, he feared for Iraq's cohesion following the end of a Coalition occupation. Other administration officials who have written of this decision supported it.[43] With the passage of time, this reasoning seems both sound and prescient given the difficulties the second Bush administration has experienced in subduing Iraq and its relative international isolation in undertaking the task.

3.5.2 *Aftermath*

The end of hostilities was to usher in important new negotiations within the Security Council on the terms of Hussein's surrender, resulting in the adoption on April 3 of SCR 687, which came to be known as the 'Mother of all Resolutions' in mockery of Saddam Hussein's description of Desert Storm as the 'Mother of All Battles'. SCR 687, drafted in Washington and London, was adopted by twelve affirmative votes, with one negative vote (Cuba) and two abstentions (Ecuador, Yemen). It contained manifold provisions, many of them highly intrusive, which would prove precedent-making in Council practice. Among its provisions: UN demarcation of the Iraq–Kuwait border, acceptance of which would be mandatory; UN observers to monitor a demilitarized zone extending 6 miles into Iraq and 3 into Kuwait—the deployment of whom would allow for withdrawal of

Coalition troops from Iraq; obligation on Baghdad to destroy unconditionally and completely or remove under international supervision all chemical and biological weapons, and all ballistic missiles with a range of more than 94 miles, and related production facilities, with similar procedures instituted to remove all material usable for nuclear weapons (with the Secretary-General to establish a Commission charged with on-site inspections and supervision by May 17—this Special Commission came to be known by its UN acronym, UNSCOM); Iraq to accept liability for damages arising from its invasion of Kuwait, with a fund to be created to meet claims drawn from Iraqi oil revenues, and a Commission established by May 2 to administer it—this body came to be known as the UN Compensation Commission, sitting in Geneva.[44] Complex arrangements were foreseen for control of Iraq's oil exports. Complaining that the resolution impinged on Iraqi sovereignty (which it clearly did, by design), Iraq nevertheless accepted its terms on April 6.

Fearing for Iraq's cohesion in the dark hour of his most devastating military defeat, Saddam Hussein turned his attention to containing a Kurdish uprising in the north and Shi'a militias in the south. As is discussed further in Chapter 4, one consequence of Bush's decision to cease the military campaign without toppling Saddam Hussein was all too obvious within days: thousands of Shi'a and Kurdish Iraqis were killed indiscriminately by a regime bent on survival at any cost. President Bush's vaunted 'New World Order' provided no guarantees to those oppressed and massacred by their own states.

SCR 686 of March 2, 1991 had purported to speed the flow of medicine to Iraq while retaining sanctions, demanding that Iraq accept liability for the extensive damage to Kuwait during the Iraqi occupation. Since the outset of the Coalition air campaign against them, Iraqi forces had systematically compounded the earlier looting of Kuwait by torching its oil installations, requiring not only rebuilding of virtually the entire production and export infrastructure of the country, but also costing it many months of forgone production. Costs for Iraq had been, in many ways, even more significant, including much of its infrastructure. Hiro suggests $190 billion, a figure arrived at by the Arab Monetary Fund, as a credible estimate of overall costs to Iraq.[45] Sent to Iraq to assess the damage, Martti Ahtisaari, formerly head of the UN's mission in Namibia, commented on March 22:

> Nothing we had seen or read had quite prepared us for the particular form of devastation which had now befallen this country. The recent conflict has wrought near apocalyptic results on the economic infrastructure of what was until recently a highly urban and mechanized society.[46]

3.5.3 *A New Peacekeeping*

The success of the peace enforcement operation led by the United States against Iraq emboldened the Security Council to take a more assertive and intrusive stance even in traditional areas of peacekeeping such as border monitoring. This became immediately apparent following the forced withdrawal of Iraqi forces from Kuwait, with the establishment of UNIKOM by SCR 689 on April 9, 1991. UNIKOM in many ways resembled earlier, classical peacekeeping operations such as UNIIMOG. But these traditional duties were grafted onto a Chapter VII mandate.[47] Using that mandate, the Security Council increased UNIKOM's strength to three mechanized infantry battalions in 1993, following a series of Iraqi transgressions, and extended its mandate to include physical enforcement of the demilitarized zone (DMZ) between Iraq and Kuwait.

This new weaponry—both literal and figurative—seemed to hail a period of muscular peacekeeping, a break from the past. It suggested the Security Council would now act as New World Order Policeman, patrolling and enforcing clearly demarcated lines in the sand. The watershed nature of UNIKOM was further underlined by the fact that all five permanent members of the Security Council (P-5)—for the first time ever—provided military staff to a UN peace operation. UNIKOM operated smoothly for almost a dozen years, standing as a symbol of the kind of international police action favored by the first President Bush with his vision of a 'New World Order'. In March 2003, his son signaled the end of that period, sending an invasion force—without specific authorization from the Security Council—to remove Saddam Hussein from power in Baghdad. On March 17, 2003, Secretary-General Kofi Annan decided to suspend UNIKOM's operations and to withdraw the Mission due to the security risks posed by Bush's invasion force and because UNIKOM could no longer operate in the DMZ. The Mission—and the DMZ—was formally terminated on October 6, 2003.

3.6 Conclusions

Iraq's invasion of Kuwait in August 1990 triggered a series of events which transformed the UN's role in maintaining world order, and the form of the peace operations it used for that purpose. Iraq's invasion of Kuwait represented more than the passage of an army across an indistinct border on the Arabian peninsula. It also signaled the transgression of two key lines in the sand: the prohibition on aggression, and the common global interest in stable oil supply and prices from the Persian Gulf. Perhaps during the Cold War, Saddam Hussein might have crossed either line with impunity; but in the post-Cold War environment, the invasion ultimately proved a fatal miscalculation. In the process, the future not only of Iraq, but of the UN, was transformed.

3.6.1 *From Police Action to a Regulatory Approach*

Embedded within the script of the Iraq–Kuwait drama, as it unfolded, were a number of clues to the future direction of UN peace operations. The sanctions regime imposed by the Security Council included, almost from its inception, a humanitarian exception which highlighted tensions between peace enforcement and humanitarian considerations that were later to dog the UN's involvement in Iraq. SCRs 686 and 687 provided the formal framework for a permanent cease-fire, pointing to the future complexity of UN roles: among other provisions, it required Iraq to accept liability under international law for war damages and to disarm, demands that would lead to a vast expansion in the Council's normative, regulatory and administrative functions, for which it was ill prepared. The complex administrative machinery that was required to implement these resolutions signaled not only the movement to a third phase of UN involvement in Iraq but also another evolution in peace operations generally, away from the police action of Desert Storm toward a more regulatory approach, discussed further in Chapters 4, 5, and 6.

3.6.2 *A New World Order?*

The UN's centrality as a geostrategic resource in this new era was clear in numerous ways. Perhaps most importantly, the United States understood that a UN Security Council mandate would harness international legitimacy to its military power. Working through the UN made geostrategic sense, not least because the USSR made clear its unwillingness to support military action except under UN auspices. Other powers and stakeholders also demonstrated their understanding of the opportunities provided by multilateralism, for example, the French through their interventions in the General Assembly and Security Council, and the OIC through its demands for Iraqi compliance with SCRs made following meetings in the margins at the UN.

After decades of limited relevance because of bipolarity, the UN acquired a new lease on life. The end of the Iran–Iraq crisis, and even more so Iraq's ejection from Kuwait under a Security Council mandate, created a central role for the UN in the conduct of international relations. That centrality was to last for some time, thanks to an unprecedented level of cooperation between the P-5, and a revitalization of the role of UN peace operations in the maintenance of world order. In the period between March 1991 and October 1993, the Council passed 185 resolutions (a rate about five times greater than that of previous decades) and launched fifteen new peace-keeping and observer missions (as against seventeen in the preceding forty-six years).[48] Vetoes also dropped by roughly 80 percent. P-5 cooperation largely continued throughout the 1990s, with Russian concerns over Yugoslavia and Chinese concerns over Taiwan mostly quarantined from other issues. There were, of course, exceptions, notably on Israel–Palestine, Bosnia, Kosovo, and increasingly on Iraq. In some ways, however, these exceptions serve to highlight the predominance of the new pattern of P-5 concord, which paved the way for UN peace operations around the globe.[49]

When that concord ultimately faded, so would the usefulness to the unipolar power—the United States—of multilateralism through the UN. At that point, in 2003, the project of a New World Order shattered once and for all. However, indications had emerged well before then that the United States, the United Kingdom, and France were unwilling to be constrained by the requirements of geostrategic compromise required for some key Security Council mandates. Instead, as the next chapter reveals, a creeping unilateralism emerged even as the embers of the Iraq–Kuwait conflict were cooling.

Notes

1. The term 'police action' was first used by President Harry S. Truman to describe the action authorized by the Security Council against Korea under Chapter VII of the UN Charter, avoiding the need for Congressional approval of a formal declaration of war.
2. Chapter VII of the UN Charter addresses both the coercive measures the Security Council can invoke and their binding nature for all states.
3. Sciolino, *The Outlaw State*, 193.
4. At the same time, Cox induced King Ibn Saud to accept Kuwait's new border with Saudi Arabia by rejecting Sabah territorial claims to the East and South and largely acceding to Saudi desiderata. This led, in due course, to irredentist Kuwaiti sentiments toward subsequent Saudi rulers.

5. The Iraqi decision not to take the border dispute with Kuwait to the ICJ can be contrasted with the recent spate of successful demarcations it has conducted, and especially the delimitation between Qatar and Bahrain. Indeed, border demarcation is now the ICJ's most routinized competency. Other delimitations involved El Salvador/Honduras/Nicaragua, Indonesia/Malaysia, Botswana/Namibia, Denmark/Norway, Canada/US, and Greece/Turkey, to name but a few.
6. See, e.g. Anthony D'Amato, 'Israel's Air Strike Against the Osiraq Reactor: A Retrospective', *Temple International and Comparative Law Journal* 10/1 (1996). For current and future ramifications, see, for example, Dan Williams, 'Eyeing Iran Reactors, Israel Seeks U.S. Bunker Bombs', *Reuters*, September 21, 2004. Israel has also publicly disavowed any desire to strike at Iran's nuclear establishment. See 'Israel "not planning Iran attack" ', *BBC News*, April 14, 2005, http://news.bbc.co.uk/go/pr/fr/-/2/hi/middle_east/4443021.stm.
7. Dilip Hiro, *Neighbours Not Friends: Iraq and Iran After the Gulf Wars* (London: Routledge, 2001), 29.
8. Hume, *The United Nations, Iran and Iraq*, 187.
9. Hume, *The United Nations, Iran and Iraq*, 188.
10. On the Council's role in Namibia, see Cedric Thornbury, 'Namibia', in David M. Malone (ed.), *The UN Security Council: From the Cold War to the 21st Century* (Boulder, CO: Lynne Rienner, 2004); Chester A. Crocker, *High Noon in Southern Africa: Making Peace in a Rough Neighborhood* (New York: W.W. Norton, 1992); and Charles W. Freeman, Jr., 'The Angola-Namibia Accords', *Foreign Affairs* 68/3 (1989).
11. The role of the OAS on Nicaragua, while not always convincingly implemented, was a harbinger of the trend toward much larger roles for regional organizations, in partnership with the UN or on their own, in conflict resolution and peacekeeping as of the early 1990s. See Shepard Forman and Andrew Grene, 'Collaborating with Regional Organizations', in David M. Malone (ed.), *The UN Security Council: From the Cold War to the 21st Century* (Boulder, CO: Lynne Rienner, 2004).
12. See Jin Song, 'The political dynamics of the peacemaking process in Cambodia', in Michael Doyle, Ian Johnstone, and Robert Orr (eds.), *Keeping the Peace: Multidimensional UN Operations in Cambodia and El Salvador* (Cambridge: CUP, 1997), 54, 76–7; see also Janet E. Heininger, *Peacekeeping in Transition: the United Nations in Cambodia* (New York: Twentieth Century Fund Press, 1994), 19–20.
13. The paragraphs below on developments within the Security Council between August 1990 and April 1991 draw heavily on Hume's insider account, *The United Nations, Iran and Iraq*, 187–202.
14. James A. Baker, *The Politics of Diplomacy: Revolution, War and Peace, 1989–1992* (New York: G.P. Putnam's Sons, 1995), 16.
15. The earlier instances of mandatory Security Council-imposed sanctions were a trade embargo against Rhodesia (1966) and an arms embargo against South Africa (1977).

16. Not all these calls were productive. According to Sciolino, *The Outlaw State*, 223, King Hussein of Jordan proved adamant in his support of Saddam Hussein. Israeli–US ties were under severe stress over the hard-line policies of Israeli Prime Minister Shamir. Bush feared Israel might involve itself in the crisis, inhibiting his own diplomacy in the Arab World. Ultimately, Israel deferred to the United States, and sat out the crisis, even refusing to retaliate when Saddam Hussein targeted Scud missiles at Israel during the fighting of Desert Storm in 1991.
17. Sciolino, *The Outlaw State*, 215.
18. Earlier purported annexations, such as those of Goa by India in 1961 and East Timor by Indonesia in 1975, involved colonies rather than existing nation-states, though East Timor later became one after exercising its right of self-determination with UN assistance.
19. Algeria and Yemen abstained. Jordan, Sudan, and Mauritania did not participate in the vote. Only Iraq, Libya, and the PLO voted against the proposal.
20. George Bush and Brent Scowcroft, *A World Transformed* (New York: Alfred A. Knopf, 1998), 315.
21. Margaret Thatcher, *The Downing Street Years* (New York: HarperCollins, 1993), 824.
22. Bush and Scowcroft, *A World Transformed*, 303.
23. On this occasion, as would be the case often again with respect to Iraq, Moscow emphasized the link between the failure to find a solution to the Israel–Palestinian crisis and the situation affecting Iraq. As would also subsequently be the case, President Bush rejected any such link but did agree in principle to an international conference on the Middle East, which was held in Madrid in 1991. At Helsinki, the Soviets also pressed their demand that somehow the Military Staff committee, the Security Council's long-dormant military subsidiary body, be involved in managing military aspects of the crisis, which would have allowed Moscow a look-in on enforcement operations in which it did not wish to participate actively.
24. Compensation was never granted to complainants through this procedure, although, subsequently, individuals, companies, and states have all been enabled to seek redress under the UN Compensation Commission (UNCC), established by Resolutions 687 and 692. The UNCC acted as an arbitral tribunal, 'examining claims, verifying their validity, evaluating losses [and] assessing payments': *Report of the Secretary-General pursuant to paragraph 19 of Security Council resolution 687 (1991)* (UN Secretariat Document S/22559), May 2, 1991, para. 20. As the first judicial organ established by the Security Council, the UNCC raised many of the questions about Security Council competence, and due process issues, that later arose in the context of the International Criminal Tribunals for the former Yugoslavia and Rwanda and individualized financial sanctions. It eventually paid out almost $19 billion in compensation. See generally Andrea Gattini, 'The UN Compensation Commission: Old Rules,

New Procedures on War Reparations', *European Journal of International Law* 13/1 (2002), 161–81; David D. Caron and Brian Morris, 'The UN Compensation Commission: Practical Justice, Not Retribution', *European Journal of International Law* 13/1 (2002), 183–99; and C. L. Lim, 'On the Law, Procedures and Politics of United Nations Gulf War Reparations', *Singapore Journal of International and Comparative Law* 4/2 (2000), 435–78. The UNCC's treatment of environmental and public health claims was particularly novel: see *Report and recommendations made by the Panel of Commissioners concerning the fifth instalment of 'F4' claims* (UN Security Council Document S/AC.26/2005/10), 30 June 2005.

25. Zbigniew Brzezinski, 'Patience in the Persian Gulf, Not War', *New York Times*, Editorial, October 7, 1990.
26. UN Security Council resolution 673, October 24, 1990.
27. See Hume, *The United Nations, Iran and Iraq*, 207–8.
28. Abraham D. Sofaer, 'Asking the U.N. is Asking for Trouble', *Wall Street Journal*, Editorial, November 5, 1990, A14.
29. George H. W. Bush, 'Address Before the 45th Session of the United Nations General Assembly in New York, New York', October 1, 1990.
30. See Michelle Mittelstadt, 'Kirkpatrick Says U.S. Cannot Allow Limited Iraqi Withdrawal from Kuwait', *Associated Press*, October 30, 1990. On speculation that the UN would now become the "world's policeman", see Warren Strobel, 'Blue line stretched thin; Peacekeepers do everything everywhere', *Washington Times*, July 19, 1992, A1; and 'Democracies must wait for sanctions to force Iraq into negotiations', *The Guardian*, September 3, 1990, 18.
31. Alert readers will recall that Soviet diplomacy had also pressed successfully for a grace period on the implementation of Resolution 598 during the Iran–Iraq war, evidence either that Moscow considered this a very good idea or that it was pretty much a one-trick pony in a game of Security Council tactics dominated by the Western powers.
32. See Sciolino, *The Outlaw State*, 237. Such personal agendas in the Security Council would again become a preoccupation of the United States prior to the critical showdown in the Security Council on force against Saddam Hussein in the winter of 2002–3, when Washington complained bitterly, in their capitals, about the stance of the Chilean and Mexican Ambassadors in New York, probably unfairly in the case of highly regarded Chilean Ambassador Juan-Gabriel Valdes.
33. At no stage did China prove obstructive, despite or perhaps because of, a chill in relations with Western powers over the violent suppression of the Tiananmen Square demonstration in 1989, which had resulted in travel strictures on Chinese officials visiting the United States, not surprisingly relaxed so that Foreign Minister Qian Qichen could join his P-5 colleagues in New York for this important Security Council vote.
34. UN General Assembly resolution 45/49, November 28, 1990.
35. See Malone, *Decision-Making*, 176 s. v. 33.

36. In spite of a US undertaking to consult its P-5 partners on every important aspect of its Iraq diplomacy, this announcement was made unilaterally, a foretaste of how difficult it was going to become for multilateral allies to influence Washington's conduct of day-to-day policy.
37. John Goshko, 'U.N. Chief Issues Plea As Peace Efforts Fail; Opposition Scuttles France's Proposal', *Washington Post,* January 16, 1991, A6; 'Middle East in Crisis: France's Gulf Peace Proposal Fails Amid Iraqi Intransigence', *Wall Street Journal Europe,* January 16, 1991, 2; 'Mitterrand's peace plan—Gulf conflict', *The Times,* January 16, 1991.
38. H. Norman Schwarzkopf and Peter Petre, *It Doesn't Take a Hero* (New York: Bantam Books, 1992), 320. Desert Storm was chosen after Peninsula Shield and Crescent Shield were considered and rejected. Schwarzkopf perhaps got a little carried away: the ground offensive was Desert Saber; the withdrawal of military forces was called Desert Farewell; the distribution of leftover food to the US poor was Desert Share: Gregory C. Sieminski, 'The Art of Naming Operations', *Parameters* 25/3 (1995), s. v. 94–8 and accompanying text.
39. This appears to have been a deliberate (and critical) allusion to Rolling Thunder, the bombing operation over North Vietnam widely criticized by many in the US Air Force for being too drawn out: see Rick Atkinson, *Crusade: The Untold Story of the Persian Gulf War* (Boston, MA: Houghton Mifflin, 1993), 59; Sieminski, 'The Art of Naming Operations'.
40. *Final Report to Congress. Conduct of the Persian Gulf War* (Washington, DC: Department of Defense, 1992), www.globalsecurity.org/military/library/report/1992/cpgw.pdf
41. Improbably, Iranian President Rafsanjani on February 4 had announced a willingness to act as a go-between in efforts to bring Baghdad and Washington together. Not surprisingly, nothing came of this.
42. The reasons may have been more technical, having to do with destruction during the air campaign of the delivery systems for chemical warheads, or a loss of potency in storage. The Coalition had also warned Iraqi commanders that they would be held responsible individually for any use of these weapons, which may have radically decreased enthusiasm for their deployment.
43. Bush and Scowcroft, *A World Transformed,* 463–4. See also, Baker, *The Politics of Diplomacy,* 435–8.
44. Iraq's creditors, including several Security Council members, were keen to ensure that this claims process did not prejudice repayment of Iraq's debts and built provisions to this effect into the text.
45. Hiro, *Neighbours Not Friends,* 34.
46. *Report on humanitarian needs in Iraq in the immediate post-crisis environment by a mission to the area led by the Under-Secretary-General for Administration and Management, March 10–17, 1991* (UN Document S/22366), March 20, 1991.
47. UN Security Council resolution 687, April 3, 1991 and UN Security Council resolution 689, April 9, 1991.

48. See David M. Malone, 'The UN Security Council in the Post-Cold War World: 1987–97', *Security Dialogue*, 28/4 (1997), 394.
49. Many of these UN operations registered disappointing results due in part to the difficulty of addressing internal conflicts often featuring a multiplicity of rebel forces. The failure of several such missions, notably in Bosnia, Angola, and Somalia contributed to a dimming of the UN's star as the 1990s progressed. Perhaps for a lack of alternatives, a new wave of UN peacekeeping missions, several moderately successful, was initiated from 1999 onward in the Democratic Republic of the Congo, Ethiopia-Eritrea, Haiti, Kosovo, Liberia, Sierra Leone, and Sudan. UNTAET in East Timor is widely recognized as the outright success of this generation of complex UN peacekeeping missions.

4

Creeping Unilateralism: Humanitarian Interventions and No-Fly Zones

With the success of the UN-mandated collective security action against Iraq, the UN took on a wide array of roles in enforcing the peace it had helped to create. That array of roles required a more multidisciplinary approach to peace operations than was traditional—an approach explored in this chapter. In Iraq, it incorporated humanitarian objectives through the deployment of UN 'Guards' to northern Iraq to protect returning refugees, and the involvement of the UN in providing humanitarian assistance to those populations. The UN system increasingly took on the role of proxy administration in areas not under sovereign Iraqi control. These developments foreshadowed much greater UN involvement in essentially internal conflicts and in complex humanitarian situations.[1] At the same time, events in Iraq were increasingly characterized by the early resort (or reversion) by several Security Council members to unilateral action. This emerged first in their launching of Operation Provide Comfort to protect Kurdish refugees in northern Iraq, but soon spilled over into the imposition by those powers of no-fly zones over northern and southern Iraq in 1991 and 1992. This creeping unilateralism was a harbinger of further unilateral enforcement measures to come that would, by 1998, sunder the unity of the Security Council's purpose on Iraq.

4.1 Operation Provide Comfort

On February 15, 1991, as the war in Iraq raged, President Bush called on the people of Iraq to 'take matters into their own hands—to force Saddam Hussein, the dictator, to step aside . . . '.[2] The Voice of Free Iraq, a clandestine radio station sponsored by the Central Intelligence Agency (CIA), reinforced this message: 'We are with you,' it broadcast into Iraq, 'in every heartbeat, in all your feelings, and in every move you make.'[3] But on February 28, Coalition military action was called to a temporary halt, and on March 2, the Security Council passed SCR 686, which established the framework for peace, including the establishment of a formal cease-fire.[4] On the same day, Shi'a militias and soldiers returning from the front rose in rebellion in southern Iraq, sensing Hussein's momentary weakness.[5] Within days, the Shi'a rebellion had spread to all major Shi'a centers—Nasiriyeh, Basra, Najaf, and Karbala—and Kurdish rebels had seized the opportunity to mount their own offensive in northern Iraq.

The Western coalition, which had spearheaded the military campaign in the Gulf, was confronted with a dilemma: support the rebellions, and Iraq might fracture into ethnic enclaves, threatening a regional firestorm drawing in Iran, Syria, Turkey, and perhaps Saudi Arabia;[6] ignore the rebellions, and Hussein would likely commit further atrocities against Iraq's ethnic minorities, just as Western media attention was focused on the region. For weeks, the US position remained guarded. President Bush issued a statement on March 15 calling on Hussein to stop combat operations against the rebels, but took no other overt action.[7] All the signals were that the United States would not intervene. It had 'made no promises to the Shi'as or Kurds', the White House spokesman reminded the press on March 27. The next day, Paul Wolfowitz, then Under-Secretary at the Pentagon, noted that 'If Iraq is just a country that treats its people decently and [does] not attack its neighbors, it'd be great progress.'[8] But with the southern rebellion extinguished by the end of March, Hussein redeployed the infamous Republican Guard into the north as the Coalition stood by. They advanced quickly.

As Iraqi military operations turned from Kuwait toward Kurdish factions in the north, 1.5–2 million Kurdish civilians began fleeing for their lives—half the entire population of the area—into the snowy mountains on the Turkish and Iranian borders.[9] Turkey took a small number into a refugee camp on its side of the border, but simultaneously signaled its unwillingness to receive the refugees in large numbers. Thanks to the presence in the region of large numbers of Western media, particularly CNN, television screens in homes throughout the United States, Europe, and elsewhere began to fill with the images of a human tide, fleeing from the threat of Hussein's reprisals, cowering in the mountains, without food, water, shelter, or sanitation near the closed Turkish border as the Iraqi military advanced.[10]

Public opinion in the United States swung quickly, backing a continued US military presence to protect these nearly 2 million Kurdish refugees.[11]

Yet having forced Iraq out of Kuwait, the US government was hesitant to deploy troops deep into Iraq, on a protective mission with no clear end-date, lest it become another 'Vietnam'. Voices in the region also cautioned against further weakening of Hussein's regime, lest Iraq fracture into ethnic enclaves.[12] Saudi Arabia was particularly concerned about the possibility of a Shi'a satellite of Iran emerging on its northern border, while Turkey and Syria both worried that the emergence of a Kurdish state in northern Iraq in the wake of a Western intervention would undermine their own territorial integrity by providing a staging base for Kurdish secessionists. Nevertheless, both Turkey and Iran wrote to the Security Council calling for international action to protect them from the floods of refugees massing on their borders.[13]

4.1.1 *A Multilateral Mandate?*

On April 3, during the Security Council's discussions of what ultimately became SCR 687, France tried unsuccessfully to insert a clause regarding the plight of the Kurds.[14] When SCR 687 was adopted without addressing the situation of the Kurds, President Mitterand declared that failure to protect them would severely affect the 'political and moral authority' of the Security Council.[15] Following informal consultations, France and Belgium submitted a resolution, co-sponsored by the United States and the United Kingdom, to the Security Council.[16] On April 5, in the face of mounting pressure, the Security Council passed SCR 688, condemning the Iraqi repression, particularly of Kurds, and calling the cross-border incursions produced by the resulting refugee flows a threat to international peace and security.[17] SCR 688 did not condemn the repression itself as a threat to international peace and security—only its transboundary effects—nor take steps under Chapter VII to put a stop to it. Russia, and perhaps also China, had indicated during negotiations that they would veto any resolution providing a specific enforcement provision.[18] Although SCR 688 established a template for action, which the Council later used in justifying its responses to crises in Yugoslavia, Somalia, Haiti, and later Kosovo, the Security Council was not yet ready to abandon the old world order of respect for sovereignty and non-interference in internal affairs.

SCR 688 was adopted by a vote of ten to three (Cuba, Yemen, and Zimbabwe). China and India abstained. No other SCR passed in the immediate aftermath of Iraq's invasion of Kuwait with so little support.[19] That is no surprise: the members of the Security Council were acutely aware, in negotiating SCR 688, of its precedential value.[20] The action to expel Iraqi forces from Kuwait was the first such Chapter VII mandate since Korea, appearing to herald a revitalization of the system of collective security.[21] But while the members of the Security Council welcomed a revitalization of the UN's role in principle, UN involvement in internal affairs of states driven by humanitarian and human rights concerns was quite another matter for some of them.

The Iraqi representative argued that the situation in northern Iraq was an internal matter, and that Security Council action would violate Article 2(7) of the Charter.[22] Yemen asserted that the Resolution set a 'dangerous precedent' marking 'an attempt to circumvent the rule of law for political ends', because as the humanitarian crisis posed no threat to international peace and security, 'the whole issue is not within the competence of the Security Council'.[23] Cuba claimed that the resolution would turn the UN 'into a system dominated by an oligarchical group, which attributes to itself powers that no one has given it'.[24] China's view on the record was subtler: it recognized 'international aspects' of the crisis, but suggested they be resolved through other channels.[25] India, too, sought a middle path.[26] Even some of the supporters of the Resolution acknowledged that it fell within the Council's competence because of the *transboundary* nature of the Kurdish refugee flows.[27] Britain and France, however, claimed that the Council was competent even to deal with some wholly internal human rights violations.[28]

4.1.2 *'Unilateral' Implementation*

In the debates over SCR 688, most of the Security Council's members affirmed traditional doctrines of sovereignty and nonintervention. But in the years that followed, the Council increasingly acquiesced in unilateralist interventions (acutely undermining Iraq's sovereignty) by the United States, the United Kingdom, and, to a lesser degree, France, under the cover of ambiguous authority of earlier Council resolutions. (This in turn set the stage for much more intrusive Council strategies in the Balkans and elsewhere as the 1990s progressed.)

On the record, Russia, China, and some other Security Council members denied that SCR 688 permitted forcible intrusion, but their rhetoric did not match the reality of their frequent unwillingness during much of the 1990s to confront the emerging unipolar Power—the United States—and whatever 'coalition of the willing' it could assemble. The Russian Federation (which had now succeeded the Soviet Union at the UN *without any debate*, in a quiet accommodation so typical of the charmed life in the Security Council of permanent members) and China for many years acquiesced in unilateral US, UK, and French implementation actions in Iraq, and only became outspoken in opposition when France switched sides.

The pattern of intervention in Iraq following the 1991 Gulf War was precedential in many ways. In particular, a new prominence emerged for human rights issues in the Council's agenda.[29] SCR 688 marked the first time, except for earlier resolutions on South Africa (and, indirectly, Rhodesia), that the Council demanded improvement of a human rights situation as a contribution to international peace and security.[30] Although SCR 688 contained none of the traditional indicia of an enforcement mandate, it did insist 'that Iraq allow immediate access by international humanitarian organizations to all those in need of assistance in all parts of Iraq and to make available all necessary facilities for their operations'.[31] It went on to request the Secretary-General to 'use all the resources at his disposal ... to address urgently the critical needs of the refugees and displaced Iraqi population', and to appeal to 'all Member States and to all humanitarian organizations to contribute to these humanitarian relief efforts'.[32]

This suggested that Member States would 'contribute' to a UN-led attempt to 'address' the humanitarian crisis. However, the same day that SCR 688 was adopted, President Bush announced that, beginning on April 7, US Air Force transport planes would begin humanitarian relief drops into northern Iraq, without any effort at coordination through or with the UN. Moreover, the United States announced the unilateral creation of a 'no-fly zone' for Iraqi aircraft in Iraqi airspace above the 36th parallel, in order to protect US aircraft engaged in the humanitarian relief drops. The US was quickly joined by the United Kingdom and France in this humanitarian effort.[33] Bush's announcement—and its backing by the United Kingdom and France—initiated a pattern of unilateral implementation and often enforcement of Security Council resolutions regarding Iraq that marked the subsequent decade, slowly driving a wedge between the Council's permanent members. Given the humanitarian objectives of the operation, however, few complained at the time.

On April 8, UK Prime Minister John Major proposed a plan to the European Community to create 'safe enclaves' inside Iraq for Kurdish refugees.[34] Across the Atlantic, the United States remained reticent to commit ground troops.[35] President Bush put it bluntly: 'We're not going to get sucked into this by sending precious American lives into this battle.'[36] In a speech in Boston on April 11—just as the Security Council president was informing the Iraqi ambassador of the coming-into-force of a cease-fire along the Kuwait border and the deployment of UNIKOM—Vice-President Dan Quayle laid the same case out in more detail:[37]

> Would America's intervention in Iraq's civil war advance vital national interests? ... I'm afraid the answer is 'no.' What are the vital interests of the United States in Iraq's civil war? Very little, if any .... What would be the clearly defined military objectives of our intervention in Iraq? Overthrow Saddam Hussein? Impose Western-style democracy? Achieve a U.S. brokered reconciliation among Kurds, Sunnis, and Shiites? Dismember Iraq? Prevent Iraq from being dismembered? Merely to pose these questions demonstrates how complicated the situation is—how easy it would be to get into Iraq, but how hard it would be to get out of the quagmire.[38]

But just five days later, on April 16, 1991, the United States, joined by the United Kingdom and France, decided to send in ground troops to support humanitarian relief efforts[39] and provide Kurdish refugees with 'safe havens'.[40] As James Mayall put it, the intervention occurred

> because the attention devoted by the Western media to the plight of the Kurds threatened the political dividends Western governments had secured from their conduct of the war itself.[41]

That political evaluation was driven home by James Baker's visit to Kurdish refugees in Turkish camps;[42] he had both the insight to realize the political cost of a failure to act, and the clout—both within the Bush administration, and overseas—to put together an effective solution.

Coalition troop access to Iraq was to be through Turkey, so the Operation—designated 'Provide Comfort'—became subject to biannual review by Turkish Parliament. The US–UK strategy overtook a French plan, hatched by the French Minister for Humanitarian Affairs, Bernard Kouchner. That plan, which had reportedly secured the support of both the Secretary-General's Executive Delegate, Sadruddin Aga Khan, and senior UNHCR official Stefan di Mistura, would have seen French troops operating as *relais humanitaires* to create safe corridors for Kurdish refugees to return home.[43]

The initial plan for Operation Provide Comfort was for the US military to build, administer, and guard six camps sheltering around 60,000 refugees.[44] Ultimately, the Operation involved 20,000 troops from thirteen nations and contributions from thirty, protecting Kurds in an area of 5,500 square kilometres in the governorate of Dohuk.[45] Its central achievement was the construction of relief camps sheltering displaced persons in Zakho and Dohuk. The US troops remained in northern Iraq until early July 1991, by which time the UN High Commission for Refugees had assumed responsibility for the refugee camps the Western troops had established.[46] The no-fly zone remained when ground troops departed.[47]

4.1.3 *Bringing the UN Back in*

Just as the US position shifted quickly in mid-April, so did Saddam Hussein's. On April 18, to the surprise of many outsiders, Kurdish rebels agreed to enter talks. Jalal Talabani, the leader of the PUK, explained that the move was prompted by the lack of outside support for the Kurds; the first priority was to allow the refugees to return home.[48] Encouraged by this development, and perhaps seeking to ensure that the creation of safe havens would not create *de facto* autonomy for the Kurds (as later occurred through another US–UK–French-led humanitarian intervention with NATO partners, in Kosovo), Hussein moved to nail down the parameters of the safe havens. First, he began quiet negotiations with the Coalition on logistics. Second, he agreed a Memorandum of Understanding (MOU) with the UN on humanitarian relief (discussed further below).[49] The MOU provided the UN with unprecedented access—perhaps in an effort to ensure that UN-hatted civilians would quickly replace Western soldiers.[50] By June, Hussein had hammered out a wider political settlement with the Kurds, thus removing one central justification for a continued Western military presence in northern Iraq.[51]

That presence was not without controversy. At first, President Bush and Prime Minister Major asserted, in a pattern that foreshadowed the arguments of their political heirs a decade later, that SCR 688 already provided them with all the authorization they needed to send troops into Iraq.[52] The US Department of State described the Western efforts as 'complementary' to the UN effort, and perhaps as a 'basis' for it—but not as part of the same effort.[53] That only served to beg the question of whence the authority for the Western intervention arose, if it was distinguishable from the UN effort contemplated by SCR 688. Even as Iraq agreed to a MOU with the UN on the provision of humanitarian relief, it denounced the presence of Western troops as interference in Iraqi internal affairs.[54] The Secretary-General's Special Envoy to northern Iraq, Eric Suy, argued that safe havens could only be established with Iraqi consent.[55] Pérez de Cuéllar himself was even more blunt. Asked whether a Western military presence could be established under UN authority without Iraqi consent, he replied 'No. No. No. We have to be in touch first of all with the Iraqis.'[56] At the same time, though, he seemed prepared to look the other way if Western forces chose to act alone, so long as the UN was not asked to use force: '... if the countries involved do not require the United Nations flag, then that is quite different.'[57] On this, the Secretary-General, Russia, and China all seem to have agreed. While the latter two might have vetoed a Security Council authorization of force, they did not speak out against Western unilateral enforcement. What they would neither authorize nor assist *de jure*, they would acquiesce in *de facto*.[58] Off the record, a senior US State Department official clarified the US position, musing that while Iraq has 'made critical comments on the U.S. effort, there is not a damn thing they can do about it'.[59]

4.1.4 *Early Warning Signals*

The United States, the United Kingdom, and France learned an important lesson about the elasticity of the Council's tolerance for unilateralism, and a no less concrete lesson about the creative use that can be made of broad authorizing Resolutions. But the legal basis for the intervention has remained the subject of much debate.[60] The UK Foreign Secretary Douglas Hurd suggested that even if SCR 688 did not specifically mandate Operation Provide Comfort, it was justified under the customary doctrine of humanitarian intervention. 'International law', Hurd stated simply, 'recognizes extreme humanitarian need.'[61] The French position prior to passage of SCR 688 was even more assertive: French Foreign Minister Roland Dumas suggested in a press interview that intervention in this case was not a right, it was a duty.[62]

This reliance on the doctrine of humanitarian intervention would have profound consequences down the track. Most obviously, it paved the way rhetorically for NATO's intervention in Kosovo in 1999, bypassing the Security Council. Equally important, though, it served as an early signal of US and UK unwillingness to give the Security Council the final say on when force might be used against Iraq. Hurd signaled that customary international law may recognize some other writ, which gives states, not the Security Council, discretion to launch offensive military action.

Operation Provide Comfort provided other early warning signals for the UN, most of them obscured by events at the time. For one thing, NGOs found themselves not only working alongside, but actively cooperating with, elite and special operations forces many of them had previously disdained.[63] The difficulties of civil–military relations in the provision of humanitarian assistance that emerged in the mountains of Kurdistan were the same ones that have confronted the UN in coordinating complex humanitarian operations for years since. The slow and at times poorly coordinated response of the UN's various humanitarian agencies to the Kurdish crisis highlighted the problems of decentralization within the UN system, triggering centralizing reform.[64]

Similarly, there is a striking similarity between the American on-the-fly approach to relief operations in northern Iraq in 1991 and its ad hoc approach to reconstruction and state-building throughout Iraq since 2003. Just as the transitional phase in 2003 was plagued by turf wars between the Departments of State and Defense, so in 1991 relief efforts were hampered by those Departments' lack of coordination.[65] In 2003, President George W. Bush seemed unprepared for the challenges of state-building, despite warnings from Colin Powell. Powell had perhaps learned from his experiences of policy-on-the-fly under Bush's father: in 1991, President George H. W. Bush gave the military—of which Powell was then Chairman of the Joint Chiefs of Staff—only two days notice of Operation Provide Comfort, and seven days into the Operation transformed it from an airlift operation to a ground operation.

A degree of doublespeak over policy also marked both periods in Washington. While George W. Bush has attracted criticism for his confused policy in the post-conflict period, it was his father who, after calling on the Iraqis 'to take matters into their own hands' in February 1991, two months later said

> ... do I think that the United States should bear guilt because of ... the implication being given by some that the United States would be there to support them militarily? That was not true. We never implied that.[66]

4.1.5 *A Leaky Umbrella*

Operation Provide Comfort undoubtedly saved many, many lives, not only in the short term, but by laying the foundation for a more effective relief and distribution system in the three northern governorates than was ever achieved elsewhere in Iraq.[67] In October 1991, Hussein decided to withdraw all Iraqi government support for the three northern governorates, ordering troops and government workers to return to Baghdad. Arab officials did, but many Kurdish officials remained, providing the backbone of a Kurdish bureaucracy that took over administration of government services across northern Iraq, allowing UN and other humanitarian relief workers to operate with a freedom they never enjoyed elsewhere in Iraq. But in other ways Operation Provide Comfort provided only a 'leaky umbrella' over the heads of the region's inhabitants.[68] Roughly 85 percent of the adult population was unemployed and malnutrition remained a serious problem.[69] Control of the oil trade into and out of Kurdistan was also murky at best, a fact at the time overlooked on the assumption that the trade assisted the struggling Kurdish population.[70] In fact, this may have been the period in which Hussein laid the groundwork for the covert oil-trading networks which he later used to circumvent the OFF Program.

Operation Provide Comfort was aimed only at humanitarian relief, and not the generation of a permanent political solution for Iraqi Kurds. Nevertheless, it did provide the foundation for positive economic and political development of the region, which was able to experiment with autonomy under international protection. Champions of Kurdish independence were able to point to the relative success of the Iraqi Kurds in managing their own affairs.[71] And Kurdish cohesion and political maturity achieved incrementally during the late 1990s gave significant weight to the region in Iraq's political evolution in 2004 and 2005 (as outlined in Chapter 8).

4.1.6 *Cold Comfort*

Operation Provide Comfort wrapped up at the end of 1996, after pressures and criticism emerged on four fronts.

First, fighting between Kurdish factions had seriously hampered relief efforts.[72] Hussein's October 1991 blockade of the north left the Kurdish factions in control of the three northern governorates. Made confident by this growing de facto authority, in May 1992 the main Kurdish factions came together to hold elections for a parliamentary assembly. The results—condemned by some observers as a sham—gave equal numbers of seats to the two main Kurdish factions, the Kurdish Democratic Party (KDP) and the PUK. By 1994, though, relations between the two factions had broken down, spawning local harassment of relief efforts and corruption.[73]

Second, in the summer of 1996, fighting between the KDP and PUK seriously escalated. The KDP allied itself with Hussein and, assisted by his troops, seized control of Irbil, inside the Safe Haven, from the PUK—just eight weeks before the US presidential election.[74] The United States responded on September 3 and 4, with a barrage of forty-four Tomahawk cruise missiles directed at defense radar installations in the south. In addition, President Clinton unilaterally extended the southern 'no-fly zone' (discussed further below) to the 33rd parallel, which included parts of Baghdad. The US move met with criticism from US allies and other powers alike—both for being unjustified and excessive and, at the same time, for being too little to stem Hussein's military campaign.[75] Undeterred, Baghdad-backed forces took Sulaimaniya, and with it, control of 80 percent of Iraqi Kurdistan.[76]

The American response to Hussein's seizure of Irbil in September 1996 drove home an important truth to observers: it demonstrated the continued resilience of Hussein's military while showing also that the United States was prepared to use SCR 688 as the basis for a wide range of policies in Iraq—even those not self-evidently designed to pursue the original objectives of the Resolution—without reference to the Security Council. But the weakness of the US response signaled that the US policy was now focused on containing Iraqi military capacity.[77] This, in itself, triggered a strategic realignment within the region, with Arab states qualifying their earlier unconditional support for the United States as they realized that not only would Hussein remain on the scene, but that he might once more emerge as an important regional player.[78] The situation of Kurds on the ground slipped down the list of priorities, and with it support for Operation Provide Comfort.

Third, a Kurdish militant group, the Kurdish Workers' Party (PKK), had increasingly used the absence of centralized authority in northern Iraq to launch attacks into Turkey. The Turkish government responded in March 1995 with its biggest military operation since World War II, Operation Steel, sending 35,000 troops into northern Iraq, creating discomfort for its NATO allies underwriting the protection to the Kurds offered by Operation Provide Comfort. Turkey remained ambivalent about Operation Provide Comfort, allowing the United States, the United Kingdom, and France to fly sorties from its base at Incirlik, but worrying that the Allied role on the ground in northern Iraq facilitated PKK operations.[79] At the end of 1996, the Turkish Parliament allowed the mandate for Operation Provide Comfort to lapse, instead permitting only a 'reconnaissance force' to operate from Turkish airspace.[80] The United States put up no overt resistance to this development.

Fourth, in late 1996 the French government withdrew its support for the Operation, officially on the basis that the situation in northern Iraq no longer required the flying of sorties to protect relief organizations, because of new guarantees that 30 percent of revenues from the OFF Program (discussed later in Chapter 5) would be distributed to Kurdish areas.[81] The French decision came, however, in a period when the Gaullist government of Chirac was beginning to flex its muscles, breaking briefly with the United States over military action to enforce the southern no-fly zone, and backing UN Secretary-General Boutros Boutros-Ghali against US attempts (ultimately successful) to oust him after only one term. The French had also been opposed to the US response to Hussein's seizure of Irbil, and to the US proposals in 1994 for a southern 'no-troop zone'.[82] France's withdrawal from Operation Provide Comfort marked an important turning point, confirming a steady divergence between the United States and France over Iraq policy that culminated in the showdown over the 'second resolution' preceding the US-led invasion in 2003. But it also reflected a broader tide of opposition to US unilateralism in Iraq, including, crucially, amongst Arab nations.[83]

Under these pressures in late 1996, Operation Provide Comfort was officially ended, to be replaced on January 1, 1997, by Operation Northern Watch, a combined US–UK operation enforcing the no-fly zone above the 36th parallel.

4.2 The UN Humanitarian Relief Program

Even as the United States and some of its allies unilaterally established Operation Provide Comfort, it was clear that a more coordinated, long-term effort was needed to discharge the UN's humanitarian obligations under SCR 688. The agreement reached between Baghdad and the UN by Sadruddin Aga Khan on April 18, 1991 contained a number of novel elements that were later used as templates for UN interventions elsewhere.[84] This MOU was structured around three basic principles: (*a*) the Iraqi government would cooperate in full; (*b*) persons displaced were entitled to return voluntarily; and (*c*) the UN was entitled to access and a humanitarian presence 'wherever ... needed' through the establishment of UN offices 'in agreement and cooperation with the Government of Iraq'.[85] These offices were empowered to 'monitor the overall situation', but only in order 'to advise the Iraqi authorities regarding measures needed to enhance their work'.[86]

These provisions exemplified the uneasy compromise between UN and Iraqi authorities, which later played out in a number of disputes over the scope and operation of the relief program. The UN could staff its offices not only with its own workers, but also with NGO and Red Cross staff seconded to the UN.[87] The MOU allowed those offices to provide not only the specified 'food aid, medical care, agricultural rehabilitation, [and] shelter' but also 'any other humanitarian and relief measures geared to the speedy normalization of life, in conformity with the principles of this memorandum'.[88] The MOU also gave the UN the power to organize airlifts and its own communications system.[89] But the MOU gave the Iraqi government control over other key decisions, particularly the location of UN offices.

This provision became contentious in relation to the Shi'a population in southern Iraq. Following reports of mass population movements into the southern marshes following the March uprising, during a visit to Iraq in July 1991, Sadruddin Aga Khan requested permission to visit the area, accompanied by media and UN experts. Thereafter, he requested a permanent UN presence in Nasariya on the edge of the marshes, stressing that 'Iraq was in breach of both the letter and the spirit of the Memorandum of Understanding' in not allowing the establishment of a Humanitarian Center there.[90] The Iraqi Foreign Minister countered that the MOU provided for the determination of humanitarian needs to be made jointly, and that to continue to insist on the establishment of an office in the area would be a political act unacceptably 'linking relief to SCR 688'.[91] The issue remained unresolved, and was eventually reported to the Security Council when it reviewed sanctions in January 1992.[92] In March, Iraq permitted the establishment of an office in Nasariya; but in the following summer, UN relief workers were ordered by the authorities to leave southern Iraq.[93]

The 'Humanitarian Relief Program' envisioned by the MOU was much more ambitious than the temporary protection provided by Operation Provide Comfort to Kurdish refugees. It aimed at providing essential humanitarian assistance to needy civilians throughout Iraq. However, personal security remained a central issue and the Iraqi military remained the primary threat. Unlike the military Operation Provide Comfort, the civilian Humanitarian Relief Program could not provide armed protection. It operated only with the agreement of the Iraqi government. How, then, could the UN ensure protection of the civilian population, and its own workers?

In private, UK Foreign Secretary Douglas Hurd went as far as suggesting that SCR 688 authorized the establishment of a 'UN police force'.[94] Prime Minister Major wrote to the Secretary-General on May 2, 1991 to formally propose the idea, and received support from both the US and the European Community.[95] Eric Suy argued SCR 688 provided insufficient authority for such a force, and Brian Urquhart warned against 'a small powerful minority' of Western states imposing their ideas on the UN.[96] In any event, Baghdad would not agree to the deployment of armed foreigners, even in a policing role, and both China and Russia resisted the notion of the Council imposing such a decision on Iraq.[97]

Instead, on May 25, 1991, Iraq and the Secretary-General reached a highly creative compromise which remains unique to this day: up to 500 UN 'Guards', drawn from the United Nations Security and Safety Service (UNSSS—the operational security arm of the UN Secretariat), supplemented by individuals seconded from national civilian police or militaries, were permitted into the country to assist with the relief effort.[98] They were permitted to be armed with pistols—provided by the Iraqi government—and were to work alongside the Iraqi authorities.[99] The objective was for the Guards to serve a confidence-building function intended to induce the voluntary return of displaced persons and potentially deter Iraqi military abuses.[100]

The Guards operated without interference—until 1996. The Guards successfully took on many roles, even negotiating local cease-fires and humanitarian evacuations.[101] The UN Guards initiative proved a creative and effective solution, operating as a security facilitator at the grassroots level. It created the conditions permitting the return of hundreds of thousands of Kurdish refugees and the safe delivery of a large international assistance program carried out by UNHCR, other UN agencies, and NGOs. These programs supported roughly 1.25 million people in northern Iraq. Sadruddin Aga Khan described the concept in this way:

> We had to improvise. The aim was a degree of security without the Security Council, of peace without peace-keeping, of international action without intervention.[102]

However, ultimately, the UN was not able to guarantee their indefinite presence. After Iraq declined to participate in the proposed OFF Program, a stalemate developed. The security situation deteriorated in 1996, with one Guard being killed and a number injured and wounded.[103] As winter approached, a new agreement was brokered, allowing temporary relief access to the Kurdish north—but leaving UN humanitarian programs in the rest of Iraq unresolved. Ultimately, this challenge was addressed through the OFF Program, discussed in the next chapter.

4.3 No-Fly Zones

4.3.1 *Creation*

From the outset, a ban on Iraqi fixed and rotary-wing aircraft above the 36th parallel was an integral part of Operation Provide Comfort, initially to ensure the safety of Coalition aircraft providing humanitarian relief to Kurdish refugees, and later to ensure the safety of Coalition ground troops.

The southern no-fly zone was established by the United States, the United Kingdom, and France in August 1992, following Iraqi military actions in southern Iraq against the Shi'a population, particularly the Ma'dan, the Arabic population of the marshes around the confluence of the Tigris and Euphrates rivers.

That this southern no-fly zone proved completely ineffective in protecting these populations from Saddam Hussein's fierce repression has received too little attention. Attacks on these groups escalated throughout the summer of 1992.[104] At the same time, the United States was coming under fire for having failed in cease-fire negotiations to limit Iraqi use of military helicopters, which provided the main assault vehicle against the Ma'dan.[105] Concerned at Baghdad's ongoing violations of both the Security Council's cease-fire resolution and its own population's human rights, the United States, the United Kingdom, France, and Belgium called a Council meeting on August 11, 1992, to which, in an unprecedented initiative, they summoned the Special Rapporteur on Iraq of the UN Commission on Human Rights, Max van der Stoel, a former Dutch Foreign Minister.[106] This followed a statement by the first ever Security Council Summit in January 1992—itself a product of the tectonic shifts in post-Cold War thinking within the Council—that noted that human rights verification was becoming one of the tasks of UN peacekeeping.[107] (That statement itself pointed to the new 'multidisciplinary' ambition of UN peacekeeping.) India, China, Ecuador, and Zimbabwe were vehemently opposed to van der Stoel's appearance before the Council.[108] India asserted:

> Deviation from the Charter, in which the nations of the world have reposed their faith and support, could erode ... confidence and have grave consequences for the future of the Organization.... The Council ... cannot discuss human rights situations *per se* or make recommendations on matters outside its competence.[109]

In the end, van der Stoel was described to the press as having appeared before the Council as a 'private citizen'.[110] He rehearsed the thrust of his earlier reports to the Commission, including the proposal to deploy UN human rights monitors inside Iraq.[111] The Security Council took no action. Instead, the United States, the United Kingdom, and France acted alone, announcing the imposition of a no-fly zone below the 32nd parallel on August 27, 1992, ostensibly to protect the southern marsh Arabs from the repression forbidden by SCR 688.[112] On December 28, 1992, a US air patrol encountered an Iraqi MiG-25 in the no-fly zone, and shot it down. As they did with Operation Provide Comfort and its successor, Operation

Northern Watch, neither Russia nor China or any other Security Council member protested this unilateral move in the Council.

Operation Southern Watch, as it was designated by the US military, differed from Operation Northern Watch in one important respect: while Hussein's control on the ground in the north was much reduced, and in places nonexistent, in the south, it remained largely intact. Parts of the north comprised a 'safe haven'; none of the south could be so described. Incongruously, ground assaults and artillery barrages remained unchallenged by the Coalition.

An intriguing question here is *why* different strategies were adopted in north and south. Some commentators have suggested that this can be explained by the US's unwillingness to see Shi'a institutions grow in the south in a manner analogous to Kurdish institutions in the north—since Shi'a development, with the possibility of Iranian sponsorship, could work against Washington's regional strategy of 'dual containment' aimed at limiting the offensive capabilities of both Iran and Iraq. Another factor may have been the lack of Western media attention to the humanitarian situation in the south immediately after the cease-fire, in part because the topography of the region allowed refugees to disperse.[113] At least as persuasive, and reflecting the recollections of David Hannay, the former UK Permanent Representative to the UN, is the suggestion that whereas the northern no-fly zone was imposed as result of significant domestic and international political pressure, the southern zone was a tactical device, intended to show Hussein the price of noncooperation with UN weapons inspectors.[114] If so, two unintended consequences emerged: Western powers in the Security Council looked inconsistent with respect to their humanitarian commitments; and for Saddam Hussein the price of noncooperation turned out, in this instance, not to be high.[115]

4.3.2 *Erosion*

For many years, the enforcement of the no-fly zones involved low-intensity confrontation between Western air commands and Iraqi military forces, with only occasional spikes of violence following Iraqi attempts to up the ante, particularly in its stalling tactics with UNSCOM (see Chapter 6). On January 13, 1993, over 100 US, UK, and French planes and ships attacked Iraqi missile sites, and on January 17, the Zafraniyah weapons facility, in response to Iraqi failures to move missiles from the south of the country. (Continuing Pérez de Cuéllar's earlier pattern of acquiescence in unilateral enforcement actions, Secretary-General Boutros Boutros-Ghali argued in a letter to US Congressional leaders that the US action was justified by a 'mandate' from the Security Council to enforce the cease-fire agreement.[116]) In mid-1993, US intelligence discovered a plan by the Iraqis to assassinate former President Bush, during a visit to Kuwait. In response, on June 27, 1993, the United States fired twenty-four cruise missiles at intelligence headquarters in Baghdad, killing eight people (according to Iraqi reports).[117]

In early October 1994, a US expeditionary army of some 54,000 troops assembled in the Persian Gulf as Iraqi troops appeared poised to attack Kuwait. What followed now bears a striking resemblance to the pattern of events in 2003. After much debate, the Security Council hammered out a unanimously adopted compromise deal in SCR 949, issuing specific demilitarization demands to Iraq.[118] As would occur with SCR 1441, the United States and the United Kingdom interpreted SCR 949 as giving them authorization to use force in the event of Iraqi noncompliance; the French and Russians were opposed to such an interpretation, and China remained silent.[119] (This was perhaps the first sign of French dissent from the Western 'authorization' orthodoxy.) In 1994, these tensions did not dissolve into war, not least because in keeping with its practice of brinksmanship, Iraq pulled back its army, complying with SCR 949.

When Hussein's troops took Irbil in September 1996, the US missile response was directed solely at targets in the south—leaving Hussein and the KDP with a free hand in the north. When the United States unilaterally extended the no-fly zone in the south to the 33rd parallel, Great Britain, Germany, Canada, and Japan offered support.[120] Russia denounced the action, while Spain argued the United States had acted too hastily.[121] France refused to patrol the expanded zone, restricting its sorties to the earlier line on the 32nd parallel.[122] This was followed a few months later by its withdrawal from the northern no-fly zone, and in 1998, after Operation Desert Fox (discussed in Chapter 6), by its withdrawal from the patrolling of its southern counterpart.

The United States and the United Kingdom continued thereafter to justify the no-fly zones as an effort to enforce SCR 688, but increasingly the other members of the P-5 challenged this interpretation, dissatisfied with the underlying strategy of containment through inspections-plus-sanctions that interpretation reflected (see Chapters 4 and 5). The US justifications for its continued presence over the south also increasingly emphasized the threat Hussein posed to his southern neighbors, suggesting the focus was on containment, rather than enforcement of SCRs 687 and 688.[123]

Following Desert Fox, the pace of sorties flown in the no-fly zone intensified dramatically, as the United States and the United Kingdom instigated a policy of 'aggressive enforcement', dropping increasing volumes of ordnance onto Iraq. US warplanes were mandated for the first time to engage not only with those parts of the Iraqi air-defense system that had targeted them, but any part. The United Kingdom followed suit in March 1999.[124] Clearly, the United States and the United Kingdom were running out of patience—and options.

4.4 Conclusions

The aftermath of Operation Desert Storm in early 1991 was a complex security environment, melding humanitarian crisis, internal repression, and tension between UN Security Council members over acceptable modes of enforcement of Council resolutions. In the years that followed, the complex challenges of a new world order have all played out in Iraq: ethnic rebellion, humanitarian crisis, black marketeering, human rights violations rapidly publicized through globalized media coverage, domestic and transnational terrorism, threats relating to the proliferation of WMD, and unilateral impulses of various powerful states. Confronted with many of these complex problems in 1991, the Security Council, its members, and the Secretariat entered a third phase of involvement in Iraq, crafting creative humanitarian solutions that provided templates for UN action used throughout the following decade.

4.4.1 *From Policing to Transitional Administration*

Operation Desert Storm demonstrated the power of a united Security Council as a New World Order Policeman. But the aftermath of the UN police action against Iraq also showed the limits of that policing role, particularly through the ease with which a tyrant could exclude international actors from what we might term 'domestic violence'. Confronted by that violence in both northern and southern Iraq, the UN was forced to take a more multidisciplinary and creative strategy to intervention, relying on lightly armed Guards and its humanitarian relief capabilities to support and protect a vulnerable population. This was a new approach to the role of humanitarian guardian. At the same time, the UN humanitarian relief operations worked in the protective shadow of unilateral military action by the Western P-3. This alignment of UN humanitarianism with Western military power was to show up again, soon and frequently.

The safe haven and no-fly zone initiatives have been cited as prototypes of the 'coercive protection' that the UN would find itself increasingly engaged in through the 1990s.[125] Other commentators see in the approach taken to the Kurds the germ of the return by the UN to the concept of the 'protectorate', and the prototype of its transitional administration projects in East Timor, Kosovo, and elsewhere.[126] Those projects have led, more recently, to calls for the renovation of concepts of 'international trusteeship', ultimately informing proposals for a UN Peacebuilding Commission.[127]

But these operational templates contained within them structural flaws, which were only later exposed. The military dimension of Operation Provide Comfort misled the United States, and the UN, into believing that humanitarian assistance could be imposed successfully in Somalia in 1992–3. In turn, highly visible failures in Somalia ushered in a decade of reliance on air power in US military strategy. Air power was useful in preparing for ground action in Iraq in 2003, but a large commitment of troops was required to remove Saddam Hussein. That pattern was equally present in the success of NATO air power in pulverizing Serb military capacity in 1999, but also in its irrelevance to policing the peace in Kosovo subsequently. Washington's post-Somalia disdain for 'nation building' and its excessive focus on air power subsequently proved unhelpful in its engagement with Kosovo, Afghanistan, and Iraq, and, ultimately, to its deterrent power.[128]

Similarly, Operation Provide Comfort and the UN Guards Contingent in Iraq both seemed to suggest vulnerable civilian populations could be shielded from local repression by lightly armed personnel operating in 'safe havens', perhaps lulling some within the UN Secretariat and the Security Council into a dangerous complacency. Ultimately, the illusion would be shattered with tragic results and to UN shame at Srebrenica in 1995.[129]

Equally, the juxtaposition of supposedly neutral humanitarian relief operations carried out by UN agencies and military intervention carried out by Security Council members was later to have profound implications for the management of UN interventions—at both strategic and operational levels. As was the case in the Iran–Iraq war, so here the bifurcation is clear between the Security Council as provider of 'hard' security and the Secretariat and agencies as guardians of 'soft' security. The struggle to align 'security', 'rights', and 'development' in the work of the Organization today bears the marks of these and other such divides.

The accommodating approach of the Security Council to the unilateralism inherent in Operation Provide Comfort and the northern and southern no-fly zones over Iraq established increasingly stressful patterns for the interaction of the United States and other Security Council members for another decade. These were repeatedly characterized by military operations led by the United States, accompanied by the United Kingdom, some other Western allies and sometimes France, purporting to effect the objectives of Security Council resolutions, but without explicit authorization for the chosen means. Within this creeping unilateralism were sheltered the seeds of the confrontation that would undermine the Council's authority in 2003.

4.4.2 *Resource or Referee?*

The P-3's resort to unilateralism in Operation Provide Comfort and the no-fly zones was cloaked in the rhetoric of humanitarian intervention, but ultimately it served both domestic political and geostrategic purposes. That blurring of humanitarianism with strategic designs was risky. At the time, though, the dangers were not apparent, because of Russian and Chinese acquiescence in the P-3's broad interpretations of Security Council 'authorizations'. That acquiescence created a veneer of P-5 consensus, creating a false perception amongst the international community that the Security Council now had a new role as international referee, whereas, for Washington, it would come to be seen increasingly as one diplomatic resource among several others.

All the same, the P-5 themselves seemed to an extent to believe their own rhetoric in these early years of the 1990s, buttressed by their frequent unity. There were important exceptions, not least on the Israeli–Palestinian conflict. Still, that division was not geostrategically crippling, given that actual progress on the conflict's resolution depends more on Washington and the parties on the ground than to any combination of other powers. Yet the struggle for dominance on strategy over Bosnia between the United States on the one hand, and the United Kingdom and France on the other, followed by the divisions over Kosovo, significantly weakened the habit of P-5 accommodation that American diplomacy in 1990 and 1991 had done so much to forge.[130] Unilateral measures became such a stock response of the Western P-5 members in Iraq, and acquiescence by the other major players early on became so routine, that neither the United States nor the United Kingdom fully anticipated the vehemence of opposition to their actions in 2003.

The creative solutions developed in the ashes of the 1991 Gulf War thus held the seeds of two developments that have shaped the Security Council since. First, the drive toward a multidisciplinary approach in peacekeeping induced increasingly hands-on, administratively intensive regulatory decisions from the Council. The specifics of those decisions on Iraq and consequences for the UN are examined in more detail in the next two chapters. Second, those solutions, though presented and often interpreted as the product of humanitarian motivations, were often driven by the political agendas of the Western permanent members. It was perhaps to be expected that these trends could run counter to each other at some point, as they were to do on Iraq very soon. This collision ultimately produced widespread disenchantment with the UN's role in Iraq and a crisis of confidence for the institution when two conceptions of the Council came into conflict in early 2003: a Council powered by rules versus a Council ruled by power.

Notes

1. In describing certain conflicts as internal, the prior qualifier 'essentially' is important. These conflicts rarely remain strictly internal for long, with neighboring countries sometimes spilling in (as in the Democratic Republic of the Congo), or the conflict spilling over (as with Colombia's turmoil affecting border areas of Ecuador and Peru and the domestic politics of Venezuela).
2. George H. W. Bush, 'Remarks to the American Association for the Advancement of Science', February 15, 1991, in *Public Papers of the Presidents of the United States: George Bush*, 4 vols. (Washington, DC: US Govt Printing Office, 1990–1993), i. 145.
3. Cited in Daniel Pipes, 'Counterpoint: Why America Can't Save the Kurds', *Wall Street Journal*, April 11, 1991, A15. For links to the CIA, see R. Jeffrey Smith and David B. Ottaway, 'Anti-Saddam Operation Cost CIA $100 Million', *Washington Post*, September 15, 1996, A1.
4. UN Security Council resolution 686, March 2, 1991.
5. Dilip Hiro, *Desert Shield to Desert Storm: The Second Gulf War* (London: HarperCollins, 1992), 400.
6. There was substantial evidence of support from Iran to the southern Shi'a rebels. See Hiro, *Desert Shield*, 401–2.
7. Hiro, *Desert Shield*, 403–4.
8. Hiro, *Desert Shield*, 406.

9. Hiro, *Desert Shield*, 407. Undoubtedly, the flight of the Kurds was prompted in part by their memories of Saddam's repression from 1985 to 1988, which culminated in the *Anfal* campaign following the release of Iraqi forces from military engagements with Iran. The Security Council had stood by while Saddam's generals massacred as many as 200,000 Kurds, and forcibly displaced another 800,000. See Michael Gunter, *The Kurds of Iraq: Tragedy and Hope* (New York: St Martin's Press, 1992), 15.
10. The crisis in northern Iraq provided one of the first instances of the 'CNN effect', referring to the effect that global media, particularly full-time television coverage, have on the determination of policy. See Steven Livingston, *Clarifying the CNN Effect: An Examination of Media Effects According to Type of Military Intervention*, Joan Shorenstein Center, John F. Kennedy School of Government, Harvard University, Research Paper R-18, June 1997. On the specifics of the humanitarian crisis, see Thomas G. Weiss, *Military-Civilian Interactions: Intervening in Humanitarian Crises* (Oxford: Rowman & Littlefield, 1999), 50–1.
11. Daniel Schorr, 'Ten Days That Shook the White House', *Columbia Journalism Review* 30/4 (1991), 23.
12. Schorr, 'Ten Days', 22. See also Hiro, *Desert Shield*, 406.
13. See *Letter dated 91/04/02 from the Permanent Representative of Turkey to the United Nations addressed to the President of the Security Council* (UN Document S/22435), April 3, 1991, and *Letter dated 91/04/04 from the Permanent Representative of the Islamic Republic of Iran to the United Nations addressed to the Secretary-General* (UN Document S/22447), April 4, 1991.
14. Nicholas J. Wheeler, *Saving Strangers: Humanitarian Intervention in International Society* (Oxford, OUP: 2000), 141.
15. Leonard Doyle, Steve Boggan, and Safa Haeri, 'Security Council abandons Kurds to their fate with non intervention policy', *Independent*, April 4, 1991, 1.
16. Wheeler, *Saving Strangers*, 142–3.
17. UN Security Council SCR 688, April 5, 1991, PP3. See Simon Chesterman, *Just War or Just Peace? Humanitarian Intervention and International Law* (Oxford, OUP: 2001), 132.
18. See Paul Lewis, 'After the War; Europeans Back Off Plan to Help Kurds', *New York Times*, April 10, 1991, A12; see also the account of David Hannay, UK ambassador at the time, in Wheeler, *Saving Strangers*, 145–6.
19. N. S. Rodley, 'Collective Intervention to Protect Human Rights' in N. S. Rodley (ed.), *To Loose the Bands of Wickedness: International Intervention in Defence of Human Rights* (London: Brassey's, 1992), 29.
20. J. E. Stromseth, 'Iraq' in L. E. Damrosch (ed.), *Enforcing Restraint: Collective Intervention in Internal Conflicts* (New York, NY: Council on Foreign Relations Press, 1993) 81; Wheeler, *Saving Strangers*, 141–6.
21. Weiss, *Military-Civilian Interactions*, 43.
22. *Provisional verbatim record of the 2982nd meeting* (UN Security Council Document S/PV.2982), April 5, 1991, 17.

23. *Provisional verbatim record of the 2982nd meeting*, 27–30.
24. *Provisional verbatim record of the 2982nd meeting*, 47. (There is, of course, some truth to this observation!)
25. See Wheeler, *Saving Strangers*, 144.
26. *Provisional verbatim record of the 2982nd meeting*, 63.
27. *Provisional verbatim record of the 2982nd meeting*, 36 on Ecuador and 58 on US.
28. See Wheeler, *Saving Strangers*, 145.
29. While the humanitarian imperative actually drove many Council decisions from 1990 onwards, human rights figure more instrumentally as an element of UN strategies designed to graduate countries from war to peace than as a driver in their own right. It was as an element of conflict resolution and peace-building strategies that China came to accept, first in El Salvador and subsequently elsewhere, that human rights needed to be respected in conflict countries for peace to take hold. See David M. Malone, 'The Security Council in the 1990s' (Proceedings of the 28th Annual Conference of the Canadian Council on International Law, The Hague & London: Kluwer, 2001, 42).
30. Rodley, 'Collective Intervention', 32.
31. SCR 688, OP3.
32. SCR 688, OP5 and OP6.
33. Elaine Sciolino, 'After the War; U.S. Warns Against Attack By Iraq On Kurdish Refugees', *New York Times*, April 11, 1991, A10.
34. Hiro, *Desert Shield*, 409; Wheeler, *Saving Strangers*, 149.
35. See Nancy Dunne, 'US cool on proposal for Kurdish enclave', *Financial Times*, April 10, 1991, 6.
36. Rita Beamish, 'Bush Says Iraqis Should Depose Saddam, But U.S. Can't Help', *Associated Press*, April 4, 1991.
37. Hiro, *Desert Shield*, 410.
38. 'Quayle: Military Intervention in Iraq Would Be Unwise', *USIA Wireless File*, April 11, 1991, www.fas.org/news/iraq/1991/910411-179992.htm.
39. See Blaine Harden, 'U.S., Iraqi Officers To Meet on Aid Plan; Americans to Stress "Noninterference" ', *Washington Post*, April 19, 1991, A1.
40. The term 'haven' had replaced 'enclave' to avoid the connotation of boundary redefinition. See Wheeler, *Saving Strangers*, 149–50. Austria, then a member of the Security Council, first floated the idea of humanitarian zones or enclaves, initially rebuffed by the permanent members. Washington, London and Paris ignored Austria's claim to paternity of the idea.
41. James Mayall, 'Non-Intervention, Self-Determination and the "New World Order" ', *International Affairs* 67/3 (1991), 421–9. For an alternative analysis, suggesting the intervention occurred as the result of John Major's conversion after viewing television images see Nik Gowing, 'Real-Time Television Coverage of Armed Conflicts and Diplomatic Crises: Does it Pressure or Distort Foreign Policy Decisions?', Joan Shorenstein Barone Centre, John F. Kennedy School of Government, Harvard University, Working Paper, June 1994.

42. See Wheeler, *Saving Strangers*, 147–9. See also John Cassidy et al., 'Haven from the Hell-Holes for the Kurds', *Sunday Times*, April 21, 1991.
43. See Franca Brilliant, Frederick C. Cuny, and Victor Tanner, *Humanitarian Intervention: A Study of Operation Provide Comfort* (Dallas, TX: INTERTECT 1995).
44. Wheeler, *Saving Strangers*, 151.
45. *Operation Provide Comfort After Action Report (U)*, Headquarters United States European Command/ECJ3, January 29, 1992.
46. Barton Gellman, 'Last Coalition Units Are Leaving Iraq; Ultimatums Issued to Protect Kurds', *Washington Post*, July 13, 1991, A1; Hiro, *Desert Shield*, 416–17.
47. Following the US withdrawal, a Western rapid reaction force ('Operation Poised Hammer') was stationed at the Incirlik airbase in Turkey, as a security guarantee for the Kurds. See Wheeler, *Saving Strangers*, 157.
48. Hiro, *Desert Shield*, 410.
49. See Hiro, *Desert Shield*, 410–11.
50. Wheeler, *Saving Strangers*, 155.
51. Hiro, *Desert Shield*, 417–18.
52. 'The President's News Conference', *Weekly Compilation of Presidential Documents* 27 (April 16, 1991), 444; Transcript of Press Conference given by Prime Minister John Major in Luxembourg (April 8, 1991), reprinted in M. Weller (ed.), *Iraq and Kuwait: The Hostilities and their Aftermath* (Cambridge: Grotius Publications, 1993), 714–15.
53. Harden, 'U.S., Iraqi Officers To Meet on Aid Plan'. US and UN efforts to address the refugees' plight appear to have been largely uncoordinated. General Shalikashvili, sent by the US to negotiate an arrangement with his Iraqi counterparts, stated that he had only 'sketchy' information about UN plans to deploy a police force in northern Iraq. See William Branigin, 'Allied Forces Will Not Move Into Key Iraqi City, U.S. Commander Indicates', *Washington Post*, May 16, 1991, A34.
54. See comments of Deputy Prime Minister Tariq Aziz, quoted in Harden, 'U.S., Iraqi Officers To Meet on Aid Plan'.
55. James Bone, 'UN Envoy Pours Cold Water on Kurd Refugee Plan', *The Times*, April 10, 1991.
56. James Bone and Robin Oakley, 'Secretary-General Clashes with West over Forces for Northern Iraq', *The Times*, April 18, 1991.
57. Leonard Doyle, 'West and UN Shamed into Aiding the Kurds', *Independent*, April 18, 1991.
58. See J. E. Stromseth, 'Iraq', 100.
59. See J. E. Stromseth, 'Iraq', 100.
60. For further discussion of the legal basis of Operation Provide Comfort and the no-fly zones see Sean D. Murphy, *Humanitarian Intervention: The United Nations in an Evolving World Order* (Philadelphia, PA: University of Pennsylvania Press, 1996), 182–97; Scott L. Silliman, 'The Iraqi Quagmire: Enforcing the No-Fly

Zones', *New England Law Review* 36/4 (2002); Gavin A. Symes, 'Force Without Law: Seeking A Legal Justification for the September 1996 U.S. Military Intervention in Iraq', *Michigan Journal of International Law* 19 (1998); Chesterman, *Just War*, 199–206.

61. 'Douglas Hurd: Parliamentary Papers 1992–93', *British Yearbook of International Law* 53 (1992), 824. See also *A. Aust, Legal Counsellor, FCO, statement before HC Foreign Affairs Committee*, December 2, 1992, *Parliamentary Papers*, 1992–1993, HC, Paper 235-iii, 85, reprinted in *British Yearbook of International Law* 53 (1992), 827. See also Christopher Greenwood, *International Law and the NATO Intervention in Kosovo, Memorandum Submitted to the Foreign Affairs Committee of the House of Commons*, reprinted in *International & Comparative Law Quarterly* 49/4 (2000), 929–30. This interpretation was later affirmed by Attorney General Lord Goldsmith in his advice to Prime Minister Tony Blair on Resolution 1441 on March 7, 2003:

    The use of force to avert **overwhelming humanitarian catastrophe** has been emerging as a further, and exceptional, basis for the use of force. It was relied on by the UK in the Kosovo crisis and is the underlying justification for the No-Fly Zones. The doctrine remains controversial, however.

    See United Kingdom, Attorney General, 'Iraq: Resolution 1441', March 7, 2003, www.number-10.gov.uk/files/pdf/Iraq%20Resolution%201441.pdf.

62. Robert Cottrell, 'Paris Calls for New UN Laws to Help Kurds in Iraq', *Independent*, April 5, 1991. These months characterized a high-water mark in French advocacy of the 'duty to intervene' advocated with panache by Kouchner. His activism was strongly supported by Danielle Mitterrand, wife of the French President and long a champion of Kurdish rights. At the UN later in 1991, France and Canada spearheaded a strong mandate for a newly recast UN humanitarian coordinator, enshrined in General Assembly resolution 46/182 of December 19, 1991. See also Weiss, *Military-Civilian Interactions*, 57.
63. Chris Seiple describes the thawing of relations between *Médicins sans Frontières* doctors and US elite forces as the former observed the clinical proficiency of the latter: Chris Seiple, *The U.S. Military/NGO Relationship in Humanitarian Interventions* (Carlisle Barracks, PA: U.S. Army College, 1996).
64. See Larry Minear et al., *United Nations Coordination of the International Humanitarian Response to the Gulf Crisis, 1990–1992*, Occasional Paper No. 13 (Providence, RI: Watson Institute, 1992).
65. See for example Colonel Philip A. Meek, 'Operation Provide Comfort: A Case Study in Humanitarian Relief and Foreign Assistance', *Air Force Law Review* 37 (1994) for an account of the confusion over how the Operation was to be funded.
66. George H. W. Bush, 'Remarks on Assistance for Iraqi Refugees and a News Conference', April 16, 1991, in *Public Papers of the Presidents of the United States: George Bush*, 4 vols. (Washington, DC: US Govt Printing Office, 1990–93), i. 380.

67. Operation Provide Comfort was only one part of the humanitarian relief effort. Relief aid of $487 million for 860,000 displaced from Kuwait by the Iraqi invasion was coordinated by the UN Disaster Relief Organization (UNDRO). See *Persian Gulf Crisis: Humanitarian Relief Provided to Evacuees from Kuwait and Iraq* (Document GAO/NSIAD-91-160), March 12, 1991.
68. Brian Whitaker and Jon Henley, 'Kurds despair under West's leaky umbrella', *The Guardian*, February 20, 2001.
69. Natasha Carver, 'Is Iraq/Kurdistan a State such that it can be said to operate state systems and thereby offer protection to its "citizens"?', *International Journal of Refugee Law* 14/1 (2002), 78.
70. See for example Laurie Mylroie, 'Kurdistan: After Saddam Hussein', *The Atlantic Monthly* 270/6 (1992), 36, 38, 49, 52.
71. See for example Peter W. Galbraith, 'How to Get Out of Iraq', *New York Review of Books* 51/8, 13 May 2004, and Peter W. Galbraith, 'Operation Save Face', *American Prospect Online*, 21 November 2004. Galbraith has long been involved in the plight of the Kurds, and was the first to uncover and report on Hussein's 'al-Anfal' campaign against Iraq's Kurds. Middle East commentator and retired US Army officer Ralph Peters has also advocated Kurdish independence in certain circumstances. See Ralph Peters, 'Kurds' success provides lesson for rest of Iraq', *USA Today*, April 26, 2004, A19.
72. See John Pomfret, 'U.S. Protection of Kurds Succeeds—But How Does It End?', *Washington Post*, April 4, 1995, A18.
73. For an extensive account of this period see Sarah Graham-Brown, *Sanctioning Saddam: The Politics of Intervention in Iraq* (London: I.B. Tauris, 1999), 213–51.
74. The KDP in turn claimed that the PUK was receiving assistance from Iran. Both the PUK and Iran denied this.
75. Craig R. Whitney, 'From Allies, U.S. Hears Mild Applause or Silence', *New York Times*, September 4, 1996, A10.
76. See Chris Nuttall and Ian Black, 'Saddam Victory Humbles Clinton', *The Guardian*, September 10, 1996, 1.
77. See Warren Richey and Scott Peterson, 'Iraqi Kurd Advance Makes Mockery of US "Safe Area" ', *Christian Science Monitor*, September 11, 1996, 1.
78. See John Donnelly, 'Stunning Shift: Arabs Want Saddam "Rehabilitated" ', *Sunday Gazette-Mail* (Charleston), September 22, 1996, 2A (detailing Jordan's call 'on the United States to start a dialogue with Iraq').
79. See Kelly Couturier, 'Turkey Says Operation Against Kurds Inside Iraq Is a Success', *Washington Post*, July 7, 1995, A27.
80. Dilip Hiro, *Iraq: In the Eye of the Storm* (New York, NY: Thunder's Mouth Press/Nation Books, 2002), 141.
81. Charles Trueheart, 'French Military to Quit Air Patrols Over N. Iraq', *Washington Post*, December 28, 1996, A18.
82. Whitney, 'From Allies, U.S. Hears Mild Applause or Silence'. After the US strikes on 3–4 September 1996, the UK introduced a draft resolution into the Security

Council, condemning Iraqi actions against the Kurds and calling for immediate troop withdrawals. France, Russia, and China all opposed the resolution. See Robert H. Reid, 'Security Council Considers Response to Iraq's Incursions Against Kurds', *Associated Press*, September 4, 1996.

83. See 'Arab League Condemns US Missile Attack on Iraq', *Agence France-Presse*, 3 September, 1996.
84. *Letter dated 91/05/30 from the Secretary-General addressed to the President of the Security Council* (UN Document S/22663), May 31, 1991.
85. *Letter dated 91/05/30*, paras. 4, 7.
86. *Letter dated 91/05/30*, para. 6.
87. *Letter dated 91/05/30*, para. 5.
88. *Letter dated 91/05/30*, para. 6.
89. *Letter dated 91/05/30*, paras. 8, 18.
90. Private letter from the Executive Delegate to the Foreign Minister of Iraq (September 2, 1991), cited in Michael Stopford, 'Humanitarian Assistance in the Wake of the Persian Gulf War', *Virginia Journal of International Law* 33 (1993), s. v. 17 and accompanying text.
91. Stopford, 'Humanitarian Assistance', s. v. 18–19 and accompanying text, citing private letter from the Foreign Minister of Iraq to the Executive Delegate (September 24, 1991).
92. Stopford, 'Humanitarian Assistance', 496.
93. Stopford, 'Humanitarian Assistance', 496.
94. Stopford, 'Humanitarian Assistance', 497, quoting private meeting between the UK Foreign Secretary and the Executive Delegate in London (April 29, 1991).
95. Wheeler, *Saving Strangers*, 155; L. Freedman and D. Boren, ' "Safe Havens" for Kurds' in N. S. Rodley (ed.), *To Loose the Bands of Wickedness: International Intervention in Defence of Human Rights* (London: Brassey's, 1992), 62.
96. Freedman and Boren, ' "Safe Havens" ', 60 and Leonard Doyle, 'Questions Hang Over UN Police Force', *Independent*, April 27, 1991, 9.
97. Wheeler, *Saving Strangers*, 152, 156; Stopford, 'Humanitarian Assistance', 497; Thomas L. Friedman, 'Baker, Rebuffed in Syria, Sees Soviets on U.N. Force for Iraq', *New York Times*, May 14, 1991, 10.
98. A similar arrangement was considered but dropped for Burundi in 1996, when the government lost control of parts of its territory, which required humanitarian assistance. See Annex to *Letter dated 91/05/30*.
99. Annex to *Letter dated 91/05/30*, paras. 6, 7.
100. Stopford, 'Humanitarian Assistance', 497, 502, s. v. 38.
101. Stopford, 'Humanitarian Assistance', 498. Some NGOs considered the UNGCI provided inadequate protection and security information, and made their own arrangements: see Graham-Brown, *Sanctioning Saddam*, 283–4.
102. Marjoleine Zieck, *UNHCR and Voluntary Repatriation of Refugees: A Legal Analysis* (The Hague: Martinus Nijhoff, 1997), 220, s. v. 239.

103. Zieck, *UNHCR*, 500.
104. Human Rights Watch, *The Iraqi Government Assault on the Marsh Arabs*, Briefing Paper (January 2003).
105. See for example Laurie Mylroie, 'Iraq's Real Coup: Did Saddam Snooker Schwarzkopf?', *Washington Post*, June 28, 1992, C1.
106. It was followed soon after, however, in the case of Yugoslavia.
107. See *Provisional verbatim record of the 3046th meeting* (UN Security Council Document S/PV.3046), January 31, 1992, and *Note [on the Summit Meeting of the Security Council to be held on 31 Jan. 1992]* (UN Security Council Document S/23500), January 31, 1992.
108. See *Provisional verbatim record of the 3105th meeting* (UN Security Council Document S/PV.3105), August 11, 1992.
109. *Provisional verbatim record of the 3105th meeting.*
110. Judy Aita, 'Iraq Systematically Repressing Kurds, Shi'a, UN Told', *USIA Wireless File*, August 11, 1992, www.fas.org/news/iraq/1992/920811-238554.htm.
111. See *Report on the situation of human rights in Iraq* (UN Document E/CN.4/1992/31), February 18, 1992, 65–6, para. 156. See also *Situation of human rights in Iraq: note* (UN Document A/47/367), 10 August, 1992, November 13, 1992 (Addendum), section 3.
112. See Norma Holmes, 'International Consensus Emerging on Iraq Intervention', *USIA Wireless File*, August 18, 1992, www.fas.org/news/iraq/1992/920818-239568.htm; 'Coalition to Impose "No-Fly" Zone in Southern Iraq', *USIA Wireless File*, August 26, 1992, www.fas.org/news/iraq/1992/920826-240538.htm
113. Weiss, *Military-Civilian Interactions*, 52.
114. See Wheeler, *Saving Strangers*, 163, s. v. 125 and accompanying text.
115. For further discussion of the politics of the no-fly zones see Graham-Brown, *Sanctioning Saddam*, 107–21.
116. 'Letter to Congressional Leaders reporting on Iraq's Compliance with UN SCRs', *Weekly Compilation of Presidential Documents* 29 (January 19, 1993), 67. Boutros-Ghali's comments suggested that Resolution 678, read with SCR 688, gave Security Council members ongoing authorization for the use of force. That was an argument the US and UK would make use of on a number of later occasions.
117. David Von Drehle and R. Jeffrey Smith, 'U.S. Strikes Iraq for Plot to Kill Bush', *Washington Post*, 27 June, 1993, A1. For a discussion of the justifications of this strike see Alan D. Surchin, 'Terror and the Law: The Unilateral Use of Force and the June 1993 Bombing of Baghdad', *Duke Journal of Comparative & International Law* 5 (1995), 459.
118. UN Security Council resolution 949, October 15, 1994.
119. See Barbara Crossette, 'Security Council Condemns Iraqis' Threat to Kuwait', *New York Times*, October 16, 1994, 12; Barbara Crossette, 'U.N. Council Unanimous In Condemning Iraq Move', *New York Times*, October 17,

1994, 10; Steven Greenhouse, 'U.S. Says Iraq Appears to Resume Pullback from Kuwait Border', *New York Times*, October 17, 1994, 10.

120. *Letter dated 96/09/03 from the Chargé d'affaires a.i. of the Permanent Mission of the United States of America to the United Nations addressed to the President of the Security Council* (UN Security Council Document S/1996/711), September 3, 1996. See also Bradley Graham, 'U.S. Launches More Cruise Missiles Against Iraq; Air Defenses Near Baghdad Hit; No-Fly Zone Extended in South', *Washington Post*, September 4, 1996, A1.
121. Graham, 'U.S. Launches More Cruise Missiles Against Iraq'.
122. Ben MacIntyre and Michael Binyon, 'France Refuses to Patrol Widened Iraq No-Fly Zone—Split Allies', *The Times*, September 6, 1996, 13.
123. See 'Text of Clinton Letter on Military Force Against Iraq Resolution', *US Newswire*, November 5, 1996.
124. Sarah Graham-Brown, 'No-Fly Zones: Rhetoric and Real Intentions', *MERIP Press Information Note 49*, February 20, 2001. See also Thomas E. Ricks, 'Containing Iraq: a Forgotten War; As U.S. Tactics Are Softened, Questions About Mission Arise', *Washington Post*, October 25, 2000, A1.
125. See Thomas G. Weiss, 'The Humanitarian Impulse', in David M. Malone (ed.), *The UN Security Council: from the Cold War to the 21st Century* (Boulder, CO: Lynne Rienner: 2004), 47.
126. See for example Michael Ignatieff, 'State-failure and nation-building', in J. L. Holzgrefe and Robert O. Keohane (eds.), *Humanitarian Intervention: Ethical, Legal and Political Dilemmas* (Cambridge, Cambridge University Press: 2003), 308.
127. See Simon Chesterman, 'Virtual Trusteeship: Security Council Authorizations of Transitional Administrations', in David M. Malone (ed.), *The UN Security Council: from the Cold War to the 21st Century* (Boulder, CO: Lynne Rienner, 2004). On peace-building, see Sebastian von Einsiedel and David M. Malone, 'Haiti, 1990–2005: Full Circle' in Mats Berdal, Spyros Economides, and James Mayall (eds.), *UN Interventionism, 1991–2004* (Cambridge: Cambridge University Press, 2006 (forthcoming)).
128. On the mixed effectiveness of and over-reliance on air power, see Daniel Byman and Matthew Waxman, 'Kosovo and the great airpower debate', *International Security* 24/4 (2000). On the focus on other theatres, see Condoleeza Rice, 'Campaign 2000: Promoting the National Interest', *Foreign Affairs* 79/1 (2000). See also Thomas Shanker, 'The Reach of War; Status of Forces: Iraq Role Limits Military Ability, Congress is Told', *New York Times*, May 3, 2005, A1, citing a report from Gen. Myers to Congress indicating that the US ability to deal with potential armed conflicts around the world would be limited because of actions in Iraq and Afghanistan.
129. *Report of the Secretary-General pursuant to General Assembly resolution 53/35: the fall of Srebrenica* (UN Secretariat Document A/54/549), November 15, 1999. The UN Secretariat did beg Member States for adequate troop numbers to

protect the safe areas of Bosnia, only to be told by the UK, France, and the US to manage with what they were given. As a Canadian representative at the UN in 1993, I attended a closed-door consultation between the principal troop contributors to UNPROFOR and Kofi Annan in the immediate run-up to adoption of the Security Council resolution on the Bosnian safe areas in which Annan argued that, in light of the ferocity of attacks against Sarajevo and some other centers, symbolic troop deployments would not prove effective. That he proved right came at great cost to Bosnians.

130. On Kosovo see Paul Heinbecker, 'Kosovo', in David M. Malone (ed.), *The UN Security Council: From the Cold War to the 21st Century* (Boulder, CO: Lynne Rienner, 2004).

5

Sanctions Enforcer: Economic Sanctions and the Oil-for-Food Program

As we have seen, SCR 661, adopted by the Security Council on August 6, 1990, imposed comprehensive sanctions on Iraq in response to its invasion of Kuwait.[1] The Council had earlier imposed an arms embargo in response to South African *apartheid* policies, and economic sanctions in response to the situation in Southern Rhodesia; but never before had it adopted sanctions in response to an act of aggression against a foreign state.[2] SCR 661 not only prohibited states from importing all commodities originating in Iraq but also any activities relating to export or trans-shipment of any commodities or products to Iraq (except for medical supplies and, in humanitarian circumstances, foodstuffs).[3] The sanctions regime was originally intended to force Iraq to conform to its obligations under SCR 660 of August 2, 1990—i.e. to withdraw from Kuwait—but, following the ceasefire, was left in place to ensure Iraqi compliance with SCR 687.[4]

Perhaps the element of this sanctions regime that was to prove the most contentious, particularly after 1996, was the absence of a sunset clause.[5] As the humanitarian toll of the Iraq sanctions grew, Russia, France, and China increasingly criticized the indefinite duration and rigidity of the regime, arguing in future sanctions decisions for a date at which a regime would lapse, unless affirmatively extended by the Security Council.[6] From the late 1990s onward, France asserted that it would never again accept open-ended sanctions regimes.[7] Nor was there any clear signal that a degree of compliance could lead to a degree of reward. When Russia and France proposed in 1991 to take note of Iraqi compliance in accepting SCR 715, they were blocked by the United States and the United Kingdom.[8] Rather, the regime embodied an 'all-or-nothing' challenge for Iraq (and for the UN), setting the compliance bar very high indeed.

Underlying the criticism of the open-ended sanctions regime were both strategic and humanitarian concerns. Strategically, there was growing alarm that rather than weakening the Baghdad regime, the sanctions were reinforcing Hussein's grip on power—while debilitating the population—through control of black markets in oil and other commodities. This phenomenon recalled events in Haiti, when, following the imposition by the Security Council of an embargo on the import of petroleum and related products, the de facto military regime vastly enriched itself through illegal imports transhipped from the Dominican Republic (and perhaps elsewhere).[9] Humanitarian concerns were articulated both by governments and the growing nongovernmental community working alongside the UN in New York and Geneva (and on the ground in Iraq).

5.1 The Humanitarian Impulse

5.1.1 *Early Response*

In the wake of Operation Desert Storm, the Secretary-General had dispatched a team, headed by Martti Ahtisaari, to assess the humanitarian situation in Iraq. His report of March 20, 1991 described conditions in Iraq as 'near-apocalyptic'.[10] Dire shortage of medicine and other humanitarian supplies was widespread. Iraq's industrial infrastructure, particularly power plants, oil refineries, water treatment plants, and pumping stations had been destroyed by Coalition bombing. The sanctions regime imposed by SCR 661 exacerbated the situation. It was clear that Iraq's humanitarian needs could not be met while the comprehensive sanctions regime remained, and that some relaxation or alteration would be necessary.[11] Independent of minor relaxations contained in SCR 687, Secretary-General Pérez de Cuéllar, therefore, dispatched a further mission to assess Iraq's civilian needs, led by his executive delegate, Sadruddin Aga Khan, in July.[12]

Sadruddin Aga Khan's report noted the folly of seeking funds from other states to reconstruct infrastructure in one of the world's largest oil-producing states:

> With considerable oil reserves in the ground, Iraq should not have to compete for scarce aid funds with a famine-ravaged Horn of Africa, with a cyclone-hit Bangladesh.[13]

Instead, he proposed that

> Iraq's 'essential civilian needs' be met urgently and that rapid agreement be secured on the mechanism whereby Iraq's own resources be used to fund them to the satisfaction of the international community.[14]

An 'Oil-for-Food' (OFF) formula (as it came to be known) was quickly adopted by the Security Council. In SCR 706, adopted on August 15, 1991, the Council established an elaborate program allowing Iraq to export a quota of oil and to use the resulting export revenues to purchase humanitarian supplies, all under the controlling eye of the UN.[15] SCR 706 established an escrow account to hold the revenues from sales of Iraqi petroleum, and a mechanism whereby those revenues would be spent on humanitarian requirements such as 'the purchase of foodstuffs, medicines, and materials and supplies for essential civilian needs'.[16] The Council was here taking the unprecedented step of controlling a sovereign state's revenues and directing its expenditures—and not only to expenses benefiting its own population, but also to other purposes, including the payment of costs incurred by the UN in the destruction of Iraqi arms in accordance with SCR 687, of compensation, and of the boundary settlement process.[17]

At the time, there was much dispute over where the oil export ceiling should be set. The Secretary-General argued for a ceiling of $2.4 billion for six months, reflecting Aga Khan's assessment of Iraqi humanitarian needs;[18] but under US and UK pressure, the Security Council authorized only $1.6 billion in SCRs 706 and 712.[19]

Since the proposal depended on Iraqi cooperation for both the production of oil and the distribution of humanitarian commodities, the proposal could not be enforced upon Iraq. Unsurprisingly, it refused to cooperate. In response, the US and the UK sponsored SCR 778, which authorized states to seize revenues from Iraqi petroleum sales and transfer them to the escrow account provided for in SCR 706, providing short-term funding for the UN relief program in northern Iraq.[20] Following that unprecedented international expropriation, the UN aid program depended from 1991 to 1995 largely on donations, beset by all of the problems of donor-funded aid programs the UN has confronted before and since.[21]

5.1.2 *Compromise*

By early 1995, opposition to continuation of the sanctions regime had developed on three fronts: within the Council, from France and Russia, and to a lesser extent, China; from Arab (and some other Muslim) countries, increasingly restless about the humanitarian situation in Iraq; and from domestic constituents in the United States and the United Kingdom.[22] The collapse in the second half of 1994 of a scheme that would have seen Iraq export oil through Turkey brought matters to a head.[23]

In March 1995, Russia, France, and China circulated a draft SCR that, if passed, would have lifted sanctions on Iraq.[24] While the United States and the United Kingdom would have vetoed any such resolution had it been brought to a vote, the need to address humanitarian concerns and the political requirements of their Security Council partners were now clear. Some compromise was therefore necessary. Thus, in April 1996, the Council passed SCR 986, providing a rare concession to Baghdad.[25] It gave Iraq the primary responsibility for the distribution of humanitarian goods under the OFF formula, except in the north where distribution would be kept under direct UN control. The launch of the OFF Program[26] is thus best understood as a product of the growing divide between the P-5 over the Iraq sanctions regime, matched by a desire to ward off a full-scale disagreement.

In negotiating the SCR, US Permanent Representative to the UN, Madeleine Albright, sought to ensure that the text addressed every one of the complaints Iraq had presented in an effort to stall and undermine the sanctions regime.[27] As Albright made clear, her objective was to back Iraq into a corner:

> If it refuses to implement this resolution, it will be clear for all to see—and especially to the Iraqi people—that the blame for the suffering of the people of Iraq rests not with the Security Council but with the government in Baghdad.[28]

At first, the Iraqi government rejected SCR 986 as 'worse and more dangerous' than SCRs 706 and 712.[29] But as Saddam Hussein's domestic position weakened through 1995, with the Iraqi economy nose-diving under the effect of sanctions, and some internal opposition beginning to grow, Baghdad's stance was reversed in January 1996. Negotiations then began between the Iraqi government and the UN Secretariat on implementation of the Program. (In another sign of growing US–UK assertiveness over Iraq within the UN and beyond, those countries intervened in the negotiations, much to the annoyance of other P-5 countries.[30]) Delayed by Hussein's seizure of Irbil in August 1996, SCR 986 came into force only in December 1996. The most comprehensive sanctions in UN history were now matched by the largest humanitarian relief operation on record.

5.2 Oil-for-Food

Over its lifetime, OFF handled $64 billion worth of Iraqi oil revenues, and served as the main source of sustenance for 60 percent of Iraq's estimated twenty-seven million people, reducing malnutrition among Iraqi children by 50 percent.[31] It underpinned national vaccination campaigns reducing child mortality and eradicating polio throughout Iraq.[32] In addition, it employed more than 2,500 Iraqis.[33]

But it became clear over time that the sanctions regime generally was being turned by the Baghdad authorities to their advantage, through the creation of black markets they controlled. The costs of sanctions were borne by the most vulnerable sections of Iraqi society, while illegal rents were devised and extracted by a cynical but still all-powerful clique in government under the initially guileless gaze of UN officials (and of the Security Council).[34] As the later Independent Inquiry Committee (IIC) under the leadership of former Chairman of the US Federal Reserve, Paul Volcker (the 'Volcker Inquiry'), would make clear, over time, UN officials, too, became entangled in the corruption of the OFF.

Revenues from the sale of Iraqi petroleum were allocated according to a strict formula dividing the resources between humanitarian programs, Gulf War compensation, and UN expenses for both weapons inspection and humanitarian purposes. They were processed through an administrative arrangement between the Government of Iraq and the UN.[35] The revenues were paid into an escrow account at the New York branch of BNP Paribas, with title vesting in Iraq, but administered by the UN. Iraq would submit draft contracts for the importation of humanitarian goods it had negotiated directly with potential suppliers. This Iraqi control over contractors was the crucial compromise that overcame Iraqi opposition and paved the way for OFF in the first place; it was also the mechanism that allowed Hussein's regime to gouge $10.99 billion in illicit commissions from the OFF Program.[36] Once approved by the '661' Sanctions Committee (on which each Security Council member country had a seat), the contract expenses were paid out of the BNP Paribas account. Thus, assisted by independent experts, the 661 Committee had oversight responsibility for OFF.[37] The humanitarian goods were distributed by the Government of Iraq in the fifteen southern governorates, and by UN agencies in the three northern governorates of Dohuk, Irbil, and Suleimaniya. Distribution in the north was organized by the UN Inter-Agency Humanitarian Program, functioning under the authority of the Department of Humanitarian Affairs (as it then was).[38]

The OFF Program was implemented in phases, each lasting approximately 180 days, rolled over by a Security Council resolution. Planning for each phase was undertaken by the Iraqi Government (in the south) and the UN Inter-Agency Humanitarian Program (in the north), in each case approved by the Secretary-General (and forwarded to the 661 Sanctions Committee). The Program also incorporated very detailed procedures for the approval of both import and export contracts, covering issues such as pricing, payment conditions, and inspection mechanisms. The contract approval process was conducted through lists of candidate companies held by Member States at the UN, which may have served significantly to align diplomatic and business interests more than is traditional at the UN.

5.2.1 *Changing the Sanctions Regime*

During the life of the OFF Program, the burden on the UN Secretariat increased markedly. The Program was overseen by the Office of the Iraq Program (OIP), established on October 15, 1997 by the Secretary-General, and mandated to consolidate and manage the activities of the Secretariat in implementing OFF. Benon V. Sevan was appointed OIP Executive Director. The Office of the Humanitarian Coordinator in Iraq (UNOHCI) reported directly to Sevan.

Initially, the OFF Program worked mainly by controlling Iraqi petroleum exports. The export ceiling was first set at $1 billion every ninety days, but was slowly lifted to $5.2 billion, until it was eliminated in 1999. This gradual raising of the ceiling was intended to allow increased humanitarian imports into Iraq. However, Iraqi oil revenues were constrained not so much by a ceiling as by the low price of Iraqi crude oil due to the dilapidated state of the Iraqi oil industry, itself a result of the sanctions regime.[39]

As the Security Council slowly permitted Iraqi exports to grow, the focus of attention shifted to controlling imports. First, in 1999, the Council introduced 'fast track' procedures for import-approval, which allowed the Secretary-General to approve contracts for the importation of specific goods on a 'green list' without reference to the 661 Committee.[40] The fast track process grew out of the Council's so-called 'Amorim Panels', set up at Canadian suggestion under the chairmanship of the widely admired Brazilian Permanent Representative, Celso Amorim, to make recommendations on new approaches with regard to Iraq on disarmament, humanitarian matters, missing persons, and stolen Kuwaiti property.

In April 1999, the Netherlands and the United Kingdom submitted a draft resolution outlining a new approach to the 661 Committee's work. When finally approved eight months later after much disputation, not only Russia and China but also France abstained, undermining the restoration of the Council's unity on the contentious sanctions issue.[41]

Nevertheless, SCR 1284 did considerably ease the humanitarian situation by removing the ceiling on the volume of Iraqi oil exports and almost all restrictions on imports of food and medicine.

The intractable problem of 'dual-use' items remained. Any delegation that considered that goods Iraq sought to import ostensibly for peaceful purposes might also be used for illicit military purposes had the capacity to place a hold on the contract, pending further investigation.[42] In reality, almost all holds were placed by the US and the UK delegations.[43] Because many contracts involved complex bundles of goods, suspicion raised by one item could block the import of a range of other, obviously harmless, goods.[44]

A number of potential solutions were considered in informal discussions undertaken by the then Chair of the Sanctions Committee, Peter van Walsum (of the Netherlands).[45] Van Walsum has hinted that he saw in the tough US approach an attempt not only to frustrate Hussein's access to WMD but also to create such pressure on Hussein as to ensure his overthrow:

> my terms of reference did not go beyond nonproliferation and the other provisions of Resolution 687, whereas the United States was also thinking in terms of regime change.[46]

Ultimately, these discussions led to the second major overhaul of import-approval procedures. In May 2002, the Security Council established the 'Goods Review List' (GRL), which reversed the presumption against importation. Import contracts were presumptively approved by the Secretary-General unless they contained a listed item.[47] The GRL also expanded the role of the UN Monitoring, Verification and Inspection Commission (UNMOVIC) and the IAEA in reviewing import contracts, to catch dual-use items, making clear the extent to which humanitarian and disarmament objectives had converged within a broader regulatory approach. This shifted the burden of responsibility for managing the approval process away from the 661 Committee and more squarely onto the OIP within the UN Secretariat and the specialized agencies, especially UNMOVIC and the IAEA.

5.2.2 *Changing the Iraqi Regime*

The overhauling of import and export procedures in the Iraqi sanctions regime marked a series of attempts to compromise between the strategic goal of disarming Iraq and the humanitarian goal of meeting its essential humanitarian needs. Support for achieving Iraqi disarmament was strongest in the US and the UK governments. But increasingly even they felt pressure—at home and abroad—on two fronts.

Some critics attacked the sanctions regime's deleterious effects on the civilian population.[48] They pointed to statistics, such as those issued by UNICEF in 2001, indicating that in the period 1990–9, Iraq had suffered an increase in child mortality of 160 percent, the highest of all 188 countries reviewed.[49] The most extreme critics drew parallels between the sanctions regime and crimes against humanity or genocide.[50] A more coherent and damning critique came from analysts such as Cortright and Lopez.[51] An insider view of the dynamics within the UN Security Council is provided by Carne Ross, the political officer ('expert', in Security Council jargon) responsible for Iraq sanctions at the UK Permanent Mission to the UN, 1998–2002. By early 2005, Ross was arguing that those denouncing the humanitarian costs had been right, while he and others seeking to prop up UK and US arguments in favor of sanctions-as-usual in the Council had been caught up in professional loyalty-induced myopia.[52]

Other critics attacked the sanctions regime's failure to produce a lasting military or political solution in Iraq. While the inspections-plus-sanctions regulatory approach had weakened Saddam's conventional military capacity and his position within the region, it had, if anything, strengthened his hold over Iraq. In 2001, Anthony Cordesman wrote:

> The end result is that we appear to be the cause of the hardships of the Iraqi people, and give Saddam Hussein aid in undercutting sanctions.[53]

The tension between the US and UK government support for continuing sanctions and growing opposition elsewhere was exacerbated by an argument increasingly clearly advocated by Washington that the only acceptable outcome of the sanctions would be regime change in Baghdad. Arguably, regime change had been a latent goal of US–UK sanctions policy for a long time. As early as May 15, 1991, Prime Minister John Major indicated that the United Kingdom would veto any Security Council resolution weakening sanctions while Hussein was in power.[54] US Secretary of State James Baker and CIA Director-Designate Robert Gates both echoed those sentiments a week later.[55] But between 1991 and 1997, the United States shifted the goals of sanctions to a policy of containment, though it continued to designate funds for Hussein's ouster.[56]

By early 1997, Clinton's Secretary of State Madeleine Albright reverbalized that regime change was back on the US sanctions agenda:

> To those who ask ... how long we will insist that the international community's standards be met, our answer is—as long as it takes. We do not agree with the nations who argue that if Iraq complies with its obligations concerning weapons of mass destruction, sanctions should be lifted.[57]

Later that year President Clinton reinforced this message in responding to Saddam's refusal to allow weapons inspectors into Presidential sites by stating that

> What he has just done is to ensure that the sanctions will be there until the end of time or as long as he lasts.[58]

As we now know, Clinton had already begun to fear the possibility of WMD developed by Hussein falling into the hands of non-state terrorists. His speech to the Joint Chiefs of Staff during the troop buildup in the Persian Gulf of early 1998 amid a confrontation between UNSCOM and Baghdad made this clear, using the rhetoric of an 'unholy axis' that now bears a striking (and largely unnoticed) resemblance to his successor's 'axis of evil':

> This is not a time free from peril, especially as a result of reckless acts of outlaw nations and an unholy axis of terrorists, drug traffickers and organized international criminals.... In the next century, the community of nations may see more and more the very kind of threat Iraq poses now—a rogue state with weapons of mass destruction ready to use them or provide them to terrorists, drug traffickers or organized criminals who travel the world among us unnoticed.... And we still have, God willing, a chance to find a diplomatic resolution to this, and if not, God willing, the chance to do the right thing for our children and grandchildren.[59]

The strategic goal of regime change became entrenched the following year when Congress passed the *Iraq Liberation Act*.[60] Washington reportedly budgeted $15 million per year toward overthrowing Hussein.[61]

5.2.3 *'Smart' Sanctions: The Last Chance*

Sanctions reform served a number of purposes: warding off calls for complete termination of the sanctions regime; focusing greater pressure on Hussein's regime, and less on the Iraqi population; and, after 9/11, focusing more specifically on proliferation issues. The US diplomatic push for 'smart sanctions' after 2001 may also have been motivated secondarily by a growing thirst for Iraqi oil in the United States. By 1999, American companies were buying roughly one-third of all oil exported from Iraq—but through Russian, French, and Chinese middlemen who substantially eroded their profits.[62] US companies were growing their oil industry repair businesses in Iraq through European subsidiaries.[63] As the global economy boomed in 2000, US policymakers assessed that any interruption of Iraqi supplies could create a spike in the price of oil, to the detriment of the US economy—in an election year.[64]

In June 2001, the United States and the United Kingdom advocated a move toward 'smart sanctions' that would have traded off stricter controls on Iraqi military procurement—including through an extended list of prohibited imports, and stricter border controls stemming the illicit flow of oil out of Iraq—in return for relaxation of controls on the civilian economy.[65] Although Russia and China rejected the longer list of prohibited imports, it was France that led resistance, sometimes aggressively, to the US and the UK interpretation of Council decisions and of guidelines for their implementation.[66] In August 2000, French Foreign Minister Hubert Védrine described the sanctions regime as 'cruel, ineffective, and dangerous'.[67] France, along with other Western countries, such as Switzerland and Norway, moved to reopen their embassies in Iraq. French oil companies began to sign contracts with the Iraqi authorities—which would become operable once sanctions had been removed. During discussions of a special working group on sanctions reform established by the Security Council further to a Canadian initiative in 2000, France, Russia, and other countries urged a majority-vote procedure in sanctions administration, attempting to short-circuit the veto power.[68]

Opposition to the smart sanctions approach diminished in the wake of 9/11, as concerns about the proliferation of WMD grew—and as it became more difficult publicly to argue against American concerns over weapons proliferation. In November 2001, the Security Council passed SCR 1382, enumerating a long list of banned items, and suggesting the future adoption of an even longer list.[69] In the second half of 2002, as the Bush administration began to push for war, it redoubled attempts to reform sanctions, expanding the GRL in an effort to catch a wider group of dual-use items.[70] The original GRL contained important compromises between members of the P-5, for example, in return for a continuing ban on foreign investment in the Iraqi oil sector—which Russia, France, and China had sought to overturn—the United States relaxed restrictions on civilian flights into Iraq. In November 2002, the United States tested those compromises by linking its support for the renewal of the OFF Program to the expansion of the GRL—that is, to a stricter regime on Iraq's military imports. France and other P-5 members resisted this linkage; the United States suggested their motivations were mercenary.[71] Eventually, a compromise was brokered, enshrined in SCR 1447.[72]

By that time, events had overtaken the OFF Program. US patience with the inspections-plus-sanctions approach had run out, and, after a series of twists and turns discussed in Chapter VII, Washington and

London unleashed Operation Iraqi Freedom in March 2003. The OFF Program was ultimately phased out on November 21, 2003.[73]

5.3 Scandal

That was not, however, the end of the OFF story.

In March 2004, reports emerged of documents in Baghdad seeming to indicate the existence of a massive scheme instituted by the Iraqi authorities to subvert OFF.[74] This scheme, as reported, was simple: the Iraqis sold oil to preferred buyers at deep discounts;[75] those buyers then resold the oil at market prices, making huge profits; the buyers then kicked back a substantial commission to Baghdad.[76] The implementation of the scheme was, however, extremely opaque, through a clandestine voucher system overseen by Saddam Hussein and high cadres of his regime.[77]

Just as the UN began to assume a meaningful role in helping to manage Iraqi political transitions at the behest of the White House (as discussed in Chapter 8), a steady drumbeat of attacks on the UN—and on Kofi Annan personally—was initiated in the United States over these emerging allegations.[78] That the timing of these attacks appeared so blatantly aimed at inhibiting any further enhancement of the UN's role and at assuaging disappointment that 'the UN had been proven right on Saddam Hussein's weapons of mass destruction' took nothing away from their seriousness.[79] Questions raised by these revelations included how the UN could have overlooked such an arrangement and whether UN and Member State officials had profited personally from the scheme.

Allegations of kickbacks were floated against the CEO of French firm SOCO International and a close political ally of President Jacques Chirac; former French Interior Minister Charles Pasqua; former French UN ambassador Jean-Bernard Mérimée; left-wing British MP George Galloway; and the Russian state itself.[80] The UN was also in the firing line, with allegations directed explicitly against the former Executive Director of the OIP, Benon Sevan, and implicitly against Annan himself, through suggestions that Cotecna, the Swiss firm hired by the UN to monitor imports, had hired his son, Kojo Annan, at the time the OFF Program was being established. The US media drew particular attention to the prominent role that French and Russian traders appeared to play in the scam, suggesting it might explain French and Russian sanctions policy.[81] Numerous investigations arose in response to the allegations, including inquiries by the US Senate Permanent Subcommittee on Investigations, other Congressional committees, a Justice Department attorney, and the Iraqi Board of Supreme Audit.[82]

The UN Secretary-General moved quickly to establish an independent panel to investigate the claims. On March 19, 2004 Secretary-General Annan advised the Security Council of his intention to create what became the IIC (or more commonly the 'Volcker Inquiry') chaired by Paul Volcker, former Chairman of the US Federal Reserve Bank, to examine the allegations. He also appointed Justice Richard Goldstone, a South African former corporate lawyer and first Prosecutor of the International Criminal Tribunal for the former Yugoslavia, along with Mark Pieth, a Swiss expert on international money-laundering and bribery. These figures each represented the epitome of public integrity and esteem in their respective spheres of professional activity. Annan gave the Volcker Inquiry guarantees of independence, and unrestricted access to UN records and personnel. This mandate was endorsed by a unanimous Security Council Resolution (which, however, did not give the IIC subpoena powers, or other coercive powers, since, unlike some other organs previously created by the Security Council, it was not created under Chapter VII of the Charter).[83]

Annan's inclination to move quickly to investigation was initially much resisted by some Member States, which complained of the UN being pushed around by its most powerful member. But further revelations were to support Annan in his determination to see the allegations investigated credibly. The Volcker Inquiry diligently investigated numerous aspects of the OFF Program over the ensuing eighteen months. The Committee presented a number of interim reports detailing the results of investigations into specific aspects of the Program, with a comprehensive Report released on September 7, 2005, just days before the World Summit at the General Assembly was to address UN reform. The picture painted through those Reports was, as the Committee ultimately acknowledged, one of 'egregious lapses' in management throughout the OFF—and the broader UN.[84] But understanding the causes of—and remedies for—those failures requires a more detailed account of the central lines of inquiry of the Volcker team. It is to that account that I now turn.

5.3.1 *Annan's role*

With respect to his son, Kofi Annan initially defended him strongly:

> Let me say that there is nothing in the accusations about my son. He joined the company even before I became Secretary-General, as a 22-year-old, as a trainee in

Geneva, and then he was assigned to work for them in West Africa, mainly in Nigeria and Ghana. Neither he nor I had anything to do with contracts for Cotecna. That was done in strict accordance with UN rules and financial regulations.[85]

But Annan's credibility was seriously wounded by later revelations (a surprise to him, he assured the world) that his son, Kojo, had been receiving payments and other benefits until as late as February 2004 from Cotecna—as well as payments from other oil companies involved in OFF.[86] At least on their face, the details of these payments created a suspicion that Kojo Annan was being paid for some reason connected to the UN.[87] At the very least, it was clear that Kojo 'took advantage of his father's position to profit from the system'.[88] Kojo responded weakly that '[a]s to using my father's name to get a discount on a car, I was young and I just didn't think it through'.[89]

Annan was reported as being 'disappointed' to learn of his son's economy with the truth, which he recognized created a 'perception problem'.[90] Actually, of course, it created a very real problem. Annan's response seemed complacent, particularly after it emerged that conflict of interest concerns had been raised as early as 1999. In a March 29, 2005 Interim Report, the Volcker Inquiry criticized Annan's failure to refer the issue of Cotecna's award to the UN's Office of Internal Oversight Services (OIOS) for investigation after being made aware that Cotecna had been awarded a contract in January 1999.[91] Annan pronounced the report a 'great relief' after 'many distressing and untrue allegations', stating that the Volcker Inquiry had 'exonerated him of any wrongdoing' in the award of the Cotecna contract.[92] Asked if he had any intention of resigning, he responded 'Hell no.'[93] Volcker retorted that the report had 'criticized him rather severely... I would not call that an exoneration.'[94]

As the *New York Times* editorialized, it was Annan's failure to act adequately against the perception of a conflict of interest in 1999, that, arguably, had sown the seeds of this more recent scandal:

Nothing has caused the United Nations more grief than the appearance of a conflict of interest. Although the Cotecna contract was a small slice of the oil-for-food program, the link to the secretary general put a face on the allegations of corruption in the program and triggered calls for Kofi Annan's resignation from critics who were enraged by his opposition to President Bush's war with Iraq....[95]

Annan was candid about the personal toll the crisis was taking:

For reasons that parents everywhere will understand, the most difficult and painful moments for me personally throughout this past year have been those when it appeared that my son Kojo might have acted inappropriately or might not have told me the full truth about his actions.... I love my son and have always expected the highest standards of integrity from him. I am deeply saddened by the evidence to the contrary that has emerged and particularly by the fact that my son had failed to cooperate fully with the inquiry.[96]

The September 2005 Report of the Volcker Inquiry indicated that while Kojo had been involved in Cotecna's bid, it appeared that Cotecna was awarded the contract on the basis of its lowest-price bid.[97] It also cleared Kofi Annan of any involvement in the Cotecna bidding process, while criticizing him for his failure earlier to conduct a more thorough investigation.[98] Annan was contrite:

I accepted then, and still accept, the conclusion that I was not diligent or effective enough in pursuing an investigation after the fact, when I learned that the company which employed my son had won the humanitarian inspection contract. I deeply regret that.[99]

But the damage was done.

5.3.2 *Secretariat Shortcomings*

Although they grabbed the headlines, the allegations of personal misconduct hanging over Kofi Annan were in one sense less critical for the UN than the allegations of broader corruption and management failure within the Secretariat. The Volcker Inquiry was damning on both fronts.

The Inquiry built strong cases of personal misconduct against a number of individuals directly involved in the OFF, and some beyond. The most significant allegations were made against the former chief of the Program, Benon Sevan, whom the Inquiry charged with improperly soliciting oil allocations worth $1.5 million, and receiving illicit commissions of $147,000 cash between 1999 and 2003.[100] Sevan was described as having a 'grave and continuing conflict of interest'. After first being suspended, Sevan eventually resigned, pointing out the achievements of the OFF Program, the Council's own failures of oversight, and drawing attention to the billions of dollars which had gone missing after funds left over from the OFF accounts were passed on to the Coalition-controlled Development Fund for Iraq.[101]

The implication of Sevan's conduct was not that the UN Secretariat was riddled with corruption, but that it was so poorly managed that serious corruption, where it did occur, was not detected and rooted out. As the *Washington Post* editorialized:

Despite a budget that ran into the millions, the inquiry did not nail large numbers of U.N. officials for personal corruption in administering the oil-for-food program. If it had done that, life would be easier; firing the wrongdoers might fix the problem. Instead, the inquiry found evidence of corruption on the part of just two officials, both of whom have since been forced out of their jobs. The real scandal that Mr. Volcker underlined is that the United Nations' culture is dysfunctional. The secretariat headed by Mr. Annan is badly managed and incapable of holding employees accountable. It is not equal to the difficult tasks that it is increasingly called upon to perform, from disaster relief to peacekeeping.[102]

In its September 2005 Report, the Volcker Inquiry directed significant criticism at the Secretary-General, the Deputy Secretary-General, and Annan's former Chef de Cabinet for their failure adequately to control Sevan.[103] It criticized them for 'minimal efforts' to address sanctions violations with Iraqi officials or to ensure that 'critical evidence' of wrongdoing was brought to the Security Council's attention.[104]

A shadow was also cast over the conduct of former Secretary-General Boutros-Ghali. The Volcker Inquiry's February 2005 Interim Report criticized Boutros-Ghali for his role in the awarding of OFF contracts. Boutros-Ghali responded, labeling the Inquiry's investigators 'ignorant' and describing the allegations against him as 'silly', perhaps because of the extent to which such decisions were understood to be made on political—and not merit—grounds. The Inquiry's September 2005 Report alleged that Iraq had tried to bribe him, through intermediaries, during the process that led to the adoption of the MOU providing the basis for the OFF; it had found no evidence, however, that he had received those funds.[105]

The Volcker Inquiry also brought to light broader corruption in the UN's procurement section. An August 2005 Interim Report fingered a Russian UN procurement official, Aleksander Yakovlev, as being on the take in a wide number of UN transactions.[106] Annan waived Yakovlev's immunity, and he immediately pleaded guilty to charges in a Manhattan Federal District Court of conspiracy, wire fraud, and money laundering.[107] As the *New York Times* editorialized, what was striking was both how 'small-bore' the corruption involved was, and, at the same time, that it underscored 'how corruption may have infected many procurement programs at the organization'.[108] The pervasiveness of the corruption was borne out a few weeks later when Annan waived the immunity of a second Russian, Vladimir Kuznetsov, who had occupied the powerful position of Chairman of the General Assembly's Advisory Committee on Administrative and Budgetary Questions (ACABQ) since February 2004. Kuznetsov, who appeared to have received bribes through Yakovlev, was arrested by the FBI on various money-laundering and fraud-related charges.[109]

The Inquiry also highlighted irregularities in the selection of the OFF Program's three major contractors, criticizing the role in the selection process of another UN official, Joseph Stephanides, who was castigated for steering a large contract to Lloyd's Register of London. A lower tender was submitted by a French rival, but the UN ultimately decided the deal should go to Lloyd's—after it lowered its bid further to confidential information obtained from UN sources—in part because a French bank had been awarded another key contract. Stephanides was fired by Annan on June 1, 2005.[110]

Those who had collaborated with Stephanides in the UK Mission to the UN went free and saw nothing to apologize for. Sir John Weston, the UK ambassador to the UN during the relevant years, made clear that the promotion of UK commercial interests was a standard part of his brief. Weston was quoted as saying that he was operating under 'ministerial instructions' from London in advising Lloyd's Register on the best tactics to win the contract. Suggestions of improper behavior were based on 'ignorance of the practices of diplomatic missions'.[111] Carne Ross, the British diplomat in charge of Iraq policy at the UN at the time, said the program was 'deeply politicized' and 'carved up' between Member States:[112]

> It was our job to lobby for British companies and we did so extremely vigorously. Nobody in Britain would have expected any less of us.... That is the way the UN operates and it seems a little harsh if Joseph Stephanides is carrying the can for this as a UN official.[113]

However, the deep cynicism over the respective roles and accountability of P-5 members and the Secretariat staff might well be summed up in the comment of a P-5 ambassador that Stephanides's plight was 'amusing'.[114] What such comments tended to highlight was the absence of leadership or even a basic sense of responsibility on the part of the Council, from the outset of the Program.

5.3.3 *The Council's Failure to Lead*

In his first days in office in early January 2001, President George W. Bush likened the sanctions regime against Iraq to Swiss cheese—both full of holes.[115] Slowly, the true extent of those holes—and US and UK knowledge of them—became clear.

The largest hole appeared to be in the area of oil smuggling. On April 7, 2004, the US General Accounting Office released a study indicating that from 1997 to 2002, the Iraqi regime derived $10.1 billion in illegal revenues from the OFF Program—$5.7 billion in smuggled oil and $4.4 billion in illicit surcharges and commissions.[116] The final figures of the Volcker Inquiry were even more stark: they suggested that while Hussein had received only $1.8 billion from kickbacks, he had amassed a staggering $11 billion from oil smuggling outside the OFF.[117]

But over the course of the Volcker Inquiry, allegations emerged of sanctions-busting in a wide range of sectors, by an equally wide range of individuals and groups, including inside Iraq.[118] An October 6, 2004 report from the Iraq Survey Group, led by former UN deputy-chief weapons inspector Charles Duelfer, detailed extensive sanctions-busting by Saddam Hussein involving not only arms (on which it implicated six countries—Syria, Belarus, Yemen, North Korea, the former Yugoslavia, and possibly Russia) but also other goods.[119] Allegations were brought against a wide range of companies from the United States and elsewhere.[120] Bernard Guillet, an adviser to Charles Pasqua, was arrested on orders of a French investigating magistrate on allegations of involvement in OFF corruption.[121] The Republican-controlled US Senate investigation released a report alleging the involvement in the OFF corruption of a top Russian aide and also of right-wing Russian politician Vladimir Zhirinovsky.[122] Congress also took on George Galloway, an outspoken left-wing British MP. Galloway had earlier faced down the *Daily Telegraph* in the United Kingdom—and won $1.4 million in libel damages, after the allegations proved to be based on forged documents. Galloway aggressively attacked the US Senate Committee when he appeared before it on May 17, 2005:

> I have never seen a barrel of oil, owned one, bought one, sold one, and neither has anybody on my behalf.... The real sanctions busters were not me or Russian politicians or French politicians ... [but] your own companies with the connivance of your own government.[123]

Those linked by the US Senate Committee to the scandal, Galloway said, had one thing in common: 'They all stood against the policies of sanctions and war which you vociferously prosecuted and which has led us to this disaster.'[124] He described the investigation as the 'mother of all smokescreens', intended to 'divert attention from the crimes you supported' in Iraq.[125]

Whatever the truth of individual allegations, all the evidence pointed to enormous leakage in the sanctions regime. In January 2005, the Volcker Inquiry released previously undisclosed UN internal audits of the OFF Program, which had failed to ask tough questions about its holes.[126] It was unclear, though, whether the failure of supervision arose from the incompetence or corruption of UN officials, on the one hand, or from the willful blindness of Security Council members (who had ultimate oversight of the Program) on the other.[127] Early signs pointed to a combination of pragmatic considerations and the adoption of a path of least resistance in a tense atmosphere as motivations for the approach of the members of the Security Council to the handling of these kickbacks.[128]

But by February 2005 it had emerged that both the Clinton and George W. Bush administrations had made formal decisions, of which they notified Congress, to allow much of the oil smuggling to continue, despite its prohibition by both Security Council resolutions and prior US law, since it was in the US 'national interest'.[129] The United States was not prepared to risk regional support for its broader policies in Iraq by pressuring Iraq's smuggling partners—primarily Jordan and Turkey—to desist, as attested by a White House official:

> We were not going to address the Jordanian smuggling.... In the case of Turkey, we tried a couple of times, but the Turks made a horrific stink. We weren't going to keep fighting, because we felt we had bigger fish to fry. ...[130]

This suggested that the United States—and perhaps the P-5 more broadly—had deliberately turned a blind eye to the corruption of the OFF Program. The realization that Hussein used oil contracts as an instrument of both domestic and international patronage was not new.[131] One senior UK official is quoted as saying:

> It was realized that a certain amount of misbehavior was going to happen on the Iraqi side if they were going to accept this [the OFF Program]. But the Iraqi government had to agree, or it wouldn't work.[132]

The Council's willful blindness played out in the 661 Sanctions Committee. The OIP raised concerns over suspicious pricing on OFF contracts with the 661 Sanctions Committee on at least seventy occasions, yet not one of these contracts was blocked by the Committee.[133] The reason seems clear: the Sanctions Committee was willing to tolerate some corruption of the program by Hussein, as the price of its very existence. A former ambassador to the UN with Security Council experience comments:

> under Resolution 986 (1995) Saddam Hussein exercised so much control over the program ... that it was only to be expected that he would find ways of turning his wide discretionary powers into money.... A total of $2bn over the whole period [1999–2000] does not seem that extravagant. Just compare this with the money Saddam would have had at his disposal if the sanctions had been lifted. From a nonproliferation point of view the issue did not seem too alarming because Saddam obviously needed a lot of money for luxury cars and the like just to keep his cronies happy.[134]

Some but too few commentators understood that Member States had been complicit in the corruption of the Program all along:

> The U.N. professionals ... were focusing on the merits, while the five permanent members of the Security Council were making political decisions according to their

own priorities. . . . Officials from the major countries understood the game in all its complexity and cynicism. It was ugly, but it worked. And then, in retrospect, the whole contraption was reduced to . . . Kofigate.[135]

The Volcker Inquiry acknowledged the Council's role in the corruption of the OFF. In the formal report, the Committee wrote of 'uncertain, wavering direction from the Security Council' and of how

differences among Member States impeded decision-making, tolerated large-scale smuggling, and aided and abetted grievous weaknesses in administrative practices within the Secretariat. An adequate framework of controls and auditing was absent.[136]

As the UN's *Daily News* saw it, the September 2005 Report found that many of the OFF's problems

were rooted in an unclear demarcation of roles and responsibilities between the Council, the 661 Committee (overseeing the programme) and the Secretariat—in particular by this Council's decision to retain substantial elements of operational control within the 661 Committee, composed of national diplomats working under highly politicized instructions from their home governments, yet willing to take decisions only when there was unanimous consent among all the 15 members.[137]

But in oral presentations to the Security Council, Paul Volcker took a stronger line, describing the OFF as 'a compact with the devil'.[138] While Kofi Annan accepted personal responsibility for his management weaknesses, few Security Council members seemed willing to shoulder their own share of the blame. Emyr Jones-Parry, UK ambassador to the UN, is quoted as saying about the report: 'We need to remember above all that it is Saddam Hussein who remains the key culprit in the OFF saga.'[139]

The exception—and all the more notable for it—was US Secretary of State Colin Powell who acknowledged prior to leaving office:

The secretary-general will have to be accountable for those management problems . . . [but] the responsibility does not rest entirely on Kofi Annan . . . . It also rests on the membership, and especially on the Security Council, and we are a member of the Security Council.[140]

5.4 The OFF Scandal and UN Reform

The OFF scandal was a major front in the ongoing struggle between US critics of the UN, who advocated extensive UN reform (if only to make it more susceptible to US influence), and those who sought to maintain the UN as a broad international church.

The attack reached a peak in December 2004 when Senator Norm Coleman, the Minnesota Republican chairing the US Senate subcommittee investigating the OFF Program, wrote a widely publicized polemic in the *The Wall Street Journal* calling for Annan's resignation.[141] In the weeks that followed the revelation of Kojo's ongoing receipt of payments from Cotecna, Kofi Annan came under further attack for the circumstances in which UN High Commissioner for Refugees, Ruud Lubbers, was forced out after allegations of sexual harassment by a number of staff. At the same time, Western media picked up on serious allegations of sexual misconduct by UN peacekeepers in DRC, further increasing pressure on the UN. Annan weathered this storm, and the inevitable calls from Conservative circles in Washington for his resignation after the release of the Volcker Inquiry Final Report.[142] But each time, he emerged with a somewhat diminished stature.

In contrast to Boutros-Ghali's dismissive tone of the Volcker Inquiry's criticism of him, Annan attempted to use the Volcker Inquiry as a trigger for deep-cutting management reform in the UN, particularly through the actions and advocacy of his energetic and impressive new chief of staff, Mark Malloch Brown. Speaking at the presentation of the Volcker Inquiry Final Report to the Security Council, Annan described the findings as 'painful' and 'deeply embarrassing to us all':

> The inquiry committee has ripped away the curtain, and shone a harsh light into the most unsightly corners of our organization.... Who among us can now claim that U.N. management is not a problem, or is not in need of reform?[143]

On its face, the Secretary-General and the Bush administration appeared to be in agreement:

> U.S. Ambassador John R. Bolton seized on the [Volcker Inquiry's September 2005] report's findings to advance his case for greater independent oversight of U.N. spending, citing the need 'to reform the U.N. in a manner that will prevent another oil-for-food scandal. The credibility of the U.N. depends on it.'[144]

But viewed more closely, the underlying tension was clear: where the United States called for greater controls on UN bureaucrats, Annan, and others, were calling for greater professionalism—and independence:

> Asked whether Annan should quit, Bolton simply smiled and waved. But he said that 'the member governments are going to lead the reform,' not the secretary-general—a signal taken by some diplomats here that Annan may have to relinquish some of his clout to stay in office.... 'He has to show that he can still be the leader of reform,' said one U.N. official, speaking on the condition he not be named. 'If not, then he might as well get out of the way.'[145]

5.5 Conclusions

In the decade and a half since SCR 661, economic sanctions have become almost commonplace in the repertoire of the Security Council, so it is important to recall how rare they had been when they were imposed against Iraq and how little experience the UN had of this potentially powerful instrument.

The sanctions regime against Iraq stands as a paradigm of both the virtues and vices of the sanctions approach. It was the Iraq sanctions regime that demonstrated the utility—and also the challenges—of Security Council subsidiary bodies operating as delegated regulators, through a supervisory committee established to monitor implementation of the sanctions. Although Haiti and other cases provided lessons, it was also the Iraq sanctions regime that demonstrated most clearly how a cunning target government could turn sanctions to its own ends, and how terrible the resulting cost to civilians might be.

5.5.1 *Lesser of Evils*

The scandal that has engulfed the UN over the administration of the OFF Program obscures the complexity of the challenges posed by Saddam Hussein's Iraq. As Harvard University's John Ruggie noted in testimony before the US House of Representatives Committee on International Relations on April 28, 2004:

> the deeper reality [was] that the United States and the United Nations often found themselves forced to choose the lesser of evils in trying to get the job done in Iraq.[146]

Ruggie explained these nuances in clear terms, for the House Committee:

> the 661 Committee ... approved roughly 36,000 [contracts].... Every member had the right to hold up contracts if they detected irregularities.... Yet, as best as I can determine, of those 36,000 contracts not one—not a single solitary one—was ever held up by any member on the grounds of pricing. Several thousand were held up because of dual-use technology concerns. What does this suggest about US and British motives ...? Stupidity? Complicity? Or competing priorities? I strongly suspect it was the last. Support for the sanctions was eroding fast. Saddam's allocation of contracts significantly favored companies in some of the countries that were also represented on the committee. So it seems reasonable to infer that the US and Britain held their noses ... in order to keep the sanctions regime in place and to put all their efforts into preventing dangerous technologies from getting into Saddam's hands.[147]

On many levels, the Program worked: it saved many lives, it drove the disarmament process, and it prevented rearmament by keeping the lion's share of Iraq's oil wealth and imports—which could be used to produce WMD—out of the hands of Saddam Hussein. Contrary to assertions that Iraq was a 'gathering' threat, the Iraqi military and weapon programs had, in fact, steadily eroded under the weight of sanctions.[148] The absence of WMD in Iraq, as confirmed by the Iraq Survey Group, points to the potential effectiveness of sanctions regimes in achieving certain security policy objectives (while creating ancillary humanitarian challenges).[149] In the words of Rolf Ekéus, first head of UNSCOM, sanctions provided the stick—and their removal the carrot—that made weapons inspections work, and through them, the entire disarmament and containment strategy.[150] Still, once it became clear to Baghdad that only regime change would induce Washington to lift the sanctions, this may have been less true.

We also now know how vulnerable sanctions regimes are to systematic corruption.[151] Hussein's government not only corrupted the Program by smuggling as much as $5.7 billion of oil out of the country, and by establishing and controlling black markets at the expense of Iraqi citizens, it also refused to countenance a number of measures, which might have alleviated Iraqi suffering.[152] Former chair of the 661 Committee van Walsum provides a good example, in an account of Iraq's refusal to agree to any one of a number of creative solutions proposed to allow Iraqi Muslims to perform the *hajj*.[153]

The Security Council and Kofi Annan faced a growing challenge in the 1990s in reconciling the UN's Iraq policies with the fundamental objectives of the UN—international peace, security, development, and human rights. On Iraq, those actors for whom security considerations outweighed others favored sanctions; those for whom the humanitarian imperative took primacy—often, notably, UN officials themselves, not least those on the ground in Iraq—argued against sanctions and for programs to blunt their impact on the population.[154] A former ambassador on the Council comments:

> the sanctions committee's brief was non-proliferation, not the development of Iraq. The more we cared about the latter, the more we could be blackmailed by Saddam. It was a lose-lose situation. If you are dealing with a dictator who has no qualms about exacerbating the suffering of his own people, you just can't win.[155]

5.5.2 *A 'Sanctions Generation'*

Saddam Hussein very effectively used the sanctions regime, and particularly US support for it, as a central plank of an anti-Western ideology that played well throughout the Muslim and much of the developing worlds.

This ideology shaped many minds in the Middle East. When US forces rolled into Iraq in 2003, they appeared to the local population not necessarily mainly as liberators, as Secretary Rumsfeld and others had hoped, but as the final coming of a power that had been laying siege to Iraq's civilian population for more than a decade. The post-invasion insurgency drew on a pool of young men—not only Iraqis, but from elsewhere in the Middle East—who had grown up on a diet of images of poverty and suffering in Iraq caused by the sanctions punctuated by sporadic barrages of Western cruise missiles. One French Foreign Minister described the resulting cohort as 'the sanctions generation'.[156]

Anthony Cordesman and Ahmed Hashim noted as early as 1997:

> The suffering caused by UN sanctions is creating broad Iraqi resentment of the US, Kuwait, and Saudi Arabia [and the] resulting revanchism may well survive Saddam Hussein, and could play an important role in shaping Iraqi politics and actions for several decades.[157]

US public diplomacy did little to defuse this time bomb prior to Operation Iraqi Freedom or thereafter, registering failures that were notorious in Washington itself.[158]

Sanctions may have served to prepare the ground for militant Islamism in Iraq in other ways, too. Between 1987 and 1997, the literacy rate plunged from 89 percent to 57 percent as a direct result of unemployment, inflation, and the collapse of the education system.[159] In the 1990s, the proportion of the Iraqi population engaged in agriculture *trebled*, as the Iraqi economy attempted to compensate for the effects of sanctions.[160] The development of Iraq over the previous decades was, in effect, being set in reverse, producing a ruralized, radicalized, increasingly undereducated, unemployed mass of young men with hatred of the West in their hearts. In many respects—the imposition of devastating embargoes and the obligation to pay war reparations, the intrusive enforcement of disarmament—the sanctions regime imposed on Iraq resembled nothing so much as the terms imposed on Germany after World War I. As Edward Luck has noted, in

> resolution 687 of April 1991, the Security Council tried to have it both ways: asserting Iraqi sovereignty yet imposing the kinds of intrusive post-war conditions that have historically been reserved for a state that had been conquered, not just defeated on the battlefield.[161]

Seen from this perspective, the anti-American insurgency that followed the Coalition invasion of 2003 should have occasioned little surprise.

5.5.3 *Geostrategies on a Collision Course*

The US approach to sanctions was part of a larger policy of 'dual containment' of Iraq and Iran after the first Gulf War.[162] That policy broke from the US' historic attempts to balance the two powers by playing them off against each other, instead promoting a strong US military presence in the Persian Gulf, which would contain both Iran and Iraq directly. While the United Kingdom, given its special relationship with the United States, was prepared to countenance and cooperate with American hegemony in the Gulf, France, Russia, and China were all more wary. As it became clear that the United States was pushing for the indefinite extension of sanctions against Iraq and that there was, as a result, no end in sight for its military dominance and control of Gulf oil supplies, sanctions became a tripwire for a showdown between the US–UK alliance and the other P-5 powers.[163]

The 1996 US–UK backing of the OFF was not the sole compromise Saddam Hussein managed to wring from the UN during this long decade. Others included the use of UN Guards rather than a continued Western military presence in northern Iraq, Boutros-Ghali's backing of BNP Paribas as the OFF bank (Hussein's first choice), the slow expansion of the humanitarian exception to the sanctions regime, the increase of the oil export ceiling, and willful Council blindness toward oil smuggling. Further concessions detailed in subsequent chapters include compromises within the weapons inspection program. Such 'fixes' sent signals to Hussein that he could rely on the UN to find peaceful solutions to his periodic showdowns with the United States and the United Kingdom, and signals to the United States and the United Kingdom that they needed to worry about the UN offering Hussein a way out. That dynamic brought with it a probability that at some point—as it turned out, early in 2003—the United States and United Kingdom would abandon the UN, and deal with Hussein themselves.

5.5.4 *Regulatory and Administrative Challenges*

The OFF scandal holds important administrative lessons for the Security Council. It highlights the risks associated with an essentially regulatory strategy relying on delegated enforcement of SCRs by the administrative action of Council agents. The ramifications of these risks were much too complex for the Council to process effectively or to manage competently. The alignment between business and diplomatic interests encouraged by

OFF operations further complicated matters. It is a first rule of efficient regulation not to give interested parties control over the administrative process that awards benefits from the regulatory regime—yet that is exactly what the OFF did.

The Council increasingly entrusts the UN system with tasks of standard-setting, performance monitoring, and enforcement that resemble the most advanced bureaucratic tasks of the modern regulatory state. The gradual increase in OIP's work reflected an increasingly tentacular and complex *modus operandi* resulting from Council decisions, illustrated clearly by the recent proliferation of expert bodies and essentially administrative committees of the Council advising on and overseeing the implementation of specific regulatory regimes.[164]

Yet the Secretariat and agencies designated as the Council's agents under these regimes are often poorly equipped (by the Council and by Member States) to play that role. As the Volcker Inquiry's comments suggested, clearer guidance is required from (and perhaps for) the Council. But the increasingly regulatory nature of the activities undertaken by the Council means that this guidance must address everything from due process rights of individuals and entities affected by administrative decision-making within these regulatory frameworks, through to limitations on the substantive considerations that Council members, Secretariat officials, or independent agents should take into account in exercising their administrative discretion.

A related issue, again highlighted by the Volcker Inquiry, is the need for meritocratic UN staffing appointments. After the Inquiry's September 2005 Report, the *Washington Post* argued that

> the United Nations' incompetence is hard-wired into the institution's DNA: the rules created by its Member States that make it impossible for the secretary general and his top staff to hire good people, fire bad ones and move resources from unneeded programs to priority ones.[165]

While many UN officials exhibit remarkable talent and resourcefulness, much of the Secretariat staffing is tied to political patrimony. James Traub highlights how this played out in the establishment of the OFF:

> In minutes of a meeting of the Iraq Steering Group from August 13, 1996, Chinmaya Gharekhan, one of then-Secretary-General Boutros Boutros-Ghali's closest advisers, said, 'Everything about implementation of 986 [the Oil-for-Food resolution] was "political", and no aspect could be assessed purely on its merits. The Secretariat had come under terrible pressure from member-states; the selection of [oil] overseers, the bank, and the firm to supply oil inspection agents had all been political.'[166]

Perhaps the scandal over OFF may offer a chance to allow in some fresh air:

> At a press briefing after the Volcker panel released the interim report, Mark Malloch Brown, Annan's new chief of staff, was asked if the report should be read as 'an indictment of United Nations culture.' Malloch Brown was candid enough to concede that 'the culture of political complicity' was a serious problem. Members, he said, should 'back off and allow us to manage this organization.'[167]

The Council does learn lessons. Paragraphs 19 and 23 of SCR 1483 offer an example.[168] They provide for the Council to establish lists of individuals and entities with links to Saddam Hussein's regime whose assets are to be frozen by UN Member States. Following criticism of earlier sanctions regimes, which had incorrectly listed individuals, and provided only limited remedies for those individuals to contest their listing, the Committee set up to implement SCR 1483 established guidelines on implementation of the Resolution.[169] Those guidelines represent the evolution of the sanctions process toward a model of delegated administrative regulation familiar in Western democracies. If the Council once again considers the use of sanctions to deal with WMD proliferation—as it most likely will on Iran and perhaps later North Korea—it would do well to remember these lessons.

Another example is provided by the GRL itself, which contains, *inter alia*, the molecular structures of prohibited chemical imports.[170] Did the participants at Dumbarton Oaks and San Francisco ever imagine that the Security Council would evolve into such a technocratic apparatus that it would publish such lists? More fundamentally, is the UN's security apparatus—distributed between the Security Council, the Secretariat, and specialized agencies—adequately equipped to administer such a technocratic regulatory apparatus? Intelligence shortcomings on Iraq confirm how dire can be the consequences of administrative failure in the regulation of security. The OFF and other such ambitious undertakings mandated by the Council require a body of independent, technically expert, international administrative staff that can implement and oversee complex administrative mechanisms—while ultimately being subject to political control by UN Member States.[171] This has important ramifications, not least for financing and resource-allocation within the UN. And if these are tasks for which the membership will not adequately equip the UN Secretariat and Agencies, then perhaps they should, as the Volcker Inquiry suggested, 'simply put their collective feet down and refuse'.[172]

5.5.5 *Legitimacy Erosion*

Another aspect of this expansion of regulatory administration is the opportunity it presents for corruption: a first form thereof now associated with the OFF scandal is corruption within the administration of the regime itself. But a second form may be more insidious, allowing, in this instance, the Ba'athist regime to turn sanctions at least partially toward its own purposes, corroding Iraqi state institutions at every level.

Perceptions of the legitimacy of the UN suffered from the humanitarian costs of the sanctions regime not just in Iraq, but more broadly in the region and beyond, as we have seen. In Iraq, the UN at once gave and took away, withholding Iraqi access to international trade, while providing humanitarian assistance. The Iraq strategy of the Council (with many of its members reluctant captives of a policy established earlier that could not be ended due to the reverse veto) contributed to a climate of antagonism between UN staff and the Council (with the Secretary-General uncomfortably caught in between). It also highlighted the increasing politicization of humanitarian assistance, with its complex effects on UN neutrality and impartiality.[173]

The intertwining of humanitarian and security objectives through the inspection-plus-sanctions regime may also have produced other largely concealed but important chasms within the UN membership. When Operation Provide Comfort triggered the creation of the Department of Humanitarian Affairs, some Third World delegates worried that it would allow northern states to dictate terms to southern states—'delivering gifts by coercion'—undermining their sovereignty.[174] The wedge these fears served to drive between members of the G-77 and some Western powers lingers still: when the Final Report of the Volcker Inquiry called for the creation of a Chief Operating Officer, many developing states argued against the proposal, fearful of a dilution of their General Assembly power.[175]

These were just some of the costs that the sanctions regime imposed. That regime, and its second iteration, through the OFF Program, were designed to maximize the freedom to maneuver of the P-5, particularly the United States and the United Kingdom. That design worked well for them, and it is important to remember that sanctions-plus-inspections ultimately worked. But the UN as a whole, unprepared for the tasks but like most large organizations always keen for new business, sustained significant damage to perceptions of its legitimacy, through corruption of its administration and a subsequent severe crisis in confidence (both internal and international).

Notes

1. UN SCR 661, August 6, 1990.
2. On South Africa: UN SCR 418, November 4, 1977 (imposing an arms embargo); UN Security Council SCR 421, December 9, 1977 (establishing a sanctions

committee); UN Security Council SCR 919, May 25, 1994 (terminating the arms embargo). On Rhodesia: UN Security Council SCR 232, December 16, 1966 (imposing sanctions); UN Security Council SCR 253, May 29, 1968 (establishing a sanctions committee); UN Security Council SCR 460, December 21, 1979 (terminating the sanctions regime).

3. See SCR 661, para. 3.
4. See SCR 687, Part F, paras. 20–9.
5. See David Cortright and George A. Lopez, 'Reforming Sanctions' in David M. Malone (ed.), *The UN Security Council from the Cold War to the 21st Century* (Boulder, CO: Lynne Rienner, 2004), 175–6. The voting constellation within the Council that these SCRs produced (establishing a program terminable only by another SCR, which could be vetoed) became known as the 'reverse veto', a phrase originally used in David D. Caron, 'The Legitimacy of the Collective Authority of the Security Council', *American Journal of International Law* 87/4 (1993). See further Lutz Oette, 'A Decade of Sanctions Against Iraq: Never Again! The End of Unlimited Sanctions in the Recent Practice of the UN Security Council', *European Journal of International Law* 13/1 (2002). Simon Chesterman suggests the problem is latent in even earlier situations, such as the establishment of the UN Military Observer Group in India and Pakistan: see Chesterman, *Just War*, 191.
6. That is, in fact, what has occurred in the Council's subsequent practice, starting with the embargo against Ethiopia and Eritrea in SCR 1298 (2000).
7. See for example *Security Council, 55th year: 4128th meeting* (UN Security Council Document S/PV.4128), April 17, 2000, 9 for French views.
8. George A. Lopez and David Cortright, 'Containing Iraq: Sanctions Worked', *Foreign Affairs*, 83/4 (2004).
9. See Malone, *Decision-Making*, 172–3.
10. See *Report on humanitarian needs in Iraq*, para. 8.
11. For a discussion of humanitarian considerations in Security Council decision making see Weiss, 'The Humanitarian Impulse', 37 and Joanna Wechsler, 'Human Rights', in David M. Malone (ed.), *The UN Security Council: From the Cold War to the 21st Century* (Boulder, CO: Lynne Rienner: 2004), 55.
12. Paragraph 20 of SCR 687 provided for expedited import of foodstuffs on the basis of notification to and no objection by the Sanctions Committee.
13. See *Letter dated 91/07/15 from the Secretary-General addressed to the President of the Security Council (Annex)* (UN Secretariat Document S/22799), July 17, 1991, Annex, 40.
14. *Letter dated 91/07/15*, 42.
15. See UN SCR 706, August 15, 1991, and UN SCR 712, September 19, 1991.
16. See SCR 706, paras. 1, 2; SCR 712, paras. 6, 8.
17. SCR 706, para. 3. See also UN SCR 778, October 2, 1992, para. 5(c)(ii).
18. See *Report of the Secretary-General pursuant to paragraph 5 of the Security Council resolution 706 (1991)* (UN Secretariat Document S/23006), September 4, 1991.

19. Some suggested the United States and United Kingdom deliberately chose a ceiling that was inadequate to meet Iraqi needs to trigger Iraqi defiance, allowing them to blame Hussein for the humanitarian situation in Iraq. See James Fine, 'The Iraq Sanctions Catastrophe', *Middle East Report* 174 (1992).
20. SCR 778, OP 1.
21. See especially Graham-Brown, *Sanctioning Saddam*, 275–80.
22. See Madeleine K. Albright, 'A Humanitarian Exception to the Iraqi Sanctions', *US Department of State Dispatch* 6/17, April 24, 1995; see also James Traub, 'Off target', *The New Republic* 232/6 (2005).
23. Albright, 'A Humanitarian Exception'.
24. Graham-Brown, *Sanctioning Saddam*, 80.
25. UN SCR 986, April 14, 1995.
26. For brief introductions to the OFF Program see Independent Inquiry Committee into the United Nations Oil-for-Food Programme, *Briefing Paper* (October 21, 2004), www.iic-offp.org/documents/Briefing%20Paper21October04.pdf; and see Kenneth Katzmann, 'Iraq: Oil-For-Food Program, International Sanctions, and Illicit Trade', *Congressional Research Service* (April 16, 2003).
27. Albright, 'A Humanitarian Exception'.
28. Albright, 'A Humanitarian Exception'.
29. Graham-Brown, *Sanctioning Saddam*, 82.
30. Graham-Brown, *Sanctioning Saddam*, 83.
31. Oil-For-Food Facts, 'Oil-For-Food: FAQ', www.oilforfoodfacts.com/faq.aspx. See especially Independent Inquiry Committee into the United Nations Oil-for-Food Programme, *The Impact of the Oil-for-Food Programme on the Iraqi People: Report of an Independent Working Group Established by the Independent Inquiry Committee* (September 7, 2005), 177, 179, indicating that OFF reduced deaths from malnutrition, but suggesting that 661 Committee 'holds' retarded this positive effect for example by impeding the distribution of medical goods; faulting the OFF for reliance on a 'relief' rather than capacity-building approach.
32. 'Oil-For-Food: FAQ'.
33. 'Oil-For-Food: FAQ'.
34. See *Adverse consequences of economic sanctions on the enjoyment of human rights* (UN Document E/CN.4/Sub.2/RES/1997/35), August 28, 1997; Cortright and Lopez, 'Reforming Sanctions' in Malone, *The UN Security Council from the Cold War to the 21st Century*; Peter van Walsum, 'The Iraq Sanctions Committee' in Malone, *The UN Security Council from the Cold War to the 21st Century*; David J. R. Angell, 'The Angola Sanctions Committee' in Malone, *The UN Security Council from the Cold War to the 21st Century*; Center for Economic and Social Rights, *Unsanctioned Suffering: A Human Rights Assessment of the United Nations Sanctions on Iraq* (May 12, 1996); Richard Garfield, 'Health and Well-Being in Iraq: Sanctions and the Impact of the Oil-for-Food Program', *Transnational Law & Contemporary Problems* 11/2 (2001). Flagrant black-marketeering by the

Baghdad government was widely recognized by the late 1990s. David Keen 'Incentives and Disincentives for Violence', in Mats Berdal and David M. Malone (eds.), *Greed and Grievance: Economic Agendas in Civil Wars* (Boulder, CO: Lynne Rienner, 2000), 34. See also Christopher C. Joyner, 'United Nations Sanctions After Iraq: Looking Back to See Ahead', *Chicago Journal of International Law* 4/2 (2003), 341–2.

35. Revenues from petroleum sales were initially allocated as follows:
    - 53 percent for humanitarian purchases for the southern Governorates;
    - 13 percent for humanitarian purchases for the northern Governorates;
    - 30 percent transferred to the United Nations Compensation Fund established by SCR 687;
    - 2.2 percent set aside for operational and administrative costs of implementation;
    - 0.8 percent transferred to a special account for UNSCOM (and later UNMOVIC) costs; and
    - 1 percent to replenish an escrow account holding frozen Iraqi assets from which funds had been borrowed for humanitarian assistance from 1991 to 1995.

    This allocation was maintained until December 5, 2000, when in SCR 1302 the share of the humanitarian sector was lifted to 72 percent (59 percent for the south, 13 for the north), with the share of the Compensation Fund reduced from 30 percent to 25 percent. NB—After the oil export ceiling was removed in 1999, more than $1 billion wound up being allocated to administration.
36. Independent Inquiry Committee into the United Nations Oil-for-Food Programmme, *Report on the Management of the Oil-for-Food Programme* (September 7, 2005).
37. The Council relied on expert overseers to report Iraqi oil exports, leaving it open to surprises such as those reported on February 12, 2005, alleging that a Portuguese contractor in UN service had received a hefty bribe from Baghdad for under-reporting the amount of oil loaded onto a tanker. See Claudio Gatti, 'Saddam bribed UN tanker monitor, investigators say', *Financial Times*, February 12, 2005, 8.
38. UN agencies involved included the Food and Agricultural Organization; International Telecommunication Union; UN Development Program; UN Children's Fund; UN Educational, Scientific, and Cultural Organization; UN-Habitat; UN Office for Project Services; World Health Organization; and the World Food Program.
39. See *Report of the Secretary-General Pursuant to Paragraph 6 of Security Council Resolution 1210 (1998)* (Introductory Statement) (UN Secretariat Document S/1999/187), February 22, 1999.
40. See UN SCR 1284, December 17, 1999.
41. For national positions see *Security Council, 54th year: 4084th meeting* (UN Security Council Document S/PV.4084), December 17, 1999, 4, 11, 15. See also van Walsum, 'The Iraq Sanctions Committee', 186–7.

42. van Walsum, 'The Iraq Sanctions Committee', 187.
43. In 2002 the US General Accounting Office estimated that of the 2,100 contracts then on hold with the 661 Committee, ninety percent of the holds were placed by the US: *Weapons Of Mass Destruction: U.N. Confronts Significant Challenges in Implementing Sanctions against Iraq* (Document GAO-02-625), May 17, 2002, 20.
44. *Weapons Of Mass Destruction: U.N. Confronts Significant Challenges*, 20.
45. van Walsum, 'The Iraq Sanctions Committee', 188.
46. van Walsum, 'The Iraq Sanctions Committee', 188.
47. UN SCR 1409, May 14, 2002.
48. See for example Roger Normand, 'A Human Rights Assessment of Sanctions: The Case of Iraq, 1990–1997', in W. J. M. van Genugten and G. A. de Groot (eds.), *United Nations Sanctions: Effectiveness and Effects, Especially in the Field of Human Rights: A Multi-disciplinary Approach* (Antwerp: Intersentia, 1999); A. Shehabaldin and W. M. Laughlin, 'Economic Sanctions against Iraq: Human and Economic Costs', *International Journal of Human Rights* 3/4 (1999).
49. UNICEF, *The State of the World's Children* (New York: UNICEF, 2001).
50. See George E. Bisharat, 'Sanctions as Genocide', *Transnational Law & Contemporary Problems* 11/2 (2001); compare Joy Gordon, 'When Intent Makes All the Difference in the World: Economic Sanctions on Iraq and the Accusation of Genocide', *Yale Human Rights and Development Law Journal* 5 (2002).
51. David Cortright et al., *Political Gain and Civilian Pain: Humanitarian Impacts of Economic Sanctions* (Lanham, MD: Rowman and Littlefield Publishers, Inc., 1997).
52. See Carne Ross, 'War Stories', *Financial Times*, January 29, 2005, 21.
53. Anthony H. Cordesman, *Proliferation in Iran and Iraq, Is There an Answer?*, CSIS Strategic Assessment, March 28, 2000, 7. See also Matthew Craven, 'Humanitarianism and the Quest for Smarter Sanctions', *European Journal of International Law* 13/1 (2002), 60.
54. Martin Fletcher and Michael Binyon, 'Special Envoy and Iraq Edge Towards Accord on Peace Force', *The Times*, May 15, 1991.
55. Martin Fletcher and Michael Theodolou, 'Secretary of State Says Sanctions Must Stay as Long as Saddam Holds Power', *The Times*, May 23, 1991; Gates stated that 'Any easing of the sanctions will be considered only when there is a new government' (cited in Hiro, *Desert Shield*, 419.)
56. Kenneth Katzman, 'Iraq: U.S. Regime Change Efforts and Post-Saddam Governance', *Congressional Research Service* (May 16, 2005).
57. Madeleine Albright, 'Preserving Principle And Safeguarding Stability: United States Policy Toward Iraq', March 26, 1997, http://secretary.state.gov/www/statements/970326.html.
58. William Clinton, 'Statement on Iraq', November 14, 1997, www.fas.org/news/iraq/1997/11/97111407_tpo.html.
59. William Clinton, *Text of President Clinton's address to Joint Chiefs of Staff and Pentagon staff*, February 17, 1998, www.cnn.com/ALLPOLITICS/1998/02/17/transcripts/clinton.iraq.

60. 'Iraq Liberation Act of 1998', H.R. 4655, October 31, 1998. See also remarks of Secretary of State Warren Christopher in 1994 ('The US does not believe that Iraq's compliance with Paragraph 22 of Resolution 687 is enough to justify lifting the embargo'), cited in Hiro, *Iraq: In the Eye of the Storm*, 102.
61. Elaine Sciolino, 'CIA Asks Congress for Money to Rein In Iraq and Iran', *New York Times*, April 12, 1995, 8.
62. Hiro, *Iraq: In the Eye of the Storm*, 165.
63. Hiro, *Iraq: In the Eye of the Storm*, 165–6.
64. Hiro, *Iraq: In the Eye of the Storm*, 167–8.
65. See George A. Lopez, 'Toward Smart Sanctions on Iraq', *Kroc Policy Brief #5*, April 2001, www.nd.edu/~krocinst/polbriefs/pbrief5.html; see also Marc Lynch, 'Smart Sanctions: Rebuilding Consensus or Maintaining Conflict?', *MERIP Online*, June 28, 2001, www.merip.org/mero/mero062801.html.
66. Lynch, 'Smart Sanctions', s. v. 69. Peter van Walsum recounts an incident where the French notified him, as Chair of the 661 Committee, of a French civilian flight to Iraq, giving him insufficient time to follow the usual practice of approval. His request that France delay the flight to allow that practice to be followed was denied. See van Walsum, 'The Iraq Sanctions Committee', 191–2.
67. 'Interview with Hubert Védrine, minister of foreign affairs', *Al Hayat*, August 1, 2000, www.info-france-usa.org/news/statmnts/2000/iraq0108.asp.
68. See *Note [on the establishment of an informal working group on improving the effectiveness of United Nations sanctions]* (UN Security Council Document S/2000/319), April 17, 2000. For the outcome of that process see Peter Wallensteen, Carina Staibano, and Mikael Eriksson (eds.), *Making Targeted Sanctions Effective: Guidelines for the Implementation of UN Policy Options: Results from the Stockholm Process on the Implementation of Targeted Sanctions* (Uppsala: Uppsala University Department of Peace and Conflict Research, 2003). For a related discussion of sanctions reform see Simon Chesterman and Béatrice Pouligny, *The Politics of Sanctions*, IPA-CERI-RIIA Policy Brief, May 1, 2002. See also Cortright and Lopez, 'Reforming Sanctions', 176.
69. See UN SCR 1382, November 29, 2001 (enumerating the extensive Proposed Goods Review List in Annex 1).
70. See Paul Kerr, 'Oil-for-food extended, goods review list revised', *Arms Control Today* 33/1 (2003).
71. Kerr, 'Oil-for-food extended'.
72. Kerr, 'Oil-for-food extended'.
73. See UN SCR 1472, March 28, 2003, UN SCR 1476, April 24, 2003, UN SCR 1483, May 22, 2003.
74. See for example Michael Soussan, 'The Cash-for-Saddam Program', *Wall Street Journal*, March 8, 2004, A16; Therese Raphael, 'The Oil-for-Food Scandal', *Wall Street Journal*, March 11, 2004, A16; William Safire, 'Scandal at the U.N.', *New York Times*, March 17, 2004, 25.

75. As a sovereign country, Iraq was entitled to negotiate export and import contracts directly with private firms.
76. Commissions were generally reflected as 'after sales service charges'. Kickbacks went to Iraqi officials at all levels. See Defense Contract Audit Agency and the Defense Contract Management Agency, *Report on the Pricing Evaluation of Contracts Awarded under the Iraq Oil for Food Program* (Washington, DC: September 12, 2003). See also Independent Inquiry Committee, *Report on the Management of the Oil-for-Food Programme.*
77. Charles Duelfer, *Comprehensive Report of the Special Advisor to the DCI on Iraq's WMD* (Washington, DC: Central Intelligence Agency, September 30, 2004), I, 28–31.
78. For an example of such coverage, sharp in every sense, see Claudia Rosett, 'The U.N.'s Secrets Grew Worse in the Dark', *Wall Street Journal Europe*, July 14, 2004, A7.
79. Ramesh Thakur, 'Beware The Rush to Condemn the UN', *Melbourne Age*, May 8, 2004.
80. Thakur, 'Beware The Rush to Condemn the UN'.
81. The Duelfer Report alleged that 30 per cent of oil vouchers were allocated to Russian nationals, 15% to French and 10 per cent to Chinese (Duelfer, *Comprehensive Report*, 31). Oil-export contracts under the Oil-for-Food Programme were, however, generally more strongly weighted to these countries: Hussein withheld contracts from US and UK firms in retaliation for their continued military opposition.
82. See William Safire, 'Kofigate Gets Going', *New York Times*, July 12, 2004, 19, and more generally Safire's columns on the UN earlier in 2004.
83. UN SCR 1538, April 21, 2004.
84. Independent Inquiry Committee, *Report on the Management of the Oil-for-Food Programme*, I, 4.
85. 'Annan says some Oil-for-Food charges "outrageous", probe will clarify issues', *The UN News Service*, April 28, 2004.
86. Independent Inquiry Committee, *Report on the Management of the Oil-for-Food Programme*, III, 228–39; Claudio Gatti, 'UN chief's son received cash from companies in probe', *FT.com*, September 7, 2005.
87. On Kojo Annan's background and business dealings, see François Soudan, 'Du Malheur d'Avoir un Fils', *Jeune Afrique l'Intelligent* 2993, December 19–25, 2004.
88. Colum Lynch, 'Oil-for-Food Panel Rebukes Annan, Cites Corruption', *Washington Post*, September 8, 2005, A1.
89. Lynch, 'Oil-for-Food Panel Rebukes Annan, Cites Corruption'.
90. 'Retraction on pay for Annan's son', *International Herald Tribune*, December 2, 2004.
91. Independent Inquiry Committee into the United Nations Oil-for-Food Programme, *Second Interim Report* (March 29, 2005).
92. 'Annan says exoneration by Iraq Oil-for-Food Report "Great Relief" ', *UN News Centre*, March 29, 2005.

93. 'Annan says exoneration by Iraq Oil-for-Food Report "Great Relief" '.
94. 'Annan and the Truth—Sort of', *Washington Times*, Editorial, April 28, 2005.
95. 'The Verdict on Kofi Annan', *New York Times*, Editorial, March 30, 2005, 16.
96. 'The Verdict on Kofi Annan'.
97. Independent Inquiry Committee, *Report on the Management of the Oil-for-Food Programme*, III, 219, 243.
98. Independent Inquiry Committee into the United Nations Oil-for-Food Programme, *Report on the Management of the Oil-for-Food Programme*, III, 227, 242–3.
99. 'Annan Stresses Vital Importance of UN Reforms in Wake of Oil-for-Food Report', UN News Service, September 8, 2005.
100. Independent Inquiry Committee into the United Nations Oil-for-Food Programme, *Interim Report* (February 3, 2005); Independent Inquiry Committee into the United Nations Oil-for-Food Programme, *Third Interim Report* (August 8, 2005).
101. Benon V. Sevan, *Letter of resignation*, August 7, 2005, on file with the author.
102. 'Reforming the UN', *Washington Post*, Editorial, September 8, 2005, A28.
103. Independent Inquiry Committee, *Report on the Management of the Oil-for-Food Programme*, I, 44–8.
104. Lynch, 'Oil-for-Food Panel Rebukes Annan, Cites Corruption'.
105. Independent Inquiry Committee, *Report on the Management of the Oil-for-Food Programme*, II, 82–97.
106. Independent Inquiry Committee into the United Nations Oil-for-Food Programme, *Third Interim Report*, August 8, 2005.
107. Warren Hoge, 'Panel Accuses Former U.N. Official of Bribery', *New York Times*, August 9, 2005, 1.
108. 'Oil-for-Food Corruption', *New York Times*, Editorial, August 10, 2005, 20.
109. Julia Preston, 'Russian Held in Scheme to Launder U.N. Bribes', *New York Times*, September 3, 2005, 8.
110. 'Annan fires Joseph Stephanides for "serious misconduct" linked to oil-for-food', *UN News Centre*, June 1, 2005. Stephanides was subsequently reinstated in his UN employment until his retirement.
111. Philip Sherwell and Charles Laurence, 'The scandal Kofi couldn't cover up', *Sunday Telegraph*, February 6, 2005, 17.
112. Sherwell and Laurence, 'The scandal Kofi couldn't cover up'.
113. Sherwell and Laurence, 'The scandal Kofi couldn't cover up'.
114. Confidential Interview, November 2004.
115. David E. Sanger and Frank Bruni, 'In His First Days, Bush Plans Review of Clinton's Acts', *New York Times*, January 14, 2001, 1.
116. *Statement of Joseph A. Christoff before the Committee on Foreign Relations* (Document GAO-04-651T), 7 April 2004. See also *Statement of Joseph A. Christoff before the Committee on Foreign Relations* (Document GAO-04-953T), July 8, 2004.
117. Independent Inquiry Committee, *Report on the Management of the Oil-for-Food Programme*, I, ch. 2.

118. Claudio Gatti and Mark Turner, 'Dealing with Saddam's regime: how fortunes were made in Iraq through the UN's oil-for-food program', *Financial Times*, April 8, 2004, 17.
119. See Duelfer, *Comprehensive Report*. See generally Douglas Jehl, 'US Report Finds Iraqis Eliminated Illicit Arms in 90's', *New York Times*, October 7, 2004, 1, and Scott Shane, 'Report Says Iraq Misused U.N. Oil Plan', *New York Times*, October 7, 2004, 28. See Thomas Catan, Mark Huband, and Steve Fidler, 'Iraq "did not have" weapons of mass destruction', *FT.com*, October 7, 2004; Eric Lipton and Scott Shane, 'US Report Says Hussein Bought Arms with Ease', *New York Times*, October 8, 2004, 1; and Alec Russell, 'Paris protests to US over bribes claim', *Daily Telegraph*, October 8, 2004, 4. Duelfer succeeded another American—former UN weapons inspector David Kay—as head of the Iraq Survey Group which searched unsuccessfully for Iraqi WMD after the invasion.
120. Jess Bravin, John D. McKinnon, and Russell Gold, 'Iraq Oil-for-Food Probe Hits US', *Wall Street Journal*, October 11, 2004, A8. The broadest accounting of corporate involvement in subversion of the OFF Program came in October 2005, with the release of a follow up report by the Volcker Inquiry on this issue: Independent Inquiry Committee into the United Nations Oil-for-food Programme, *Report on the Manipulation of the Oil-for-Food Programme*, October 27, 2005, www.iic-offp.org/documents/IIC%20Final%20Report%20Oct2005.pdf.
121. Claudio Gatti, 'Oil-for-Food Inquiry Targets French Minister', *Financial Times*, April 28, 2005, 1.
122. Justin Blum and Colum Lynch, 'Oil-for-Food Benefited Russians, Report Says', *Washington Post*, May 16, 2005, A01.
123. Brian Knowlton, 'Briton puts senators on defensive on Iraq', *International Herald Tribune*, May 18, 2005, 3.
124. Knowlton, 'Briton puts senators on defensive on Iraq'.
125. 'Oil for What?', *Washington Post*, Editorial, May 21, 2005, B06.
126. See Independent Inquiry Committee into the United Nations Oil-for-Food Programme, *Briefing Paper* (January 9, 2005). The Committee's provisional assessment suggested the 58 audits conducted by the OIOS had focused excessively on operations of the OFF Program outside UN Headquarters in New York, that they had on occasion not been followed up adequately, that they did not evince an overall strategy based on risk assessment, and that they did not focus adequately on pricing and quality in contracts.
127. Compare 'The Oil-for-Food audits', *New York Times*, Editorial, January 17, 2005, 16.
128. Duelfer, *Comprehensive Report*.
129. Elise Labott and Phil Hirschkorn, 'Documents: US condoned Iraq oil smuggling', *CNN.com*, February 3, 2005, http://edition.cnn.com/2005/WORLD/meast/02/02/iraq.oil.smuggle; Mark Turner, 'US and Congress knew Saddam was smuggling oil', *FT.com*, January 19, 2005.

130. Traub, 'Off target'.
131. See for example Coalition for International Justice, *Sources of Revenue For Saddam & Sons: A Primer on the Financial Underpinnings of the Regime in Baghdad*, September 18, 2002; Tish Durkin, 'The U.N.'s Oil-for-Food Program is a Windfall for Saddam', *National Journal*, 34/38 (September 21, 2002), 2681.
132. Traub, 'Off target', 14. See also *Statement for the Record of Ambassador John Negroponte, Permanent Representative US Mission to the UN, Before the Committee on Foreign Relations, United States Senate, on Oil-for-Food Program*, Second Session, 108th Congress (April 7, 2004); and see *Statement by Ambassador Patrick F. Kennedy, United States Representative for UN Management and Reform on the UN Oil-For-Food Program, before the House Committee on Government Reform Subcommittee on National Security, Emerging Threats, and International Relations* (April 21, 2004). See also *Weapons Of Mass Destruction: U.N. Confronts Significant Challenges*, 7 and Appendix I (estimating illegal oil surcharges at $2.3 billion since 1997).
133. Traub, 'Off target', 14–17.
134. Confidential correspondence with the author, February 11, 2005.
135. Traub, 'Off target', 14–17.
136. Independent Inquiry Committee, *Report on the Management of the Oil-for-Food Programme*, I, 2.
137. 'Annan Stresses "Vital Importance" of UN Reforms in Wake of Oil-for-Food Report', *UN News Service*, September 8, 2005.
138. Mark Turner, 'Annan accepts claim of failure on oil-for-food', *FT.com*, September 7, 2005.
139. Ewen MacAskill, 'Annan call for reform in wake of report', *The Guardian*, September 8, 2005, 16.
140. See Nicholas Kralev, 'Powell urges UN Council to take blame for scandal', *Washington Times*, January 12, 2005, A11. The 661 Committee did take some steps to curtail surcharges, including by moving from the proactive to the reactive pricing mechanism; but it remains unclear what measures, if any, it adopted against illegal commissions.
141. Norm Coleman, 'Kofi Annan Must Go', *Wall Street Journal*, December 1, 2004, A10.
142. See for example the comments of Sen. Norm Coleman (R-Minn.) in Betsy Pisik, 'U.N. corruption cited in Iraq oil-food scandal', *Washington Times*, September 8, 2005, A01.
143. Warren Hoge, 'Annan Failed to Curb Corruption in Iraq's Oil-for-Food Program, Investigators Report', *New York Times*, September 7, 2005, 6.
144. Lynch, 'Oil-for-Food Panel Rebukes Annan, Cites Corruption'.
145. Maggie Farley, 'Accepting Criticism, Annan Seeks to Make Use of It', *Los Angeles Times*, September 8, 2005, A7.

146. John G. Ruggie, 'Hearing on The United Nations Oil-for-Food Program: Issues of Accountability and Transparency', United States House of Representatives Committee on International Relations, April 28, 2004.
147. Ruggie, 'Hearing on The United Nations Oil-for-Food Program'.
148. Lopez and Cortright, 'Containing Iraq', 97.
149. See Duelfer, *Comprehensive Report.*
150. Lopez and Cortright, 'Containing Iraq', 97.
151. Cortright and Lopez, 'Reforming Sanctions', 171.
152. 'Oil-For-Food: FAQ'. Hussein sold oil to neighboring countries at significant discounts, gaining their support against military pressure on Iraq which might disrupt these cheap sources of oil.
153. Van Walsum describes a range of solutions from redeemable vouchers to out-of-country reimbursements to Saudi Arabian reimbursement, all of which were rejected by the Iraqi government. See van Walsum, 'The Iraq Sanctions Committee', 188–9.
154. See for example Denis J. Halliday, 'End The Catastrophe Of Sanctions Against Iraq', *Seattle Post-Intelligencer,* Editorial, February 12, 1999, A17; Denis J. Halliday and Jennifer E. Horan, 'A new policy needed for Iraq', *Boston Globe*, Editorial, March 22, 1999, A19; H. C. Graf Sponeck, 'Sanctions and Humanitarian Exemptions: A Practitioner's Commentary', *European Journal of International Law* 13/1 (2002). See also William F. Donaher and Ross B. DeBlois, 'Is the current UN and US policy toward Iraq effective?', *Parameters* 31/4 (2001).
155. Correspondence with the author, February 11, 2005.
156. See 'France Calls for Lifting of Sanctions Against Iraq', *Xinhua News Agency,* August 1, 2000.
157. Cordesman and Hashim, *Iraq: Sanctions and Beyond*, 4.
158. See for example a televised interview of Madeleine Albright in which she was backed into stating that Hiroshima-dimension human losses in Iraq due to sanctions were 'worth it': *60 Minutes* (CBS), May 12, 1996. The State department's high-profile public diplomacy portfolio produced so many gaffes and so little progress that it became a revolving door for senior Republican operatives after 2002.
159. See International Study Team, 'Our Common Responsibility: The Impact of a New War on Iraqi Children', January 26, 2003.
160. Graham-Brown, *Sanctioning Saddam*, 184, citing Peter Boone et al., *Sanctions Against Iraq: Costs of Failure* (Brooklyn, NY: Center for Economic and Social Rights, 1997), 51.
161. *Statement of Edward C. Luck to the Subcommittee on National Security, Emerging Threats and International Relations Committee on Government Reform of the United States House of Representatives*, April 21, 2004.
162. See Martin Indyk, 'The Clinton Administration's Approach to the Middle East', Keynote Address to the Soref Symposium on 'Challenges to US Interests

in the Middle East: Obstacles and Opportunities', *Proceedings of the Washington Institute for Near East Policy*, May 18–19, 1993. See also Zbigniew Brzezinski, Brent Scowcroft, and Richard Murphy, 'Differentiated Containment', *Foreign Affairs* 76/3 (1997).

163. For an early analysis along these lines see Gary Sick, 'Rethinking Dual Containment', *Survival* 40/1 (1998).
164. See, for example, the Committees established by SCRs: 1540 (2004) (WMD); 1533 (2004) (DRC); 1521 (2003) (Liberia); 1518 (2003) (Iraq); 1373 (2001) (Counterterrorism Committee); 1343 (2001) (Liberia); 1298 (2000) (Ethiopia and Eritrea); 1267 (1999) (Al Qaeda and the Taliban); 1160 (1998) (Kosovo); 1132 (1997) (Sierra Leone); 985 (1995) (Liberia); 918 (1994) (Rwanda); 864 (1993) (UNITA); 751 (1992) (Somalia); 748 (1992) (Libya). The ICTY and ICTR can also be considered as subsidiary organs of the Security Council designed to enforce detailed administrative standards—namely those regulating the conduct of hostilities.
165. 'Reforming the UN'.
166. Traub, 'Off target'.
167. Traub, 'Off target'.
168. SCR 1483.
169. See 'Guidelines For The Application Of Paragraphs 19 And 23 Of Resolution 1483 (2003)', www.un.org/Docs/sc/committees/1518/1483guide.pdf.
170. See Annex to *Letter dated 2002/05/03 from the Deputy Permanent Representative of the United States of America to the United Nations addressed to the President of the Security Council* (UN Security Council Document S/2002/515), May 3, 2002.
171. For some of the problems of day-to-day administration of the OFF Program, see Graham-Brown, *Sanctioning Saddam*, 286–7.
172. Independent Inquiry Committee, *Report on the Management of the Oil-for-Food Programme*, I, 7.
173. See generally Christopher Greenwood, *Humanitarian Intervention: Law and Policy* (Oxford: OUP, 2001).
174. Paul Lewis, 'Disaster Relief Proposal Worries Third World', *New York Times*, November 13, 1991, 9.
175. See Louise Fréchette, 'L'ONU doit réformer sa gestion', *Le Figaro*, September 8, 2005.

6

Weapons Inspector: UNSCOM, UNMOVIC and the Disarming of Iraq

Weapons of mass destruction (WMD) in Iraq had long been a source of international concern.[1] On June 19, 1981, the Security Council strongly condemned Israel's destruction of Iraq's nuclear reactor at Osiraq, which Israel claimed was being used in the preparation of nuclear weapons—an ironic response in light of later developments, but one very much in keeping with international conceptions of sovereignty and aggression during the Cold War years.[2] In 1986 an Australian scientist working near Iraqi frontlines for one of the UN inspection teams developed by Pérez de Cuéllar came across an unusual shell. He picked it up and drained its brownish, liquid contents into the nearest receptacle—a Coca Cola bottle. It was mustard gas. Clearly, Iraq's WMD ambitions were not limited to nuclear weapons. By 1991, Iraqi possession of WMD posed a widely appreciated threat to the region—and to Iraq's own people, as Saddam Hussein's use of chemical weapons at Halabja in 1988 made clear.[3] Iraq's continued possession of WMD threatened not only the region but also—and of greater geostrategic significance—global energy security.

In the aftermath of the First Gulf War, SCR 687 made disarmament the centerpiece of a formal end to hostilities. The system of inspection and monitoring it established was, in the words of US Vice President Richard Cheney, 'the most intrusive system of arms control in history'.[4] This battle was fought internationally 'by the dark arts of bureaucratic trench warfare: campaigns for influence, diplomatic offensives and the deployment of the weapons of public opinion, economic incentive and false information'.[5]

6.1 UNSCOM

The central trade-off envisaged in SCR 687 was the lifting of economic sanctions in return for 'progress toward the control of armaments in the region', the latter to be evaluated by unimpeded monitoring of Iraqi weapons.[6] The focus on the elimination of WMD as a key objective first came from the United Kingdom during negotiation of SCR 686, which provided for a provisional cease-fire, and was agreed in SCR 687.[7] The United Kingdom advocated destruction of Iraq's stock of biological and chemical weapons and a mechanism to prevent it from acquiring new capabilities. The United States proposed the addition of nuclear controls. The Soviet Union, France, and China sought to introduce a reference to the need to rid the entire Middle East of all WMD—a veiled reference to Israel's suspected possession of nuclear weapons.[8] The United States suggested linking the lifting of existing sanctions to Iraqi disarmament. (The USSR, France, and China all initially suggested that the lifting of sanctions should depend only on the fulfillment of the more conventional conditions set out prior to the UN-authorized military action, in SCR 660.)[9]

To oversee Iraqi disarmament, the Council took the unprecedented step of creating a subsidiary organ charged with monitoring the destruction, removal, or neutralization of all Iraqi chemical and biological weapons, including the stocks of agents, related subsystems, components and all research, development, support, and manufacturing facilities. This organ was the United Nations Special Commission (UNSCOM). The Security Council charged the IAEA with similar responsibilities in relation to Iraqi nuclear capability and activity.

The first Executive Chairman of UNSCOM was Rolf Ekéus, a Swede.[10] Ekéus remained in the post until 1996, when he was replaced by Richard Butler, an Australian diplomat and arms control expert. The triangular relationship between UNSCOM, the Secretary-General, and the Security Council established by SCR 687 was unusual. The Executive Chairmen were appointed by the Secretary-General, after consultation with the Council, and formally reported to the Council through the Secretary-General. Otherwise, though, the Secretary-General exercised no control over UNSCOM.[11] While this arrangement worked well in UNSCOM's early years, it was to prove highly problematic in 1998, when Kofi Annan and Richard Butler differed on issues of substance.

UNSCOM was set up at UN Headquarters in New York, with offices in Bahrain and Baghdad. UNSCOM's staff in New York included technical experts and diplomatic and administrative staff. The Bahrain office served as the assembly and training point for inspection teams as well as a logistics and supply point, while the Baghdad office provided communications and logistical support in the field. The total staff (excluding the forty-five aircrew inside Iraq) was approximately 120 people.

6.1.1 *Early Resistance*

Iraq accepted SCR 687 on April 6, 1991. The resolution gave it fifteen days to provide a complete disclosure of the location, amounts, and types of all WMD. On April 17, 1991, Baghdad provided an 'initial declaration', disclosing details of some chemical weapons and materials and fifty-three long-range ballistic missiles. But soon a pattern of noncooperation set in. In late June, Iraqi guards fired warning shots to prevent UNSCOM and IAEA inspectors from intercepting and inspecting Iraqi vehicles thought to be carrying nuclear equipment. In July, IAEA officials were obstructed from visiting two sites that Iraq had not listed as nuclear facilities, and soon afterwards discovered several kilograms of highly enriched uranium.[12]

In response, the Council issued SCR 699, confirming that the mandate of UNSCOM and the IAEA included the arms control provisions of SCR 687, and deploring Iraq's lack of cooperation.[13] Under pressure, Baghdad reversed its initial declaration that it possessed no biological weapons capability, indicating that it had in fact conducted 'biological research activities for defensive military purposes'. The Council then passed SCR 707 demanding that Iraq fully disclose its weapons programs, and authorized the use of fixed-wing and helicopter flights inside Iraq for inspections purposes. Iraq objected strongly, aware that on August 11 the United States had overflown Iraq with a U-2 spy plane, ostensibly undertaking surveillance for UNSCOM.[14]

With tensions rising, on September 6, 1991, Iraq blocked the first UNSCOM inspection team from inspecting Iraqi weapons sites. On September 21, 1991, IAEA inspectors led by David Kay discovered documentation revealing Iraq's efforts to acquire nuclear weapons. Iraqi officials were successful in confiscating only some of the documents, and refused to allow the IAEA inspectors to leave the site, detaining them in a parking lot. For four days, this incongruous standoff continued. Confronted by a direct threat to its authority, the Council threatened enforcement action. Conforming to an emerging pattern of cat and mouse maneuvering, Iraqi officials then backed down and allowed the IAEA inspectors to leave—with the most damning portion of the documents.[15]

Concerned by the flagrancy of Iraq's defiance, the Council concluded that sustainable arms control required more than just a temporary program of inspections, and so issued Resolution 715, which approved a more intrusive Ongoing Monitoring and Verification (OMV) regime. The Resolution directed that Iraq must 'accept unconditionally the inspectors and all other personnel' designated by UNSCOM, and that OMV would remain in place until the Security Council decided to remove it.[16] Iraq rejected the OMV as unlawful. For two years, this tug of war continued, with information trickling out from Iraq of small numbers of ballistic missiles. It was not until November 1993 that Iraq finally accepted Resolution 715.[17]

6.1.2 *Raising the Stakes*

Upping the ante, Iraq announced its own deadline of October 10, 1994, for the completion of weapons inspections, after which it would cease cooperation. Indeed, Saddam Hussein deployed troops toward the Kuwaiti border in October 1994. In turn, the United States began a massive troop buildup in the Persian Gulf (dubbed Operation Vigilant Warrior). Resolution 949 of October 15, 1994 demanded Iraq 'fully cooperate' with UNSCOM and withdraw its troops from southern Iraq.[18] The troops were withdrawn, and in March 1995 Iraq made a second 'Full, Final, and Complete' disclosure of prohibited biological and chemical weapons programs to UNSCOM.

UNSCOM benefited significantly from Iraqi defections in 1994, including those by General Wafiq Samarai (a former head of Iraqi military intelligence) and Khidhir Abdul Abbas Hamza (a senior Iraqi nuclear scientist).[19] But the greatest coup came on August 20, 1995, when General Hussein Kamel Hassan, Saddam Hussein's son-in-law, defected to Jordan. Kamel was a former Director of Iraq's Military Industrialization Corporation and had been responsible for all of Iraq's weapons programs. Questioned by UNSCOM, he revealed extensive details of Iraqi weapons programs proscribed by SCR 687—details that had been deliberately withheld from the UN through a 'Concealment Operations Committee' chaired by Saddam Hussein's son, Qusay.[20]

Now in serious damage control mode, Baghdad announced a new policy of complete cooperation and transparency with UNSCOM and the IAEA. It withdrew its latest disclosure and admitted, for the first time, that it had successfully weaponized biological agents. It also revealed previously undisclosed success in long-range missile production. It turned over large amounts of documentation to UNSCOM and the IAEA, claiming it had been hidden by Hussein Kamel. In one of the rare comical moments of this saga, Iraqi authorities took weapons inspectors to a chicken coop on a farm allegedly owned by Kamel, where the documents had allegedly been hidden.[21] These documents led to further disclosures, including the revelation that Iraq had produced the deadly nerve agent VX and was working to develop nuclear weapons. This episode for a time undermined a growing French and Russian drive to lift sanctions.[22] But Saddam Hussein had hardly turned over a new leaf. In November 1995, Jordan intercepted a shipment of high-grade missile components on their way to Iraq, which led UNSCOM to uncover an Iraqi program to acquire sophisticated missile guidance and control systems.

The pattern of feints and taunts continued through 1996, with the Security Council repeatedly calling on Iraq to cooperate unconditionally with UNSCOM and the IAEA, to no avail.[23] In the middle of the year, Hussein moved troops back into Kurdistan, taking Irbil (as discussed in Chapter 4). The United States responded with missile strikes in southern Iraq, deepening tensions between Iraqi officials and UNSCOM inspectors—particularly the Americans among them. The United States also raised the stakes by sponsoring a failed coup attempt against Hussein by a group of army generals.[24] Tensions rose steadily, with Iraqi officials adopting an increasingly hostile approach toward UNSCOM inspectors, barring them from several 'sensitive' sites, destroying files, and interfering with UNSCOM helicopter flights.

6.1.3 *The 'Presidential' Precedent*

One of the arguments used by the Iraqis to bar access to sensitive sites in the spring of 1996 was that they were 'Presidential'. The Iraqis argued that the preambular provision of SCR 687 indicating the Security Council's respect for Iraq's sovereignty and integrity prevented inspection of such sites. In Resolution 1060,[25] the Council rebuffed this argument. Ekéus has confirmed that the US made explicit to him that it stood ready to take unilateral military action against Iraq.[26] Ekévs then traveled to Baghdad, where he met with Tariq Aziz, the Deputy Prime Minister.

Continuing the pattern of Iraqi backdowns in the face of US military pressure, Aziz agreed, in writing, to grant 'immediate, unconditional and unrestricted access' to sites UNSCOM and the IAEA wished to inspect. Ekéus argues that

> [w]ith this accomplishment we avoided a break out of violence, the Security Council requirements . . . had been met and most important from my perspective,

UNSCOM and IAEA could continue their activity [through] to the successful completion of Iraq's disarmament....[27]

Yet Ekéus agreed to 'modalities'—what others considered 'conditions'—of access to sites in which 'the President of Iraq was present'.[28] His argument today that the agreement did not prevent UNSCOM from successfully disarming Iraq is hard to refute.[29] However, it did carve out a precedent providing apparent exceptions to the inspections regime, which the Iraqis would soon manipulate into a wedge to drive between the P-5. In retrospect, this was not the finest hour in a long, wearying, and very successful tenure overall (and one much praised by his former American deputy Bob Galluci.)[30]

6.1.4 *Active Resistance*

By early 1997, with the OFF Program under way and France recently withdrawn from Operation Northern Watch, Saddam Hussein may have sensed the tide turning in his favor. In an important development, any pretence that mere satisfaction of the disarmament obligations imposed by SCR 687 would induce the United States to allow sanctions to be lifted had disappeared by early 1997, as documented in the previous chapter. Only regime change could satisfy Washington. Madeleine Albright's comments to this effect (repeated in variations by other administration officials) encapsulated a unilateral reinterpretation of Council resolutions, in effect moving the goalposts. It removed from Saddam Hussein any real incentive to comply with the resolutions.[31]

Not surprisingly, as 1997 wore on, Iraqi obstructionism grew. Recognizing new opportunities to drive a wedge between the members of the P-5, Iraq slowly turned the screw.[32] On November 3, 1997, the Iraqis blocked an UNSCOM inspection of a short-range missile site because the team contained too many Americans. In response, Annan sent a team, led by Lakhdar Brahimi, to mediate. But on November 12, Baghdad expelled six US inspectors. President Clinton reacted angrily, dispatching an aircraft carrier to the region.[33] Resolution 1137 of November 12 termed Iraq's actions 'unacceptable', and warned of 'serious consequences' (code for possible use of force), if Iraq failed to comply with earlier resolutions.[34] However, the rift within the P-5 was becoming more and more obvious: presented with a resolution drafted by the United States threatening travel bans on Iraqi officials obstructing UNSCOM work, France, China, Russia, Kenya, and Egypt all abstained.[35]

Russia soon brokered a deal with Hussein that saw him allow all UNSCOM inspectors back in. Rather than UNSCOM playing the role of neutral and objective intermediary between Iraq and the Council, dispassionately discharging its inspections mandate, UNSCOM and Iraq had now become the adversaries, with some of the P-5 playing the role of intermediary. The danger of polarization within the P-5—with UNSCOM identified as an instrument of the United States, in particular—was clear.

6.1.5 *The Threat of Force*

Perhaps sensing that its serial provocations were successfully widening the rift among the P-5, Iraq struck again: on January 13, 1998, Iraq withdrew its cooperation from several inspection teams, once again on the pretext that they included too many individuals of US or UK nationality. Despite a Security Council Presidential Statement terming Iraq's actions unacceptable, Iraq continued to assert that it would not permit access to eight so-called 'Presidential sites'.[36] A serious US military buildup in the Gulf followed, with token support from only a few of its allies (Great Britain sent ships, the Netherlands dispatched frigates, Canada and Australia pledged logistical support). The broad coalition to confront Iraq, built by George Bush and Jim Baker in 1990 under the Desert Storm umbrella, had withered away. In contrast to the cooperation from the USSR and France, which had underpinned the coalition in 1990, America was now confronted by Russian and French obstructionism. They deplored the threat of force and pressed for change in the sanctions regime.[37] At their insistence, the Security Council continued to encourage Iraq to comply with past Resolutions, holding out the prospect of some sort of relaxation of sanctions as 'light at the end of the tunnel'.[38] President Yeltsin went further, pledging to secure a timetable for the lifting of sanctions, in return for Iraqi consent to the unconditional return of UNSCOM inspectors.[39] At the end of the month, Richard Butler, who had taken over as UNSCOM Executive Chairman on July 1, 1997, made the alarming (and alarmist) assertion that Baghdad had enough biological weapons and missiles 'to blow away Tel Aviv'.[40] Security Council members, who had been presented with no such evidence, were shocked. Butler backpedaled.[41] Hussein had little to lose from bombing—especially if it reinforced his position at home, and drove a further wedge between the P-5. Hostilities seemed likely.

In an effort to build support for military action—and, cynics claimed, to detract attention from a growing scandal relating to President Clinton's relationship with Monica Lewinsky—the White House dispatched Secretary of State Madeleine Albright, Secretary of Defense William Cohen, and National Security Adviser Samuel Berger to nudge along public opinion through a 'town hall' meeting on US policy toward Iraq at Ohio State University on February 18. This maneuver backfired badly. With CNN and other television channels carrying vociferous protest and often penetrating questions critical of US policy, it became a 'self-inflicted ... public relations disaster'.[42] A February 22 *Newspoll* showed US public support for military action against Iraq drastically down.[43] Washington's interest in a negotiated outcome suddenly increased markedly.

Offering his good offices, Kofi Annan now stepped in.[44] In doing so, Annan staked out a position as a neutral peacemaker between the Council and Iraq. This initiative, perhaps unintentionally, showed up the Council's failure to find a common position that might allow compromise with Iraq. His intervention forced the P-5 to consent to a serious attempt at compromise. Fortified (and seriously constrained) by detailed guidance from the P-5 ambassadors in New York on the parameters of an acceptable agreement (the bottom-line being defined by the US and UK positions), Annan set off for Baghdad, in a move reminiscent of Pérez de Cuéllar's intervention in the Iran–Iraq conflict (see Chapter 2).[45] On February 22, Annan secured the agreement of Iraq for 'unlimited access' by UN inspectors to the Presidential sites. A Memorandum of Understanding (MOU) included several face-saving provisions for Saddam, but seemed to achieve the Council's objectives.[46]

Behind closed doors in the Security Council on his return, Annan offered a pointed (and culturally specific) characterization of some UNSCOM inspectors as 'cowboys'.[47] Perhaps stung, the US government failed to display much appreciation for his mediation efforts:

> Annan left Baghdad believing that he had achieved not only personal but also institutional vindication—vividly demonstrating the merits of diplomacy and multilateralism. He arrived back in the United States and heard himself denounced as a latter-day Neville Chamberlain by the Senate Majority Leader, Trent Lott. The Clinton Administration, which had arguably been saved from itself, issued not so much as a thank-you.[48]

Many in Washington were dismayed by a comment Annan ill-advisedly made about Saddam Hussein in New York following his return from Baghdad: 'I think I can do business with him.'[49] The remark reinforced an impression already held by some in Washington that Annan was too accommodating to be entrusted with negotiations affecting vital US interests. On this occasion, Butler disagreed: 'He brought home the bacon.'[50]

6.1.6 *Desert Fox*

Although Butler evoked a 'new spirit of cooperation between the two sides' after a visit to Iraq from March 22 to March 26, and in spite of visits to the Presidential sites in the period March 26–April 2 by UNSCOM and IAEA inspectors accompanied by a gaggle of senior diplomats, Iraqi compliance with the MOU soon flagged.[51] Iraq refused in August to entertain UNSCOM verification proposals, viewing them as 'endlessly prolonging the process on irrelevant and trivial issues'.[52] Further crises led to a renewed break in Iraqi cooperation with UNSCOM in October 1998. UNSCOM inspectors were readmitted to Iraq in November (after considerable US and UK saber-rattling), but the Iraqi government systematically obstructed their work.

Butler's December 15 report, detailing persistent Iraqi non-compliance, was the final straw for an increasingly frustrated United States and United Kingdom. Though they pressed for a more forceful response, there was growing exasperation with the inspections melodrama, and a sense on the part of the other P-5 members that Iraq had mostly been disarmed. An advisor to Kofi Annan expressed the prevailing mood:

> You can never have 100 percent proof disarmament because it is too easy to develop, manufacture and hide biological weapons, so at some point technical exercise gives way to political judgment.... At some point it becomes impossible to prove the negative.[53]

Additionally, the Council's integrity had been assaulted in the latter months of 1998 by the sordid revelations of former UNSCOM senior inspector Scott Ritter on UNSCOM's troublingly close relationship with Washington. The fact that Butler's report had apparently been circulated through US hands before being shown to other Council members also created an uproar.[54]

Washington and London could not be placated, however, and, in a sign of how far unilateralism had become embedded in the practice of the Council, decided to engage in a bombing campaign without seeking Council authorization, relying instead on Iraqi noncompliance with earlier Council resolutions as sufficient legal justification. UNSCOM inspectors were withdrawn from Iraq during the night of December 15–16 at US request, leaving behind other UN staff, including humanitarian personnel. Immediately following the evacuation of UNSCOM personnel, US and UK bombing of Iraq commenced, in an operation dubbed Desert Fox. For four days, US and UK forces conducted roughly 650 air strikes against approximately 100 Iraqi targets, with the US launching 400 cruise missiles.[55] The strikes appeared to do little to 'degrade' Iraqi WMD capacity (President Clinton's stated objective), and even less to change Saddam Hussein's behavior. As Anthony Cordesman noted, the Iraqi President had again shown the world that he could survive US attack.[56]

6.2 Goodbye UNSCOM

UNSCOM now became a political football. Attacks on Butler by France, Russia, and China grew unrelenting. With little support for the bombing campaign among UN Member States, the United States was now in a weak position to defend UNSCOM effectively. Ultimately, Washington sacrificed UNSCOM in order to protect the sanctions regime, which it saw as more vital to its ability to contain the Iraqi government's capacity to destabilize its region.[57]

Indications soon emerged in the US media of a concerted effort by the United States to use UNSCOM cover for US intelligence activities targeted at the Iraqi regime. These revelations, while eliciting little surprise from those at the UN informed of the presence among UNSCOM staff of intelligence personnel from several countries, nevertheless seemed to shock much of the UN community. The assertions were flatly denied by US spokespeople, but subsequent leaks only reinforced the credibility of the allegations. UN staff and the US administration were soon trading brickbats over this use of UN cover.[58] Butler defended UNSCOM's record with panache and apparent conviction: 'I am entirely satisfied with the answers I received [from Washington]. I do not believe that the US piggybacked on us.' However, Scott Ritter claimed that a US listening device that Butler had ordered him to install in Baghdad had been under Washington's complete control from July to December 1998: 'What Butler did was allow the United States to take over.'[59] It was left to the *Wall Street Journal Europe* to question the extent to which successive crises in relations with Iraq and the year-end bombing campaign were designed to detract attention from President Clinton's travails in the Monica Lewinsky case:

> When convenient, the reports of UNSCOM inspectors were ignored by the US. At other times, the reports appeared to be geared to the Clinton Administration's political needs, which compromised Mr. Butler. The events that led up to the Desert Fox bombings looked suspiciously as if they had been orchestrated to delay an impeachment vote in the US Congress.[60]

6.2.1 *Scapegoating Annan?*

Typically, relations between Annan and Washington were an immediate casualty: 'US officials in the Clinton Administration and on Capitol Hill said the incident was likely to damage relations, already chilly, between Washington and Annan.'[61] A senior State Department official was quoted on January 30 as stating:

What Washington expects of Mr. Annan is that he start each sentence on Iraq by accusing Saddam Hussein of being the direct cause of all suffering by Iraqi civilians. If he does not, Washington will not be able to work with him, or, by extension, with the UN.[62]

A widely read *Washington Post* column seemed to convey the city's conventional wisdom:

Annan's people misjudge the temper of Washington. 'Their undermining of UNSCOM and economic sanctions will drive people who want to clear up the problem of US back dues and other problems into the confrontation camp and provoke a serious US–UN crisis' a senior administration aide said to me.[63]

This administration view was echoed elsewhere:

Mr. Annan ... brought into his expanding role great charm and wit, and a clear concept of how to handle Saddam—with diligent appeasement. By himself, he has become Saddam's greatest single asset at the UN.[64]

The Clinton administration's penchant for scapegoating the UN was once again on display.[65] That Annan was stoutly defended in the rest of the world for pointing to the consequences of any US spying under UN cover may have further excited the US administration's irritation.[66] Once it became clear that allegations of US intelligence gathering for its own account were true, the editorial line of some leading US publications, including traditional strong supporters of the UN, shifted to justifying the US practice. The *Los Angeles Times* opined: 'Iraqi behavior has simply allowed no alternative to using every intelligence means possible to uncover and destroy its provocative and threatening secret arms program.'[67] However, some US news media belatedly admitted that the UN had fallen victim to shoddy treatment by Washington. On March 2, 1999, the *Washington Post* editorialized:

It turns out that American intelligence used UN cover to conduct a secret, Americans-only operation spying on Iraqi communications. All this took place while the United States was denying Iraqi charges that it was exploiting the agreed-upon UN inspections for purposes of American espionage.... What happened is not a moral crime, but it is a blunder.[68]

Annan meanwhile moved to calm the very troubled waters between Washington and the UN headquarters. In a speech to the Council on Foreign Relations, he argued that the Secretary-General's office cannot be seen as serving the 'narrow interests of any one state or group of states'.[69] Rather plaintively, he argued that as Secretary-General of the UN he could only seek to achieve his ends peacefully:

> Whatever means I have employed in my efforts in dealing with Iraq, my ends have never been in question: full compliance with all relevant Security Council resolutions. ... By precedent, by principle, by charter and by duty, I am bound to seek these ends through peaceful means.[70]

In fact, the Secretary-General's emphasis on peaceful means here contrasts starkly with his assertion in February 1998 that it was diplomacy 'backed by force' (or rather, its threat) that led to the signing of the MOU with Iraq on access to 'Presidential sites'.[71] Annan's discourse more broadly has veered between implied sympathy for the use of force in pursuit of humanitarian goals in extreme circumstances (as in his statement following the launch of the NATO campaign against Serb forces in Kosovo) and adherence to the primacy in international law of the UN Charter's provisions on authorization of the use of force.[72]

John Ruggie, of Harvard University, then a Special Adviser to Annan, drew attention to a comment by Annan to the Council after his return from Baghdad:

> 'No promises of peace and no policy of patience can be without limits'.... These are hardly the words of an appeaser....[73]

Throughout all of this, Hussein must have watched from the sidelines with something approaching glee. The unparalleled unity of the Gulf War coalition was now a thing of the past. In its place lay a deep and abiding division within the ranks of the Council, and even between America and the candidate it promoted for Secretary-General in 1996.

6.2.2 *Spillover?*

The bitterness generated within the Security Council by events pertaining to Iraq spilled over into an unrelated item on the Security Council's agenda: Kosovo. The split within the P-5 on the unilateral use of force, raised but not settled by Operation Desert Fox, arose even more starkly over the prospect of NATO military action against Serbia to put an end to its depredations in Kosovo. Russia, strongly averse to use of force against

Serbia by NATO, overplayed its hand, threatening to veto any Council authorization of such force. The failure to pursue seriously the option of mediation by the Secretary-General was at least in part attributable to the deterioration in relations between Washington and Annan. It was also due to the conviction held by many NATO governments that dilatory diplomatic tactics, following the 'last chance' Rambouillet conference, could only serve to allow a slow-motion repetition of earlier Serb aggression in the Balkans—which disastrous Western and UN tactics had failed to stop until convincing force was applied by the Croatian armed forces and by NATO air-strikes. In part due to its frustration with the Security Council's performance on Iraq, Washington was increasingly lionizing NATO and its 'out of region' capabilities in the run-up to the April 1999 NATO Summit.[74]

In spite of Russia's veto threat at the UN, NATO launched massive air-strikes against Serb targets. In a further humiliation for Moscow, two days later the Council failed to uphold a Russian condemnation of NATO action, with only three members (China, Namibia, and Russia) supporting the Russian view—and twelve voting against. The G-8 (including Russia as well as the major Western powers) then negotiated agreement on May 6 on a face-saving, UN-led, postconflict transitional administration for Kosovo.[75] The UN played no role in these negotiations, with Annan reduced to commenting from the sidelines. Strategic leaks in Washington invited Annan to butt out of negotiations: 'The United States told the United Nations ... not to meddle in the Kosovo peace talks....'[76] While the desire to keep channels to Milosevic clear and unencumbered was understandable, and the risk of mixed signals through multiple negotiators very real, the message was couched in characteristically dismissive tones.

The G-8 proposal was adopted by a wide majority in SCR 1244 on June 10, 1999. The UN was given the lead role in civilian administration of Kosovo while significant roles were reserved for NATO (military enforcement through KFOR), the European Union (economic reconstruction) and the Organization of Security and Cooperation in Europe (rule of law and human rights issues) without the UN having had any opportunity to shape any of these roles or prepare for its major new responsibilities in a timely way. On the one hand, the UN seemed resentful that it had been called upon to play a role more thankless than that of NATO in restoring order and civilian life to Kosovo. On the other, Annan had signaled that he wanted a lead role for the UN in running the Kosovo protectorate (presumably if only as a means of reasserting the UN's centrality in the international system and overcoming the embarrassment over its marginalization in the search for an outcome to the conflict).[77] While the UN's umbrella role in Kosovo was championed by some European states, Canada, and Russia, it rapidly attracted criticism in Washington for its pace of police deployment into Kosovo.[78]

A portent of things to come for the UN on Iraq in 2003? Damned if it did, and damned if it did not, events in Iraq in 1998–9 and in Kosovo in 1999 pointed to a rising tide of disenchantment with the UN in Washington.

6.3 Hello UNMOVIC

Desert Fox, prickly Council member relations, and recriminations about the politicization of UNSCOM combined to encourage Baghdad to launch a full offensive campaign of defiance and obstruction, making UNSCOM weapons inspections increasingly difficult. Faced with rapidly deteriorating working conditions and little support at home, Butler decided to close shop. On January 12, 1999, he suspended flights over Iraq of US U-2 aircraft gathering information for UNSCOM. The Commission was now history.[79]

On January 13, France proposed the replacement of UNSCOM by a 'renewed control commission' that would 'have its independence ensured and its professionalism strengthened'. With the US and UK increasingly isolated and other UN Member States now eager to map out a new strategy, hints soon emerged of new flexibility in Washington on modalities for the sanctions regime and of a recognition that UNSCOM was doomed. Ekéus describes the situation as follows:

> The Clinton administration's policy vis-à-vis Iraq was inconsistent and hesitant. The French and the Russians were going full speed ahead for ending the inspection activities, no matter what. The British were confused and the Chinese were lying low.[80]

Seymour Hersh captured the essence of the outcome: 'The result of the American hijacking of the UN's intelligence activities was that Saddam survived but UNSCOM did not.'[81] It was now imperative for Council members to devise a strategy to recover from this institutional shock and to reach agreement on further steps. On January 30, the Security Council established three panels chaired by Brazilian ambassador, Celso Amorim, to provide a 'comprehensive review' on UN approaches to Iraq (see Chapter 5).[82] The French position was that Iraq had been effectively disarmed to the extent possible (the French having asserted that complete disarmament would be impossible to prove) and that, in these circumstances, the maintenance of sanctions could no longer be justified. The Russians hewed closely to the French line. On the other hand, bereft of any new ideas, and with an administration edging into 'lame duck' status and increasingly distracted by domestic politics (not least the Monica Lewinsky affair), Washington continued to insist that sanctions be maintained. Privately, it admitted that the nuclear sector at least appeared to present few short-term risks.[83]

The relevant panel report, transmitted to Annan on March 27, 1999, concluded that 'although important elements still have to be resolved, the bulk of Iraq's proscribed weapons programs has been eliminated'. It nevertheless endorsed the continuation of inspections-based monitoring as the best way to guard against rearmament.[84] With respect to UN machinery, the report reflected concerns over undue influence of intelligence organizations over UNSCOM and advocated more neutral arrangements under which the UN inspections unit accepted intelligence information but did not share its own information with intelligence agencies.

The United Kingdom worked hard to bridge Washington's views with those of other Security Council members in order to create a successor unit. The French suggested a multilayered approach. First, they advocated continuing the IAEA role in monitoring Iraqi nuclear development. Second, they suggested requiring Iraq to join the Chemical Weapons Convention, and receive monitoring from its Secretariat, just then being established in The Hague. Biological weapons posed a dicier challenge: there was, as yet, no satisfactory international agreement either prohibiting them or governing their use. Furthermore, they are exceptionally difficult to detect and monitor. In the words of one French diplomat: 'Three pots of yogurt in a basement can be developed into biological weapons with the right additives and know-how.'[85] Further control would be exerted through the escrow accounts into which the proceeds of Iraqi oil sales are deposited.

The United States seemed content to do without inspections, as long as sanctions remained in place. For other P-5 members, the exact reverse arrangement was preferable.[86] Relations between the Permanent Members on Iraq were sufficiently frayed, and their views on the Amorim reports sufficiently divergent that it was not until December 1999 that they were able to agree on alternative arrangements, enshrined in Resolution 1284.[87]

Resolution 1284 established a new body, the UN Monitoring, Verification, and Inspection Commission (UNMOVIC), with important structural differences to UNSCOM: the recruitment, status, training, and behavior of its personnel were to be consistent with UN standards and rules on impartiality and professionalism; control over UNMOVIC was given to a college of commissioners; and there was to be only one-way intelligence traffic.[88] In an important affirmation of the Council's intention that sanctions should be temporary, paragraph 33 of the Resolution held out the Council's 'intention' to suspend sanctions in the event of adequate Iraqi cooperation, while paragraph 38 indicated that the Council intended 'to act in accordance with the relevant provisions of SCR 687 (1991) on the termination of prohibitions'. Although this text was approved, the approach failed to achieve broad consensus. When the text was put to a vote on December 17, 1999, a year after Operation Desert Fox, China, France, Russia, and Malaysia abstained.[89]

In a clear nod to the Amorim panel's recommendations, UNMOVIC inspectors were to be recruited independently and work for the United Nations (UNSCOM inspectors had often been 'on loan' from their home governments, raising questions about divided loyalties). This staffing independence was secured by a 0.8 percent share of funds raised by the OFF Program—which, despite the small fraction, totaled roughly $100 million per year.[90] The Secretary-General now needed to identify a chair of UNMOVIC less in the mould of the confrontational Richard Butler and more in that of Rolf Ekéus. In fact, Ekéus's name briefly circulated, but France and Russia made clear he would not be acceptable to them, perhaps perceiving him as having worked too closely with the Americans during his years with UNSCOM. In late January, the Secretary-General nominated and the Security Council confirmed Hans Blix, the former head of the IAEA, like Ekéus a Swede. Blix had known a good deal about Iraq at the IAEA.

The mere fact that all five of the permanent members could agree on his nomination in the poisonous atmosphere that enveloped many of their discussions on Iraq suggested that he might prove both inoffensive and ineffective. But he confounded such expectations. While understated, and largely invisible to the public for nearly three years after his appointment, in the crucible of fierce international pressure and media attention from November 2002 to March 2003 he proved committed to his mandate, independent in his views (over time infuriating several camps within the international community), cool under attack, and possessed of a dry sense of humor.

The IAEA, under the terms of Resolution 1284, remained responsible for nuclear inspections and certification. Blix's successor at the IAEA, the tough-minded and widely admired Mohamed El Baradei, was thus to become his counterpart in much of the drama of late 2002 and early 2003. ElBaradei, an Egyptian, helpfully undermined any impression that the UN inspections were an all-Western operation indentured to the Americans.

Baghdad, believing itself to be in a position of greater strength than several years previously, did not accept the terms of Resolution 1284 and continued to hope that French and Russian influence within the Council might achieve the suspension of sanctions without further significant compromises on its own part. At the same time, it may have considered the concept of the 'suspension' of sanctions, a further indication that sanctions would never be entirely lifted.[91] On February 27, 2001, after discussions with Kofi Annan, Iraqi Foreign Minister Mohammed Saeed Al Sahaf referred to UNMOVIC as a 'non-entity' and to Blix as a 'detail'.[92]

In his memoir of his years with UNMOVIC, Blix takes pride in his systematic approach to assembling a new, independent, and highly professional team at the service (and in the pay) of the UN. This team, operating as a skeleton staff while steeping itself in research and contingency planning on how to enlarge and deploy rapidly should the opportunity arise, remained barred from inspection roles in Iraq until after the adoption of Resolution 1441 in November 2002.[93] During these fallow months, Blix communicated regularly with Security Council members, including in their capitals. Yet he took careful steps to ensure UNMOVIC's independence from the P-5, particularly the United States:

> When I began to organize UNMOVIC all of the P-5 accepted that we should be independent. Thus the US accepted without a problem that I would abolish the post of Deputy Executive Chairman (which had always been held by an American) . . . and no one objected to our decision no longer to use Gateway—the US naval base in Bahrein—for briefing and debriefing inspectors.[94]

All the same, during a meeting in Washington on August 22, 2000, Albright and Berger made clear to Blix that Washington hewed to a restrictive interpretation of Resolution 1284. This contrasted with the French and Russians who wished Annan and UNMOVIC to explore with the Iraqis arrangements for suspending sanctions as Iraq complied with 'key' disarmament issues—thus seeking to create a carrot to supplement the stick of sanctions.[95] Washington's pressure on Iraq did not relent; the endgame was nigh.

6.4 Conclusions

6.4.1 *Inspections Calculus*

Disarmament controlled by inspections and monitoring was the cornerstone of the vision set out for Iraq by SCR 687 in 1991. Weapons inspections were the administrative mechanism for the verification of Iraqi disarmament, with sanctions and the threat of force providing the incentive for Iraq to disarm. But for over a decade, Saddam Hussein successfully obscured the degree to which actual disarmament had been achieved, an uncertainty assessed very differently by Paris and Washington. Although the inspections-plus-sanctions approach did, ultimately, turn out to have ensured substantive disarmament, the United States eventually abandoned the uncertainties of regulatory pressure for the more categorical and immediate outcomes of military intervention.

The fact that UNMOVIC was necessary shows just how uncertain the results of UNSCOM's efforts were. In many ways, the inspections calculus was weighted in Hussein's favor from the start. As Pascal Teixeira da Silva, a senior French negotiator has noted:

> The very logic of Resolution 687 is that Iraq declares, discloses and provides evidence, then UNSCOM and the IAEA verify. It requires not only Iraq's acceptance of the rules but also Iraq's active cooperation with these two bodies. Unfortunately Iraq never abided by its obligations in good faith, instead adopting a reverse logic: UNSCOM and the IAEA search, then Iraq explains.[96]

To adapt US Secretary of Defence Donald Rumsfeld's famous phrase, Iraq needed only to ensure 'the absence of evidence', while the inspectors had to produce 'evidence of absence' to satisfy the United States. The architects of SCR 687 assumed that Iraq would swiftly disarm—the continuation of the Resolution 660 sanctions was at first envisaged as a temporary measure. But Iraq's failure to cooperate led to those sanctions becoming entrenched.[97] From that, in turn, Saddam Hussein reaped public relations benefits and the opportunity to create black market and other rents for the regime. He also benefited greatly for a time from the resulting disunity among the P-5.

It is now clear that the controversy and multiple deceptions Saddam Hussein generated with respect to Iraq's WMD programs blinded many analysts, including professional intelligence analysts, to the remarkable success of the inspections-plus-sanctions approach in containing Iraq's military machine. Due in part to Saddam Hussein's deliberately erratic behavior, and to *idées fixes* in certain capitals, what the inspectors could not find caused more concern than what they could, contributing to a sense of crisis among decision-makers. As a result of Iraqi noncooperation,

> the inspection bodies and members of the Security Council became suspicious and more demanding. The more they doubted the sincerity of Iraq, the narrower was the acceptable margin of uncertainty. But this dynamic could lead to an endless process.[98]

The US and UK insistence on the continuation of sanctions and inspections seemed increasingly to resemble 'tunnel vision'. That sat uncomfortably with an increasing acceptance by other members—reflected in the Amorim Report—that:

> some uncertainty is inevitable in any country-wide technical verification process which aims to prove the absence of readily concealable objects or activities. The extent to which such uncertainty is acceptable is a policy judgment. Both UNSCOM and IAEA have therefore been adopting a pragmatic approach which assumes that 100% of verification may be unattainable.[99]

Uncertainty was to take on a different weight relative to risk when the possibility of transnational non-state terrorism was added to the equations. As we saw in Chapter 5, President Clinton recognized this changed calculus as early as 1998.[100]

Even such worries do not fully explain why the United States and the United Kingdom were unwilling to offer the partial lifting of sanctions as a reward for partial Iraqi compliance with Security Council resolutions. Russian and French diplomats, among others, repeatedly encouraged the adoption of such an approach, believing that the prospect of eased sanctions would entice Iraq to comply with monitoring.[101] But the United States and the United Kingdom rejected the proposition. The rigidity in the US/UK position probably negated the most positive potential effect of sanctions: that of inducing negotiations, along with a possibly large degree of compliance and compromise by the Iraqi regime.[102] The contrast to the approach taken over Libya, where the United States and the United Kingdom adopted a more flexible approach, compromised their positions, and offered incentives to Libya through access to the economic fruits of engagement with the European Union, achieving Libyan renunciation of a nascent nuclear weapons program in December 2003, are stark.[103] The lessons for handling Iran, North Korea, and other countries are many and complex.

The beauty of calculus lies in its instrumentalism. Its symbols stand in the place of real numbers, expressing generic relationships. In some ways, there was a similar kind of instrumentalism at play in the attitudes of the different players involved in inspections policy vis-à-vis Iraq. Iraq used all the opportunities presented to it by SCRs to stall, evade, and manipulate the inspections process. But equally, the United States and the United Kingdom treated those same SCRs instrumentally, using the weapons inspection process as an instrument of espionage, of hostile intrusion, and as a trigger for military action. For the Americans, even UNSCOM itself was a legitimate instrument of national policy, serving as cover for US intelligence gathering, and perhaps also for the fomenting of a coup attempt inside Iraq.

Nor were they alone. Russia, France, and China used the inspections process as a vessel for their own strategic objectives, particularly financial ones. Russian and French industry were displeased with US dominance of reconstruction contracts in Kuwait after 1991, and China had an increasing interest in energy security in the Gulf as its economy boomed through the 1990s.[104] These countries' major oil companies pre-positioned themselves for the lifting of sanctions against Iraq by signing 'agreements in principle' for oil development that did not formally break the Security Council's embargo on signing new contracts with Iraq, but would instead become operative on the termination of sanctions. These moves cast doubt on the motivations behind the insistence by these P-5 members that sanctions against Iraq be lifted. A related matter was Russia's reported request for 'flexibility' from UNSCOM, so that sanctions might be lifted and Russia's $7 billion debt from Iraq be discharged.[105] All of these doubts were further fueled when, later, serious allegations about French and Russian involvement in the corruption of the OFF Program emerged (see Chapter 5).

In sum, *all* of the P-5 players treated the inspections instrumentally. But this process could not, ultimately, produce the convergence of the interests at play. What it makes clear, though, is that the Security Council, and its organs, remains for the P-5 a resource to be used to further their own interests. When, instead, it seems to represent an obstacle to those interests, it can be sidelined, as it was in the G-8 assumption of control of the Kosovo peace process in 1999, and again over Iraq in 2003.

6.4.2 *Balancing UN Objectives*

As weapons inspections and sanctions became increasingly permanent, difficult questions about how those mechanisms should allow for the nonsecurity objectives of the UN—such as human rights and human welfare—came to the fore. It is hardly surprising that Annan chose to be attentive not only to the United States and the United Kingdom, who championed this enforcement aspect of the UN's mandates in Iraq, but also to other voices in the Security Council and in the General Assembly emphasizing the UN's role as a humanitarian guardian. UNSCOM was, from Annan's perspective, but one of many UN agencies and programs in Iraq. Several other UN units on the ground disagreed strenuously with both UNSCOM's mandate and the manner in which it was being implemented. While the Security Council looms supreme in its sphere of competence, other UN actors can and do challenge its strategies when they interfere with their own developmental, humanitarian, or social mandates.

The only way to ensure that the various UN mandates can be properly balanced is through careful design and coordination. It seems to have been a mistake to establish UNSCOM with an executive chair whose mandate did not require him to reconcile the purposes of UNSCOM with the larger purposes of the UN. To some extent the problem was institutional. Perhaps creating UNSCOM as an organ of the Security Council substantively independent of the Secretary-General made it inevitable that there would be both institutional clashes between UNSCOM and the UN Secretariat, and individual clashes between Butler and Annan's staff. Many of these same issues arise in relation to the concept of 'integrated' peace operations. Even more directly, the Council will be forced to balance the humanitarian needs of civilian populations against the military aspirations of their rulers if it resorts to sanctions against Iran or North Korea. Again, careful design will be key to ensuring than an inspections-plus-sanctions regime effectively targets those leaders, without allowing the costs to be displaced onto the civilian population.

At the same time, the Weapons Inspector role of the Council and its subsidiaries highlight the importance of key management personalities in ensuring that the diverse members of the UN family work together. Both Rolf Ekéus and Hans Blix seem, through a low-key but tough approach, to have achieved more than Butler, with his publicly more aggressive posture. That said, Butler remains a hero to many in Washington, where Blix is still widely reviled.

6.4.3 *A permanent Weapons Inspection Role?*

Lessons are learned from time to time at the UN, contrary to conventional wisdom. In setting up UNMOVIC, note was taken of the Amorim report and some of UNSCOM's more obvious flaws were not repeated. But in the next chapter, the limitations of any such weapons inspection process are explored. One pressing issue, particularly in the context of Iran and North Korea, is the question of whether a permanent analog of UNMOVIC may be needed in the Security Council's arsenal.[106] Hans Blix has suggested that while there may not be a brisk demand for challenge inspections [as opposed to inspections by invitation of the inspected state], a small standing group under the Security Council would be very useful. It would not be an intelligence body. There is plenty of stuff in open sources. However, it would be as objective as you can be. It would thus be of interest for Great Powers to check how their intelligence compares and it could help the [non-permanent 10], who mostly do not have a great deal of information of their own. In addition, it would have a roster of inspectors and could 'surge' quickly, if needed.[107]

France has been the major proponent of making UNMOVIC 'permanent' in some form, and the fact that it was UNMOVIC that identified the alarming disappearance of dual-use items after the US invasion points to its continued usefulness;[108] the United States and China have openly opposed the idea, citing unnecessary costs (and privately preferring ad hoc arrangements they can more easily control). Other Council members including Russia have expressed concern about the purposes of such an institution. The Council's inability, in spite of much discussion, to agree on any successor organization, permanent or temporary, universal in mandate or more crisis-specific, by the end of 2005, is sobering, while the remnants of UNMOVIC are allowed to wither.

6.4.4 *Peace Through Regulation*

The previous chapter argued that the growing resort to sanctions in the 1990s can be read as a movement toward a regulatory approach to international peace and security, relying on the Council to establish binding standards, which are then implemented, monitored, and enforced by subsidiary administrative apparatus. The inspections process—with its list of dual-use goods, Council texts containing the molecular structures of prohibited chemicals, and its meticulous inspection and remote monitoring of potential WMD sites in Iraq—was the other major manifestation of this turn in the Council's practice in Iraq. Iraq was a laboratory for these techniques, from the level of scientific approaches to inspections through to the institutional arrangements used to organize such a regulatory approach.[109] Since those experiments, the approach has been replicated in a number of other areas: the development of sophisticated, individualized sanctions regimes and accompanying administrative apparatus to monitor their enforcement and assess their effects; the establishment of the counter-terrorism and counter-proliferation regimes under Resolutions 1373 and 1540; increasing resort to Expert Panels and ad hoc investigative commissions; and perhaps even in the use of individual criminal sanctions administered through ad hoc criminal tribunals under the Security Council's mandate. Given this increasing importance of the regulatory approach to international peace and security in the Council's practice, it is worth considering some lessons from the inspections process.

First, SCRs may not always provide a sound basis for administrative control. The creative ambiguity embedded in the language of SCR 687 and subsequent Council resolutions was often designed mainly to foster unity (at least outwardly), despite actual divergences in opinion and interests. Ambiguous language opens the door to conflicting interpretation, as was so fatefully to prove the case with the notion of the 'serious consequences' of Resolution 1441 of November 2002. This ambiguity, so crucial to diplomatic drafting, is a weak basis for the creation of effective and authoritative administrative regimes, only deferring submerged differences for debate at a later stage. That debate will often manifest itself through attempts to control and influence the administrative discretion of regulatory delegates and agents, as occurred with both UNSCOM and the OFF Program. What begins as an attempt to establish independent, expert regulatory capacity quickly becomes infected with politicking. The problem is even clearer where the agents authorized to implement the regulatory mandate are not independent third parties, but the principals themselves. This was repeatedly the case in Iraq, where the United States and the United Kingdom would offer one interpretation of a Resolution, arguing the existence of a 'material breach' or that 'severest' or 'serious consequences' authorized Member States to take enforcement action, while other Member States offered a very different interpretation. Such divergences serve only to undermine the legitimacy of a regulatory regime, and with it, the authority of the Council.[110]

Regulatory regimes relying on administrative enforcement can only be efficient and effective if they feature clear chains of command and responsibility. The confusion over the ultimate source of authority over UNSCOM—was it the Security Council, the Secretary-General, or ... the US?—demonstrated the dangers of inadequate clarity on this point. Part of the problem was that the Council stumbled into this new administratively-intense approach through SCR 687; it was never expected to provide a semi-permanent regime, but a transition to a stable outcome. Rolf Ekéus comments that

> UNSCOM enjoyed exceptional political support in the Security Council up 'til summer 1997. In 1998 the unity among the P-5 broke. Whether this was a consequence of Security Council patience running out, UNSCOM's shortcomings or of a clever Iraqi policy of spreading confusion and division in the ranks of the Security Council members is difficult to judge. At least one lesson can be learned, namely that 9 years is too long a period for the Council to maintain the 'pressure-cooker' attention that is required to sustain a technically and politically complex, constantly challenged operation like the UNSCOM one.[111]

Additionally, as argued at the conclusion of Chapter 5, administrative mechanisms need to be independent of the parties that set them up, and that are to be affected by their exercise of administrative discretion. All too often, UNSCOM did not demonstrate that independence, and relied excessively on material assistance from the United States.[112]

The regulatory approach forces exactly the kind of impartial, judicious examination of evidence, which is routine in scientific inquiry and the administration of justice—but historically alien to politics, and the decision to go to war. The Council may be no better equipped today than it was fifteen years ago to oversee complex subsidiary machinery, much of it relying on experts for analysis and operations—or to engage in this impartial assessment of evidence.

6.4.5 *Fleeting Favor in Washington*

Washington had been chief among Kofi Annan's backers as a candidate for Secretary-General in 1996, blocking re-election of Boutros Boutros-Ghali and using its full diplomatic weight to ensure Annan's election. Washington was tired of Boutros-Ghali's cerebral but autocratic approach to the job, deemed insufficiently sensitive to Washington's requirements. American antipathy toward Boutros Boutros-Ghali intensified after the October 1993 Mogadishu fiasco for which Washington unfairly blamed the UN. Boutros-Ghali's efforts to set the record straight enraged the White House. His other displays of independence, his arrogance, and his inability to communicate well with the American public and political world in English were all held against him.[113]

Annan enjoyed broad support among Member States who admired his tenure as Under-Secretary-General for Peacekeeping Operations from 1991 to 1996. The United States had reason to be pleased with its choice early on. Annan made clear that he shared and wished to advance internationally 'values' shared by Washington, championing human rights and humanitarian action to a greater extent than had Boutros-Ghali. His low-key charm and discreet but real charisma helped usher in a more civil tone in relations between the United States and the UN, at a time when the US Congress was refusing to pay American dues. Senator Jesse Helms, Chairman of the Senate Foreign Relations Committee and a sharp antagonist of Boutros-Ghali, reacted positively to Annan's efforts to improve perceptions of the UN within the US legislature. Prodded by US Secretary of State Madeleine Albright, with whom he had established a working relationship, Helms soon helped craft a bill to pay off a large amount of the US arrears to the UN.

But the events of 1998 and 1999, culminating in the implosion of UNSCOM, provided a taste of things to come for Annan in his relationship with Washington. If the United States and the United Kingdom wished to circumvent the Security Council, who was the Secretary-General to stand in their way?

The United States might have been expected to work hard to retain good relations with a UN Secretary-General universally seen as well-disposed toward it. But a poor choice of words by Annan on his return to New York from Baghdad in February 1998 and Saddam Hussein's repeated violations of his agreement with Annan were sufficient in Washington to cast the Secretary-General as an appeaser hostile to US interests. Annan's known reservations over Richard Butler's modus operandi were interpreted in Washington as an attack on its own policies. When detailed allegations of US spying against Iraq under UNSCOM cover came to light, Washington seems to have considered that the best defense would be a strong offense—against Annan, who became the target of a concerted administration campaign to discredit him. The UN, never particularly adept at 'spin', and the Secretary-General, notoriously unconfrontational by nature, were ill equipped to fight back. By the time allegations of US spying became irrefutable through the accumulation of damning leaks (mostly in Washington), the damage had been done. The administration had undermined the potential usefulness in Washington (and consequently some of the usefulness elsewhere) of a Secretary-General of its own choice.[114]

At the same time, Washington's irritation with Annan and his decision to stand his ground elicited a sympathetic response from the vast majority of other Member States who saw him cleaving to the impartiality that lies at the heart of his functions. This support was not insignificant, propelling Annan and the organization to the Nobel Peace Prize a year later. That upswing in Annan's fortunes, accompanied as it was by a thaw in relations with Washington was enough to secure him early re-election in 2001. Ultimately, though, it only proved a temporary respite before the resumption of the now consistent pattern of attacks from US sources on the Secretary-General and his institution, mostly centered on the Oil-for Food-scandals. In commenting on the sour grapes conveyed in Boutros Boutros-Ghali's autobiography, State Department Spokesman Jamie Rubin stated that Boutros-Ghali had neglected his core duty:

'smooth cooperation with the United States'.[115] At the time, it seemed fair to suppose Rubin's comment was made tongue-in-cheek; today, after a consistent pattern of attacks on Secretaries-General—even those it has itself picked and backed—that is far from clear. Washington definitely wants a secretary, not a general at the UN helm.

Beyond that, though, there is something deeply disquieting about the vicious personal attacks mounted time and again by Washington on international public servants whose views it dislikes or has found inconvenient. The unceremonious replacement of José Bustani as head of the Organization for the Prohibition of Chemical Weapons in a special session under extreme US pressure in July 2002, and the vigouros US campaign to oppose a third term for Mohammed El Baradei at the IAEA in 2005, smack of bullying.[116] The case against El Baradei was simple: 'Before the war, he upset [Washington] by declaring more or less that there was no evidence that Iraq had an active nuclear weapons program. After the war, he rubbed salt in the wound by being right.'[117] This is reasoning unbecoming for a great nation.

Annan and his key advisers do seem to have drawn conclusions from the events of February 1998. The risks of the Secretary-General himself conducting sensitive negotiations engaging the interests of key Member States rather than designating credible representatives to do so on his behalf became better understood. On many delicate issues to do with Iraq in 2003 and beyond he referred to trusted advisers such as Lakhdar Brahimi for this reason.

In covering the events chronicled here, the editorial pages of several US newspapers hewed disturbingly close to the Washington administration's line, seemingly suspending disbelief. Here, again, was a taste of things to come later in Iraq. While much reporting proved excellent, editorial bombast in support of what later proved to be misleading positions peddled by the administration (or segments thereof) already suggested in 1998 and 1999 both the depths of the UN's problems with US media opinion-makers (even those not inherently hostile to the organization), and editorial standards that seem to fall well below those achieved in countries whose media organizations are more skeptical of their governments' spin operations.

To note these pathologies is not to suggest anything singularly disturbing about US governance. Quite the contrary: checks and balances work well in the United States over time. Public debate is dynamic, democracy vibrant. US international leadership has mostly advanced global interests, sometimes spectacularly so, as during the twentieth century's two world wars. That said, the United States displays tremendous difficulty in managing equably its relations with international organizations (and sometimes their members), which has often damaged its international standing, never more so than in the circumstances examined in the next two chapters.[118]

Notes

1. See Richard Butler, *Talk* (September 1999), 198.
2. UN Security Council resolution 487, June 19, 1981.
3. See the excellent 1991 Human Rights Watch report on the Halabja tragedy and related events: 'Whatever Happened To The Iraqi Kurds?', March 11, 1991.
4. 'Vice President Honors Veterans of Korean War', *White House Office of the Press Secretary*, August 29, 2002.
5. James D. Cockayne, correspondence with the author, April 20, 2005.
6. Resolution 687, paras 22, 28.
7. Pascal Teixeira da Silva, 'Weapons of Mass Destruction: The Iraqi Case', in David M. Malone (ed.), *The UN Security Council from the Cold War to the 21st Century* (Boulder, CO: Lynne Rienner, 2004), 206.
8. Teixeira da Silva, 'Weapons of Mass Destruction', 206.
9. Teixeira da Silva, 'Weapons of Mass Destruction', 206.
10. Ekéus, after a stint as Swedish Ambassador in Washington, later became the OSCE High Commissioner for Minorities, succeeding Max van der Stoel—also earlier an actor in the Iraq saga. These appointments underscore the much greater role human rights have played in international relations in the post–Cold War world.
11. The 20 members of the Commission, from 20 Member States, were appointed by the Secretary-General, after consultation with the Security Council. See Bailey and Daws, *The Procedure of the UN Security Council*, 377.
12. Hiro, *Iraq: In the Eye of the Storm*, 98–9.
13. UN Security Council resolution 699, June 17, 1991.
14. Hiro, *Iraq: In the Eye of the Storm*, 99.
15. See Tim Trevan, *Saddam's Secrets: The Hunt for Iraq's Hidden Weapons* (London: HarperCollins, 1999), 103–9.
16. UN Security Council resolution 715, October 11, 1991.
17. UNSCOM used a range of visual, video, chemical, and temperature sensors to remotely monitor 150 sites throughout Iraq.
18. Resolution 949. See also the discussion of the French role in this episode in Chapter 4.
19. See Graham-Brown, *Sanctioning Saddam*, 84.
20. Hiro, *Iraq: In the Eye of the Storm*, 97.

21. See *Note [transmitting report on the status of the implementation of the Special Commission's plan for the ongoing monitoring and verification of Iraq's compliance with relevant parts of section C of Security Council resolution 687 (1991)]* (UN Security Council Document S/1995/864), October 11, 1995.
22. Astonishingly, Kamel returned to Iraq a few months later, perhaps relying on family connections for protection. He was dead within ten days.
23. See UN Security Council resolution 1051, March 27, 1996, and UN Security Council resolution 1060, June 12, 1996.
24. See Hiro, *Iraq: In the Eye of the Storm*, 81–8.
25. Resolution 1060.
26. Rolf Ekéus interview, May 28, 2005.
27. Rolf Ekéus interview, May 28, 2005.
28. Rolf Ekéus interview, May 28, 2005.
29. Rolf Ekéus interview, May 28, 2005.
30. In conversation with the author.
31. Madeleine Albright, 'Preserving Principle And Safeguarding Stability'.
32. Scott Ritter, *Endgame: Solving the Iraq Problem—Once and For All* (New York: Simon and Schuster, 1999), 190.
33. Steven Lee Myers, 'Clinton is Sending 2d Carrier to Gulf', *New York Times*, 15 November 1997, A1.
34. UN Security Council resolution 1137, November 12, 1997.
35. UN Security Council resolution 1134, October 23, 1997.
36. Presidential Statement, 'The situation between Iraq and Kuwait', UN Doc. S/PRST/1998/1, January 14, 1998.
37. John M. Goshko, 'Security Council Debate Reflects Continued Split on Iraq', *Washington Post*, December 19, 1997, A20.
38. Teixeira da Silva, 'Weapons of Mass Destruction', 210. The term seems to have originated within the ranks of the British Labour government. See Graham-Brown, *Sanctioning Saddam*, 87.
39. Hiro, *Iraq: In the Eye of the Storm*, 112.
40. Christopher S. Wren, 'Weapons Inspection Chief Tells of Iraqi Tricks', *New York Times*, January 27, 1998, 6.
41. Hiro, *Iraq: In the Eye of the Storm*, 114.
42. Martin Kettle, 'Iraq crisis: The debate: White House scores a PR own goal', *The Guardian*, February 19, 1998, 13.
43. Hiro, *Iraq: In the Eye of the Storm*, 116.
44. Hiro, *Iraq: In the Eye of the Storm*, 116.
45. The issuance of guidelines was disclosed to the media at the time by the UK Permanent Representative to the UN, John Weston: Laura Silber et al., 'UN Chief in Baghdad Mission', *Financial Times*, February 18, 1998, 1; see also John Weston, 'Books—Hidden Arms Still Within the Gates', *Financial Times*, May 27, 2000, 5. Butler erred in his own book—claiming that Annan had 'no specific

instructions': Richard Butler, *The Greatest Threat: Iraq, Weapons of Mass Destruction, and the Crisis of Global Security* (New York: PublicAffairs, 2000), 138.

46. *Letter dated 98/02/25 from the Secretary-General addressed to the President of the Security Council* (UN Security Council Document S/1998/166), February 27, 1998.
47. 'Reversing Course on Iraq', *Washington Post*, Editorial, February 26, 1998, A14.
48. James Traub, 'Kofi Annan's Next Test', *New York Times Magazine*, March 29, 1998, 46.
49. John M. Goshko, 'U.S. Says Questions Remain on Iraq Pact', *Washington Post*, February 25, 1998, A01.
50. Traub, 'Kofi Annan's Next Test'.
51. *Letter dated 98/03/27 from the Executive Chairman of the Special Commission established by the Secretary-General pursuant to paragraph 9 (b) (i) of Security Council resolution 687 (1991) addressed to the President of the Security Council* (UN Security Council Document S/1998/278), March 27, 1998.
52. *Letter dated 98/08/05 from the Executive Chairman of the Special Commission established by the Secretary-General pursuant to paragraph 9 (b) (i) of Security Council resolution 687 (1991) addressed to the President of the Security Council* (UN Security Council Document S/1998/719), August 5, 1998.
53. Barton Gellman, 'U.N. Team Downcast About Iraq Mission; Inspectors Note Eroded Authority', *Washington Post*, November 22, 1998, A01.
54. *Letter dated 98/12/15 from the Secretary-General addressed to the President of the Security Council* (UN Security Council Document S/1998/1172), December 15, 1998; see Christopher Hitchens, 'Weapons of Mass Distraction', *Vanity Fair*, March 1, 1999, 104. See also Ritter, *Endgame*, 195–6 discussing the daily coordination of Sandy Berger and Richard Butler in November and December 1998; and see Amin Saikal, 'Iraq, UNSCOM and the US: A UN Debacle?', *Australian Journal of International Affairs* 53/3 (1999).
55. See Tom Clancy with Tony Zinni and Tony Koltz, *Battle Ready* (New York: G.P. Putnam's Sons, 2004).
56. See Tim Weiner, 'U.S. Long View on Iraq: Patience in Containing the Ever-Deadlier Hussein', *New York Times*, January 3, 1999, 10.
57. Confidential interviews in Washington, January 1999.
58. Most of the US media unquestioningly took Washington's side in the dispute, arguing that US ends justified the UN means.
59. Cameron Stewart, 'Butler: I Never Served US Interests', *The Australian*, 11 January 1999, 8. Ritter's revelations (and speculations) can be found in greater detail in *Endgame*. An insightful review by Brian Urquhart ('How not to Fight a Dictator', *The New York Review of Books* 46/8, May 6, 1999, 25–29) places Ritter's material in context. Charles Duelfer, the American UNSCOM Deputy Chairman, later famous for his 2004 report detailing corruption in the Oil-for-Food Program, was sanguine on where weapons inspectors were to be found:

'When we ask for good non-proliferation people, where do they come from? . . . The Red Cross doesn't have chemical weapons experts.' See Barbara Crossette, 'Reports of Spying Dim Outlook for Inspections', *New York Times*, January 8, 1999, 8.

60. 'Goodbye, UNSCOM', *Wall Street Journal Europe*, Editorial, January 12, 1999, 10.
61. Colum Lynch, 'US Spying Goals in Iraq Called Difficult', *Boston Globe*, January 7, 1999.
62. Author's translation, Afsané Bassir-Pour, 'Le secrétaire général de l'ONU est attaqué sur son role au Rwanda et face à l'Iraq', *Le Monde*, February 1, 1999.
63. Jim Hoagland, 'Time to Face the Super-Thug Alone', *Washington Post*, January 8, 1999, A21.
64. A. M. Rosenthal, 'The Carpet of Contempt', *New York Times*, Editorial, January 8, 1999, 19. The title of his *New York Times* column on January 15, 1999 aptly sums up his view of Annan's approach to Iraq: 'The UN Suicide Road', *New York Times*, Editorial, January 15, 1999, 23.
65. This penchant was most evident following the deaths of 18 US soldiers in Mogadishu on October 3–4, 1993, while under US command and control on an operation aimed at hunting down war-lord Mohamad Farah Aideed, neither authorized nor pre-cleared by UN authorities. Much of the quality US media had played along.
66. See 'UNSCOM Scandal', *Nation* (Islamabad), Editorial, January 8, 1999; 'UN as US Spy—surprise?', *HindustanTimes.com*, Editorial, January 8, 1999; 'Stepping over the Line', *Japan Times*, Editorial, January 11, 1999.
67. 'Justified Spying', *Los Angeles Times*, Editorial, January 12, 1999, B6; see also Amos Perlmutter, 'What if UNSCOM Was Used?', *Washington Times*, January 12, 1999, A13.
68. 'Under UN Cover', *Washington Post*, Editorial, March 3, 1999, A22.
69. Kofi A. Annan, 'Walking the International Tightrope', *New York Times*, Editorial, January 19, 1999, 19.
70. Annan, 'Walking the International Tightrope'.
71. At a press conference in Baghdad, February 23, 1998, Annan said: 'You can do a lot with diplomacy, but of course you can do a lot more with diplomacy backed up by firmness and force.'
72. On March 24, 1999, Annan stated: 'It is indeed tragic that diplomacy has failed, but there are times when the use of force may be legitimate in the pursuit of peace.'
73. John G. Ruggie, 'Kofi Annan's Goals on Iraq', *Washington Post*, Editorial, January 18, 1999, A23.
74. Dana H. Allin, *NATO's Balkan Interventions*, Adelphi Paper 347 (London: International Institute for Strategic Studies, 2002).
75. Paul Heinbecker has presented an insider's account of this G-8 process in 'Kosovo', in Malone, *The UN Security Council: From the Cold War to the 21st Century*.

76. Ben Barber, 'U.S. asks U.N. to implement, not broker, peace deal', *Washington Times*, May 14, 1999.
77. See *Report of the Secretary-General on the United Nations Interim Administration Mission in Kosovo* (UN Security Council Document S/1999/779), July 12, 1999 on the Secretary-General's approach to implementing SCR 1244.
78. Eric Schmitt, 'U.N. Drags Feet in Kosovo, Pentagon Leaders Declare', *New York Times*, July 21, 1999, 10.
79. Butler's term was up in late June 1999. Earlier that month, the Council on Foreign Relations in New York announced that he would be joining it for a period as a diplomat-in-residence.
80. Rolf Ekéus interview, May 28, 2005.
81. Seymour M. Hersh, 'Saddam's Best Friend', *New Yorker* 75/6, April 5, 1999.
82. Teixeira da Silva, 'Weapons of Mass Destruction', 212.
83. See David M. Malone, 'Goodbye UNSCOM: A Sad Tale in US-UN Relations', *Global Governance*, 30/4 (1999).
84. *Letter dated 99/03/27 from the Chairman of the panels established pursuant to the note by the President of the Security Council of 30 January 1999 (S/1999/100) addressed to the President of the Security Council* (UN Security Council Document S/1999/356) March 30, 1999.
85. Confidential interview with the author, December 2000.
86. Butler quotes French diplomat Jean de Gliniasty as concluding in December 1998: 'Of the choices available, it would be better to continue some arms-control monitoring in Iraq without sanctions rather than to retain sanctions with no monitoring'. See Butler, *The Greatest Threat*, 200.
87. UN Security Council resolution 1284, December 17, 1999. Amorim's tenure at the UN was cut short in mid-1999 when he was abruptly shifted, in mid-Security Council term, to Brazil's Geneva Mission, occasioning UN corridor chat suggesting that American complaints on his panel conclusions had convinced Brasilia that it needed a new pair of hands in New York to calm waters with the Americans. Amorim later became President Luiz Inacio Lula da Silva's influential Foreign Minister.
88. See Teixeira da Silva, 'Weapons of Mass Destruction', 213.
89. Teixeira da Silva, 'Weapons of Mass Destruction', 213.
90. Hans Blix, 'Disarming Iraq: Hans Blix's Story. A Vernon Center Conversation and Spring Break Special Event', Speech at New York University, March 15, 2004. Blix put a great deal of effort into ensuring that UNMOVIC did not repeat UNSCOM's organizational flaws: see *Note [transmitting the organizational plan for the UN Monitoring, Verification and Inspection Commission (UNMOVIC) prepared by the Executive Chairman]* (UN Secretariat Document S/2000/292), April 6, 2000.
91. Teixeira da Silva, 'Weapons of Mass Destruction', 213.
92. Hans Blix, *Disarming Iraq: The Search for Weapons of Mass Destruction* (New York: Pantheon, 2004), 59.

93. Blix, *Disarming Iraq*, 47–53.
94. Hans Blix interview, May 18, 2005.
95. Blix, *Disarming Iraq*, 55.
96. Teixeira da Silva, 'Weapons of Mass Destruction', 207.
97. As Teixeira da Silva notes, even the institutionalization of the OFF as a humanitarian exception to the sanctions can be construed as sending a signal to the Iraqis that sanctions were here to stay. Teixeira da Silva, 'Weapons of Mass Destruction', 209.
98. Teixeira da Silva, 'Weapons of Mass Destruction', 208.
99. *Letter dated 99/03/27*, sec. 27.
100. *Text of President Clinton's address to Joint Chiefs of Staff.*
101. F. Gregory Gause III, 'Getting it backward on Iraq', *Foreign Affairs* 78/3 (1999).
102. See David Cortright and George A. Lopez, *The Sanctions Decade: Assessing UN Strategies in the 1990s* (Boulder, CO: Lynne Rienner, 2000), 223–4.
103. Flexibility was, of course, only one of the elements involved in the Libyan case. Different trade patterns, leader personalities, the 'demonstration effect' of the American invasions of Afghanistan and Iraq, and other elements all factored into Col. Qadhafi's decision to renounce terrorism and WMD and reintegrate Libya into the world community.
104. See Seymour M. Hersh, 'The Spoils of the Gulf War', *New Yorker*, September 6, 1993.
105. Reported in Butler, *Talk*.
106. See Trevor Findlay, *A Standing United Nations WMD Verification Body: Necessary and Feasible* (Stockholm: VERTIC, 2005).
107. Hans Blix interview, May 18, 2005.
108. *Note [transmitting the 21st quarterly report on the activities of the UN Monitoring, Verification and Inspection Commission, in accordance with para. 12 of Security Council resolution 1284 (1999)]* (UN Security Document S/2005/351), May 27, 2005.
109. Blix has pointed out how experience in Iraq has contributed significantly to the development of scientific techniques used in sanctions. For example, after some UNSCOM inspectors were prevented from leaving an inspection site in 1991, UNSCOM learnt to use chemical analysis of the inspectors' own clothes as a way to test for the presence of certain chemicals and radioactivity at inspection sites. Blix, 'Disarming Iraq: Hans Blix's Story'. (UNMOVIC's experiences with overhead imaging were also used significantly in the UN's response to the December 26, 2004 tsunami.)
110. See Michael Byers, 'The Shifting Foundations of International Law: A Decade of Forceful Measures against Iraq', *European Journal of International Law* 13/1 (2002).
111. Rolf Ekéus interview, May 28, 2005.
112. See further Chantal de Jonge Oudraat, 'UNSCOM: Between Iraq and a Hard Place', *European Journal of International Law* 13/1 (2002); Hélène Ruiz Fabri, 'The UNSCOM Experience: Lessons from an Experiment', *European Journal of International Law* 13/1 (2002).

113. For a self-regarding but lucid account of the deteriorating relationship between one Secretary-General and the sole remaining superpower, see Boutros Boutros-Ghali's autobiography, *Unvanquished: a US-UN Saga* (New York: Random House, 1999).
114. For a balanced assessment of Annan's difficulties in maintaining good relations with Washington at this time, see John Goshko, 'Iraq Dilemma Erodes Annan's Bond with US', *Washington Post*, February 23, 1999, A13.
115. Hubert B. Herring, 'Diplomacy and Betrayal', *New York Times*, May 31, 1999, 2.
116. On Bustani, see 'Argentine Named Head of Organization for the Prohibition of Chemical Weapons', *UN News Centre*, July 26, 2002.
117. Steven Fidler, 'IAEA chief ready to serve another term', *Financial Times*, February 28, 2005, 38.
118. International perceptions of this syndrome are discussed in David M. Malone and Yuen Foong Khong (eds.), *Unilateralism and US Foreign Policy: International Perspectives* (Boulder, CO: Lynne Rienner, 2003).

7

Sidelined: From 9/11 to August 19, 2003

Despite the erosion of public support for the sanctions regime, and increasing skepticism in Washington and London about the prospects of a successful outcome to the inspections process, there seemed little prospect entering 2001 of any radical change to the UN's approach in Iraq. In part, this was a result of the 'reverse veto', which prevented changes to the inspections-plus-sanctions machinery without P-5 unanimity; in part, due to a lack of political energy on the file. The only other real option—military intervention—seemed far off, not least because of the stated antipathy of the incoming Bush administration to the concept of 'nation-building', which would inevitably follow any invasion of Iraq to depose Saddam Hussein.[1] Condoleezza Rice made this clear: 'The 82nd airborne should not escort kids to kindergarten.'[2]

Still, the current approach was not working for the United States. On January 10, 2001, outgoing Secretary of Defense William Cohen issued a report asserting that Iraq had rebuilt its weapons production capabilities.[3] In the middle of 2001, US Secretary of State Colin Powell led a push for streamlining the sanctions machinery in line with newly popular ideas on 'smart sanctions'.[4] Eventually, the Council adopted Resolution 1382, simplifying sanctions processes but still rooted in the logic of containment. Implementation quickly ran into significant obstacles, not least the hostility of Iraq's neighbors to improved border controls, without which 'smart' sanctions could not function effectively, and which threatened the significant, illegal trade of those countries with Iraq—long acquiesced in by the P-5.

This chapter tracks developments in the Security Council and beyond relevant to the march toward war against Saddam Hussein in 2003, and some consequences for the UN of its marginalization by Coalition military action against Iraq that year.

7.1 Terror and its Consequences

7.1.1 *Al Qaeda and the Axis of Evil*

On September 11, 2001 (9/11), Al Qaeda terrorists brought down the World Trade Center and breached the walls of the Pentagon. The strategic calculus used in Washington and London was transformed. Hussein's presumed pursuit of WMD no longer represented a nuisance, but was now perceived as a potentially mortal threat, to be eliminated as soon as possible.

The scale and devastation of the attacks on lower Manhattan was clearly discernable from the highest floors of the UN Secretariat building. Equally clear from there must have been the certainty that the attacks would have profound impacts on the UN. The US government quickly pointed the finger at the Al Qaeda network and the Taliban regime in Afghanistan that had sheltered it. Al Qaeda's rhetoric drew frequently on the history of American-led—but UN-branded—sanctions and military action in Iraq through the 1990s, and the American presence in the Gulf reinforced since 1990. An earlier plan by Al Qaeda to attack UN headquarters in New York had fortunately been foiled, but its import had perhaps not been fully appreciated at the time.[5]

The Security Council was galvanized by the 9/11 attacks, unanimously adopting a French text the next day expressing solidarity with the United States and anticipating its resort to self-defense against Afghanistan.[6] Several days later, at US initiative, the Council unanimously adopted sweeping provisions under Chapter VII of the Charter, binding on all Member States, against the financing of terrorism and the provision of safe haven for terrorists, establishing a subsidiary body, the Counter-Terrorism Committee (CTC), to monitor compliance.[7] In effect, the Council here took on a legislating role, imposing domestic regulatory requirements that previously had been the preserve of the treaty-making process at the UN and elsewhere. While the action against terrorism was broadly supported at the UN, the precedent of the limited-membership Security Council legislating on behalf of all Member States inspired some concern, expressed more strongly in 2004 when the Council again resorted to legislating on terrorism and WMD proliferation.[8] The move to establish a supranational administrative apparatus to monitor counter-terrorist measures at the national level simultaneously heralded an expansion of the Council's legal-regulatory approach to peace and security.

Unwisely, Iraq could not resist the temptation to draw the UN's attention to itself in the wake of 9/11, with Iraq's ambassador claiming that it would be 'hypocritical to condemn the [World Trade Center] bombings, given the sanctions and bombings against Iraq'.[9] In fact, it later emerged that within days of the 9/11 attacks, President Bush and Secretary of Defense Donald Rumsfeld were urging military action against Iraq once Al Qaeda and the Taliban had been disposed of. Richard A. Clarke, responsible for counter-terrorism in both the Clinton and Bush administrations, asserted that Rumsfeld broached the idea of bombing Iraq in response to 9/11. Soon after,

> The president dragged me into a room with a couple of other people, shut the door, and said, 'I want you to find whether Iraq did this.' The entire conversation left me in absolutely no doubt that George Bush wanted me to come back with a report that said, 'Iraq did this.'[10]

The administration soon found the links it sought. During a November 2001 visit to Washington, Czech Prime Minister Milos Zeman told Secretary of State Powell that Muhammad Atta, the best known of the 9/11 hijackers, had visited Prague in April 2001 to confer with Ahmad Ani, an Iraqi intelligence officer.[11] While the claim was later widely discredited, it—and other tenuous data suggesting links between the secular nationalist Ba'ath regime in Iraq and the Wahabist religious fundamentalists of Al Qaeda—was seized in Washington. In November–December 2001, Rumsfeld instructed General Tommy Franks to start preparing war plans for Iraq.[12]

7.1.2 *Faith and Ideology*

A widely read book by Bob Woodward published in early 2004 documented not only how the focus of White House planning shifted quickly from Al Qaeda to Iraq in the months following 9/11, but also the quasi-religious fervor pervading the war thinking. Brian Urquhart reflected the alarmed sentiments the President's Manichean rhetoric elicited in many in the international security community:

> It is when the President's personal faith appears to enter into policy, in the talk of 'evil' and 'evildoers' or ... of a war that is carrying out the will of Almighty God, that serious concerns arise. Our most immediate and dangerous enemy, the Islamic fundamentalist terrorists, have already declared a holy war against our society and all its cherished values. If we are to face this enemy united and confident in ourselves, we need the widest possible coalition of allies, including the governments of Islamic states. It would be disastrous if ... the United States were somehow to talk itself and its allies into a religious war.[13]

A more sharply critical view was also on offer in the *Financial Times*: 'Faith-based intelligence abroad and faith-based initiatives at home reflect the essence of the Bush administration.'[14] Yet it was not only his 'higher' father that Bush Jr. seemed determined to vindicate. His own comments fuelled a perception that he was bent on revenge against 'the guy who tried to kill my dad'.[15] Nonetheless, Bush made it clear that his temporal father was 'the wrong father to appeal to in terms of strength',[16] and indeed his foreign policy is proudly closer to the radicalism of Reagan than the conservatism of his own father.[17] In fact, many of its architects occupied key positions in the Reagan administration. The hard core of these was a group of so-called 'neoconservatives'. *The Economist* portrayed the group thus:

> This group, including Paul Wolfowitz, John Bolton and Douglas Feith inside the administration, Richard Perle on its fringes and influential journalists such as William Kristol of the *Weekly Standard* on the outside—share ... a belief in the need and ability of America sometimes to use its overwhelming military power, even against the wishes of the UN, and in the exportability of American values.[18]

Several of these figures and others had collaborated in an ambitious charter for a more assertive US policy in 'A Project for the New American Century'. Its driving propositions were

> that American leadership is good both for America and for the world; that such leadership requires military strength, diplomatic energy and commitment to moral principle; and that too few political leaders today are making the case for global leadership.[19]

The 'neocons' had championed Ahmed Chalabi's Iraqi National Congress (INC), envisaging Iraqi regime change as the first move in the democratization of the Middle East.[20] Their ideas were challenged by 'realist' conservatives including John Lewis Gaddis, John Mearsheimer and, on certain issues such as the pre-emptive use of force, Henry Kissinger.[21] As events unfolded in Iraq in 2003, and particularly 2004, a number of other conservative icons, such as George Will, and self-styled 'paleoconservatives', such as Patrick Buchanan, joined more libertarian Cato Institute members in denouncing the administration's conduct of the Iraq venture.[22] But in mid-2002, the neocons were at the zenith of their influence, itching to take on Iraq.

7.1.3 *A New Strategy*

Whatever the background influences, Bush's perception that 9/11 marked a historical turning point is clearly signaled in his repeatedly likening the

World Trade Center attack to Pearl Harbor.[23] Confronted by the risks of foreign tyranny combining with transnational terrorism, Bush decided to move American military power onto the front foot, taking the fight to these combined enemies. Through 2002, his administration slowly developed and rolled out a new policy to deal with this new strategic calculus. Iraq was to be its first test.

In his January 29, 2002, State of the Union address, Bush signaled a paradigm shift in US strategic thinking, describing a need to 'prevent regimes that sponsor terror from threatening America or our friends and allies with weapons of mass destruction', and named Iraq, Iran, and North Korea as an 'axis of evil, arming to threaten the peace of the world'.[24] President Clinton's use of similar language four years earlier had not presaged the fundamental strategic revision that Bush was now embarking upon, cheered by much of Washington. The swelling chorus calling for the invasion of Iraq was led by Kenneth Pollack in his much-discussed book, *The Threatening Storm: The Case for Invading Iraq.*[25] The 'humble' foreign policy that Bush had advocated in 2000 was now shelved.[26] The shock engendered by the attacks of 9/11 had produced an appetite for military solutions in Washington that was not satiated by the Afghan expedition. More significant targets representing more serious threats would have to be found and combated in order to deter further attacks on US soil. Saddam Hussein's hour had come.

The new assessment of the Iraqi threat was not solely concerned with the possibility of Hussein providing WMD to non-state terrorists but also encompassed a growing unease about the threat posed by Hussein to regional security—and through oil, by extension to global security—should he acquire nuclear weapons. Neocon advocacy of a democratic reshaping of the Middle East also appears to have met with considerable success in the White House.[27] Iraq became the 'central front in the war on terrorism'.[28]

The imminence of military action grew more clear as the months passed. In June 2002, Bush addressed graduating cadets at West Point:

> The war on terror will not be won on the defensive. We must take the battle to the enemy, disrupt his plans, and confront the worst threats before they emerge. In the world we have entered, the path to safety is the oath of action. And this nation will act.[29]

In September 2002, this rhetoric was fleshed out in a new US *National Security Strategy,* outlining a position in favor of pre-emptive military action that came to be known as the 'Bush doctrine':

Traditional concepts of deterrence will not work against a terrorist enemy .... The overlap between states that sponsor terror and those that pursue WMD compels us to action .... The greater the threat, the greater is the risk of inaction—and the more compelling the case for taking anticipatory action to defend ourselves, even if uncertainty remains as to the time and place of the enemy's attack. To forestall or prevent such hostile acts by our adversaries, the United States will, if necessary, act preemptively.[30]

By the first week of October, the administration had begun openly to connect the dots between Iraq, terrorism, and pre-emptive military action. After releasing a National Intelligence Estimate that characterized Iraq as possessing WMD and being in active pursuit of nuclear weapons production capability, Bush stated

The time for denying, deceiving, and delaying has come to an end. Saddam Hussein must disarm himself—or, for the sake of peace, we will lead a coalition to disarm him.[31]

On October 16, the US Congress passed a joint resolution authorizing military action.[32] President Bush responded by stating: 'I have not ordered the use of force. I hope the use of force will not become necessary.'[33]

7.1.4 *The 'UN Route'*

Bush was not alone in his analysis of the threats posed by the possible connection between Iraqi WMD and transnational terrorism. In the United Kingdom, Prime Minister Blair had drawn similar strategic conclusions from 9/11, although he saw a central role for the UN in meeting the new threats it heralded:

[A]ll those worries I'd had about W.M.D. and proliferation were thrown into sharp relief .... What does that mean? It means sending the right signal across the world that from now on if you develop this in the face of U.N. resolutions you're going to be in trouble.[34]

It was clear that Blair saw Hussein as a chief troublemaker: as early as April 3, 2002, Blair asserted that London knew Iraq to possess stockpiles of chemical and biological weapons.[35] But the United States and United Kingdom differed significantly over what role the UN should play in the decision to go to war. This is made clear by a confidential 'Downing Street Memorandum', published by *The Times* of London on May 1, 2005, which contains minutes from a July 2002 meeting of Prime Minister Blair with principals, including Geoff Hoon (UK Defence Secretary), Lord Goldsmith (UK Attorney General), and John Scarlett (head of the Joint Intelligence Committee). Scarlett indicated that in Washington,

> [m]ilitary action [against Iraq] was now seen as inevitable. Bush wanted to remove Saddam, through military action, justified by the conjunction of terrorism and WMD. But the intelligence and facts were being fixed around the policy. The NSC had no patience with the UN route .... There was little discussion in Washington of the aftermath of military action.

Scarlett's assessment suggests that President Bush had determined by the third week of July 2002 to go to war with Iraq, with intelligence being 'fixed' to that end.[36] Many indications have since emerged that an atmosphere developed in Washington influencing intelligence officials as to what they should find and report. Vice President Cheney visited CIA headquarters personally numerous times through 2002.[37] The memorandum also suggested, as the anarchy in post-invasion Iraq would bear out, that post-conflict planning was not high on the US agenda. Most revealing, though, was what the memorandum revealed about the differing US and UK attitudes to the UN. The memorandum records Jack Straw, UK Foreign Secretary, opining:

> It seemed clear that Bush had made up his mind to take military action, even if the timing was not yet decided. But the case was thin. Saddam was not threatening his neighbours, and his WMD capability was less than that of Libya, North Korea or Iran. [The UK] should work up a plan for an ultimatum to Saddam to allow back in the UN weapons inspectors. This would also help with the legal justification for the use of force.

Thus, UN weapons inspections could serve as means and not only ends. This was acknowledged publicly in mid-2003 by US Deputy Secretary of Defense Paul Wolfowitz, who stated that WMD were 'settled on' as 'the one reason that everyone could agree'.[38] Yet, as Mark Danner points out,

> [t]he key negotiation in view at this point ... was not with Saddam over letting in the United Nations inspectors.... The key negotiation would be between the Americans, who had shown 'resistance' to the idea of involving the United Nations at all, and the British, who were more concerned than their American cousins about having some kind of legal fig leaf for attacking Iraq.[39]

Within the administration, the Vice President opposed Secretary of State Colin Powell's advocacy of the UN route:

> A return of inspectors would provide no assurance whatsoever of his compliance with U.N. resolutions. On the contrary, there is a great danger that it would provide false comfort that Saddam was somehow 'back in his box.' ... [T]here is no doubt that Saddam Hussein now has weapons of mass destruction....[40]

Danner concludes that the hard-liners in the administration 'feared "the UN route" not because it might fail but because it might succeed and thereby prevent a war that they were convinced had to be fought'.[41] For a time, though, Powell seemed to gain the upper hand, with Bush influenced by Blair's indication at Camp David on September 7 that he could not guarantee UK troops without a commitment from the US to take the UN route.[42] The push to sell military action at the UN had begun.

7.2 With or Without the UN?

7.2.1 *War: A Hard Sell*

While Bush's Manichean rhetoric earlier in 2002 may have helped prepare the ground at home for action against Hussein, it produced skepticism elsewhere. Even traditional allies expressed concern that the US was seeking to use WMD as a pretext for regime change in Iraq. The European Commission President Romano Prodi warned that 'unilateral US military action could destroy the keystone of US diplomacy, the global antiterrorist alliance'.[43] His Commissioner for external relations, Chris Patten, criticized the notion of the 'axis of evil' as 'absolutist and simplistic', and warned of pending 'unilateralist overdrive'.[44] Canadian Deputy Prime Minister John Manley stated: '[a]s for going in and changing the regime, as opposed to going in and ensuring that there are no weapons of mass destruction, we haven't signed on to that.'[45] German Chancellor Gerhard Schröder ruled out German participation in an invasion of Iraq, whether or not there was a UN mandate,[46] while French President Chirac expressed 'great reservations'.[47]

Iraq engaged France, Russia, and China to assure them that Baghdad represented no threat to international peace and security. Scott Ritter reemerged, arguing ubiquitously that all the evidence suggested Iraq was 90–95 percent disarmed.[48] To counter, on September 12, 2002, as President Bush traveled to UN Headquarters to engage world attention on Iraq, the White House released a twenty-page document on Iraq entitled *A Decade of Deception and Defiance*, advancing evidence of Iraqi noncompliance with disarmament obligations, much of it apparently supplied by Ahmed Chalabi's INC.[49] Kofi Annan spoke before the President in the General Assembly:

> I stand before you as a multilateralist—by precedent, by principle, by charter, by duty.... Every government that is committed to the rule of law at home must also be committed to the rule of law abroad.[50]

Bush offered an ultimatum:

> If Iraq's regime defies us again, the world must move decisively to hold Iraq to account.... Are Security Council resolutions to be honored and enforced? Will the United Nations serve the purpose of its founding, or will it be irrelevant?[51]

The uncomfortable implications for the UN were clear: either the Security Council backed the US demand for forceful disarmament of Iraq—and by implication regime change—or it would be sidelined. For many in the UN, this was a lose-lose situation: kowtow to the hegemon, or face irrelevance.

7.2.2 *Breakthroughs?*

In November 2002, Republicans assumed control of both houses of Congress and the White House, for the first time in living memory. For the old hands—Cheney, Rumsfeld—who had been locked in the political hand-to-hand combat of Washington for most of their lives, this was a moment to be savored, one of vindication. November 2002 also provided a moment of triumph for Colin Powell, who appeared, at least for a time, vindicated by the Security Council's adoption of Resolution 1441.[52]

The substantive genesis of SCR 1441 was a Carnegie Endowment for International Peace (CEIP) report of August 2002 advancing a proposal outlining a middle path between unarmed weapons inspections and military intervention. The proposal called for coercive inspections, positing a 'powerful, multinational military force, created by the UN Security Council' that would force access to—and if necessary destroy—a suspected site, impose no-drive zones in inspection target areas, carrying out a 'comply or else' system of inspections.[53] In retrospect, it is not clear that the CEIP proposal would have achieved more than buy time, had Washington been willing to do so. As became clear when UNMOVIC moved into Iraq, the real challenge was not access to sites but apparent Iraqi concealment. The International Crisis Group characterized the proposed compromise as, 'one of those rarest of ideas that both Iraq and the US are likely to reject'—too strong for the Iraqis and too weak for the US.[54] All the same, it was a brave, articulate policy proposal at a time when no others were being broached in the US. It signaled that a middle road *might* be possible. French and German officials apparently gave the proposal detailed consideration.[55] The idea even found its way into the original US draft for a final attempt at weapons inspection, introduced into the Security Council on October 25, 2002.

Two issues dominated Council negotiations over this text: (*a*) what would constitute the 'failure' of renewed weapons inspections; and (*b*) what would occur if—or when—that failure became apparent. The United States argued for a Resolution authorizing Member States to determine Iraqi non-compliance with an imposed inspections regime, and to take enforcement action to produce that compliance.[56] Predictably, Russia, France, and China were not prepared to support any such 'automaticity' that could serve as a blank check for the United States. They sought to defer the authorization of the use of force to a second resolution.

The compromise that emerged gave Iraq one last chance. Resolution 1441 found Iraq had been and continued to be in 'material breach' of its disarmament obligations. Second, it afforded Iraq one 'final opportunity' to meet its disarmament obligations through an enhanced inspections regime. The special inspections regimes for both 'sensitive' and 'Presidential' sites were terminated. It charged Iraq with providing 'a currently accurate, full, and complete declaration of all aspects of its programs to develop' WMD and missiles. This latter provision aimed to assist UNMOVIC and the IAEA to establish new baselines for inspections and to give Iraq a last opportunity to state the whole truth.[57]

Council hard-liners considered the outcome potentially a neat trap: if Hussein admitted possessing WMD, he was acknowledging a violation of UN resolutions; if he did not, he would be deceiving the world, and again violating those resolutions.[58] Either way, the UN would have enhanced the legitimacy of armed intervention. That, of course, assumed that Hussein *had* WMD—as we now know a misreading of the situation on the ground.[59]

The devil was, as always in the Council, in the details. In deliberately ambiguous language, SCR 1441 determined that in the event of a further 'material breach' by Iraq, the Council would reconvene to 'consider the situation', make an 'assessment', and impose 'serious consequences'.[60] This left unsettled whether the Council merely would *discuss* the material breach, after which states could themselves take enforcement action, or whether such enforcement would have to be authorized by a 'second' Resolution.

That ambiguity was clear in the text but obfuscated by the members of the Council in their self-congratulatory comments. The US indicated that, under its interpretation, SCR 1441 did not require a second resolution, but permitted states to enforce UN resolutions.[61] On the other hand, Mexico and Ireland considered enforcement to require a second resolution. Syria stated that 1441 did not 'authorize' the use of force. Decidedly straddling the fence, Jeremy Greenstock, the UK ambassador to the UN, stated:

> We heard loud and clear during the negotiations about 'automaticity' and 'hidden triggers'.... Let me be equally clear ... There is no 'automaticity' in this Resolution. If there is a further Iraqi breach of its disarmament obligations, the matter will return to the Council for discussion as required ... We would expect the Security Council then to meet its responsibilities.[62]

An opaque joint statement of France, Russia, and China left everyone guessing as to their ultimate intentions.

Resolution 1441 represented a paradigmatic example of creative ambiguity in diplomatic drafting and forged the way for the return, after four years of absence, of weapons inspectors to Iraq. Whether it was fated to prove a blind alley is open to debate. For some, it represented the ultimate diplomatic 'fix' at the UN, a convenient but substantively meaningless improvisation that immediately spawned new wrangles over its interpretation. Jeremy Greenstock argues that 'the fact that there was unanimity, while it did not help provide a basis for a second resolution in March, did in my view help to bring the Security Council together [in 2003] after the conflict in 1483 and 1512.'[63] His French colleague, Jean-David Levitte, who shortly after the adoption of SCR 1441 moved on to represent France in Washington, believes that the Resolution could have provided a good basis for negotiation between Europeans and Americans, had the Europeans been united.[64] Recalling that France was then quite open to the use of force against Saddam Hussein as long as it was authorized by the Security Council, he notes that his first senior visitor in Washington, mid-December 2002, was a French military officer offering the Americans 15,000 troops, the nuclear-powered aircraft carrier *Charles de Gaulle*, and other military assets under the right political dispensation.[65] However, with the United Kingdom increasingly lined up behind the United States diplomatically and as an unconditional military partner, Washington had little reason to negotiate with Paris (or the rest of the Council members) to meet conditions on its use of force. Greenstock to a degree concurs:

> The UK was not only trying to avoid a bust up in the Council—it was also trying to avoid the use of force at all. Looking back, its attempt to keep the Council together in the early months of 2003 was forlorn for two primary reasons: the Americans had no further incentive, once they assumed that the UK would be with them on the basis of 1441, to worry deeply about Security Council diplomacy; and the French (in particular) refused to condone the American approach—not least because they saw American lack of interest in UN consensus.[66]

7.2.3 *'Just do what we did for Kosovo . . .'*

Confronted by this 'final opportunity', on November 13, 2002, Iraq agreed to the return of weapons inspectors.[67] In early December, Iraq presented its 'currently accurate, full and complete declaration'. The US pointed to omissions in this declaration as material breaches in themselves. National Security Adviser Rice later described the document as a

'12,200 page lie'.[68] But most Council members were disposed to give UNMOVIC and the IAEA a genuine chance. The weapons inspectors quickly set to work, conducting 237 inspections at 148 sites between November 2002 and March 2003.[69]

These were not the only positive signals. By early January, Paris had realized that the US was intent on going to war. President Chirac's personal envoy to meet the National Security Adviser Rice was given a clear signal that the US was intent on a military solution.[70] Paris privately offered Washington a significant compromise. The new French ambassador there, Jean-David Levitte, quietly met Steve Hadley, Deputy National Security Adviser. He gave an amber light for war, promising a degree of accommodation by Paris as long as a clash in the Council was avoided:

> We understand that you will push for war. We think it's a big mistake, but don't add another mistake. Just do what we did for Kosovo—act on the basis of existing resolutions, and you go. And then it will be easier after the war to come together.[71]

That compromise would not, however, suit Prime Minister Blair, who had promised his public a second Resolution. In the end, it may have been the UK need for a second Resolution that precipitated the clash within the Security Council. Taking advantage of France's role as Security Council President for January, de Villepin called a Council meeting at Foreign Minister level, ostensibly on terrorism, perhaps inadvertently setting it for January 20, (Martin Luther King Day, highly significant for Powell's community in the United States). Powell reluctantly came to New York, only to suffer what was perceived as a media ambush by de Villepin. Characterizing war as 'the worst possible solution'[72] he told a waiting media after Powell's departure from the UN that France 'will not associate ourselves with military intervention that is not supported by the international community'.[73] De Villepin's comments might have been intended to reinforce the signal that while France would 'not associate' with military action not explicitly authorized by the Council, it would not actively block it.

The pattern of P-5 mutual accommodation in the post-Cold War era seemed to make a veto by one Western power of an initiative vital to others unlikely.[74] Yet Washington seemed to respond dismissively to France's overtures, with Donald Rumsfeld denigrating France and Germany as 'old Europe'.[75] Perhaps stung, the signals from Paris changed, with President Chirac declaring that as 'the worst of solutions' and 'an admission of defeat', 'everything must be done to avoid' war.[76] The prospect of a French veto in the Council was clear, if still implied. Chirac's move helped generate a wave of public sentiment well beyond France intensely opposed to

American militarism. Two days later, German Chancellor Gerhard Schröder, with Germany presiding over the Council, indicated that Germany, too, would do all it could to avert war. The same day, Russian Foreign Minister Igor Ivanov said that 'Russia deems that there is no evidence that would justify a war in Iraq.'[77] On January 23, China described its position as 'extremely close' to that of France.[78]

7.2.4 *Endgame*

On January 27, Hans Blix and Mohammed El Baredei reported to the Security Council. Although both UNMOVIC and the IAEA were making progress, Blix made a crucial assessment:

> Iraq appears not to have come to a genuine acceptance—not even today—of the disarmament which was demanded of it and which it needs to carry out to win the confidence of the world and to live in peace.

Blix himself later suggested that he was, by this time, already doubtful of Iraqi possession of WMD:

> How could there be 100 percent certainty about the existence of WMD, but zero percent knowledge of their location?[79]

His comment about Iraqi acceptance perhaps aimed to underscore that Iraq had not publicly renounced the pursuit of WMD. Yet Blix might have foreseen the reaction this comment would elicit from Washington, which jumped on it as an independent verification of its claims to Iraqi possession of WMD. Stung, Iraq significantly increased its cooperation with UNMOVIC. The United States and United Kingdom interpreted the resulting information and materials, such as the surrender and destruction of over seventy Samoud 2 missiles, as evidence of past and likely further deception; others on the Council suggested it proved that SCR 1441 was bearing fruit.[80]

On February 5, Colin Powell, reprising Adlai Stevenson's role in the Cuban Missile Crisis, presented a multimedia dossier detailing 'evidence' of Iraqi WMD to the Security Council.[81] The presentation was broadcast live around the world, in an atmosphere of real tension, but failed to produce a 'smoking gun', focusing instead on shadowy photographs and assertions of connections between Iraq, Al Qaeda, and nuclear proliferators. He detailed 'mobile biological weapons laboratories' (now thought to be mobile hydrogen generation plants), 'decontamination vehicles' (now thought to be fire trucks), and aluminum tubes for use in nuclear weapons (actually spare parts from missiles).[82] Only his claims that Iraq was manufacturing prohibited missiles has held up well.

Meanwhile, UNMOVIC and the IAEA began to produce tentative evidence of Western intelligence failures, visiting sites identified by the United States and the United Kingdom without finding anything of substance.[83] The IAEA declared that Iraq was not in the process of reconstituting its nuclear program.[84] When on February 14, Blix not only cast doubt on some of Powell's claims but also claimed that Iraq had decided to cooperate with inspectors, the United States seemed to fulfill an earlier promise by Vice President Cheney that it would, if necessary, 'discredit inspections in favor of disarmament'.[85] The American media's blistering attacks on Blix did not seem to ruffle his Scandinavian calm;[86] he claims to have been mildly amused by the email he received describing him as a 'French poodle'.[87] He continued to work, particularly with the British, to find benchmarks that might convince the United States of serious movement by Iraq toward disarmament.[88] Sensing that unilateral military action by the United States and the United Kingdom was in the offing, France, Russia, and Germany agreed to list 'benchmarks' for Iraqi compliance and to consider a second resolution setting out an inspections timetable stretching over the coming months. But with over 200,000 troops in the Persian Gulf and the summer heat and sand storms fast approaching, Washington was in no mood to wait.

The tension between Washington and Paris rose. De Villepin traveled to several African capitals to lobby for their votes in the coming Council showdown. At the February 14, 2003, meeting of the Council, de Villepin played on Rumsfeld's earlier comment in underscoring the depredations of war:

> It is an old country, France, of an old continent such as mine, Europe, that speaks before the Council today, that has known war, occupation, barbarity.[89]

A few days later President Chirac, perhaps presciently, argued that

> A war of this kind cannot help giving a big lift to terrorism. It would create a large number of little bin Ladens.[90]

Massive street protests unfolded throughout Europe on February 15—with up to one million marching in each of London, Rome, and Madrid. In Germany, a poll had earlier showed that 53 percent of respondents considered Bush more of a threat to international peace and security than Hussein.[91]

On February 24, 2003, the United States, Britain, and Spain introduced a draft resolution, which stated that the Council '[d]ecides that Iraq has failed to take the final opportunity afforded to it in resolution 1441 (2002).'[92] Although the draft did not specify what the consequences of the decision were, legal advisers of both the United States and the United Kingdom indicated that this would revive the authorization to use force provided by SCR 678.[93] Pointing to a preambular paragraph in the draft finding Iraq in noncompliance with SCR 1441, France described the text as a 'declaration of war "by preamble" '.[94]

Council vote counting had begun. Washington was confident (London less so) of its ability to secure the nine votes needed for the Resolution to pass.[95] But success was to prove elusive. On February 22, the NAM signaled from Kuala Lumpur that it opposed military intervention in Iraq, putting pressure on several Council members to refrain from supporting the draft resolution. The United States deployed all the diplomatic, financial, and military leverage at its disposal to influence votes in the Council.[96] Not least among the controversies this spawned was a US intelligence surveillance operation targeting Council diplomats and UN officials.[97] Particularly targeted were said to have been the Council's 'swing votes': Angola, Cameroon, Chile, Guinea, Mexico, and Pakistan—and Annan. Annan's response to the revelation of this espionage, while condemning such practices as contrary to international law, seemed to accept the reality that such bugging of senior UN officials was routine.[98]

The UK Prime Minister Blair was in a bind, apparently committed to a war his constituency—and even large sections of his own party—opposed. On February 26, the House of Commons voted against the use of force, after 120 Labour MPs joined with the opposition. British diplomats worked frantically to bridge the gap between the United States and France, vigorously pursuing the possibility of a combined benchmarks-and-timetable approach. The British quietly encouraged a Canadian initiative that month to set a deadline for Iraqi compliance in a few weeks, an idea torpedoed by active US and French opposition; instead, in an effort to secure more support for the draft resolution, a provision allowing Iraq just a few days to disarm was added.[99]

On March 5, the Foreign Ministers of France, Germany, and Russia met in Paris, and agreed to block any resolution authorizing the use of force. For weeks, such capitals as Mexico City and Santiago had been under intense pressure from the P-5 antagonists and from their own public. On March 7, another meeting of the Security Council at Foreign Minister level failed to break the deadlock. A French proposal to allow a further 120 days of inspections was rejected by the United States.[100] Jack Straw announced a last-ditch change to the draft text, which now held out one *more* chance for Saddam, and at the same time seemed to leave the Security Council a role in determining whether force would be used. The new draft called on Iraq immediately to 'take the decisions necessary in the interests of its people and region'. It then declared that Iraq would be considered to have 'failed to take the final opportunity' unless on or before March 17 the Council concluded that Iraq had demonstrated full, unconditional, immediate, and active cooperation.[101] This shifted no country's vote.

Public utterance of a deadline of March 17 may have precipitated Chirac's statement on March 10, making explicit what had until then been implied: France would veto any resolution that would lead to war. With perhaps three vetoes imminent, and lacking the affirmative votes to force even these vetoes, Blair, Bush, and Spanish Prime Minister José Maria Aznar, after an hour-long meeting in the Azores Islands on March 16, withdrew the draft resolution.

7.2.5 *An Unexpected Obstacle*

Meanwhile, the US had encountered an unexpected obstacle to military action: its close ally Turkey.[102] Ankara had much to lose from a war in Iraq, particularly if it led to a strengthening of the Kurdish hand and autonomy within Iraq. Despite massive public opposition in Turkey to US war plans, Recep Tayyip Erdogan's Justice and Development Party, elected only in February 2003, had attempted to accommodate US basing and overflight needs. The United States in return offered a sizable package of development assistance, but it sent mixed signals on how it would react if Turkish forces intervened in northern Iraq once hostilities commenced. On March 1, the Turkish Parliament voted to reject the deal, forcing significant changes to military planning for Operation Iraqi Freedom. On March 18, the United States offered to allow up to 20,000 Turkish troops to establish a 20-km buffer zone inside Iraq, ensure that Kurdish forces stayed out of Mosul and Kirkuk, and undertake a joint operation with the Turkish forces to disarm the Kurdish *peshmerga*.

On March 19 (as hostilities began), the Turkish Parliament voted not to accept this offer but nevertheless to allow US overflight. While helpful, this forced the US military command to abandon its plans of a northern front in the invasion of Iraq. This in turn reduced the US troop presence once the fight was won, arguably facilitating the widespread looting that eventuated (discussed in the following section). Moreover,

US–Turkish relations had been badly damaged. At the same time, the US offer to allow Turkish forces to occupy a strip of northern Iraq revealed that the United States now saw itself as the final arbiter of security in the region and the authority to use force. The Security Council had been sidelined.

7.3 Operation Iraqi Freedom

On March 17, President Bush addressed the nation:

> Saddam Hussein and his sons must leave Iraq within 48 hours. Their refusal to do so will result in military conflict, commenced at a time of our choosing.... The United Nations Security Council has not lived up to its responsibilities, so we will rise to ours.[103]

Bush's ultimatum built on earlier calls from Gulf States for Saddam Hussein to leave Iraq voluntarily. Although Coalition Special Forces had already been operating in remote areas of Iraq for a day or two, major hostilities commenced on March 19, 2003, when Bush—reacting to intelligence about Hussein's whereabouts—ordered an air strike against him at Dora Farms, which proved unsuccessful.[104] The ground war began the next day. Just over two weeks later, after meeting weak resistance from a dispirited Iraqi military, US troops took control of the Baghdad airport. By April 9, US troops had taken control of central Baghdad, pulling down an iconic statue of Hussein in Firdos Square. Hussein himself, and many of his top Ba'ath regime leaders, vanished.

7.3.1 *Shock and ORHA*

The US military had promised to begin the war in Iraq with a campaign of 'shock and awe', a devastating aerial barrage of such precision and power that it would 'shock and awe' the Iraqi military into submission. But in their haste to take Baghdad, Coalition troops had become overextended. There were insufficient 'boots on the ground' to secure key locations beyond the Oil Ministry—and US troops lacked instructions to do so.[105] The sporadic looting that often breaks out when a vacuum of authority develops quickly mutated into something more systematic and fierce, as US troops mostly stood aside. The targeting of infrastructure by looters and vandals undermined the Coalition's ability to maintain basic services throughout the country; electricity, sanitation, and medical services were all severely damaged. The damage to cultural treasures, such as the National Museum and National Library, initially attracted much attention.

Even more seriously, evidence has emerged that looters ransacked weapons storage facilities with impunity—even the Tuwaitha nuclear complex, stealing yellowcake. Having justified the invasion on the grounds of preventing the proliferation of WMD, this was a major Coalition failure.[106]

In a battle over control of Iraq policy between the US Departments of State and Defense, the latter had secured control of almost every significant aspect, including postwar planning. The detailed plans put together by State—through a $5 million interagency process known as the Future of Iraq Project, which produced 2,000 pages in thirteen volumes, including recommendations on topics from education to health, sanitation, agriculture, finance, energy, security, governance, rule of law, and transitional justice—were largely ignored by the Pentagon and its agents on the ground in Iraq.[107] Only weeks before the invasion, on January 21, 2003, President Bush established within the Pentagon the Office for Reconstruction and Humanitarian Assistance (ORHA), henceforth responsible for planning and implementing the post-conflict management of Iraq, placing in charge a retired General, Jay Garner, who had played a major role in Operation Provide Comfort. Oddly, Garner did not even enter Iraq until April 9, 2003—three days *after* the US military airlifted the INC's Ahmed Chalabi and a posse of supporters into Nasariya. By then, looters had wreaked havoc. As Garner himself admitted,

> They stole everything. They stripped the wiring out of the walls, took the plumbing, and they torched the buildings.[108]

The reasons for this debacle are manifold. Chalabi, the Iraqi exile who had played such a key role in US regime-change planning in previous years, had promised an underground security network that failed to materialize.[109] Secretary of Defense Rumsfeld's long-term advocacy of a Revolution in Military Affairs, reducing manpower and increasing mechanization, prompted Pentagon planners to opt for a streamlined invasion force. Senior military commanders, such as Army Chief of Staff General Eric Shinseki, who suggested a larger force—'something on the order of several hundred thousand soldiers'—were rebuked as 'wildly off the mark' and sidelined.[110] 'Choices had to be made' between speed of military victory and policing needs, Deputy Secretary of Defense Paul Wolfowitz asserted.[111] Rumsfeld downplayed the consequences:

> Freedom's untidy. Free people are free to make mistakes and commit crimes and do bad things.[112]

7.3.2 *From Bad to Worse*

Given the inept performance of ORHA, which never established a firm grip in Baghdad, US military authorities were perceived as running the country (to the extent that it was under control). European countries, already concerned about contributions to humanitarian assistance funds legitimizing a war they had opposed, now objected to the militarization of humanitarian aid.[113] With the costs of reconstruction of Iraq rising exponentially as looting spiraled out of control, Iraq's medium-term economic future looked bleak.

The political outlook seemed no brighter. ORHA was to hand over power to an interim Iraqi administration, expected to draw significantly on Iraqi exiles close to Washington. Nine months later, a constituent assembly would meet to draft a new Iraqi constitution, leading to elections within two years. Although this scenario has, in fact, been broadly implemented, ORHA soon fell by the wayside. Its planning had been based on postconflict scenarios—including widespread oil-fires, a massive refugee crisis, and regional instability—that proved inaccurate.[114] Garner himself admitted that ORHA 'didn't really have enough time to plan'.[115] A senior official present in Baghdad at the time describes the situation candidly:

> The initial post-war situation in Baghdad was a nightmare—the military and civilian components of the American deployment were not working together and, until Bremer arrived, it looked as if the [situation] might spin out of control altogether.[116]

With ORHA nearly completely ineffective, the White House changed tack. On May 6, President Bush appointed L. Paul ('Jerry') Bremer III, a career diplomat close to the Pentagon with recent experience in counter-terrorism, to head a new Coalition Provisional Authority (CPA). Bremer moved decisively, making some significant policy mistakes, but establishing control, not least over the US military in Iraq. On May 16, he issued a decree 'disestablishing' the Ba'ath Party and removing its members from positions of authority. The edict targeted not only senior leaders and those who had participated in the abuses of Hussein's regime but also removed teachers, doctors, and mid-level civil servants from Iraq's reconstruction. Bremer appointed Ahmed Chalabi to oversee the 'de-Ba'athification' process, and members of his INC to key oil, finance, trade, and central bank posts.[117] On May 23, he banned the Iraqi Army, instantly creating some 500,000 unemployed, highly trained, armed enemies of occupation, most of them Sunni. These today are considered to have been serious errors, greatly complicating reconstruction and fueling the subsequent insurgency, but they were popular with both exiles and the Shi'a majority community of the country.[118]

7.3.3 *Mission Accomplished?*

Sunni resentment of the occupation and the specter of Shi'a political dominance grew quickly. Attacks against electricity, oil, and water infrastructure, and military convoys, escalated, soon compounded by frequent carjackings, kidnappings, and suicide bombings. Sunni insurgents were soon operating alongside foreign *jihadist* fighters flowing into Iraq. Among those fighters, a Jordanian terrorist, Abu Musab al-Zarqawi, was soon singled out by the US, not least for his close ties to Al Qaeda. Having invaded Iraq to prevent the supply of WMD to terrorists, the Coalition now seemed to have created a powerful platform for terrorist recruitment, just as President Chirac had predicted a few months earlier.

While US military leaders on the ground recognized that the 'terrorist problem [was] emerging as the number-one security threat', Washington initially seemed unperturbed.[119] Asked about the escalating attacks, Bush responded 'Bring 'em on.'[120] On May 1, he co-piloted a fighter jet onto the flight deck of the aircraft carrier *USS Abraham Lincoln* and, against the backdrop of a giant banner proclaiming 'Mission Accomplished', announced the end of major combat operations.[121]

7.4 What Role for the UN?

The US and the UK decision to go to war sidelined the UN. Addressing the Security Council, Kofi Annan asserted that '[w]e must all feel that this is a sad day for the UN and the international community.'[122] The way forward for the UN, and the role it would play in Iraq, were not clear. In early April, Annan appointed Rafeeuddin Ahmed, a low-key, senior Pakistani UN official with development experience, as a Special Adviser, to coordinate thinking on the role the UN could play in post-conflict Iraq. This was potentially controversial, as any UN presence could be seen as legitimating the Coalition's actions. However, at a senior level the majority UN view was that the UN could not shirk its humanitarian and peace-building vocations in Iraq. The Coalition, however, early on seemed uninterested in any significant UN role beyond humanitarian assistance.

7.4.1 *Resolution 1483*

On May 22, the Council adopted SCR 1483, through which the P-5 sought to chart a new working relationship on Iraq, despite lingering bitterness in some quarters. The text, including both aspirational and regulatory elements, was described as 'as much ... an invitation to further dialogue as ... a detailed blueprint' for how the Council would address occupied Iraq.[123] The text reflects a compromise between the United States and United Kingdom, who sought an omnibus blessing recalling SCR 687, and the French, Russians, and Chinese, who were eager to avoid repeating the *post facto* validation that was widely seen as characterizing SCR 1244 in the wake of NATO's Kosovo intervention. Specific provisions included, *inter alia*, measures for recovering public property, the denial of safe haven to Ba'ath regime figures implicated in international crimes, the termination of sanctions against Iraq (except the military embargo), and measures to stimulate Iraq's economy.

But the real significance of SCR 1483 was political. After some tough negotiating, the resolution affirmed that the United States and United Kingdom were occupying powers, a provision initially resisted by Coalition countries. This affirmation was important because, by acknowledging individual liability and state responsibility for their administration of occupied Iraq, the United States and United Kingdom recognized that this remained a US–UK venture, not a UN-sanctioned one. At the same time, in contradiction to much traditional occupation law, the resolution gave the Coalition Provisional Authority a central role in transforming Iraq's political and constitutional landscape.[124]

Council discussions over the UN's role in this political transformation proved contentious. The preamble suggested that the UN would 'play a vital role in ... the restoration and establishment of national and local institutions for representative governance', and Operational Paragraph 8(c) tasked a Special Representative of the Secretary-General (SRSG) to that end. The SRSG was additionally mandated to coordinate action in the areas of humanitarian relief, reconstruction, infrastructure rehabilitation, legal and judicial reforms, human rights and return of refugees, and also to assist with civilian police.[125] Additionally, the resolution authorized the Coalition Provisional Authority, 'working with' the SRSG, to appoint an interim Iraqi administration.[126]

Annan appointed Sergio Vieira de Mello, the charismatic former head of the UN's post-conflict mission in East Timor (UNTAET) to the key post of SRSG, 'borrowing' him from his responsibilities as UN High Commissioner for Human Rights for a projected four months. Soon after de Mello's arrival in Baghdad, it became clear that the United States would allow him only a very limited role in the development of an Iraqi constitution, the holding of elections, and the establishment of a government (thus rejecting a template for UN involvement in such tasks successfully implemented in East Timor and in Afghanistan). The UN was to be confined to a largely technical role with the United States continuing to call the shots.[127] This was not to be a UN peace operation. That said, de Mello, always creative, found ways to involve himself usefully in the transitional process, for example working on regional governments to 'embrace' the new Iraqi authorities.[128] Still, the Coalition tactic was clear: it would revert to the Security Council only when its stamp of approval was perceived to be both available and useful.

The extent to which the UN had become subordinate through the provisions of SCR 1483 became clear through the administration of the US-controlled Development Fund for Iraq (DFI). The resolution allowed funds remaining in the OFF Program UN escrow account to be administered through the DFI, to be spent on reconstruction contracts. The United States announced in December 2003 that only companies from Coalition partner states would be entitled to bid for these contracts—a move it justified as 'necessary for the protection of the essential security interests of the United States', but it seemed designed to punish erstwhile antagonists in the Council.[129] (Indeed, National Security Adviser Rice was rumored to have advocated a policy, which would 'punish France, ignore Germany, and forgive Russia'.)[130] These views soon yielded to calmer sentiments, with other countries, including Canada, which had not joined the Coalition, invited to bid. But it later emerged that perhaps as much as $9 billion of these funds went 'missing', with the CPA unable to account for them.[131]

7.4.2 *Moving Toward a Larger Role?*

In this uncertain atmosphere, Annan prepared the ground for the UN to have the support it needed in the capitals when it could play a more meaningful role—clearly not yet. In early April, Presidents Chirac and Putin and Chancellor Schröder met in St Petersburg, calling 'the political, economic, humanitarian and administrative reconstruction of Iraq . . . a matter for the United Nations and for it alone'.[132] The next week, Secretary-General Annan attended a summit of the European Union in Athens. The EU issued a call for the UN to take control of postwar Iraq. Signs emerged, too, that the United Kingdom desired a greater UN role in political transition.[133]

Annan quietly advocated a broad, multidisciplinary assistance operation, including the World Bank and the IMF from the outset. In a report to the Security Council in July, he suggested a range of tasks the UN might undertake in Iraq, relevant to the constitutional process, judicial and legal reform, police training, demobilization and reintegration of former military forces, public administration, economic reconstruction and sustainable development, and technical assistance to Iraqi ministries.[134] These activities could be discharged by a UN Assistance Mission for Iraq (UNAMI), totaling around 300 local and international staff. At the same time, he brought pressure to bear on the Coalition to lay out a clear timetable for the withdrawal of occupying forces. Given the complex security situation in Iraq, it was widely thought at that time that any such withdrawal would ideally be followed by the deployment of a significant UN (or Arab or Islamic) security force.

The United States disregarded calls for greater UN involvement. On July 13, Bremer announced the formation of an Interim Governing Council (IGC). The twenty-five members of this group, picked by him, included thirteen Shi'a, four Sunnis, six Kurds, one Turkmen, and one Assyrian Christian. Three were women.[135] In its ethnic diversity and balance, the IGC represented an important step forward in the history of Iraqi governance. A month later, the Security Council in SCR 1500 cautiously welcomed the IGC as 'broadly representative' and 'an important step toward the formation by the people of Iraq of an internationally recognized, representative government'. (De Mello was more enthusiastic.[136]) It also established UNAMI, with a mandate already established under Resolution 1483.[137]

The IGC's composition troubled some international actors, given the inclusion of Ahmed Chalabi and Iyad Allawi, another Iraqi exile with close ties to the US administration, who later became Iraqi Prime Minister. The IGC had no authority over foreign affairs, security issues, or oil, and could only propose, not approve, budgets. It operated out of the fortified Coalition Green Zone in the center of Baghdad. Leading Shi'a figures, notably the increasingly influential al-Sistani, rejected the IGC as an 'unelected body'.[138] Al-Sistani, the leading Shi'ite cleric and *marja' al-taqlid* (source of emulation) in Iraq, had already made clear that a new constitution would only be acceptable to the Shi'a if drafted by a constitutional conference directly elected by the Iraqi people—and therefore dominated by Shi'a representatives.

Much of the time, the IGC was dysfunctional. It took until September 2, to name twenty-five ministers, who often clashed among themselves. Still, the international community's acceptance of the IGC was confirmed when

Hoshyar Zebari, a Kurd, was permitted to take the Iraqi seat at an Arab League meeting in Cairo on September 9, 2003. Zebari cannily used the occasion to assure the Arab states of Kurdish commitment to Iraq's 'Arab' identity, and ongoing support for the Palestinian people (despite links between Israel and the Kurds).[139] Confronted by Arab reporters on the question of whether the IGC was an American tool, Zebari responded ambiguously:

> The legitimacy of the Governing Council is definitely stronger than the legitimacy of the one-man totalitarian regime of Saddam Hussein.[140]

7.4.3 *The UN's 9/11*

On August 19, 2003 the UN suffered the largest loss of life of its civilian employees in its history. A massive truck-bomb was detonated at the corner of the UNAMI headquarters in Baghdad, directly under de Mello's office, killing him and twenty-one others, and wounding 150 more. This terrorist attack shocked the UN community and cast doubt over the security of its remaining staff in Iraq. A second attack within a month left twenty injured. The International Red Cross headquarters in Baghdad was decimated by a similar attack. Annan downsized the UN presence radically.[141] These attacks profoundly shook the UN, with consequences explored in the next chapter.

7.5 Conclusions

The terrorist attacks of 9/11 shook the confidence of the world's greatest military power, inducing it to flex its military muscle, first in Afghanistan (where the UN played a central political role) and then in Iraq. In Iraq, the UN was sidelined by the United States, and, having nevertheless sought to play a useful role through UNAMI on the ground, experienced a serious crisis of self-confidence following the devastating terrorist attack against its headquarters there. The fourth phase of UN involvement in Iraq between 2001 and 2003 developed into one of widespread disappointment and disillusionment.

7.5.1 *Terrorism and the UN*

September 11, 2001, and August 19, 2003, have forced a reappraisal, at a number of levels, of the implications for the UN of the new breed of transnational terrorism.

The first level is that of operational security. An independent inquiry launched by Kofi Annan into the August 19 bombing condemned what it described as a failure to provide adequate security to UN staff in Iraq.[142] The UN's security management structures proved woefully inadequate and required deep surgery if the UN was to continue to deploy to the world's hottest spots. Key changes resulted from this report. First, in a much-publicized and rare move, Annan took disciplinary measures against senior UN staff.[143] That, in turn, reflects movement toward greater accountability in UN administration later accelerated by the OFF scandal. Second, in a largely unheralded move, the UN proposed engaging a private firm to provide security for its global operations—an idea later abandoned.[144] Third, in subsequent SCR 1546, the Security Council for the first time approved the creation of a distinct component within a UN-authorized multinational force devoted specifically to UN security (see Chapter 8).[145] Fourth, UN security structures were overhauled, with the creation of a newly powerful Department of Safety and Security.

Another consequence of the August 19 bombing was an arguably exaggerated reaction among UN staff that risked paralyzing the UN's capacity to respond meaningfully to those Iraqi needs that the Organization might best be placed to address. Grief and rage among UN staff over the carnage ran deep. Internal criticism of Annan and his senior staff for allowing a UN deployment to Baghdad grew. UN staff expressed resentment at Annan's (actually, mostly de Mello's) attempts to forge a bridge between the Coalition occupiers and the rest of the international community in support of Iraqi needs. Increasingly, it seemed to be Annan's political judgment, not the UN's security mistakes, that some staff were targeting. Over time this discontent led to perverse results. The UN's new representative in Baghdad, Ashraf Jehangir Qazi, insisted in mid-2004 that security is 'not only the first consideration, it is the first priority, the second priority, and the third priority' for his Baghdad mission.[146] But if UN staff security is the UN's only significant priority and if Annan's margin for diplomatic and operational maneuver is to be constrained by staff challenges to his judgment, the UN will simply not be able to play much of a role in Iraq, or indeed in any of the theatres of war where it is most needed.[147]

The attacks on UNAMI made clear two other aspects of the new operational environment. First, they signaled that the UN's image of impartiality was under attack from Islamic fundamentalists who saw the UN as a stooge for Western interests. The UN had long been a target of violence in states in which it operated. It had also learned, in Bosnia and Rwanda, that impartiality cannot be equated with moral equivalence among the parties to a conflict or with unwillingness to intervene to prevent atrocities.[148] Second, the attacks drove home that terrorism posed a fundamental threat not only to the United States, but also to the UN.[149] The diffuse and asymmetric nature of terrorism calls for a different kind of international policing than the UN has traditionally been able to supply, with a greater focus on cooperative regulation and enforcement by states (as demanded by SCR 1373 and SCR 1540).[150] Thus, in the future, UN peacekeeping may have to compete for scarce resources with other forms of UN-mandated security regulation.

The terrorism of 9/11 and 8/19 has also forced a reappraisal at the legal level. In SCR 1502, the Security Council characterized the August 19 attack as a 'violation of international humanitarian law'.[151] That is certainly the case; but, at what point the threat of terrorist attack may trigger the right of states to use force has proven a thornier issue. In the 9/11 case, the Council acknowledged (in SCR 1368) that a massive terrorist attack triggered a right to self-defense against the state that harbored those terrorists. But on Iraq, the Security Council faced a much knottier test. There, the United States alleged that the advent of transnational terrorism transformed the strategic threat posed by a tyrannical regime with WMD aspirations, and sought authorization from the Council to use force to pre-empt the conjunction of these threats. The Council declined to offer such authorization, and the United States and the United Kingdom acted unilaterally.

In this action, we may see the seeds of an entirely new set of parameters for international (including, conceivably, UN) peace operations.[152] Terrorism offers a new justification for intervention, not only as a response to state failure, but also as a measure to prevent state failure lest it provide the conditions for the incubation of transnational terrorism. The rise of transnational terrorism may also affect the strategies of state-building adopted by the UN, placing a premium on the establishment of a strong state that can combat terrorism, with the transition to democratic statehood a secondary longer-term goal.[153] That could undermine long-held goals relating to the centrality of the rule of law in state-building, as we have seen with the early support for warlords in post-Taliban Afghanistan.[154]

7.5.2 *An Inevitable Crisis? Two Contending Instrumentalisms*

The United States and United Kingdom presented their decision to go to war in Iraq as an effort to enforce the resolutions of the Security Council. But for many, it demonstrated a willingness to sideline the UN when the Council refused to play ball. For the UN, these contending positions pointed to two perceived failures of containment: for some, a failure to contain Iraqi WMD aspirations, and for others, a failure to contain US–UK unilateralism. Michael Doyle reflects:

> The Council's performance on Iraq in March 2003 was both—and in about equal measure—a massive disappointment and a surprising relief. It disappointed all hopes that this essential international forum for multilateral policy could achieve a viable policy. At the same time, it demonstrated to the surprise of many that it would not let itself be bullied or bribed by any power, permanent or even hyper. The so far unanswered question is: Can it meet the challenge of keeping intact its integrity while improving its effectiveness?[155]

Yet, set against the sweep of earlier Council involvement in Iraq, the crisis takes on a certain inevitability. It appears the logical conclusion of two potentially contradictory trends highlighted earlier in our tale: on the one hand, a drift toward an increasing reliance on a legislative-regulatory approach to containing the Iraqi threat, working through strong UN institutions drawing legitimacy and effectiveness from an underlying P-5 consensus; and on the other, a creeping willingness by United States and United Kingdom to take unilateral enforcement action when no P-5 consensus could be mustered.

Until late 2002, a dangerously ambitious institutional system of regulation through inspections-plus-sanctions coexisted with P-5 willingness (under protest frequently) to accept unilateralist uses of force to further humanitarian interests and to provide the inspections-plus-sanctions regime some teeth. By late 2002, US and UK patience with this accommodation had run out, influenced by a new strategic calculus placing a premium on preventive action. These two impulses—toward strengthened institutions, and toward unilateral action—were set on a collision course.

Both impulses—multilateralist institutionalism and unilateralist realism—treat the Council instrumentally, but with different understandings of the timeline for payoffs from resort to the Council (or other global institutions). The multilateralist institutionalism symbolized in President George H. W. Bush's notion of a 'New World Order' sought instrumentally to generate long-term stability and value through investment in global institutions and a rule of law restricting even US power. The unilateralist realism symbolized by his son's opportunistic treatment of the 'UN route' reflects an appreciation of the Security Council as one coalition formation among many available to the Great Powers to achieve foreign policy objectives. This seemed to represent a major shift in Washington away from its commitment, dating back to World War II and its midwifery of the UN's birth, to global institutionalism.

The unique features of UN legitimacy, including its alignment with international legality, were no doubt understood in Washington; but in the end, if the UN did not offer the path of least resistance for the achievement of US foreign policy goals, the United States could dispense with it.

In retrospect, the fear of WMD seems to have been instrumentalized to sell a decision to go to war that had already been made in Washington.[156] The UN was certainly a useful partner for the United States in much of its strategy: the existing UN resolutions offered a plausible, ready-made *casus belli* linking Iraq with the threat of WMD proliferation. But, without UK insistence that a Security Council authorization had to be sought, would the United States, in this instance, have viewed the UN as the most suitable framework for assembling a Coalition? (It did not on Afghanistan, in spite of strong Security Council support for its aims.) And will we again see the United States placing its vital national interests before unpredictable and sometimes unreliable partners in the UN Security Council for deliberation and decision?

President Bush's speech to the General Assembly on September 12, 2002, warning the UN of an imminent choice between supporting the United States or being deemed irrelevant, had not been an idle talk: it could prove a self-fulfilling prophesy.[157] Lawrence Freedman has characterized the invasion of Iraq as 'something of an experiment' by the Western powers, using a pre-emptive strategy rather than a responsive one.[158] But it was equally an experiment in US–UN relations, in which the United States tested whether UN legitimacy could, on balance, serve the achievement of its (new) foreign policy goals. The outcome could prove unsettling for those who hold multilateral approaches to collective security sacred.

The United States, the new champion of a 'realist' approach recognizing its power, was and still is to a degree, opposed by defenders of 'institutionalism' in the Security Council. France was certainly keen to present itself in that light (Russia and China prudently less so, allowing France to take the lead). In part, this explains why revelations of French and Russian involvement in the corruption of the OFF Program have become so symbolically charged: such revelations can be taken to suggest that, while they purported to champion idealism and institutionalism, those powers in fact treated the Council, its decisions and its implementing machinery, with a mercantilism even more reprehensible than US instrumentalism.

In fact, the impulses and behavior of the P-5 may resemble each other much more than is immediately clear. As explored in Chapter 9, France's mixture of unilateralist realism and multilateralist institutionalism toward Côte d'Ivoire reminds us that within its own geostrategic sphere of influence, it is not so much France's principles as the now limited extent of its military, economic, and political power that dictate more multilateral strategies. What this may, in turn, suggest is that the Council's spawning of thick, powerful institutions intruding on state sovereignty to which we may have begun to become accustomed—UNSCOM, UNMOVIC, the CTC, the 1540 Committee, even the new child soldiers monitoring mechanism—will occur only where the P-5's interests are aligned. This may most likely be the case where the threat comes from non-state sources with which all the P-5 struggle equally. To date, this has included transnational terrorism and WMD proliferation; perhaps, in the future, it will include other non-state threats such as fast-moving pandemics.

Notes

1. Condoleezza Rice, 'Campaign 2000: Promoting the National Interest'.
2. Michael Gordon, 'Bush Would Stop U.S. Peacekeeping in Balkan Fights', *New York Times*, October 21, 2000, 1.
3. *Proliferation: Threat and Response*, Office of the Secretary of Defense, January 10, 2001, 38–42.
4. See Lopez, 'Toward Smart Sanctions on Iraq'; see also Lynch, 'Smart Sanctions: Rebuilding Consensus or Maintaining Conflict?'; and see David Cortright and George A. Lopez, 'Reforming Sanctions' in Malone, *The UN Security Council from the Cold War to the 21st Century*, and Pascal Teixeira da Silva, 'Weapons of Mass Destruction: The Iraqi Case', 214.
5. See Joseph P. Fried, 'Sheik Sentenced to Life in Prison in Bombing Plot', *New York Times*, January 18, 1996, 1.
6. UN Security Council resolution 1368, September 12, 2001. Council members reported privately that France was keen to have the Council authorize the use of force against Al Qaeda, but Washington, preferring to rest its action on the right to self-defense, refused.
7. UN Security Council resolution 1373, September 18, 2001. The CTC, which got off to a strong start under the chairmanship of the United Kingdom, soon disappointed the high hopes invested in it by engaging in an endless loop of correspondence with Member States on the degree of their compliance with the terms of Resolution 1373. The CTC was also slow to grasp that it could not duck the issue of respect for human rights in the fight against terrorism. Nevertheless, the Committee adopted unusually transparent procedures, including an innovative website—www.un.org/Docs/sc/committees/1373—on which much of the correspondence was reproduced. Under the Chairmanship of Spain, as of mid-2003, respect for performance of the CTC declined precipitously among Member States, interested experts, and commentators. This, in turn, inspired

the reforms enshrined in UN Security Council resolution 1535, March 26, 2004, revitalizing the CTC by establishing an Executive Directorate to coordinate and oversee its activities.

8. See UN Security Council resolution 1535, March 26, 2004, *Letter dated 2004/02/19 from the Chairman of the Security Council Committee established pursuant to resolution 1373 (2001) concerning counter-terrorism addressed to the President of the Security Council* (UN Security Council Document S/2004/124), February 19, 2004, and UN Security Council resolution 1540, April 28, 2004.
9. Hiro, *Iraq: In the Eye of the Storm*, 173–4.
10. Richard A. Clarke, interview with Leslie Stahl, 60 Minutes, CBS, March 21, 2004.
11. Walter Pincus, 'No Link Between Hijacker, Iraq Found, U.S. Says', *Washington Post*, May 1, 2002, A09.
12. Bob Woodward, *Plan of Attack* (New York, NY: Simon & Schuster, 2004), 8, 38.
13. Brian Urquhart, 'A Cautionary Tale', *New York Review of Books* 51/10, June 10, 2004.
14. See Jonathan Steinberg, 'One man and his god', *Financial Times*, June 12, 2004, 26; see further Peter Waldman, 'Evangelicals Give U.S. Foreign Policy Activist Tinge', *Wall Street Journal*, May 26, 2004, A1.
15. See 'Bush calls Saddam "the guy who tried to kill my dad"', *CNN.com*, September 27, 2002, http://archives.cnn.com/2002/ALLPOLITICS/09/27/bush.war.talk/index.html.
16. Woodward, *Plan of Attack*, 421.
17. See Bill Keller, 'Reagan's son', *New York Times*, January 26, 2003, 26.
18. 'Fumbling the Moment', *The Economist*, May 29, 2004, 23. Some of these figures do not fit comfortably with the idealism implicit in the neoconservative ideology, notably John Bolton, a stern advocate of American power unswayed by notions relating to the promotion of values.
19. Project for the New American Century, 'Welcome to the Project for the New American Century', www.newamericancentury.org.
20. See Seth Lipsky, 'Bush's Contras? The new president should support Iraq's democrats in exile', *Wall Street Journal* (*OpinionJournal.com*), February 21, 2001. The rhetoric of the US bears striking similarity to the US case against Panama in 1989—minus WMD—citing self-defense and the spread of freedom. See the comments of US Ambassador Thomas Pickering in *Provisional verbatim record of the 2902nd meeting* (UN Security Council Document S/PV.2902), December 23, 1989, 7–16.
21. John Lewis Gaddis, 'Grand Strategy in the Second Term', *Foreign Affairs* 84/1 (2005); John J. Mearsheimer and Stephen Walt, 'An unnecessary war', *Foreign Policy* 134 (2003); Roland Watson, 'Bush risks isolating US, cautions Kissinger', *The Times*, August 13, 2002, 12; Henry A. Kissinger and George P. Shultz, 'Results, Not Timetables, Matter in Iraq', *Washington Post*, January 25, 2005, A15.

22. See Franklin Foer, 'Once Again America First', *New York Times Book Review*, October 10, 2004, 22, for an analysis of trends within the American conservative movement relevant to Iraq.
23. 'President Discusses War on Terror', *White House Office of the Press Secretary*, March 8, 2005.
24. 'President Delivers State of the Union Address', *White House Office of the Press Secretary*, January 29, 2002.
25. Kenneth Pollack, 'Next Stop Baghdad?', *Foreign Affairs* 81/2 (2002) and *The Threatening Storm: The Case for Invading Iraq* (New York, NY: Random House, 2002). After the war, Pollack argued that at the 'very least we should recognize that the Administration's rush to war was reckless even on the basis of what we thought we knew in March of 2003. It appears even more reckless in light of what we know today.' See Kenneth Pollack, 'Spies, Lies, and Weapons: What Went Wrong', *Atlantic Monthly*, 293/1 (2004), 90–1.
26. 'I think the United States must be humble and must be proud and confident of our values, but humble in how we treat nations that are figuring out how to chart their own course', President Bush stated during the Presidential Debate at Wake Forest University. See Commission on Presidential Debates, '2000 Debate Transcript: The Second Gore-Bush Presidential Debate', October 11, 2000.
27. See Philip H. Gordon, 'Bush's Middle East Vision', *Survival* 45/1 (2003).
28. Jonathan S. Landay, Warren P. Strobel, and John Walcott, 'Doubts Cast on Efforts to Link Saddam and Al-Qaeda', *Knight Ridder/Tribune News Service*, March 3, 2004.
29. 'President Bush Delivers Graduation Speech at West Point', *White House Office of the Press Secretary*, June 1, 2002.
30. United States, President of the United States, *The National Security Strategy of the United States of America* (Washington, DC: The White House, 2002), 15.
31. 'President Bush Outlines Iraqi Threat', *White House Office of the Press Secretary*, October 7, 2002.
32. United States Congress, *Authorization for the Use of Military Force Against Iraq*, Public Law 107–243, 116 Stat. 1498, H.J. Res. 114, October 16, 2002.
33. Mark Danner, 'The Secret Way to War', *New York Review of Books* 52/10, June 9, 2005, 70.
34. David Remnick, 'The Masochism Campaign', *New Yorker* 81/11, May 2, 2005, 84.
35. UK Prime Minister Tony Blair, NBC TV News, April 3, 2002.
36. A much overlooked *Knight Ridder* report of February 13, 2002 had laid out much the same conclusion, pointing to an ultimatum on cooperation with weapons inspectors as the likely *casus belli*: John Walcott and Walter P. Strobel, 'Bush Has Decided to Overthrow Hussein', *Knight Ridder News Service*, February 13, 2002.
37. Walter Pincus and Dana Priest, 'Some Iraq Analysts Felt Pressure From Cheney Visits', *Washington Post*, June 5, 2003, A1.

38. Deputy Secretary Wolfowitz Interview with Sam Tannenhaus, *Vanity Fair*, May 9, 2003.
39. Danner, 'The Secret Way to War', 71–2.
40. 'Vice President Honors Veterans of Korean War'.
41. Danner, 'The Secret Way to War'.
42. Woodward, *Plan of Attack*, 178; Christopher Bluth, 'The British road to war: Blair, Bush and the decision to invade Iraq', *International Affairs* 80/5 (2004), 879.
43. Karen DeYoung, 'Bush to Challenge U.N. on Iraqi Threat; President Will Demand Action Soon on Hussein', *Washington Post*, September 11, 2002, A13.
44. Jonathan Freedland, 'Patten lays into Bush's America: Fury at president's "axis of evil" speech', *The Guardian*, February 9, 2002, 1.
45. Brian Knowlton, 'Bush presses case for international support to strike Iraq', *International Herald Tribune*, September 10, 2002, 8.
46. Steven Erlanger, 'Stance on Bush Policy Could Swing Election in Germany', *New York Times*, September 9, 2002, 3. For analysis, see Anja Dalgaard-Nielsen, 'Gulf War: The German Resistance', *Survival* 45/1 (2003).
47. 'French Leader Offers America Both Friendship and Criticism', *New York Times*, September 9, 2002, 9.
48. 'Former weapons inspector: Iraq not a threat', *CNN.com*, September 9, 2002, http://archives.cnn.com/2002/WORLD/meast/09/08/ritter.iraq/index.html.
49. 'A Decade of Deception and Defiance', *White House Office of the Press Secretary*, September 12, 2002.
50. *General Assembly official records, 57th session: 2nd plenary meeting* (UN General Assembly Document A/57/PV.2), September 12, 2002, 1.
51. *General Assembly official records, 57th session: 2nd plenary meeting*, 8.
52. UN Security Council resolution 1441, November 7, 2002.
53. Jessica T. Mathews, 'A New Approach: Coercive Inspections', in Jessica T. Matthews (ed.), *Iraq: A New Approach* (New York, NY: Carnegie Endowment, 2002).
54. International Crisis Group, *Iraq Policy Briefing: Is There An Alternative To War?*, Middle East Report No. 9, February 24, 2003, 20.
55. ICG, *Is There An Alternative To War?*
56. James Traub, *The Best Intentions: Kofi Annan and the UN in the Era of American World Power* (New York, NY: Farrar Straus and Giroux, 2006 (forthcoming)).
57. Teixeira da Silva, 'Weapons of Mass Destruction', 215.
58. Comments of White House spokesman Ari Fleischer, cited in Woodward, *Plan of Attack*, 232.
59. Lawrence Freedman, 'War In Iraq: Selling The Threat', *Survival* 46/2 (2004), 29.
60. UN Security Council resolution 1441, November 8, 2002.
61. *Security Council, 57th year: 4644th meeting* (UN Security Council Document S/PV.4644), November 8, 2002.
62. Cited in Danner, 'The Secret Way to War', 72; see also *Security Council, 57th year: 4644th meeting*, 4–5.

63. Correspondence with the author, June 6, 2005.
64. Interview, June 7, 2005.
65. Interview, June 7, 2005.
66. Correspondence with the author, June 6, 2005.
67. *Letter dated 2002/11/13 from the Secretary-General addressed to the President of the Security Council* (UN Security Council Document S/2002/1242), November 13, 2002, annex.
68. Condoleezza Rice, 'Why We Know Iraq is Lying', *New York Times*, February 23, 2003, 25.
69. Lopez and Cortright, 'Containing Iraq', 92.
70. Quentin Peel et al., 'How the US Set a Course for War with Iraq', *Financial Times*, May 26, 2003.
71. James Traub, *The Best Intentions: Kofi Annan and the UN in the Era of American World Power* (New York, NY: Farrar Straus and Giroux, 2006 (forthcoming)).
72. Quentin Peel, et al., 'How the US Set a Course for War with Iraq'.
73. Quentin Peel, et al., 'How the US Set a Course for War with Iraq'.
74. I, for one, overestimated the inclination of the P-5 to accommodate each other's priorities, believing that a confrontation would ultimately be avoided. See Malone, 'The UN will come around to the Bush-Blair view', *International Herald Tribune*, February 1, 2003, 4.
75. See Steven R. Weisman., 'U.S. Set To Demand that Allies Agree Iraq is Defying U.N.', *New York Times*, January 23, 2003, 1.
76. Quentin Peel et al., 'How the US Set a Course for War with Iraq'.
77. 'No evidence yet to justify war on Iraq: Ivanov', *Agence France-Presse*, January 23, 2003.
78. 'China adds voice to Iraq war doubts', *CNN.com*, January 23, 2003, http://edition.cnn.com/2003/WORLD/asiapcf/east/01/23/sprj.irq.china/index.html.
79. Hans Blix, 'Disarming Iraq: Hans Blix's Story'.
80. See Philip H. Gordon and Jeremy Shapiro, *Allies at War: America, Europe and the Crisis over Iraq* (New York, NY: McGraw Hill, 2004); and Michael Clarke, 'The diplomacy that led to war in Iraq', in Paul Cornish (ed.), *The Conflict in Iraq 2003* (London: Palgrave/Macmillan, 2004).
81. See 'U.S. Secretary of State Colin Powell Addresses the U.N. Security Council', *White House Office of the Press Secretary*, February 5, 2003.
82. 'U.S. Secretary of State Colin Powell Addresses the U.N. Security Council'.
83. Blix, *Disarming Iraq*, 157, 167.
84. Mohammed El Baradei, 'The Status of Nuclear Inspections in Iraq: An Update', March 7, 2003.
85. Blix, *Disarming Iraq*, 86.
86. See for example Steven R. Weisman, 'To White House, Inspector Is Now More a Dead End Than a Guidepost', *New York Times*, March 2, 2003, 13.
87. Blix, *Disarming Iraq*, 239.
88. Blix, *Disarming Iraq*, 246.

89. *Security Council, 58th year: 4707th meeting* (UN Security Council Document S/PV.4707), February 14, 2003.
90. James Graff and Bruce Crumley, ' "France Is Not a Pacifist Country"; The target of U.S. scorn, France's Jacques Chirac tells *Time*'s James Graff and Bruce Crumley of his objection to war and his love of American junk food', *Time*, February 24, 2003, 32.
91. 'Euro polls show little appetite for war', *Daily Telegraph Online*, January 18, 2003.
92. United States Department of State, 'Iraq: U.S./U.K./Spain Draft Resolution', February 24, 2003.
93. This argument is laid out most cogently in the secret legal advice provided by UK Attorney General Lord Goldsmith on March 7, 2003 and released to the public on April 28, 2005, 'Iraq: Resolution 1441'. As Adam Roberts has persuasively pointed out, the argument that hostilities may lawfully be recommenced in the event of a lapse of a ceasefire (which is what SCR 687 purported to impose) is supported by Article 30 of the 1907 Hague Regulations. See Adam Roberts, 'The Use of Force', in Malone, *The UN Security Council from the Cold War to the 21st Century*.
94. Blix, *Disarming Iraq*, 213.
95. An 'absolute majority' of nine—not eight—votes is required on the Council, despite the fifteen members. See Bailey and Daws, *The Procedure of the Security Council*, 225.
96. Sarah Anderson, Phyllis Bennis, and John Cavanagh, 'Coalition of the Willing or Coalition of the Coerced?', Institute for Policy Studies, February 26, 2003, www.ips-dc.org/COERCED.pdf.
97. Martin Bright, Ed Vulliamy, and Peter Beaumont, 'Revealed: US dirty tricks to win vote on Iraq war', *The Observer*, March 2, 2003, 1.
98. See Warren Hoge, 'On Bugging News, Annan Had Low-Key Reaction to Old Practice', *New York Times*, February 28, 2004, 6.
99. Blix, *Disarming Iraq*, 217.
100. Blix, *Disarming Iraq*, 212.
101. Blix, *Disarming Iraq*, 212–13.
102. See generally David L. Phillips, *Losing Iraq: Inside the Postwar Reconstruction Fiasco* (New York, NY: Westview, 2005), 111–20.
103. 'President Says Saddam Hussein Must Leave Iraq Within 48 Hours', *White House Office of the Press Secretary*, March 17, 2003.
104. Douglas Jehl and Eric Schmitt, 'Errors Are Seen in Early Attacks on Iraqi Leaders', *New York Times*, June 13, 2004, 1.
105. The US Army Third Division's *After Action Report* for this period states: 'Higher headquarters did not provide ... a plan for ... stability operations.... [We] transitioned ... in the absence of guidance.' Quoted in Phillips, *Losing Iraq*, 133–4.
106. See Zainab Bahrani, 'Days of Plunder', *The Guardian*, August 31, 2004, 13.

107. When Jay Garner brought one of the leaders of the State Department project, Thomas Warrick, into his staff, he was ordered to remove him by Cheney and Rumsfeld. James Fallows, 'Blind into Baghdad', *Atlantic Monthly* 293/1 (2004). See also Phillips, *Losing Iraq*, 37, 134.
108. *Lt. Gen. (Ret.) Jay Garner testimony before the House Committee on Government Reform Subcommittee on National Security*, May 13, 2003.
109. Phillips, *Losing Iraq*, 68.
110. See John Hendren, 'Showdown With Iraq: A Huge Postwar Force Seen', *Los Angeles Times*, February 26, 2003, A1, and *Deputy Secretary of Defense Paul Wolfowitz testimony before the Senate Foreign Relations Committee*, May 22, 2003; see also David Rieff, 'Blueprint For A Mess', *New York Times Magazine*, November 2, 2003, 28.
111. *Deputy Secretary of Defense Paul Wolfowitz testimony before the Senate Foreign Relations Committee*.
112. Defense Department news briefing, April 11, 2003.
113. Judy Dempsey, 'Keep Aid Neutral, Urges EU Relief Chief', *Financial Times*, March 31, 2003, 4.
114. Phillips, *Losing Iraq*, 131.
115. Eric Schmitt and David E. Sanger, 'Looting Disrupts Detailed U.S. Plan to Restore Iraq', *New York Times*, May 19, 2003, 1.
116. Confidential interview, June 2, 2005.
117. Phillips, *Losing Iraq*, 147.
118. Bush later awarded Bremer—along with General Tommy Franks and CIA Director George Tenet, who famously described the intelligence case on Iraqi WMD as a 'slam dunk'—the Medal of Freedom, the highest US public award.
119. Defense Department news briefing, August 21, 2003.
120. Defense Department news briefing, August 21, 2003.
121. David Ignatius, 'Lessons for Iraq From Gettysburg', *Washington Post*, May 4, 2005, 19.
122. *Security Council, 58th year: 4721st meeting* (UN Security Council Document S/PV.4721), March 19, 2003, 22.
123. See Thomas D. Grant, 'The Security Council and Iraq: An Incremental Practice', *American Journal of International Law* 97/4 (2003), 824.
124. See David Scheffer, 'Beyond Occupation Law', *American Journal of International Law* 97/4 (2003).
125. UN Security Council resolution 1483, May 22, 2003, para. 8.
126. SCR 1483, para. 9.
127. See *Deputy Secretary of Defense Paul Wolfowitz testimony before the Senate Foreign Relations Committee*, July 29, 2003.
128. 'Goal In Iraq Is Early End To Occupation, Formation Of Representative Government, Secretary-General Tells Security Council' (UN Press Release SC/7821), July 23, 2003. For this, he was quietly criticized by many in the UN Secretariat.

129. Douglas Jehl, 'Pentagon Bars Three Nations from Iraq Bids', *New York Times*, December 10, 2003, 1.
130. 'Audit: U.S. lost track of $9 billion in Iraq funds', *CNN.com*, January 31, 2005, http://edition.cnn.com/2005/WORLD/meast/01/30/iraq.audit/index.html.
131. 'Report of the International Advisory and Monitoring Board of the Development Fund for Iraq', IAMB, December 14, 2004, 3: 'IAMB believes that controls were insufficient to provide reasonable assurance (i) for the completeness of export sales of petroleum and petroleum products, and (ii) whether all DFI disbursements were made for the purposes intended.' See also Christopher Cooper and Greg Jaffe, 'Audit Splits U.S. and U.N.—Inquiry Centers on a $20 Billion Account for Projects in Iraq', *Wall Street Journal*, September 17, 2004, A4; 'Audit: U.S. lost track of $9 billion in Iraq funds'; Thomas Catan, Stephen Fidler and Demetri Sevastopulo, 'Big Spender: was the US-led coalition a careless steward of $20bn of Iraqi funds?', *Financial Times*, December 10, 2004, 17.
132. 'Chirac says U.N. must handle rebuilding Iraq', *Reuters*, April 8, 2003.
133. 'Goal In Iraq Is Early End To Occupation'.
134. See *Report of the Secretary-General pursuant to paragraph 24 of Security Council resolution 1483 (2003)* (UN Security Council Document S/2003/715), July 17, 2003.
135. Phillips, *Losing Iraq*, 171.
136. John Daniszewski, 'Iraqis OK Plan for Temporary Governing Council', *Los Angeles Times*, July 8, 2003, A1.
137. UN Security Council resolution 1500, August 14, 2003.
138. Jonathan S. Landay, 'Bush Administration Split Over How to Restore Iraqi Self-Rule', *Knight Ridder/Tribune News Service*, January 27, 2004.
139. Abeer Allam, 'Iraqi Takes Seat at Arab League', *New York Times*, September 10, 2003, 11.
140. Allam, 'Iraqi Takes Seat at Arab League'.
141. See Alex Berenson, 'U.N. Chief Orders Further Reduction of Staff in Baghdad', *New York Times*, September 26, 2003, 8.
142. See 'Report of the Independent Panel on the Safety and Security of UN Personnel in Iraq', Independent Panel on the Safety and Security of the United Nations Personnel in Iraq, October 20, 2003; and see 'Report of the Security in Iraq Accountability Panel (SIAP)', Security in Iraq Accountability Panel, March 3, 2004.
143. See 'Annan takes strong disciplinary measures after probe reveals security failures in Iraq,' *UN News Centre*, March 29, 2004.
144. See Edith M. Lederer, 'U.N. Intends to Hire a Security Firm', *Associated Press*, March 4, 2004.
145. See *Text of letters from the Prime Minister of the Interim Government of Iraq Dr. Ayad Allawi and United States Secretary of State Colin L. Powell to the President of the Council*, Annex to UN Security Council resolution 1546, June 8, 2004, 11.

146. See *Secretary-General's press encounter with his Special Representative for Iraq, Ashraf Qazi*, July 22, 2004.
147. See David M. Malone, 'Nobody said it would be safe: UN anger over Iraq', *International Herald Tribune*, October 1, 2004, 9.
148. See especially *Report of the Secretary-General pursuant to General Assembly resolution 53/35: the fall of Srebrenica; Letter dated 99/12/15 from the Secretary-General addressed to the President of the Security Council [Report of the Independent Inquiry into the Actions of the United Nations During the 1994 Genocide in Rwanda]* (UN Security Council Document S/1999/1257), December 16, 1999; and the Brahimi Report, *Identical letters dated 2000/08/21 from the Secretary-General to the President of the General Assembly and the President of the Security Council [Report of the Panel on United Nations Peace Operations]* (UN General Assembly-Security Council Document A/55/305-S/2000/809), August 21, 2000, which argued for the primacy of 'impartiality' over 'neutrality' in peace operations.
149. See generally Edward C. Luck, 'Tackling Terrorism', in Malone, *The UN Security Council from the Cold War to the 21st Century*, and Andrés Franco, 'Armed Nonstate Actors', in Malone, *The UN Security Council from the Cold War to the 21st Century*.
150. SCR 1373; SCR 1540.
151. UN Security Council resolution 1502, August 26, 2003.
152. See 'The Future of UN State-Building: Strategic and Operational Challenges and the Legacy of Iraq', International Peace Academy, New York, December 2003.
153. See 'The Future of UN State-Building', 6. The American approach in Iraq employs the reverse logic: the accelerated grafting of an unstable democracy onto the Iraqi polity in order to generate 'legitimacy', which can eventually lend support to the foundation of a strong state, which can then fight terrorism.
154. See Antonio Donini, Norah Niland, and Karin Wermester (eds.), *Nation-Building Unraveled? Aid, Peace and Justice in Afghanistan* (Bloomfield, CT: Kumarian Press, 2004).
155. See David M. Malone, 'Conclusions', in Malone, *The UN Security Council from the Cold War to the 21st Century*, 644.
156. See Woodward, *Plan of Attack*, 220.
157. *General Assembly official records, 57th session: 3rd plenary meeting* (UN General Assembly Document A/57/PV.3), September 12, 2002.
158. Freedman, 'War In Iraq', 39.

8

Crisis of Confidence: *Annus Horribilis* and a 'Vital' Role

The deadlock in the Security Council early in 2003, followed by the terrorist bombing of UN headquarters in Baghdad on August 19, 2003, triggered a profound crisis of confidence in the UN, inducing soul-searching and calls for reform. The sidelining of the UN during 2003 represented a fourth phase, discussed in the previous chapter, in the UN's involvement with Iraq since 1980. Now, it entered a fifth, attempting to find its feet in Iraq, and contemplating meaningful reform in its way of doing business.

The path to rehabilitation was not to be easy. No amount of activity elsewhere (notably in Africa), much of it useful and on its own terms successful, was capable of recovering its credibility. Shortcomings in past UN activities in Iraq, particularly the OFF Program, weighed heavily; successes, such as the weapons inspections regime, were given little credit. Warning of a possible 'proliferation of the unilateral and lawless use of force', Annan told the General Assembly in September 2003 that the UN had 'come to a fork in the road'.[1] The reform imperative was clear, but Member States were recalcitrant to significant change. Annan announced the appointment of a High-Level Panel on Threats, Challenges and Change, to chart a new course.

The contrast between the Council's rhetoric, entrusting a 'vital' role to the UN, and the reality of its marginal presence on the ground was stark. The UN's potential there was circumscribed on the one hand by the continuing strong guiding hand of the United States in Iraqi affairs and on the other by the dreadful security situation in Iraq precluding deployment of a large UN international staff. The toll on Kofi Annan, in particular, was heavy; he described 2004 as his '*annus horribilis*'.

8.1 A Vital Role?

8.1.1 *The Coalition under Pressure*

The terrorists' targeting of the UN and other symbols of the international community was only one feature of a much wider deterioration in security in Iraq. On August 29, an explosion in Najaf killed a leading figure in the Iranian-backed Shi'a Supreme Council for Islamic Revolution in Iraq (SCIRI), Muhammad Bakr al-Hakim. Attacks on Italian troops, the Jordanian Embassy, the Turkish Mission, and the International Committee of the Red Cross soon followed. A missile attack on the al-Rashid Hotel on October 26 barely missed Paul Wolfowitz. By October 29, 2003, more US troops had died in combat deaths *since* President Bush's declaration on the deck of the *USS Abraham Lincoln* of 'Mission Accomplished' than prior to it. The Coalition appeared at times to drift, unable to meet the most basic security needs of Iraq's citizens and increasingly abandoning its vaunted economic reconstruction objectives.[2]

An October 2003 resolution of the Security Council reaffirmed the 'vital role' of the UN in humanitarian relief, reconstruction, development, and the transition to representative government, but did not significantly broaden its mandate beyond calling on the UN to support the constitutional drafting processes established by the Iraqi Governing Council.[3] The resolution also authorized the presence of a multinational security force in Iraq under US command, providing a degree of international cover for the Coalition's military operations and indicating that the UN would not take over security obligations in post-conflict Iraq any time soon.

By November, the situation had become so dire for the Coalition that Bremer was called to meetings in Washington. A senior CPA official recounts the effect this had on Bremer:

> Bremer did not work for the Administration as a whole. Rather he responded to the Department of Defense and to the Republican Party. Even he did not retain the Administration's undivided confidence beyond November 2003, when he started being micro-managed by the Pentagon (for example on the Fallujah campaign during the Spring of 2004) and increasingly shadowed by the National Security Council's Robert Blackwill.[4]

The Bush administration now reversed course and agreed to create an Iraqi interim government prior to the completion of the drafting of a constitution. A November 15 agreement set out a timetable for the drafting of a 'Transitional Administrative Law' by February 28, 2004 and for local caucuses in each of Iraq's eighteen governorates to elect delegates to a Transitional National Assembly, which would then elect an interim government assuming full power by June 30, 2004. By March 15, 2005, direct elections would be held for a conference that would draft a permanent constitution, under which national elections for a post-transition government would be held by December 31, 2005.

Support for this plan, which involved much else, was uneven. The Kurds opposed it because it did not give them Kirkuk, and because it left the existing eighteen governorates intact, entrenching the division of Kurdish areas into three governorates. Leading Shi'a opposed it because it did not allow them immediately the dominant political role they would derive from direct elections and because it did not give a special normative place to *shari'a*. Ayatollah al-Sistani vigorously opposed the suggestion of regional caucuses, insisting on direct elections. He even refused to deal with the CPA. Assessing the challenges to Bremer and his performance, a senior CPA official offers:

> On balance, Bremer performed creditably in a difficult environment about which he initially knew nothing. He was decisive, and even when wrong in his decisions, telegraphed a sense of command to which the Iraqis generally responded. That said, Sistani never trusted him, never believed he would deliver on his promises of elections, control for the Shi'a etc.—which, of course, ultimately he did.[5]

Given al-Sistani's lack of trust in the CPA, what was needed was an impartial third party to broker a way forward. *Faute de mieux*, the United States now turned to the UN 'to bring all the parties together to support the November 15 plan'.[6]

8.1.2 *Brahimi the Kingmaker?*

With the UN in shock after the August 19 bombing, Annan waited until December 10 to name even an acting replacement for de Mello. Coalition forces captured Saddam Hussein on December 13, 2003, but this did not reduce insurgent violence.[7] Sensing that the moment might provide 'an opportunity for a new beginning in the vital task of helping Iraqis take control of their destiny', Annan pushed for the Security Council to clarify the UN's future role in Iraq.[8] By mid-January 2004, consensus emerged that the UN should play an advisory role on the timing and organization of elections.[9] Helpfully, al-Sistani indicated he would accept a ruling by the UN on whether credible elections would be feasible within six months.

On February 3, in a sign of the rapprochement, Annan was invited to the White House to nail down the UN's role. By February 7 a UN team led by Lakhdar Brahimi had arrived in Iraq to explore with Iraqis and the

Coalition ways forward toward representative government.[10] Brahimi, urged on personally by President Bush who met with him in Washington, now entered into a delicate partnership with the CPA. A veteran of difficult UN missions, Brahimi first distinguished himself leading the UN mission in Haiti, 1994–6, working well with, but never subordinating himself to, the United States—which had significant interests there. He had also been involved in negotiations over Iraqi cooperation with UNSCOM in the late 1990s. In his earlier years, Brahimi had been an FLN student activist in his native Algeria, and eventually Algeria's Foreign Minister, 1991–3. His political philosophy and modus operandi are unusual at the UN:

> He does not see it as his business to engineer new democracies or to impose outside visions on reluctant societies. On the contrary, he is a tough-minded realist who respects and understands power; his approach ... has been to figure out which players are in charge on the ground and how to meet their minimum requirements.[11]

This approach was appreciated in Washington, which saw Brahimi's pragmatism up close in Afghanistan, where he had been UN supremo after the US-led invasion. The same pragmatism characterized his perception of the challenges he faced in Iraq:

> After more than three decades of despotic rule, without the basic elements of the rule of law, a ruined economy, a devastated country, the collapse of state institutions, low political will for reconciliation and distrust among some Iraqis, conditions in Iraq are daunting.... [The political process] remains limited to a few actors, with varying credibility.[12]

Brahimi met with all the key players, including Ayatollah al-Sistani, and agreed to back al-Sistani's call for elections, working at the same time to bury the idea of elections by June.[13] Instead, the UN would work with the Coalition and Iraqis to generate a widely acceptable interim government until elections could be held (ultimately on January 30, 2005).[14] He had managed to do what the United States could not, engaging with Iraqi society such that the United States hoped he could 'cultivate legitimacy for a step-by-step political process'.[15]

On March 8, Bremer signed into force a 'Transitional Administrative Law' (TAL), to serve as a constitutional framework in the period until elections allowed for the drafting of a new Iraqi constitution.[16] It contained important compromises, particularly from the Kurds, who in exchange for the concession of administrative unity and the elevation of Kurdish to the status of an official national language alongside Arabic, allowed a census prior to the determination of the final status of Kirkuk.[17] But al-Sistani remained concerned about its failure to deliver Shi'a dominance of Iraqi politics.[18]

In April, Brahimi met with a wide cross-section of Iraqi society in Baghdad, Basra, and Mosul. This time, he did not meet with al-Sistani, who may have been miffed by Brahimi's refusal to support his calls for constitutional enshrinement of *shari'a*. Brahimi recommended that the IGC be replaced by a transitional government that would prepare for elections, made up of men and women known for their honesty, integrity, and competence—code for 'technocrats'—to be selected by the UN after consultation with the CPA and Iraqis.[19] A consultative assembly of perhaps 1,000 Iraqis was recommended to help promote stability. Annan fully backed Brahimi's plan and so did Washington, through the voice of Colin Powell, who described him as 'quite skilled at these kinds of things'.[20] Brahimi had suggested that the IGC should not be represented in the new government, but intense maneuvering from within the IGC, which displayed a predictable reluctance of turkeys to acquiesce in Christmas, produced a nominee from within its ranks, Iyad Allawi, as transitional Prime Minister.[21] (Brahimi's first choice, Hussein Shahristani, a scientist, had been marginalized.[22]) Bremer and Washington were comfortable with this development as, in exile, Allawi had long been in close contact with the CIA. Indeed, Bremer's role in this critical choice may have been responsible for Brahimi branding him as the 'dictator of Iraq'.[23]

While the broader Government and Cabinet bore the stamp of Brahimi's consultations, with posts carefully allotted to the main religious and ethnic groups, an impression remained that the UN had been traduced.[24] However, Brahimi—always a realist—had emphasized all along that the UN's capacity to influence events in Iraq should not be exaggerated.[25] In briefing the Security Council, he lauded the active role Iraqi political voices played in formation of the Interim government. A CPA official familiar with the negotiations characterized Brahimi's role in the following terms:

> Brahimi's role ... was made much more difficult by the absence of a UN team on the ground and by security factors that prevented him from meeting freely with Iraqis all over the country. He did play a role, but, ultimately, the top leadership of the Interim Government was determined more by the Iraqis themselves—Sistani, the Governing Council and several individuals, including Adnan Pachachi, who withdrew from the Presidency at the last moment. The key problem was that no genuinely credible Sunnis ever came forward.[26]

Reflecting later on his role, Brahimi noted:

> I ... accepted that mission very reluctantly. The US needed the UN ... and it was true they could not have done what was to be done without the UN. But the situation had deteriorated considerably and there was ... very little space to

manoeuvre. Am I happy with what we did during those months in Baghdad? No, I am not.... The one thing which we thought was necessary—and I still believe it was, and still is—was to talk to those insurgents who had what one might call a patriotic agenda. And that was not part of our mission.

The UN, of course made the election possible (people forget that it was my meeting with Ayatollah Sistani that led to him and the Shi'a to accept the postponement of the election to January 2005) and was instrumental in securing whatever credibility that election ultimately had. But neither the formation of that new Government in May 2004 and our role in it, nor the election and our role in making it relatively credible has contributed to the restoration of security which is the key to the future of Iraq.[27]

Security was the key, too, to the limited involvement of the UN. While some advocates were soon calling for the UN to take a leading role in guiding the Iraqi transition after June 30, UN officials were reluctant, traumatized by the August 2003 bombings, and chastened by a realization that the UN's legitimacy had been repeatedly tarnished in Iraq.[28]

8.2 Rocky Waters

8.2.1 *Conduct Unbecoming*

In April 2004, US forces launched 'Operation Desert Scorpion' against insurgent militia in Fallujah, meeting stiff resistance.[29] The Coalition then tried alternative approaches, such as introducing Iraqi army units to patrol Fallujah, and negotiating in Najaf with Moqtada al-Sadr, reversing earlier strategies of the CPA.[30] Soon bombardments of both cities with their attendant civilian casualties had ceased. This progress was obscured, however, by media reports of harsh, indeed bizarre, treatment of Iraqi prisoners involving psychological, physical, and sexual abuse and torture by US interrogators at the Abu Ghraib prison. Further evidence leaked out rapidly—including from the International Committee of the Red Cross.[31] Photographs of naked detainees in degrading postures were racing around the Internet and onto the front pages of newspapers the world over.[32] Many of the worst allegations were confirmed in a searing investigation by US Major General Antonio Taguba.[33]

The international reaction of disgust (and grim satisfaction in some quarters) can hardly be exaggerated. President Bush cast the incidents as the product of six or seven 'bad apples', but an avalanche of documents leaking out of Baghdad and Washington made clear that extreme interrogation methods had been authorized up the chain of command, prompting questions about methods at the US detention facilities in Afghanistan (where detainees had died while under interrogation) and at Guantánamo Bay.[34] Subsequent revelations underscored that Pentagon and White

House policies on interrogation had been challenged vigorously by the State Department, but to little avail.[35] The policy of 'rendering' suspects to countries in which information might be extracted under duress was highlighted by the case of Maher Arar, a Canadian citizen deported by the United States to and allegedly tortured in Syria, and gave rise to friction when Italy, a close US ally on Iraq, complained about CIA tactics of concealed rendition from Italian soil.[36]

In June 2004, the US Supreme Court granted legal rights of review to detainees at Guantánamo in a decision interpreted by many as a rebuke to the US administration.[37] In time, the administration did introduce new interrogation rules for detainees in Iraq, involving a 'more limited set of techniques' and 'additional safeguards'.[38] And the Justice Department recast its definition of torture, retreating from the much-criticized guidelines the administration had instituted in 2002.[39] But the administration often manifested an unshakable belief that 'legally and politically ... the measures simply raise no problem of constitutionality or civil rights'.[40]

The damage to the international standing of the United States was real and lasting. At home, some conservative commentators were unapologetic.[41] Others, including some who had supported the war based on purported intelligence findings and the undeniable horrors of the Saddam Hussein regime, felt bitterly let down. Michael Ignatieff wrote:

> Someone like me who supported the war on human-rights grounds has nowhere to hide: we didn't suppose the administration was particularly nice, but we did assume it would be competent. There isn't much excuse for its incompetence, but equally, there isn't much excuse for our own naiveté either.... The United States did one thing well in Iraq ... it overthrew a dictator. Everything else was badly done, and some of what was done—Abu Ghraib—was a moral disgrace and a strategic catastrophe.[42]

The international community was equally dismayed.[43] Jakob Kellenberger, President of the ICRC commented:

> The world should not need any photographs of torture and ill treatment to remember that the protection of human life and dignity is everyone's concern and requires action.[44]

There were consequences even in the Security Council. On June 23, 2004, Washington was compelled to withdraw a proposed 'technical rollover' of a 2002 resolution providing blanket immunity from criminal prosecution in the International Criminal Court (ICC) for American troops participating in UN peacekeeping.[45] Unable to muster the nine affirmative votes it would require, Washington suffered the further humiliation of chiding by China.[46] China's UN Ambassador, Wang Guangya, stated, 'Clearly from the very beginning, China has been under pressure because of scandals and the news coverage of the prisoner abuse.'[47]

Unsurprisingly, the Abu Ghraib scandal seemed to further radicalize the booming Iraqi insurgency, now targeting non-Iraqi individuals. On May 11, a video on the internet showed the beheading of a 26-year-old American businessman, Nick Berg, claimed to be in retaliation for American prisoner abuse in Iraq. Suicide bombings also increased in Iraq following the Abu Ghraib scandal, targeting the emerging transitional administration's personnel and credibility. Nowhere in central Iraq seemed safe for Iraqis or foreigners.[48]

8.2.2 *Losing Partners and Allies*

The Abu Ghraib scandal did not help the United States in implementing its already troubled Iraqi reconstruction agenda. By mid-2004, of the $18.6 billion appropriated by Congress in reconstruction funds, only $3.7 billion had been spent, the largest portion of it on electricity installations. Contractors—particularly convoy truck drivers and personal security details—proved enticing targets for insurgent attack.[49] By late summer, the US Embassy in Baghdad had recommended reallocating some of the unspent funds to security—perhaps a necessary response to the security situation, but one sending profoundly negative signals to Iraqis about the prospects of reconstruction.[50]

The scandal also brought extra pressure on several Coalition governments to bring their troops home. In many cases, Iraq was beginning to eat away at their electoral appeal domestically. Honduras and the Dominican Republic withdrew their (small) military contributions. More significantly, so did the new Spanish government that took power after a shattering terrorist attack on commuters in Madrid in March 2004.[51] Norway quietly withdrew its military personnel from Iraq, and the Netherlands and Poland laid the groundwork for doing so the following year. The Philippines, in the wake of a highly emotive kidnapping saga involving a Filipino national, abruptly withdrew its troops. It was not all bad news for the United States. Japanese troops arrived in Iraq on February 8, 2004. And after an election victory on October 9, 2004, Australian Prime Minister Howard in early 2005 increased his country's troop commitment in Iraq. But in general, the trend was clearly toward a shrinking Coalition base, and rising costs for the United States.

Friends were hemorrhaging elsewhere too. By late May, festering differences between the CPA and erstwhile local US ally Ahmed Chalabi had broken into open confrontation. Chalabi had been seeking to reposition himself as a credible Shi'a political leader by calling for an end to US military occupation.[52] The charge, from Washington, was that Chalabi had been leaking intelligence to Tehran—perhaps an early sign of just how far the US occupation strategy may have unwittingly benefited Tehran.[53] His offices in Baghdad were raided days after the Pentagon had cut off the INC's monthly stipend.[54] This falling out, while long in the making, was embarrassing for the United States.[55] But it may have played into Chalabi's hands, assisting him to make common cause with Shi'a forces and to recover a leading role—Deputy Prime Minister—in Iraqi politics in 2005.[56]

8.2.3 *Transatlantic Squalls*

Prime Minister Blair's decision to back Washington's venture in Iraq remained controversial domestically. Under attack over the death of a British public servant and former UN inspector in Iraq, David Kelly, Blair was cleared in an inquiry led by Lord Hutton in January 2004. He also came under fire from fifty-two former senior British diplomats, decrying his growing alignment with Bush on the Israel/Palestine conflict and Iraq.[57] An inquiry into the quality and uses of UK intelligence on Iraq, led by Lord Butler, found the intelligence assessment dossier behind the government's decision to go to war 'severely flawed'.[58] The subdued Labour Party conference of September 2004, confirmed that Blair's popularity remained weighed down by 'his war'.[59] Even in the United States, Blair's support of Washington had its critics. Zbigniew Brzezinski wrote:

> It is ... difficult to understand why an ally with an intimate knowledge of the Arab world and a deep grasp of Islamic culture would have been so feckless as not to urge a wiser course of action. Had the UK, America's most trusted ally, spoken firmly as the stalwart voice of Europe instead of acting as the supine follower in an exclusive Ango-American partnership, it could have made its voice heard.... Superior personal eloquence in making the case for a historically reckless course of action is no badge of merit ....[60]

But it was not until the general election of May 5, 2005, that Blair ultimately paid a political price. The campaign was marked by leaking of legal advice by the Attorney General, Lord Goldsmith, prepared during the run-up to the invasion, which seemed not only to throw doubt on the legality of the war, but also to indicate legal advice might have been 'fixed'.[61] The reduction of Blair's House of Commons majority from 161 to 66 was widely perceived as a rebuke for his decision to go to war in Iraq.

Calls for his resignation grew but Blair did not buckle, instead throwing himself with relish into management of the G-8 and EU, both of which he chaired in 2005.[62] Terrorist attacks on the London transit system on July 7, 2005, and again two weeks later, which might have hurt Blair politically, especially after Al Qaeda figures claimed they were justified by London's policy on Iraq, in fact seemed to have the opposite effect, uniting British resolve against terrorism. The attacks of '7/7', as they became known, seemed to allow the British public to rule a line under Blair's decision, however mistaken in their view, to go into Iraq. Blair had survived the worst of the storm.

Broader European public opinion and many European politicians continued to be highly critical of Bush's policies in Iraq.[63] At the 2004 G-8 Summit, German Chancellor Gerhard Schröder was less hostile to American policies than he had been, but French President Jacques Chirac refused to tone down opposition by Paris to a NATO role in Iraq.[64] Paris was also increasingly experiencing 'splendid isolation' (in the words of *Le Monde*) in Europe and within NATO.[65] The 'pole' positions of the United States and France in the Iraq debate increasingly were leaving both countries looking extreme and petty—each thoroughly exceptionalist.[66] The new French Foreign Minister, Michel Barnier, sought to imprint a more conciliatory tone on French diplomacy, repudiating de Villepin's more flamboyant rhetoric, declaring: 'France is not great when it is arrogant. France is not strong if it is alone.' But French President Chirac continued to single out differences with Washington.[67] Through 2005, France saw its standing within the EU eroded, in part due to its impulsive and unnecessary spat with new EU members in early 2003 and the defeat of a referendum on the EU Constitutional Treaty in May 2005.

EU affairs remained strained by divisions on Iraq. Some in Europe continued to see in US policy a blessing in disguise for European security ambitions.[68] Spanish Prime Minister José Luis Rodríguez Zapatero asserted: 'Europe must have faith in the prospect of becoming the most important global power in 20 years.'[69] But US problems in Iraq did not seem meaningfully to benefit Europe, particularly with the Union remaining sharply split on participation in the multinational force there. As Andrew Moravcsik, an astute analyst of European affairs has noted, these divisions meant that 'Europeans were utterly discredited in American domestic politics. Today, Europe's standing is so low that it scarcely figures in ... US geopolitical calculations.'[70] A slight thawing in relations was detectable in the first half of 2005. In February, Condoleezza Rice, newly appointed Secretary of State, traveled to Europe on gusts of personal style, her visit characterized as a 'charm offensive'. Donald Rumsfeld joked about his own past rhetorical sallies with respect to Europe, attributing these to the 'old Rumsfeld'.[71] Nevertheless, former US Defense Secretary William Cohen commented: 'The tone [is] different, but the music is the same.'[72]

8.2.4 *And at the UN*

With NATO offering only limited support, and the Coalition slowly unraveling, the United States was increasingly reliant on symbolic support from the UN to underpin its efforts in Iraq. Resolution 1546, adopted in June 2004, endorsed the arrangements negotiated by Brahimi, the US, and Iraqi parties. The relationship of coordination and partnership between the interim government and the United States was spelled out in an annex to the Resolution, following intricate negotiations over the extent of the government's control over Coalition military operations.[73] The Resolution was viewed by some as legitimating the path the Coalition had followed since Saddam Hussein's overthrow, although it was mostly seen as an effort to support the new Iraqi authorities in the run-up to handover of qualified sovereignty to them on June 30.[74] But Russian President Putin spoke for many when he commented: 'It will take quite a long time before this ... document will have any real impact on the real change on the ground.'[75]

The Resolution authorized the continuing presence in Iraq of a US-led 'multinational force', though only with the consent of the Iraqi government, and subject to review within a year by the Security Council. The Resolution gave the government control over Iraq's oil revenues and the Development Fund for Iraq, subject to transitional monitoring by the UN-mandated International Advisory and Monitoring Board (IAMB). Yet SCR 1546 was conspicuously silent about the Transitional Administrative Law. Al-Sistani had warned against its endorsement by the Security Council. (The Kurds were infuriated by the loss of protection the TAL offered them.[76])

The Resolution purported once again to give the UN a 'leading and vital role' in navigating these rocky waters. But this depended on security. Annan acknowledged this reality:

> Security affects everything.... It affects elections. It affects reconstruction and recovery. It affects the lives of ordinary Iraqis....[77]

On July 12 Annan named a Pakistani, Ashraf Jehangir Qazi, as his Special Representative for Iraq. In an attempt to break out of dependence on the

United States for security, at French instigation, the Security Council included a separate provision creating a dedicated force to protect the UN mission, but the requisite troops were hard to find.

8.2.5 *Sovereign Iraq*

On June 28, 2004, Bremer handed over to Iyad Allawi before departing Baghdad. Iraqi sovereignty was restored. Shortly thereafter, John Negroponte presented his credentials as US Ambassador to Iraq.[78]

As in 1932, when the British government had transferred sovereignty to the Iraqi monarchy, foreign troops remained very much in evidence. Simon Chesterman commented:

> An Iraq where the US controls foreign policy, [has] an embassy with 2,000 staff, and [more than] 100,000 troops, is not that dissimilar from the Soviet Union's relations with eastern bloc states.[79]

In August 2004, a US National Intelligence Estimate posited three potential scenarios for the near future of Iraq: in the best case, 'tenuous stability'; in the worst, civil war.[80] Spasms of violence, such as the running confrontation between US troops and those of al-Sadr's militia in Najaf, served to remind how serious security challenges required American involvement front and center, large-scale training efforts of Iraqi troops and police notwithstanding.[81] Such violence inevitably overshadowed such events as Iraq's 'national conference' convened to choose a broadly based National Council to advise the government until elections were held.[82] The interim government was continually upstaged by US leadership of the war on insurgents.[83] Insurgents continued to target contractors, journalists, and aid workers; after the abduction (and later brutal slaying) of the director of the CARE office in Baghdad, Margaret Hassan, that organization left Iraq, soon followed by many others, further undermining recovery.[84] In late October, insurgents dressed as Iraqi police massacred forty-nine Iraqi military trainees.[85] The heterogeneity of the violence in Iraq suggested that the Coalition was not facing a single insurgency, but a range of violent opponents, including an increasingly radicalized Sunni community, a range of Shi'a groups, some possibly with backing from Iran, and foreign terrorists, championed by Abu Musab al-Zarqawi.

October produced some good news for the Bush administration, including the beginning of voluntary disarmament by Moqtada al-Sadr's militia.[86] But October also brought a report in *The Lancet* claiming

98,000 Iraqi deaths since March 2003 that would not have occurred absent the military intervention.[87] While a degree of caution is required in assessing figures advanced under so broad a heading—the very notion of 'excess deaths' being debatable—the report sparked much commentary:

> For every 100 dead Iraqis (most of them civilians), only one U.S. combatant has been killed. The huge mostly unreported Iraqi civilian death toll helps explain why Washington is losing the hearts-and-minds battle in Iraq and just why there is so much Iraqi rage over the occupation.[88]

By November 2004, security was so bad that a US Army unit refused to carry out a supply mission on the grounds that it was too dangerous.[89]

8.3 Democracies in Action

8.3.1 *The US Election*

Comment on Iraq within the United States throughout 2004 was colored by the Presidential election to be held in early November. A sense grew that Secretary of Defense Rumsfeld and his most senior civilian associates had displayed incompetence in planning for the occupation of Iraq.[90] Fareed Zakaria cuttingly quoted former IBM Chief Louis Gerstner: 'Strategy is execution'.[91] Some moderates within the Republican Party were highly critical of Washington's handling of Iraq. Brent Scowcroft, National Security Advisor to the first President Bush, lambasted the administration, saying that US engagement with the UN and NATO in Afghanistan and Iraq was 'as much an act of desperation as anything else ... to rescue a failing venture'.[92] The military and political situation in Iraq was sufficiently worrying as to prompt occasional calls in the United States for American military withdrawal, although neither candidate in the US Presidential election countenanced the option.[93]

Bush's election strategists sought to portray him as a man of conviction and strength, in contrast to a John Kerry they painted as weak and indecisive. In late August, Bush did acknowledge that he had made a 'miscalculation of what the conditions would be' in post-war Iraq.[94] But mostly he stuck to his guns:

> Knowing what I know today we still would have gone on into Iraq.... He had the capability of making weapons. He had terrorist ties.... The decision I made was the right decision. The world is better off without Saddam Hussein in power.[95]

The administration was also successful in focusing accountability for prisoner abuse at Abu Ghraib on lower-level officials. (Bush twice rejected

Rumsfeld's offer to resign.[96]) But one potentially troubling issue for the President was flawed US intelligence in the lead-up to the invasion of Iraq. Intelligence confidently advanced in the run-up to the Iraqi war as a 'slam dunk' justification for war, had turned out to be in many respects embarrassingly wrong.[97] The Senate Intelligence Committee confirmed egregious errors, making it 'abundantly clear' that many claims made by the White House based on intelligence analysis were 'either substantially or completely wrong'.[98] In June 2004, long-serving CIA Director George Tenet, he of 'slam dunk' fame, resigned. Also potentially problematic were the conclusions of the independent '9/11 Commission' established (reluctantly) by the President to inquire into the circumstances under which the 9/11 attacks occurred.[99] The bipartisan Commission concluded that no links existed between Al Qaeda and the Saddam Hussein regime relevant to the events of 9/11.[100] (Later, the Silberman-Robb Commission recommended sweeping changes to US intelligence structures, finding that US intelligence on Iraq had been 'dead wrong' and that in early 2005 the United States still knew 'disturbingly little about the nuclear programs of many of the world's most dangerous actors'.[101])

The realization of the gross errors in pre-war intelligence estimates also led to soul-searching by some of the press over its acquiescent stance toward administration claims on purported Iraqi links with Al Qaeda and on the existence of WMDs in Iraq.[102] But Senator Kerry failed to achieve traction, even with reports emerging of the disappearance of 377 tons of high-grade Iraqi explosives following the Coalition campaign of 2003.[103] Ultimately, concern within the United States over involvement in Iraq had little impact on the result of the November 2 election. Iraq in the end counted for less to voters than such issues as whether homosexuals should be allowed to marry and whether discarded embryos should be used for stem cell research.[104] The administration strengthened its grip on power significantly, not just through a majority of the popular vote, but also through significant Republican gains in the Senate and the House of Representatives, both of which it continued to control.

Despite his electoral success, Bush's victory did little to improve public backing for the war in Iraq, with 56 percent of the population believing the war 'not worth fighting'.[105] Media reports soon emerged of 'detailed scenarios for withdrawal' circulating in London.[106] US Ambassador in Baghdad Negroponte was at pains to confirm whenever asked that if, following the January 30, 2005 elections, a new Iraqi government asked the Coalition to withdraw, it would do so. In his year-end press conference President Bush noted that the performance of Iraqi security forces was uneven, increasingly emphasizing that it would be up to Iraqis to ensure their own security in the future.[107]

8.3.2 *The Iraqi Election*

Attention now turned to the looming end-of-January 2005 deadline for elections in Iraq. An international conference involving neighbors of Iraq (including Iran), the G-8 countries, China, and several Arab States met in Sharm el Sheikh, Egypt, on November 22–23 and issued a stirring communiqué of support for the transition to democracy in Iraq. NATO also agreed to expand its training role, pointing to an increasing 'out-of-area' footprint for that organization. But behind the scenes, Arab governments expressed the opinion that their publics would view the upcoming elections in Iraq as a US-inspired sham to prop up Iraqi authorities.[108]

Washington and Baghdad had hoped that the deadly campaign in Fallujah would break the back of the insurgency. But, by early December, car bombs and other attacks were again ravaging the ranks of the Iraqi security authorities. The Governor of Baghdad was assassinated.[109] Preparation of the elections represented a 'nightmarish logistical operation' according to a UN official in Baghdad.[110] The UN played a major supporting role, first in developing the Electoral Law and then in providing technical assistance, fielding Carlos Valenzuela as a non-voting member of the Independent Electoral Commission of Iraq (IECI). But, due to security worries, its presence was tiny—in the dozens. As January 30 approached, there was growing criticism of an electoral system grounded in national slates of candidates rather than one set up along district or provincial lines (which would, at the very least, have guaranteed reasonable Sunni representation). Under strong pressure from the Shi'a community, some polling stations were established abroad.[111] A coalition of national election assessors, led by Jean-Pierre Kingsley of Canada, was assembled to gauge the outcome.[112] In face of growing evidence that voting in Sunni areas would be severely limited, calls for postponement of the election were increasingly voiced but resisted by Washington and the Interim Government.[113]

Thanks to the courage of Iraqi citizens, the elections proved a remarkable success—within limits.[114] Fifty-eight percent of the electorate voted, even though at least forty-four people were killed and many others wounded in up to 260 incidents of election-day violence (the highest number on any single day since March 2003).[115] As one commentator put it, '[n]ever have elections been held under such difficult conditions.'[116] Indeed, allegations would emerge later of US attempts to 'rig' the election outcome.[117] The success of the poll was largely due to a massive security operation, closing off virtually all road traffic, declaring a three-day holiday, and imposing a curfew. Most Iraqi police and army forces were assigned to the task for this period, with at least thirteen men at each of the 5,232 polling centers. A substantively happy outcome was politically undermined by an almost complete boycott by Sunni voters. Final results on February 13 gave the Shi'ite religious list forty-eight percent of the votes—well below the 60 percent some had predicted, but still reflecting a quiet success for the Shi'a parties, and their main backer, Tehran. The second-largest bloc in the assembly (25 percent) went to the main Kurdish alliance. Allawi's secular group came in a distant third, scoring just 14 percent. (The largest Sunni-led ticket, topped by Interim President Ghazi al-Yawar, came in fourth, with less than 2 percent.) Others winning enough votes to be represented in the assembly included a Turkmen party, the Communist party, a labor alliance, and a group of Assyrian Christians.[118]

An outpouring of international support followed. On January 31 the United States sought and obtained Security Council agreement on a press statement welcoming the vote.[119] Iraq's Sunni insurgents were soon reported to be seeking an 'exit strategy' in exchange for security and political guarantees, although violence redoubled.[120] President Bush, who called Annan to thank him for UN assistance with the elections, hailed the outcome: '[Iraqis] have demonstrated the kind of courage that is always the foundation of self-government.'[121] Annan, while declining to characterize the election as 'free and fair' looked ahead to the political bridge-building to the Sunni community now required:

> It is important to ensure that all individuals, groups and parties who, for whatever reason, were unable or unwilling to take part in the election are now brought into the constitution-making process.[122]

8.3.3 *Searching for Constitutional Consensus*

The horse-trading on a new Iraqi government soon began, despite the absence of much Sunni representation, and proved such a drawn-out and painful process that it was described as 'birth by caesarian section'.

It was clear that the new government leader must come from the Unified Iraqi Coalition, the coalition of sixteen Shi'a groups endorsed by al-Sistani. But it took those sixteen groups five weeks to negotiate a candidate among themselves. In late April, Ibrahim al-Ja'afari's largely Shi'a

Unified Iraqi Coalition, the Kurdish list, and a collection of Sunni representatives agreed to a formula for allocation of the key posts—eighteen for the Shi'a, eleven for the Kurds, six for the Sunnis, and one for Iraq's Christian population. The largely ceremonial Presidency went to Jalal Talabani, a Kurd, and the Prime Ministership to al-Ja'afari, with Ahmed Chalabi emerging as a Deputy Prime Minister. Allawi was shut out. Significantly, seven posts went to women. Ayatollah al-Sistani reaped much of the credit for the new Iraqi politics, given his insistence—maintained in the face of many American, UN, and other reservations—that early elections be held.[123]

In May 2005, Sunni leaders formed a coalition to ensure that they had a voice.[124] Moqtada al-Sadr indicated that—for now—he was turning away from violence in favor of the political process.[125] But the drafting of the constitution got off to a slow start, and despite reassurances by Iraqi politicians, the self-imposed deadline of August 15, 2005, elapsed without agreement being reached. Instead, the National Assembly granted itself an extra week to reach agreement, though this was technically not permitted by the TAL, which called for dissolution of the Assembly and new elections at this point.[126] The US Ambassador to Iraq described this as 'an exciting time for Iraq and Iraqis';[127] others warned that the divisions—over the role of Islam, women's rights, the distribution of oil wealth, and regional autonomy—signaled a growing 'lack of enthusiasm about the very notion of an Iraqi state'.[128]

Each of Iraq's ethnic communities had interests it sought to defend in the constitutional bargaining process. One key question was the form of government that should emerge, with champions of a loose federation (particularly the Kurds) vying with partisans of a strong central government (particularly the Sunnis). Some in the United States hinted that a breakup of the country into three separate political entities, each with their own governance structures—ultimately perhaps three independent countries—should be considered.[129] Such ideas aimed principally at protecting Kurdish autonomy. But most international experts rejected the notion of partition, arguing that balkanization of Iraq would lead to destabilization of the region as a whole, drawing Iran, Turkey, and possibly Syria into conflicts over irredentist claims.[130]

The specter of civil war continued to loom darkly over the constitutional process. Lakhdar Brahimi worried that civil war could indeed result from a lack of capacity for compromise.[131] The UN anticipated playing a key role in efforts to avoid such a result. Annan stated that the UN remained 'committed to doing everything possible to assist Iraq to move forward to the next phase of its political transition.'[132] His SRSG in Iraq, Ashraf Qazi, told the Security Council that

> Almost without exception, Iraqi interlocutors want the UN to assume greater responsibilities and a greater visibility in Iraq.... We will be assessing the scope for increased humanitarian and development initiatives, consistent as always with the security of UN staff.[133]

Others, like Jeremy Greenstock, also recognized the important role the UN had to play in fostering a common Iraqi political project:

> The responsibility for making hard choices has to stimulate a new leadership and inspire a collective spirit beyond the experience of any living Iraqi. And the awareness of international support for the process has to be a comforting one, without suspicion of outside manipulation or the primacy of other interests.[134]

The implication of Greenstock's comments was that the US presence did *not* have such an effect. Former British Foreign Secretary Robin Cook was more explicit in his comments, just months before his untimely death:

> Training of Iraqi troops and police is necessary but not sufficient for Iraqi sovereignty to reassert itself. The motivation and morale to take on the insurgents will be more difficult to muster while they serve US commanders. If they are to risk their lives, Iraqi security personnel will need to be accountable to Iraqi political direction rather than being ultimately directed by Coalition forces.[135]

Yet this did not happen. Instead, Iraqi politicians relied increasingly on sectarian militias.[136] Insurgents sought to exploit the lack of Iraqi 'ownership' of centralized security services by stimulating sectarian violence, shifting focus onto Iraqi targets.[137] In a spectacularly gruesome incident, a suicide bomber managed to kill 122 among a crowd of Iraqi police and army recruits on February 28, a feat surpassed in its scale of devastation when around 160 job-seekers were killed by a van-load of explosives in September 2005.[138] In April, mass kidnappings of Shi'a civilians and their subsequent murders were announced by President Talabani. With few signs of improvement in the security situation, on May 31 the Security Council approved an extension of the mandate of the multinational force. Bush administration officials remained upbeat, with Vice President Cheney describing the insurgency as 'in its last throes'. But US military advice was much less confident.[139]

8.3.4 *Spillover in the Broader Middle East*

In November 2003, the United States launched a Broader Middle East and North Africa (BMENA) initiative, intended to promote democracy and reform throughout the region in follow-up to the UN Development Program (UNDP)'s excellent *Arab Human Development Report*.[140] Allies dutifully—but in some cases unenthusiastically—joined in this effort (that somewhat duplicated the European Union's Barcelona process).[141] The launch of the US-sponsored *al-Hurra* (The Free One) television network in the Middle East, a centerpiece of US efforts to win hearts and minds in the region, also proved anticlimactic. Potential audiences deemed it propagandistic, preferring the sensationalist effusions of the *al-Jazeera* network. US efforts to win over Arab opinion were undermined by new homeland security regulations severely restricting and delaying visa issuance within the Muslim World, a fusillade of anti-Muslim comments from (generally marginal) political figures in the West, and a perception that President Bush was determined to impose US political and social values on the Islamic World by force of arms if necessary.

But there were more positive signals too. The death of Yassir Arafat on November 1, 2004 was viewed by many as an opportunity, not only for the Palestinians, but more broadly for the Middle East. The smooth transition to power of Mahmoud Abbas stirred hopes for democratic reform within the Palestinian movement. Global developments as well suggested real returns from Washington's focus on democracy and freedom,[142] highlighted most in Bush's 21-minute inauguration address on January 20, 2005, in which the words 'freedom' and 'liberty' were used twenty-seven and fifteen times, respectively.[143]

The outcome of rigged elections in Ukraine (initially endorsed by President Putin of Russia) was overturned due to a peaceful popular uprising in December 2004, followed by further reverses for Moscow in elections in Moldova in March 2005. These developments came on the heels of the victory of radically pro-Western democracy advocate Mikhail Saakashvili as President of Georgia in January 2004 after his predecessor, Eduard Shevardnadze (the USSR's Foreign Minister in the beginning of our narrative), was run out of office by demonstrators.

Just over two weeks after the success of the Iraqi elections, much discussed in the Middle East, former Lebanese Prime Minister Rafiq Hariri was assassinated by a massive bomb in Beirut on February 15, 2005.[144] France and America had on September 2, 2004 sponsored SCR 1559, calling on all foreign (i.e. Syrian) military forces to leave Lebanon, an initiative aimed not only at strengthening Lebanese sovereignty but also allowing Washington to create pressure on a country it had found unhelpful on Iraq.[145] Hariri's assassination provoked international outrage and massive demonstrations in the streets of Beirut—both for and against Syrian withdrawal.

By the end of April 2005, the Secretary-General's envoy, Terje Roed Larsen, had secured Syrian commitment to a full withdrawal, which was carried out largely without incident. People power seemed to have come to the Middle East.

Sensing the shift, in Egypt President Mubarrak uncharacteristically encouraged the Egyptian parliament to permit contested presidential elections later in 2005—which he unsurprisingly won—and freed opposition leader Ayman Nour following the protest of his arrest by cancellation of a visit by US Secretary of State, Condoleezza Rice.[146] In Kuwait, women were given the vote. The tide of democracy seemed to be coming in. Even on the Left in France, former Foreign Minister Hubert Védrine asked: 'Is George W. Bush right?'[147] The new democracies of Europe responded fervently to Washington's democracy agenda.[148] Although Washington's claims to vindication in Iraq seemed premature to many, advances on democracy there undoubtedly helped create more hopeful times for democrats in the Arab World at least.[149] Still, as Madeleine Albright commented, given the frightening levels of violence in and around Baghdad in mid-2005, 'no country wishes to take Iraq today as a model'.[150] If there was 'freedom' in Iraq, it could not be much enjoyed.

8.4 In Larger Freedom

8.4.1 Annus Horribilis

At the UN in September 2004, President Bush argued that Iraq was on its way to stability and called for a new 'definition of security'—i.e. one which allowed greater unilateral, pre-emptive action to those who could take it. But Kofi Annan responded: 'Those who seek to bestow legitimacy must themselves embody it, and those who invoke international law must themselves submit to it.'[151] Annan's relations with Washington grew increasingly tense. On September 16, he commented that the invasion of Iraq had been 'illegal'.[152] Then, ahead of a much-heralded assault by Coalition troops on Fallujah, on October 31 Annan, in a move that puzzled even some of his own advisers, wrote to leaders of the United States, Britain, and Iraq to warn that another full-scale assault would further alienate Iraq and disrupt the January elections.[153] The letter caused fury among US, UK, and Iraqi leaders. By the time this letter leaked, Bush was re-elected and Washington was in no mood to forgive Annan for his inconvenient presumption. 'We're beyond anger', a senior US official stated.[154] The assault on Fallujah went ahead, as did attacks on Annan's management of the UN, particularly the OFF Program, in the US media and Congress.[155] While Colin Powell, the departing US Secretary of State, strongly endorsed Annan's record overall, the administration as a whole equivocated. But the *Financial Times* echoed much of the world's media, editorializing that 'the witch-hunt against Kofi Annan and the UN over the OFF scandal is, quite simply, a scandal all on its own'.[156] The *Economist* opined:

> Many of Mr. Annan's accusers are not friends of the UN. Wishing the organization ill, they are using him as a means to castigate it. Most governments continue to express their confidence in Mr. Annan. Innocent until proven guilty is not a bad rule, even at the United Nations.[157]

Reeling from these pressures, Annan described how he saw 2004: it was his *annus horribilis*.[158] Soon, things got worse. Reports from the Volcker Inquiry criticized a number of UN officials and, to a degree, Annan himself (see Chapter 5). A scandal relating to the sexual conduct of UN peacekeepers in the Congo undermined the UN's largest peacekeeping operation, MONUC.[159] Annan was also harshly blamed by UN staff and others for initially whitewashing a controversy embroiling UN High Commissioner for Refugees Ruud Lubbers, who had been found by UN investigators to have committed sexual harassment. Lubbers ultimately resigned on February 20, 2005, seemingly heedless of the damage the case had inflicted on UN credibility.[160] As if that was not enough, in March 2005 news broke that the UN's Electoral Assistance Division, led by Carina Perelli, which had played an important role in Iraq since 2003, had been criticized in a review undertaken at the UN's request by a Swiss consulting firm, notably for an abusive atmosphere in which unwanted sexual advances had occurred.[161]

8.4.2 *The Reform Imperative*

With the UN confronting a genuine crisis of confidence, the drive for 'reform' was clear. The High Level Panel on Threats, Challenges, and Change reported on December 2, 2004.[162] It addressed a range of issues relevant to collective security, including intervention, WMD, terrorism, peace-building, crime, health crises (such as AIDS), environmental degradation, and poverty. It also, at the insistence of Annan personally, included some options for Security Council reform that rapidly proved controversial.[163] (Anti-Japanese demonstrations in China in April 2005 revealed just how potentially corrosive Security Council reform could be.) Annan's weakened standing did not bode well for his role in reform leadership.[164] That the Panel went 'a long way to meet US concerns' and much of its report 'could have been written by Mr. Bush's national security advisers' did not guarantee it a dispassionate reading in Washington.

American friends of the UN, including Tim Wirth, the president of the United Nations Foundation (funded by Ted Turner), met with Annan on December 5 to suggest drastic remedial action. Richard Holbrooke described this group as people 'who care about the UN and believe that the UN cannot succeed if it is in open dispute and constant friction with its founding nation, its host nation and its largest contributor nation'.[165]

Responding to these concerns, Annan took a broom to upper management, leading to the departure of several long-time advisers. He appointed as new Chief of Staff Mark Malloch Brown, already Administrator of the UNDP, a political fixer and spinmeister extraordinaire. Meeting with the media, Malloch Brown intimated that the UN needed to do a much better job of getting its story across.[166] Repairing ties with the United States became a key objective.[167] With Malloch Brown in the lead, the UN began directly courting Congressional leaders. He noted that there had not been 'a time in the UN's 60-year life when the organization has prospered and done well that it hasn't rested on a strong, effective relationship' with the United States.[168]

Yet after a catastrophic tsunami devastated a number of Indian Ocean countries on December 26, 2004, President Bush announced that the United States would lead a coalition of countries (including Japan, India, and Australia) in responding to the crisis. The United States reacted angrily to a remark by UN humanitarian coordinator Jan Egeland that western donors had generally proved stingy.[169] Intense efforts were required by Colin Powell and others to bring subsequent international relief operations under a UN umbrella.[170]

In May, Malloch Brown, appearing before the House Committee on International Relations chaired by Henry Hyde, cast the UN as 'under-funded and over-managed'.[171] He noted that the UN was operating eighteen peacekeeping missions, with 67,000 uniformed personnel, on a budget of $4.5 billion—less than 0.5 percent of the world's military spending—'a unit cost for peacekeeping that is a fraction of that spent by the United States and the United Kingdom in comparable operations'.[172] He pointed not to bureaucratic incompetence but to poor administrative design and practice and micromanagement by Member States as the core of the UN's problems. He suggested elsewhere that über-hawk John

Bolton—appointed as the United States' new Permanent Representative to the UN through a special Congressional 'recess' process invoked by the President—might convince Congress to avoid the 'nuclear' option of withholding or freezing US dues to the UN.[173]

Before Malloch Brown's Congressional testimony, UN Deputy Secretary-General Louise Fréchette unveiled reforms made in response to internal staff criticism and interim reports from the Volcker Inquiry.[174] These included strengthening of the Office of Internal Oversight Services and anti-corruption measures, and broader financial disclosure requirements. Whistleblower policies were to be overhauled.[175] The signals to the United States were reinforced by the appointment of a former US Marine reservist who had served in the 1991 Gulf War, as Under-Secretary-General for Management.[176]

Annan also sought to induce debate on substantive improvements at the UN, issuing his own conclusions on the High Level Panel Report, and on follow up to the Millennium Development Goals. Using a phrase drawn from the Preamble of the UN Charter, but with one eye clearly on the *Zeitgeist* in Washington and elsewhere, the report was entitled *In Larger Freedom*.[177] It endorsed many of the HLP's recommendations, but was unable to agree on others. The notion of a 'grand bargain' between industrialized and developing states involving concessions on development and security issues respectively, that had earlier been bruited about, was frustrated by uncompromising positions adopted late in the negotiations by the United States on the one hand, and leading NAM members such as Egypt, India, and Pakistan on the other (with China unyielding on the specifics of new human rights architecture at the UN). The Outcome Document proved both patchy and vapid in parts.[178]

The outlook for the UN at the center of an effective multilateral system of collective security had never looked bleaker.

8.4.3 *Towards withdrawal and new challenges for the UN*

Many of these threads wove together as 2005 drew to a close. Milestones in the Iraqi electoral process were achieved in the last quarter of the year, the themes of reform and scandal continued to weigh heavily upon the UN, and based on a patina of success in Iraq the US began to set the stage for its gradual withdrawal.

In Iraq, the constitutional minuet paused momentarily for the October 15 vote, which witnessed high Sunni turnout and a narrow but satisfying passage of the constitution.[179] US ambassador Zalmay Khalilzad intervened energetically to secure Sunni participation in the voting process by suggesting that many of the most contentious issues could be punted later to the new parliament.[180] The October 25 release of voting results coincided with two grim new milestones: the 2,000th American battle fatality a day later, and an estimate by the US military that a minimum 26,000 Iraqi civilian casualties had been inflicted by insurgents since the beginning of 2004.[181]

Public debate on torture, in Iraq and elsewhere, continued, as Secretary Rice fought off suggestions in Europe that the policy of 'rendition', which she described as necessary, was practiced mainly in order to extract information under duress. Guantánamo continued to be short-hand the world over for judicial and interrogation practices seen as unworthy of the United States.[182] The final months of 2005 witnessed skirmishing between the Administration and Senator McCain over a congressional ban the latter instigated against torture by US government officials, including the CIA (much resisted, on grounds of executive privilege, by Vice-President Cheney among others). The most damaging international consequence of 'these affronts to both the idealism and the respect for the rule of law on which the US has built its authority' in the words of Philip Stephens 'has been the collapse of trust in America's motives'.[183]

All eyes turned then to the December 15 Iraqi parliamentary elections. In a positive sign, three major Sunni political parties joined forces to field common candidates, signaling growing Sunni assimilation into the political process.[184] At a reconciliation conference hosted by the Arab League in Cairo, participants agreed to recognize the legitimacy of national resistance and for the first time called for gradual Coalition withdrawal from Iraq—significant concessions to Sunnis.[185] Failure by the Sunnis to translate these achievements into success at the ballot box on December 15—the Shi'ites still achieved a reduced majority—led to cries of foul play. A particularly gruesome two-day bombing spree in the early days of 2006, in which over 200 Iraqis were killed, suggested that Sunni political parties would continue to play 'Sinn Fein' to the insurgency's 'IRA'.[186] The role of the Shi'ite-dominated Interior Ministry in allegations of torture and murder of Sunnis also tempered optimism on long-term Iraqi reconciliation.[187]

At the UN, the Security Council adopted SCR 1637 on November 11, 2005, extending the term of multinational forces in Iraq for one year, allowing for 'a review of that mandate at any time, no later than mid-June 2006, or for its termination, at the request of the Iraqi Government'.[188] The much-anticipated UN Peacebuilding Commission was established, but US Ambassador Bolton kept up the pressure for reform by asserting that the UN was but one 'competitor' in the global conflict resolution marketplace.[189] OFF aftershocks also reverberated not only with the final Volcker Inquiry report documenting large-scale OFF-related corporate corruption but also with news that former French Ambassador (and Special UN Envoy) Jean-Bernard Mérimée had admitted to receiving kickbacks from Iraq through the scheme.[190]

In the US, armed with the achievement of three recognizable 'deliverables' in 2005—two elections and a constitutional referendum—and faced with growing domestic dissent, the White House began to turn discernibly towards questions of military 'draw-down' as circumstances allowed. In January 2006 the White House quietly stated that once its initial allotment of about $18 billion in Iraqi reconstruction funds was spent, there would be no supplementary funds.[191] US military assessments of the situation on the ground in Iraq remained sombre.[192] The costs of war had already proved staggering, conservatively estimated at an absolute minimum of $250 billion not counting many knock-on effects and future direct and indirect expenditures.[193] Serious volatility in international oil markets in late 2005, with prices spiking upwards prior to and following Hurricane Katrina, underscored that if the war in Iraq had been about oil, it was 'a dubious investment'.[194] The President found a new groove in messaging on Iraq—admitting mistakes but predicting ultimate victory—that worked for him better than had previous White House approaches.[195] Following the Iraqi elections in December, his polling numbers recovered somewhat. But Iraq remained a millstone around his and the Republican Party's necks as the November 2006 congressional elections loomed.

At the UN, Iraq remained a painful topic. In his year-end interview, Kofi Annan described the war there as having 'brought . . . division within this Organization and the international community'.[196] Some Member States were beginning to wonder what role the UN could and should play in support of the Iraqi people as the Coalition withdrawal took shape, but most UN staff and delegations shied away from the subject. In spite of the UN's 'credibility deficit' of which Annan had spoken earlier in the year, UN reform efforts were meeting stiff resistance, in particular those aimed at creating a UN Human Rights Council and those aimed at greater transparency, flexibility, and decisiveness in management.[197] The Organization frequently seemed to be sleep-walking, waking briefly only to speculate on who Annan's successor (to be selected by late 2006) might turn out to be.

8.5 Conclusions

The confrontation over Iraq in the Security Council in early 2003 had, by the end of 2005, yielded no clear winners, but had produced many losers.

The United States and the United Kingdom remained tied down militarily in Iraq, absorbing very significant economic costs and, for the Americans, heavy casualties. US deterrent capacity—particularly in relation to Iran and North Korea—was seriously undermined. France saw its standing within the European Union eroded, in part due to its 2003 spat with new members and the failure of the EU Constitution in 2005. The Russian Federation could do little more than monitor developments in Iraq nervously, while its 'near abroad' bubbled alarmingly with democratic impulses. Beijing bided its time, worrying over energy supplies for its increasingly thirsty economy. The Iraqi people, so long repressed by a brutal state, now suffered from arrested recovery; as Phebe Marr has noted, '[i]n two years, Iraq [went] from being a rogue state to being an ailing, if not failing, one'.[198]

But, above all, the UN was the loser, not in terms of compromise to its principles, but in perceptions of its effectiveness and centrality.

8.5.1 *A Flexible Instrument*

Partly because of the military constraints imposed by its commitments in Iraq, the United States was limited in 2004 and 2005 in its options for response to the humanitarian crisis in the Darfur region of Sudan.[199] The inability to forestall further violence in Sudan frustrated John Danforth, the US Permanent Representative to the UN in 2004. 'Why have this building? What is it all about?' he was quoted as wondering aloud.[200]

Part of the answer came in early 2005 when, despite Chinese, Russian, and American reservations, the Security Council referred the cases of those suspected of war crimes and massive human rights violations in Darfur to the International Criminal Court.[201] The United States, prior to abstaining on the relevant resolution, had first secured an exemption for citizens of countries not party to the ICC serving with the UN or the African Union in Sudan.[202] But, given the administration's hostility to the ICC, the referral represented a major concession, recognizing the utility of addressing some issues at the heart of security not by the use of economic or military sanctions, but through criminal law enforcement, a further step toward the legal-regulatory approach to international peace. The referral also pointed to how flexible an instrument the Council can be, when the political stars align.

The Security Council can confer international legitimacy on a wide range of processes—for example, in relation to Iraq, the generation of a timetable for the transition; the recognition of a government in mid-2004; and assistance with elections in January 2005. That conferral requires flexibility in the modalities of UN action—from the brokering role of Lakhdar Brahimi, to the work of small teams of experts on elections. The Coalition also rediscovered that the UN's usefulness lies in the unique legitimacy it draws first from its universality (and impartiality), and second from its unparalleled experience in peace-building and related functions such as the management of political transitions and elections.[203] Mats Berdal writes:

> The occupation has also revealed how parts of the Secretariat have managed to adapt functionally to changing circumstances, acquire expertise and assume responsibilities sharply at odds with the image of incompetence that is so widespread, especially in neo-conservative circles.[204]

Throughout 2004, imparting a sense of the occupation's internationally sanctioned character became ever more important to Washington and London as they were denied the type of legitimacy that easy success on the ground would have conferred. This, in part, explains why the Coalition countries reverted to the Security Council, despite its refusal to retrospectively legalize the intervention.

The utility and inherent currency of a Security Council resolution is clear in contrasting the cases of Kosovo and Iraq. The 'Contact Group' of countries on Kosovo papered over their differences through adoption of a resolution in the Security Council in June 1999 to secure, not narrowly—*post facto* legitimization of NATO intervention there, but rather the legitimacy of all that was to follow. This was beneficial, as Jochen Prantl writes, because 'the prospect of re-engaging the United Nations via the adoption of SCR 1244 helped to create broader acceptance and the perception of legitimacy'.[205] On Iraq, because the Council's resolutions in May 2003 and subsequently bear so little relation to reality on the ground, they have not had a similar effect. Decreeing a 'vital' role for the UN does not confer the same benefits as actually creating one would. As Lakhdar Brahimi put it:

> Is there a 'vital role' for the UN today?... There is not enough political space for the UN to take initiatives and to do what most people in the organization think we should be doing. 'United Nations a la carte'—to be used when the Iraqi

Government and or the coalition think they need it and pushed aside when they think it is not needed—is not my idea of a 'vital role'.[206]

8.5.2 *The US and the UN—Conceptions of Legitimacy*

Senior officials in the UN openly acknowledged in 2005 that in a unipolar world, the UN's relationship with Washington has special significance, with US pre-eminence posing both an opportunity and a fundamental challenge to the UN, particularly the Security Council.

If the Iraq saga has taught the United States and the UN anything, it is that each needs the other. Following the events of early 2003, those who, like Michael J. Glennon, declared the demise of the Security Council's relevance, underestimate both the short-term and long-term costs of acting outside the framework of the Council and of international law.[207] These costs are both financial—as US taxpayers have learnt—and reputational, as powerfully argued by Thomas Franck.[208] But the clash of visions for the UN's role inherent in speeches by US President George W. Bush and UN Secretary-General Annan before the UN General Assembly on September 21, 2004 suggests continuing divergence, however much the United States may need the UN instrumentally.[209]

The Dayton Accord (on Bosnia) of 1995, brokered by Washington, was a turning point in UN affairs, consecrating the United States, according to one Security Council Ambassador in early 1996, as 'the supreme power'.[210] The challenge for the Security Council in the future will remain to engage the United States on the major security challenges without acquiescing in dangerous initiatives; to 'have the courage to disagree with the United States when it is wrong and the maturity to agree with it when it is right'.[211] It must 'keep intact its integrity, while improving its effectiveness'.[212] It must be seen in Washington, as elsewhere, as more and better than just one coalition among many available to Member States.

If this is to occur, it will be because the costs of unilateral action—especially in a difficult economic climate—are realized. Assessing prospects for President Bush's second term, Richard Haass wrote:

> The United States will not remain a Great Power for long if the economic foundation of its power erodes. It must rein in domestic spending. [This will lead to] a more restrained America. New wars of choice are less likely.[213]

James Dobbins pointed out that while the US President had often sounded strident in his unilateralist discourse, he had tacked significantly toward approaches advocated by his multilateralist critics following the overthrow of Saddam Hussein, co-opting many of their ideas. In 2004

more traditional American notions of burden sharing and multinational leadership began to reassert themselves. The administration began to register the staggering costs of stabilizing and reconstructing Iraq and Afghanistan and to recognize, if not admit, the inadequacy of American resources for these tasks.[214]

In Afghanistan, the US-led war-fighting Operation Enduring Freedom, the NATO-led peacekeeping and peace-building ISAF, and the UN's political, humanitarian, and economic development operations have, together, achieved relative success. In particular, they have achieved extensive burden-sharing across the international community. This stands in sharp contrast to the quandary the Coalition faced in 2005 in Iraq. Here, the UN is not much able to help, NATO is largely absent (except in a limited training role), and the Coalition is bearing the full burden of significant risks to its personnel and staggering expense for operations that remain highly controversial at the international and regional levels.

8.5.3 *State-Building and Peace-Building*

One attendant risk is that Washington may begin to perceive the UN's role as, at best, one of long-term peace-building following short and sharp US or Western-led military interventions (mandated by the Council or not). The UN would be confined to 'picking up the pieces', as we saw in 2004 in Haiti and Afghanistan, providing an exit strategy for intervening powers.[215] But the security situation in Iraq has conspired against the willingness of Member States and UN staff to volunteer for UN service in Iraq.

The UN will have to engage more deeply with Iraq in order to sow more seeds of peace before it could 'dig up the roots of war', as Ralph Bunche termed the UN's mission.[216] Brahimi's role in 2004 laid the groundwork for the UN to take on a political role in state-building in Iraq; but without a larger role in advising the Iraqi transitional government, it stood little chance of meaningfully contributing to state-building there.[217] The difficulties which the Iraqi constitutional process ran into in the second half of 2005 attested to the Coalition's failure to generate a common political project in Iraq. As Richard Haass commented, 'In the end, toppling Saddam Hussein was easy compared with putting in place a new Iraqi government that could run a secure, viable country.'[218] The Coalition clearly underestimated the challenge of state-building in Iraq, not least through a startling unpreparedness for its sectarian realities. Too much attention was focused on the Shi'a community, and also, possibly on the Kurds, with insufficient focus on the newly disenfranchised Sunnis. On being asked why the specificity of the British experience in Iraq in the 1920s and 1930s seemed to have played no role in post-war planning, a senior British official stated simply:

> We were driven by events, by the difficulty of lining up UN resolutions and troops on the ground, and by the absolute priority of winning the war. We had done some post-war thinking, but we'd been working with the wrong crowd in Washington (the State Department team) whose work was torn up by the Pentagon.[219]

Another commented:

> For the CPA, ensuring that the Shi'a remained on-side was paramount—in the face of challenges by Moqtada el Sadr and others. In the 1920s, the Shi'a were marginalized, as they were again by the Baath regime. We did not imagine that the most critical problem would turn out to be the alienation of the Sunni community as a whole.[220]

These miscalculations, refracted through violence on the ground, produced new challenges. Numbers published in early June 2005 not only confirmed increased political freedom (as measured through an exploding number of commercial television and radio stations, independent newspapers, and magazines) but also stagnating economic growth and collapsing security. While fuel supplies had risen since May 2003 from 10 percent of estimated needs to 94 percent, and oil production had largely recovered, wheat production had actually fallen and economic activity had stagnated, falling victim to non-stop and frequently very murderous security incidents.[221] The Iraqi government itself put direct Iraqi deaths at a staggering 12,000 since the beginning of 2004.[222]

The operational environment in Iraq stands as a catalogue of all the obstacles which a post-conflict society faces in its transition to stable governance: a brutalized and disintegrated population, society, and economy; an easy supply of small arms and large numbers of disgruntled soldiers struggling with demobilization and reintegration; ethnic and religious divisions; corruption; and terrorism.[223] The UN, with its experience of many post-conflict situations, can help, and has in Iraq. Mats Berdal has pointed to the comparative efficiency of the World Food Program, UNICEF, UNDP, and other UN specialized agencies and programs there.[224] Still, expectations of what the UN can achieve in Iraq as the Coalition begins to withdraw must be carefully managed.[225] As I explore in more detail in the final chapter, the new UN Peacebuilding Commission could play a helpful role in such management processes in Iraq, and beyond.[226]

Notes

1. *General Assembly official records, 58th session: 7th plenary meeting* (UN General Assembly Document A/58/PV.7), September 23, 2003.
2. See Galbraith, 'How to Get Out of Iraq', and 'Iraq: The Bungled Transition', *New York Review of Books* 51/14, September 23, 2004; Seymour M. Hersh, 'Chain of Command', *New Yorker* 80/12, May 17, 2004. Richard W. Stevenson, Seeing Threat to Iraq Elections, U.S. Seeks to Shift Rebuilding Funds to Security, *New York Times*, September 15, 2004, 12.
3. UN Security Council resolution 1511, October 16, 2003.
4. Confidential interview, June 2, 2005.
5. Confidential interview, June 2, 2005.
6. Jonathan S. Landay, U.S. Says It Will Stick with Plan on Transfer of Power in Iraq , *Knight Ridder/Tribune News Service*, January 17, 2004.
7. Farnaz Fassihi et al., 'Winning the Peace: Early U.S. Decisions on Iraq Now Haunt American Efforts', *Wall Street Journal*, April 19, 2004, A1.
8. 'Annan asks Security Council for greater clarity on UN role in Iraq', *UN News Centre*, December 16, 2003.
9. Elaine Sciolino and Warren Hoge, 'UN to Send Expert Team to Help in Iraq, Annan Says', *New York Times*, January 28, 2005, 10.
10. See *Letter dated 2004/03/18 from the Secretary-General addressed to the President of the Security Council* (UN Security Council Document S/2004/225), March 19, 2004.
11. Laura Secor, 'The Pragmatist', *Atlantic Monthly* 294/1, July 1, 2004. In Afghanistan, Brahimi was criticized for early accommodation of the warlords and for giving priority to viable politics over considerations of justice. That said, the societal fabric in the country was almost certainly unprepared to withstand an undiluted focus on retributive justice in the immediate post-conflict period.
12. Warren Hoge, 'U.N. Chief Says Iraq Elections Could Be HeldWithin a Year', *New York Times*, February 24, 2004, 10.
13. 'UN Envoy Backs al-Sistani on Poll', *Al-Jazeera.net*, February 13, 2004.
14. See *Letter dated 2004/02/23 from the Secretary-General to the President of the Security Council* (UN Security Council Document S/2004/140), February 23, 2004.
15. Edward Joseph, 'A balancing act for the UN s Brahimi Between Iraqis and Americans', *International Herald Tribune*, May 15, 2004, 9.
16. For a detailed discussion see *Iraq s Transitional Law* (Document GAO-04-746R), May 25, 2004.
17. See International Crisis Group, 'Iraq's Kurds: Towards An Historic Compromise?', *Middle East Report* No. 26, April 8, 2004.
18. See Galbraith, 'Iraq: The Bungled Transition'.
19. *See Transcript of press conference by Secretary-General Kofi Annan at United Nations Headquarters* (UN Secretariat Document SG/SM/9281), April 28, 2004. For

further details, see Christine Hauser, 'Politicians React to Plan from the UN for Iraqi Rule', *New York Times*, April 17, 2004, 7.

20. Colin Powell, interview by Katie Couric, Today, NBC, May 25, 2004. Complicating the picture, Brahimi made controversial comments on French radio describing Israeli policy and the US support it received as the great poison in the region . Annan distanced the UN from these personal views. For reaction thereto, see William Safire, 'Brahimi's Two Mistakes', *New York Times*, April 26, 2004, 19. See also Phillips, Losing Iraq, 2067. It is not clear that Brahimi's currency ever fully recovered in Washington.
21. For an excellent profile of Allawi, see Jon Lee Anderson, 'A Man of the Shadows', *New Yorker*, 24/31 January 2005.
22. Roula Khalaf, Mark Turner, and James Drummond, 'The US and UK say they are putting Iraq on the path to sovereignty; From Baghdad to the UN, doubts remain', *Financial Times*, May 26, 2004, 21.
23. Patrice Claude, 'Aux Critiques adressées à l'ONU, M. Brahimi répond que Paul Bremer est "le dictateur de l'Iraq" jusqu'au 30 juin', *Le Monde*, June 4, 2004.
24. Mats Berdal, 'The UN after Iraq', *Survival* 46/3 (2004), 88; Rajiv Chandrasekaran, 'Envoy Bowed to Pressure in Choosing Leaders', *Washington Post*, June 3, 2004, A10.
25. Anthony Sampson, 'Brahimi—The UN Can Play Only a Limited Role in Exit Strategy', *Independent*, May 18, 2004, 4.
26. Confidential interview, June 2, 2005.
27. Correspondence with the author, June 20, 2005.
28. See International Crisis Group, 'Iraq's Transition: On a Knife Edge', *Middle East Report No. 27*, April 27, 2004, 12–13.
29. Charles Clover, 'The Fighters of Falluja', *Financial Times Weekend*, April 25, 2004, 18.
30. Phillips, *Losing Iraq*, 200.
31. 'Report of the International Committee of the Red Cross (ICRC) on the Treatment by the Coalition Forces of Prisoners of War and Other Protected Persons by the Geneva Conventions in Iraq During Arrest, Internment and Interrogation', International Committee of the Red Cross, February 2004; see, for example, Demetri Sevastopulo and Frances Williams, 'Red Cross reignites US torture dispute', *Financial Times*, December 1, 2004, 1.
32. An incisive account of these developments is to be found in Mark Danner, 'Torture and Truth', *New York Review of Books* 51/10, June 10, 2004.
33. *Article 15-6 Investigation of the 800th Military Police Brigade* (The Taguba Report), May 5, 2004.
34. See Seymour M. Hersh, 'Torture at Abu Ghraib', *New Yorker* 80/11, May 10, 2004. The key memoranda are gathered in Karen J. Greenberg and Joshua L. Dratel (eds.), *Torture Papers: the Road to Abu Ghraib* (New York: Cambridge University Press, 2005).
35. See John Barry et al., 'The Roots of Torture', *Newsweek*, May 24, 2004.

36. See Jane Mayer, 'Outsourcing Torture', *New Yorker*, February 14, 2005, and Stephen Grey and Don van Natta Jr., 'In Italy, Anger at US Tactics Colors Spy Case', *New York Times*, June 26, 2005, 1.
37. See *Hamdi et al. v. Rumsfeld, Secretary of Defense, et al.*, US Supreme Court, No. 03-6696, June 28, 2004; *Rasul et al. v. Bush, President of the United States, et al.*, US Supreme Court, No. 03-334, June 28, 2004; *Rumsfeld, Secretary of Defense v. Padilla et al.*, US Supreme Court, No. 03-1027, June 28, 2004.
38. Eric Schmitt, 'New Interrogation Rules Set for Detainees in Iraq', *New York Times*, March 10, 2005, 1.
39. See Neil A. Lewis, 'U.S. Spells Out New Definition Curbing Torture', *New York Times*, January 1, 2005, 1, and Tim Golden, 'U.S. Is Examining Plan to Bolster Detainee Rights', *New York Times*, March 27, 2005, 1.
40. Anthony Lewis, 'Bush and the Lesser Evil', *New York Review of Books* 51/9, May 27, 2004, 9.
41. George Will, 'No Flinching From the Facts', *Washington Post*, May 11, 2004, A19.
42. Michael Ignatieff, 'The unbearable burden of destiny', *International Herald Tribune*, June 30, 2004, 6.
43. Kishore Mahbuhbani, formerly Singapore's Ambassador to the UN, claims that Abu Ghraib and especially Guantánamo 'had a profound impact on Chinese intellectuals. Before Guantánamo, they had accepted the right of Americans to stand on a moral pedestal and lecture China on human rights issues. After Guantánamo, the pedestal had vanished. [A young intellectual] said to me with masterful understatement: "We Chinese have discovered that Americans are not really different from us. We thought they were special. Now we know that they are just like us." ' See Kishore Mahbuhbani, *Beyond the Age of Innocence* (New York: Public Affairs, 2005), 133.
44. Jakob Kellenberger, 'No War Is Above International Law', *Financial Times*, May 19, 2004, 19.
45. UN Security Council resolution 1422, July 12, 2002; UN Security Council resolution 1487, June 12, 2003; see also UN Security Council resolution 1497, August 1, 2003, OP7 (exempting portions of the Liberian peacekeeping mission from ICC jurisdiction). And see Benny Avni, 'U.N. Defeats U.S. On Bid To Shield GIs From Court', *New York Sun*, June 24, 2004.
46. See Warren Hoge, 'Annan Rebukes US for Move to Give its Troops Immunity', *New York Times*, June 18, 2004, 10. See also David Scheffer, 'Article 98(2) of the Rome Statute: America's Original Intent', *Journal of International Criminal Justice* 3/2 (2005).
47. Warren Hoge, 'US Drops Plan to Exempt GIs from UN Court', *New York Times*, June 24, 2004, 1.
48. See Roula Khalaf, 'Support surges for rebel Iraqi cleric', *Financial Times*, May 20, 2004, 1.
49. See Rajiv Chandrasekaran, 'As Handover Nears, U.S. Mistakes Loom Large', *Washington Post*, June 20, 2004, A1.

50. See Anne Ellen Henderson, *The Coalition Provisional Authority's Experience with Economic Reconstruction in Iraq: Lessons Identified*, United States Institute for Peace, Special Report 138, April 2005.
51. Guy Dinmore and James Harding, 'Bush attacks Spanish troops pull-out', *Financial Times*, April 20, 2004, 10.
52. A fine profile of Chalabi is to be found in Jane Mayer, 'The Manipulator', *New Yorker* 80/15, June 7, 2004.
53. Peter Slevin, 'Chalabi Denies Charges he Spied for Iran', *Washington Post*, May 24, 2004, A19.
54. 'Busted neo-con icon', *Financial Times*, Editorial, May 22–3, 2004.
55. The significance of Chalabi's marginalization for intra-Administration dynamics in Washington was made clear in 'The Chalabi Fiasco', *Wall Street Journal*, Editorial, May 26, 2004, A16.
56. Phillips, *Losing Iraq*, 210. By the end of 2005, Chalabi's star had dimmed again somewhat, as he failed in his bid to be elected to Iraq's Parliament.
57. See Owen Bowcott and David Palliser, 'Butler Report: Evidence stretched to "outer limits" ', *The Guardian*, July 15, 2004, 6. For the UK diplomats' letter, see 'Doomed to failure in the Middle East: A letter from 52 former senior British diplomats to Tony Blair', *The Guardian*, April 27, 2004, 23. A similar initiative in Australia is detailed in 'Our military and diplomatic elders on truth in democracies and the downside of invading Iraq', *Sydney Morning Herald*, August 9, 2004.
58. United Kingdom, *Review of Intelligence on Weapons of Mass Destruction: Implementation Of Its Conclusions* (London: The Stationery Office, July 14, 2004). For the original dossier see *Iraq's weapons of mass destruction: the assessment of the British government* (London: The Stationery Office, September 24, 2002).
59. 'The damage Iraq has done him', *The Economist*, October 2, 2004, 55.
60. Zbigniew Brzezinski, 'America's policy blunders were compounded by Britain', *Financial Times*, Editorial, August 6, 2004, 17.
61. 'Iraq: Resolution 1441'.
62. See for example Andy Mcsmith and Francis Elliott, 'General Election 2005: The war is over. Now the big guns prepare for battle', *The Independent*, May 8, 2005, 10; David Cracknell, 'Labour MPs tell Blair to quit Downing Street', *Sunday Times*, May 8, 2005, 1.
63. See Patrick Jarreau, 'Laurent Fabius expose à Chicago le "paradoxe du 6 juin" ', *Le Monde*, May 27, 2004, 1.
64. Glenn Kessler and Dana Milbank, 'Leaders Dispute NATO Role in Iraq', *Washington Post*, June 10, 2004, A06; and see Guy Dinmore, James Drummond, and Nicolas Pelham, 'NATO plans Iraq mission despite Chirac', *FT.com*, July 2, 2004, and Lee Feinstein and Anne-Marie Slaughter, 'Iraq needs more backers on board', *Financial Times*, Editorial, June 29, 2004, 21. Relations between France and the US continued to plumb new depths in 2004 on issues beyond Iraq: see John Carreyrou and Glenn R. Simpson, 'Foreign Policy: How

Insurance Spat Further Frayed U.S.-French Ties', *Wall Street Journal*, April 16, 2004, A1.

65. See 'Splendide Isolement', *Le Monde*, Editorial, July 1, 2004, 16.
66. See Deb Riechmann, 'Bush Looks to Europe for Help in Iraq', *Associated Press*, June 25, 2004.
67. See Elaine Sciolino, 'Latest French Policy on U.S.: Don't Say Anything at All', *New York Times*, August 27, 2004, 8.
68. See Daniel Dombey and Eric Jansson, 'EU seeks show of intent on defence', *FT.com*, December 1, 2004.
69. Quoted in the Charlemagne column, 'A European Superpower', *Economist*, November 13, 2004, 58.
70. Andrew Moravcsik, 'How the World Sees It', *Newsweek Online*, November 15, 2004.
71. Elaine Sciolino, ' "New" Rumsfeld is Seeking Stronger Ties with Europe', *New York Times*, February 12, 2005, 17.
72. Daniel Dombey and Peter Spiegel, 'US and EU tensions remain beneath Munich bonhomie', *Financial Times*, February 14, 2005, 7.
73. UN Security Council resolution 1546, June 8, 2004, Annex. See also James Bone, 'Struggle as Allies Seek Backing at UN', *The Times*, June 3, 2004, 15.
74. Warren Hoge, 'Security Council Backs Resolution on Iraq Turnover', *New York Times*, June 9, 2004, 1.
75. David E. Sanger and Richard W. Stevenson, '8 Leaders Welcome UN Backing for Iraq Transition', *New York Times*, June 9, 2004, 3.
76. William Safire, 'The Resolution's Weakness', *New York Times*, June 9, 2004, 23.
77. *Transcript of press conference by Secretary-General Kofi Annan at United Nations Headquarters.*
78. Phillips, *Losing Iraq*, 211–12.
79. See Khalaf, Turner, and Dummond, 'The US and UK say they are putting Iraq on the path to sovereignty'.
80. Douglas Jehl, '2 C.I.A. Reports Offer Warnings on Iraq's Path', *New York Times*, December 7, 2004, 1.
81. See Johanna McGeary et al., 'The Lessons of Najaf', *Time*, August 30, 2004, 30–3.
82. See Mark Turner, 'Iraq brushes off UN on forum to build consensus', *Financial Times*, July 24, 2004, 10.
83. 'Power-play in Najaf', *Financial Times*, Editorial, August 28, 2004, 10.
84. See Daniel B. Schneider, 'Driven from Iraq, Aid Groups Reflect on Work Half Begun', *New York Times*, November 15, 2004, 13.
85. Edward Wong, 'Allawi Blames "Negligence" by US-led Force for Ambush Deaths of 49 Iraqi Soldiers', *New York Times*, October 27, 2004, 10.
86. Dexter Filkins and Edward Wong, 'Cleric's Militia Begins to Yield Heavy Weapons', *New York Times*, October 12, 2004, 1.
87. Slightly less alarming figures have surfaced in other reports. See FAFO, *Iraq Multiple Indicator Rapid Assessment*, May 12, 2005.

88. Andrew Mack, 'Now we know: the high cost of war in Iraq', *Globe and Mail*, November 3, 2004, A27.
89. Eric Schmitt and Ariel Hart, 'Punishment Urged for Reservists Who Disobeyed', *New York Times*, November 16, 2004, 13.
90. See Bryan Burrough, Evgenia Peretz, David Rose and David Wise, 'The March to War', *Vanity Fair*, May 2004, 228–44, 281–3.
91. Fareed Zakaria, 'Why Kerry is Right on Iraq', *Newsweek*, August 23, 2004, 35.
92. Daniel Dombey, 'Scowcroft lambasts core Bush foreign policies', *FT.com*, October 13, 2004. On the potential for UN-NATO synergy, see Gwyn Prins, *The Applicability of the NATO Model to UN Peace Support Operations Under the Security Council* (New York: UNA-USA, 1996).
93. 'Time to consider Iraq withdrawal: US forces are part of the problem rather than the solution', *Financial Times*, Editorial, September 10, 2004, 18. Francis Fukuyama, 'America's next president will need to rethink Iraq', *Financial Times*, Editorial, September 14, 2004, 23. These ideas reflected his thesis in *State Building: Governance and World Order in the 21st Century* (Ithaca, NY: Cornell University Press, 2004). See also Edward N. Luttwak, 'Iraq: The Logic of Disengagement', *Foreign Affairs* 84/1 (2005).
94. David E. Sanger and Elizabeth Bumiller, 'Bush Dismisses Idea That Kerry Lied On Vietnam', *New York Times*, August 27, 2004, 1.
95. 'President's Remarks on Intelligence Reform', *White House Office of the Press Secretary*, August 2, 2004.
96. Donald Rumsfeld, Larry King Live, *CNN.com*, February 3, 2005.
97. Thomas Powers, 'The Failure', *New York Review of Books* 51/7, April 29, 2004, 4–6.
98. Thomas Powers, 'How Bush Got it Wrong', *New York Review of Books* 51/14, September 23, 2004, 91. See also 'Report on the US Intelligence Community's Prewar Intelligence Assessments on Iraq', Senate Select Committee on Intelligence, July 7, 2004.
99. See National Commission on Terrorist Attacks upon the United States, *The 9/11 Commission report: final report of the National Commission on Terrorist Attacks upon the United States* (New York: Norton, 2004).
100. Thomas Catan, 'Al-Qaeda link with Iraq over attacks ruled out: September 11 Inquiry', *Financial Times*, June 17, 2004, A8.
101. Commission on the Intelligence Capabilities of the United States regarding Weapons of Mass Destruction, *Report to the President of the United States*, March 31, 2005.
102. See Sylvie Kauffmann, 'Tempêtes au "New York Times" ', *Le Monde*, July 2, 2004, 1, and Michael Massing, 'Unfit to Print?', *New York Review of Books* 51/11, June 24, 2004.
103. See 'The UN's Revenge', *Wall Street Journal*, Editorial, October 29, 2004, A14. For relevant UN documentation, see Annex to *Letter dated 2004/10/25 from the*

Secretary-General addressed to the President of the Security Council (UN Security Council Document S/2004/831), October 25, 2004.

104. Michael Massing, 'Iraq, the Press & the Election', *New York Review of Books* 51/20, December 16, 2004.
105. See Joanna Chung and Ben Hall, 'Majority in US believe Iraq war a mistake', *FT.com*, December 22, 2004.
106. Ewan MacAskill, Richard Norton-Taylor, and Rory McCarthy, 'US and UK look for early way out of Iraq', *The Guardian*, January 22, 2005, 1.
107. See James Harding, 'Bush admits Iraq bombers are having effect', *Financial Times*, December 21, 2004, 1.
108. Confidential interviews with Arab Foreign Ministers and officials.
109. See, for example, 'Sistani aides murdered in double attack', *Daily Star* (Beirut), January 14, 2005.
110. Bourzou Daragahi, 'Fear reigns across Iraq on the eve of election', *Globe and Mail*, January 29, 2005, A1.
111. Edward Wong, 'Vote Officials Move to Let Expatriates Cast Ballots', *New York Times*, November 19, 2004, 14. The International Organization for Migration oversaw this polling in a dozen or so countries.
112. This operation, the International Mission for Iraqi Elections, was criticized by some for its failure to deploy observers on the ground. See Steve Negus, 'UN worried over monitoring of Iraq election', *Financial Times*, January 21, 2005, 10.
113. See 'Facing Facts about Iraq's Election', *New York Times*, Editorial, January 12, 2005, 20.
114. Michael Ignatieff, 'The Uncommitted', *New York Times Magazine*, January 30, 2005, 15.
115. See John F. Burns, 'US Shouldn't Cut Force Soon, Iraqi Leaders Say', *New York Times*, February 2, 2005, 10.
116. Marina Ottaway, 'Iraq: Without Consensus, Democracy Is Not the Answer', *Policy Brief 36*, Carnegie Endowment for International Peace, March 2005. On the grim realities of the election, see also Mark Danner, 'Iraq: The Real Election', *New York Review of Books* 52/7, April 28, 2005, 41–4.
117. Seymour M. Hersh, 'Get Out the Vote', *New Yorker*, July 25, 2005, 52–7.
118. Challiss McDonough, 'Iraq Election Officials Announce Final Results', *Voice of America Press Releases and Documents*, February 13, 2005.
119. See *Press Statement by Security Council President on Iraq Elections* (UN Secretariat Document SC/8303-IK/477), February 1, 2005.
120. Steve Negus, 'Iraq's insurgents "seek exit strategy" ', *Financial Times*, March 26, 2005, 9.
121. 'President Congratulates Iraqis on Election', *White House Office of the Press Secretary*, January 30, 2005. See also David Stout, 'Bush Hails Iraq Vote as "A Resounding Success" ', *New York Times Online*, January 30, 2005.
122. See *Statement from the Secretary-General on the Iraqi Elections*, January 30, 2005.

123. See Thomas Friedman, 'A Nobel for Sistani', *New York Times*, March 20, 2005, 13. See also Hendrik Hertzberg, 'Landmarks', *New Yorker*, 14/21 February 2005.
124. Sabrina Tavernise and Richard A. Oppel Jr., 'Sunnis in Iraq Unite to Compete With Shiites in Politics', *New York Times*, May 22, 2005, 14.
125. Richard A. Oppel Jr., 'Rebel Iraq Cleric Hints He'll Shift To Political Path', *New York Times*, May 23, 2005, 1.
126. Dexter Filkins and James Glanz, 'Leaders in Iraq Extend Deadline on Constitution', *New York Times*, August 16, 2005, 1.
127. Interview with Ambassador Zalmay Khalilzad, *Al-Iraqiya TV*, August 14, 2005.
128. Filkins and Glanz, 'Leaders in Iraq Extend Deadline on Constitution'.
129. See Leslie H. Gelb, 'What Comes Next?', *Wall Street Journal*, May 20, 2004, A12.
130. See Carl Bildt, 'The Dangerous Idea of Partitioning Iraq: A Balkan Lesson', *International Herald Tribune*, May 20, 2004, 8.
131. Hamza Hendawi, 'Iraq May Be Slipping Into Civil War', *AP Online*, February 16, 2004.
132. 'New Iraqi Government is Important Step in Transition, Says Annan', *UN News Service*, April 28, 2005.
133. 'Nearly All Iraqis Seek Greater UN Role in Political Transition, Security Council Told', *UN News Centre*, April 11, 2005.
134. Jeremy Greenstock, 'What must be done now', *The Economist*, May 8, 2004.
135. Robin Cook Interview, May 27, 2005.
136. See Peter W. Galbraith, 'Iraq: Bush's Islamic Republic', *New York Review of Books* 52/13, August 11, 2005, 6, 8–9.
137. See Steven Komarow, 'Troop Deaths drop to lowest point in a year', *USA Today*, March 31, 2005.
138. See Warzer Jaff and Robert F. Worth, 'Blast Kills 122 at Iraqi Clinic In Attack on Security Recruits', *New York Times*, March 1, 2005, 1.
139. Jim VandeHei and Peter Baker, 'Bush's Optimism on Iraq Debated', *Washington Post*, June 5, 2005, A01; John F. Burns and Eric Schmitt, 'Generals Offer Sober Outlook on Iraqi War', *New York Times*, May 19, 2005.
140. See *Arab Human Development Report 2003* (New York: United Nations Development Program, 2003).
141. See Quentin Peel, 'A big idea that Europe won't buy', *Financial Times*, February 5, 2004, 17.
142. See 'A gentle glow: How much credit should President Bush get for recent changes in the Middle East?', *The Economist*, March 12, 2005.
143. See Julian Borger, 'Heartfelt flow of fire and brimstone', *The Guardian*, January 22, 2005, 17. For the President's address, see 'President sworn in to Second Term', *White House Office of the Press Secretary*, January 20, 2005. Even Republican mainstay Peggy Noonan deplored the President's 'mission inebriation' in 'Way Too Much God', *Wall Street Journal*, January 21, 2005, A8.
144. See 'Something Stirs', *The Economist*, March 5, 2005.

145. UN Security Council resolution 1559, September 2, 2004. See also 'Syria to UN: Drop Dead', *Wall Street Journal*, Editorial, September 8, 2004, A18.
146. The Egyptian elections held later in the year were marked by much violence. Nour, to the consternation of Egypt's Western allies, was jailed after highly questionable court proceedings. Egypt had, by the end of 2005, regressed deplorably in the practice of democracy.
147. Hubert Védrine, 'George W. Bush a-t-il raison ?', *Le Monde*, March 26, 2005, 1.
148. Philip Stephens, 'It is time for Old Europe to turn back towards liberty', *Financial Times*, February 25, 2005, 19.
149. 'Two Years Later', *New York Times*, Editorial, March 18, 2005, 20.
150. Madeleine Albright, interview with the author, May 19, 2005.
151. Warren Hoge, 'Annan Reiterates His Misgivings About Legality of War in Iraq', *New York Times*, September 22, 2004, 10.
152. Kofi A. Annan, interview with Owen Bennett-Jones, *BBC World Service*, September 16, 2004, http://news.bbc.co.uk/1/hi/world/middle_east/3661640.stm.
153. Confidential interviews. See also Maggie Farley, 'U.N.'s Annan Seeks to Prevent an Assault on Fallouja', *Los Angeles Times*, November 5, 2004, A7.
154. Warren Hoge, 'U.S. and U.N. Are Once Again the Odd Couple Over Iraq', *New York Times*, November 14, 2004, 15.
155. Phillips, *Losing Iraq*, 216.
156. 'Destroying the UN: US should worry about the witch-hunt against Kofi Annan', *Financial Times*, Editorial, December 4, 2004, 12.
157. 'Blaming Annan: Calls for the secretary-general to resign over the oil-for-food scandal are premature', *The Economist*, December 11, 2004, 11. See also Quentin Peel, 'Stop this demonising of the UN', *Financial Times*, December 9, 2004, 19.
158. Edith M. Lederer, 'Annan: U.N. and U.S. Must End Disputes', *AP Online*, December 22, 2004.
159. While serious abuses were discussed seriously, *Emergency Sex and Other Desperate Measures* provided a more light-hearted account of UN horizontal shenanigans in exotic war-torn locales: Kenneth Cain, Heidi Postlewait, and Andrew Thomson, *Emergency Sex and Other Desperate Measures* (New York: Hyperion, 2004). See also Ben McGrath, 'Just Whistle; the Diplomats', *New Yorker* 80/40-41, December 20/27, 2004.
160. Andrew Gumbel, 'UN chief quits over sex abuse allegations', *Independent*, February 21, 2005, 1.
161. See Colum Lynch, 'Report Cites Mismanagement in UN Elections Office', *Washington Post*, March 31, 2005, A13.
162. *Note [transmitting report of the High-level Panel on Threats, Challenges and Change, entitled 'A more secure world: our shared responsibility']* (UN General Assembly Document A/59/565), December 2, 2004. See Mark Turner, 'UN puts its future up for debate in biggest challenge yet', *Financial Times*, December 21, 2004, 3. See also 'A U.N. for the 21st Century', *New York Times*, Editorial, December 7,

2004, 26, and Kofi Annan, 'Courage to Fulfil our Responsibilities', *The Economist*, December 4, 2004.

163. Warren Hoge, 'U.N. Tackles Issue of Imbalance of Power', *New York Times*, November 28, 2004, 26.
164. See Jim Hoagland, 'Failure of Nerve in U.N. Reform', *Washington Post*, December 6, 2004, B07.
165. Warren Hoge, 'Secret Meeting, Clear Mission: 'Rescue' U.N.', *New York Times*, January 3, 2005, 1.
166. *Transcript of Press Conference by Secretary-General Kofi Annan at United Nations Headquarters* (UN Secretariat Document SG/SM/9664), January 3, 2005.
167. Colum Lynch, 'Repairing Ties With U.S. Is Key, U.N. Officials Say', *Washington Post*, February 26, 2005, A14.
168. Lynch, 'Repairing Ties With U.S. Is Key'. Many developing countries at the UN resented Malloch Brown's courting of Congress, but few of them seemed to understand how deeply anti-UN Sentiment then ran in Washington.
169. For one US view of this contretemps, see 'Far From Stingy', *Wall Street Journal*, Editorial, December 31, 2004, A10.
170. See Martin Fackler and Timothy Mapes, 'The Tsunami's Aftermath: UN Takes Lead in Tsunami Relief: US and Other Nations Constituting "Core Group" End Their Separate Effort', *Wall Street Journal*, January 7, 2005, A7.
171. 'Annan's Chief of Staff Tells US House that UN is Under-Funded, Over-Managed', *UN News Centre*, May 19, 2005.
172. 'Annan's Chief of Staff Tells US House that UN is Under-Funded, Over-Managed'.
173. Michael Hirsh, 'The Hyde Factor', *Newsweek Online*, June 1, 2005.
174. 'Fréchette Unveils UN Reforms Responding to Volcker Panel's Criticisms', *UN News Centre*, May 17, 2005.
175. 'Fréchette Unveils UN Reforms Responding to Volcker Panel's Criticisms'.
176. 'Veteran US Official Appointed New Chief of UN Management', *UN News Centre*, May 17, 2005.
177. See *In larger freedom: towards development, security and human rights for all: report of the Secretary-General* (UN General Assembly Document A/59/2005), March 21, 2005.
178. On the lead-up to the summit, see Mark Turner, 'Last year, the UN, criticised in the wake of the war in Iraq, commissioned a high-level panel to examine its role. Out this week, the resulting report is expected to be a blueprint for the UN's future, 60 years after its foundation', *Financial Times*, November 29, 2004, 17. The fracas produced by the final Volcker Inquiry report threatened to overwhelm the process, providing 'a splendid pretext for everybody to do nothing', see 'A nasty smell', *The Economist*, August 13, 2005. The Draft Outcome Document was adopted by the General Assembly on September 17. See *2005 World Summit Outcome: draft resolution referred to the High-level*

Plenary Meeting of the General Assembly by the General Assembly at its 59th session (UN General Assembly Document A/60/L.1), September 15, 2005.

179. Steve Negus, 'Fears Yes vote could divide Iraq further', *FT. com*, October 25, 2005. With rules dictating that the constitution would fail if three provinces rejected it by a two-thirds majority, the Sunni region of Iraq fell short by one province—Nineveh—which only voted 55 percent against.
180. On January 11, 2006, Abdul Aziz al-Hakim, leader of SCIRI, disavowed the understanding with Sunnis which called for allowing the new parliament to decide many of the most contentious articles. His rejection of any 'major changes' raised serious doubts over the sustainability of the constitution over time.
181. Sabrina Tavernise, 'U.S. Quietly Issues Estimate Of Iraqi Civilian Casualties', *New York Times*, October 30, 2005, 10. On December 12, 2005, President Bush stated: 'I would say 30,000 [Iraqis], more or less, have died as a result of the initial incursion and the ongoing violence against Iraqis.' See Demetri Sevastopulo, 'Bush acknowledges about 30,000 Iraqis have died since war began', *Financial Times*, December 13, 2005, 3. The death toll for the American Military in Iraq for 2005 was 844, near the level of 848 in 2004.
182. See Jane Mayer, 'A Deadly Interrogation: Can the CIA Legally Kill a Prisoner', *New Yorker*, November 14, 2005, 44–52.
183. Philip Stephens, 'The world needs a powerful but more humble America', *Financial Times*, September 9, 2005, 15.
184. Dexter Filkins, '3 Sunni Parties Form Bloc to Take Part in Iraq Vote', *New York Times*, October 27, 2005, 14.
185. Hassan M. Fatah, 'Iraqi Factions Seek Timetable for U.S. Pullout', *New York Times*, November 22, 2005, 1.
186. Filkins, '3 Sunni Parties Form Bloc to Take Part in Iraq Vote'.
187. Ellen Knickmeyer, 'Abuse Cited In 2nd Jail Operated by Iraqi Ministry: Official Says 12 Prisoners Subjected to "Severe Torture" ', *Washington Post*, December 12, 2005, A01.
188. Iraq's Interior Minister, Bayan Jabr, suggested that this extension would probably be its last. See Hassan M. Fatah, 'Iraqi Factions Seek Timetable for U.S. Pullout', *New York Times*, November 22, 2005, 1.
189. Evelyn Leopold, 'UN creates new body to help states out of war', *Reuters*, December 20, 2005; and Colum Lynch, 'Bolton Admonishes U.N.', *Washington Post*, November 23, 2005, A07.
190. See 'Under the UN Table: Volcker highlights corporate complicity in Hussein's bribery', Editorial, *Financial Times*, October 29/30, 2005; and Francis Harris and David Rennie, 'I took Saddam's cash, admits French envoy', *Daily Telegraph*, November 18, 2005, 16.
191. Stephen Farrell, 'Iraq must rebuild itself after £11bn fund is exhausted', *The Times*, January 3, 2006, 33.

192. See Eric Schmitt, 'Iraq Facing Hurdles, U.S. General Warns', *New York Times*, January 6, 2006, A6.
193. Martin Wolf, 'America failed to calculate the enormous costs of war', *Financial Times*, January 11, 2006, 15.
194. John Gault, 'Has Iraq Helped America's Energy Security? A Dubious Investment', *International Herald Tribune*, December 14, 2005.
195. Admitting mistakes was all the rage. Paul Bremer published a memoir owning up to several, but shifting blame for others to the Pentagon, which refused to respond. See L. Paul Bremer III, *My Year in Iraq: The Struggle to Build a Future of Hope* (New York: Simon & Schuster, 2006); and see L. Paul Bremer III, 'In Iraq, Wrongs Made a Right', *New York Times*, January 13, 2006, A23. Admitting to no mistakes of his own, former UK Ambassador in Washington Christopher Meyer published a cringe-inducing sensationalist memoir blaming Prime Minister Blair for not doing enough to restrain President Bush in his rush to war retailing principally for its gossip value: Christopher Meyer, *DC Confidential* (London: Weidenfeld & Nicolson, 2005).
196. UN Document SG/SM/10280, December 21, 2005.
197. See Warren Hoge, 'Officials at U.N. Seek Fast Action on Rights Panel', *New York Times*, January 1, 2006, A1.
198. Phebe Marr, 'Occupational Hazards: Washington's Record in Iraq', *Foreign Affairs* 84/4 (2005).
199. Stryker McGuire, 'Tony's Second Chance: The Crisis in Sudan gives Britain's Prime Minister a Shot at redemption', *Newsweek*, August 9, 2004, 22.
200. Philip Gourevitch, 'Power Plays', *New Yorker* 80/39, December 13, 2004.
201. See Stephen Glain, 'Yet Another Great Game: Beijing's aggressive petrodiplomacy in Africa has put it on a collision course with Washington', *Newsweek*, December 20, 2004, 24.
202. UN Security Council resolution 1593, March 31, 2005.
203. On the peace-building aspect, see Winrich Kühne (ed.), *Winning the Peace: Concept and Lessons Learned of Post-Conflict Peacebuilding* (Ebenhausen: Stiftung Wissenschaft und Politik, 1996).
204. Berdal, 'The UN after Iraq', 87.
205. Jochen Prantl, 'Informal Groups of States and the UN Security Council,' *International Organization* 59/3 (2005). The Quint was composed of five NATO allies: US, Britain, France, Italy, and Germany.
206. Correspondence with the author, June 20, 2005.
207. Michael J. Glennon, 'Why the Security Council Failed', *Foreign Affairs* 82/3 (2003). See also Ruth Wedgwood, 'The Multinational Action in Iraq and International Law', ch. 25 in Ramesh Thakur and Waheguru Pal Singh Sidhu (eds.) *The Iraq Crisis and World Order: Structural, Institutional and Normative Challenges* (Tokyo: United Nations University Press, forthcoming).
208. Thomas M. Franck, 'What Happens Now? The United Nations after Iraq', *American Journal of International Law* 97/3 (2003).

209. See *General Assembly official records, 59th session: 4th plenary meeting* (UN General Assembly Document A/59/PV.4), September 21, 2004. In the wake of Hurricane Katrina, and severe domestic criticism of his Administration, President Bush struck a much more conciliatory note in his address to the UN Summit on September 14, 2005. See 'President Addresses United Nations High-Level Plenary Meeting', *White House Office of the Press Secretary*, September 14, 2005.
210. Interview with then-Egyptian Ambassador to the UN Nabil Elarabi, January 1996.
211. Interview with then-Mexican Ambassador to the UN Adolfo Aguilar Zinser, January 26, 2003.
212. Correspondence with Michael W. Doyle, New York, May 16, 2003.
213. Richard Haass, 'The World on His Desk', *The Economist*, November 6, 2004.
214. James Dobbins, 'We're all multilateralists now', *International Herald Tribune*, November 13, 2004, 6.
215. For a cogent view on such worries, see Ingrid Lehmann, 'Bush's Monkey on the UN's Back', *Financial Times*, May 26, 2004, 23.
216. James Cockayne and David M. Malone, 'The Ralph Bunche Centennial: Peace Operations Then and Now', *Global Governance* 11 (2005), 346.
217. International Peace Academy, 'The Future of UN State-Building: Strategic and Operational Challenges and the Legacy of Iraq', Kirsti Samuels and Sebastien von Einsiedel, Rapporteurs, June 2004, 8.
218. Richard Haass, 'Regime Change and Its Limits', *Foreign Affairs* 84/4 (2005), 70.
219. Confidential Interview with British official, June 2, 2005.
220. Confidential Interview with second British official, June 2, 2005.
221. See Adriana Lins de Albuquerque, Michael O'Hanlon and Amy Unikewicz, 'The State of Iraq: An Update', *New York Times*, Editorial, June 3, 2005, 23.
222. Ellen Knickmeyer, 'Iraq Puts Civilian Toll at 12,000', *Washington Post*, June 3, 2005, A01.
223. Knickmeyer, 'Iraq Puts Civilian Toll at 12,000', A3–4.
224. Berdal, 'The UN after Iraq', 86–7.
225. See IPA, *The Future of UN State-Building*, June 2004, 3.
226. José Manuel Durao Barroso and Joaquim Chissano, 'We need a new way to prevent conflicts', *International Herald Tribune*, May 8, 2004, 4.

9

Conclusions: Serious Consequences: How Twenty-Five Years of Involvement with Iraq Has Changed the Security Council

After twenty-five years of dealings with Iraq, the Security Council at the end of 2005 was much changed. That quarter-century of Council activity paints a remarkable portrait of political developments at the global level, and of their effect on the practice and prospects of the Security Council. In this concluding chapter, I highlight four major trends derived from this narrative: (*a*) the instrumental multilateralism of all five permanent members on the Council; (*b*) the manner in which its encounters with Iraq forced the Council to confront new threats, and to address questions of legality and legitimacy, representation, and democracy; (*c*) the underlying evolutionary trajectory of Council practice, away from a politico-military mode in which it mediated between warring states, to a mode in which it sits at the apex of a global legal-regulatory architecture; and (*d*) the emergence of a comprehensive approach to peace, justice, security, and development, in which the Council occasionally and controversially legislates for all states on critical new security threats such as terrorism and WMD.

In order to secure Iraqi compliance with its decisions, the Council repeatedly threatened Iraq with serious or severe consequences of non-cooperation, perhaps most famously in its ambiguous Resolution 1441 of November 8, 2002. In fact, serious consequences occurred all around when the Council failed to demonstrate unity in following up on that Resolution: the UN, trans-Atlantic relations, the European Common Foreign and Security Policy, the Arab League, and Iraqis soon found themselves rent by the fallout of the Council's divisions.

The Council's credibility, always under a degree of attack, was seriously undermined by its inability to unite on a strategy for Iraq in early 2003, and prospects for its continued relevance to the hardest security challenges at the end of 2005 seem uncertain.

9.1 Instrumental Multilateralism[1]

In twenty-five years of dealings with Iraq, the Council has played a number of roles—Cold War Peacemaker, New World Order Policeman, Weapons Inspector, and Sanctions Enforcer—some with more success than others. The Council received its most euphoric reviews for its performance as a New World Order Policeman in Iraq in 1990–91, contrasting starkly with the disillusion widely experienced following its handling of Iraq in 2002–3. As James Cockayne comments:

> The crisis over Iraq is, by many reckonings, evidence of a transformative disintegration of an existing UN-centered world order. The prohibition against aggression is challenged by an emerging doctrine of pre-emption. International relations are undermined by the maintenance and proliferation of weapons of mass destruction (WMD) and the asymmetrical warfare of non-state armed groups. A Hobbesian race for security replaces a growing global interdependence.[2]

The Council has always been endowed with unique powers under the UN Charter, but its structural peculiarities also contain the seeds of its failures. No other institution in world history has been granted by its near-universal membership the authority to mandate coercive measures, including the use of force against sovereign states; however, the vetoes required to induce the adhesion of several great (and some lesser) powers also allow five states with often diverging interests to block these and other measures. For the duration of the Cold War, superpower rivalry produced a degree of paralysis. But as *glasnost* and *perestroika* took effect, the Council found a way to work together on the Iran–Iraq conflict, signaling (in the words of Jan Eliasson) 'the end of the Cold War'.[3] In the heady new post-Cold War era, the success of Council-mandated Operation Desert Storm made international police action seem both obvious and easy. However, the necessary alignment of Great Power interests remained a prerequisite for such action. Tony Judt writes:

> for ten years following the end of the cold war the US and the 'international community' appeared, however fortuitously, to share a common set of interests

and objectives; indeed, American military preponderance fueled all manner of liberal dreams for global improvement. Hence the enthusiasms and hopes of the Nineties—and hence, too, the angry disillusion today.[4]

The Council's inability to manage successfully the Iraq crisis of 2002–3 was sobering, especially as the costs of this failure have been high for all concerned. An inability, perhaps an unwillingness, to see the pattern of Iraq's dangerous behavior as a shared problem requiring a shared solution—an approach central to the concept of collective security—highlighted the tendency of each of the P-5 to view the value of the Council as at least largely instrumental. As discussed in the conclusions of Chapter 7, this crisis pointed to two contending forms of instrumentalism possible for the P-5: one realist, treating the Council as just one available legitimizing resource among many; the other, institutionalist, treating the Council as a long-term investment in international stability. The positions of the five permanent members represent five different variations on these two basic leitmotifs.

9.1.1 *Five Variations on Instrumental Multilateralism*

It is instructive to review how the strategies of the P-5 on Council membership as an instrument of foreign policy (including in relation to each other) have played out during the Council's quarter-century of dealings with Iraq. Non-permanent members, often colorful but rarely central to the action, play a significant role in Council decision-making only when the P-5 split, a rare occurrence as they have every interest in agreeing to the extent necessary to 'control the game'—though the crisis of 2002–3 precipitated just such a split.[5]

THE UNITED KINGDOM: STUCK IN THE MIDDLE

The United Kingdom, increasingly aligned with Washington since the Suez Crisis and the Vietnam War episodes divided them, sought consistently to build bridges between Washington and other Council members on Iraq (and other issues), leveraging its own close ties with the United States. This involved a willingness to shoulder a significant proportion of the military burden on the ground in Iraq (and in the no-fly zones over it), and to lead on much of the diplomatic heavy-lifting in New York, for Foreign Office negotiating skills are widely recognized. British diplomats were often dismissive in private of US strategies, but at the political level, particularly under Prime Minister Tony Blair (after 1997), London's commitment to Washington became absolute. While this provided British diplomacy with a degree of authority it otherwise might not have had, it also seriously constrained the leeway of the United Kingdom within the Security Council and beyond.

When the chips were down in February 2003, London, incapable of finessing positions as starkly delineated as those of Paris and Washington (although it had been open itself to a number of compromise options), opted for Washington. Blair was widely credited with forcing the United States to take the 'UN route', but when the United States and the United Kingdom failed to secure a resolution clearly authorizing military action, his emphasis on Security Council authorization worked against his own arguments that the war was legal regardless. By initially insisting on such a Council resolution only later to abandon that position, Blair confused his public and was caught in between the unilateralism of the United States—which had seen the elusive Council resolution as an optional extra—and the institutionalism of the British and broader European publics.

While UK forces on the ground generally performed with distinction, and the UK's military sector anchored by Basra proved much more peaceful than the Sunni triangle (no doubt at least in part due to UK management), London increasingly seemed very much Washington's junior partner on the ground. UK input to post-conflict management was characterized more by the professionalism and expertise of its personnel (Jeremy Greenstock, David Richmond, John Sawers) than by their apparent influence on US decision-making.

The United States owed the United Kingdom a great deal, since without its support it would have seemed even more isolated internationally than it was; yet the outcome to date of the Iraq adventure is not a further deepening of the 'special relationship', but rather an increased questioning within the British public of the merits of that relationship and Blair's Iraq strategy.

The United States and the United Kingdom will likely continue to display much mutual affinity in the Council in years ahead. But their foreign policies diverge sharply on global issues, such as the necessary underpinnings for economic development, the need for robust multilateral action on climate change, and their instincts on how to support failing states. Blair was successful in the run-up to the Gleneagles G-8 Summit in 2005 in prodding Washington into a more generous engagement with Africa. But the United Kingdom will continue to differ from Washington in its commitment to the International Criminal Court and the Kyoto Protocol.

Thus, ties between Washington and London are more complex than they would seem viewed solely through the prism of Iraq policy. But the 'special relationship' remains the strongest and most stable axis in international relations, with profound implications for the Security Council, where the United Kingdom will continue with its instinctive bridge-building and its interpretation of Washington to the rest of the members and vice versa—even as large sections of the British public demand unambiguous advocacy of institutionalism and the global rule of law. Blair's ability to overcome his public's skepticism of his Iraq policy, however much Iraq has eroded his early domestic standing, reminds us that he remained, in 2005, the most energetic and talented international politician of his generation.

FRANCE: THE OTHER EXCEPTIONALIST

As Stephen Schlesinger notes, France at first turned down the invitation to be a Permanent Member of the Security Council in 1945, only changing its mind halfway through the San Francisco Conference.[6] Sixty years later, the United States may regret extending that invitation. Paris characteristically sought a central role in the Council's dealings with Iraq on numerous occasions, including during the lead-up to Operation Desert Storm in 1991, signaling its unwillingness to cede the stage to Washington. By 1996, it had claimed that central role, as its defection from the Western P-3 fuelled international opposition to Iraqi sanctions and, ultimately, to military intervention.

The reasons for Paris's shift in the mid-1990s on Iraq policy are not entirely clear, but spawned from an increasingly assertive nationalism under the newly elected Jacques Chirac, possibly combined with a re-reading of French strategic and commercial interests in Iraq. Chirac reintroduced a more Gaullist perspective in French foreign policy, valuing independence and French leadership in their own right. The Council would prove a valuable instrument for the expression of France's policy shift, Paris holding, as it does, the 'swing' vote in the P-5 much of the time. Washington can usually rely on support from the United Kingdom on major geostrategic issues (with the important exception of the Israeli–Palestinian question, where the calculus is more complex) and Russia and China can often be co-opted into acquiescence when the United States, the United Kingdom, and France present a united front. When the United States and France unite purposefully, the Council generally acts forcefully: witness Council action on Haiti and Lebanon in 2004.

But when they are divided, the United States faces difficulties, as the Iraq crisis in 2002–3 showed.

Newly re-elected in 2002 after an acrimonious campaign in which the far-right National Front had bested the Socialist candidate, President Chirac had little to offer domestically given the slumbering economy and a European conjuncture decreasingly open to French leadership. Thus, the Iraq crisis of 2002–3 provided the President with an opportunity to focus French public opinion on a foreign policy question on which he was virtually unopposed domestically. While the President cast himself as a sage, regretting American adventurism and advising words of wisdom,

Box 9.1 A SUCCESSFUL FRENCH APPROACH TO INSTRUMENTALIZING THE COUNCIL

The recent French intervention in Côte d'Ivoire began as an action to protect French civilians from unrest in Abidjan in September 2002. But the French, unlike the other intervening Western militaries (including US Special Forces), stayed on.[1] Without a mandate from the Security Council, France rapidly became enmeshed in the growing internal conflict, eventually using a strong arm to produce Ivorian consent for a settlement (the *Linas Marcousis Agreement*) between the parties, partly brokered through ECOWAS. The UN had maintained a modest political presence in Côte d'Ivoire as of 2000, but the Security Council did not become involved in the Ivorian turmoil until an ECOWAS request, prompted by France, in early 2003. On February 4, 2003, SCR 1464 endorsed French and ECOWAS actions under Chapter VII and VIII mandates;[2] a UN liaison mission, MINUCI, was authorized somewhat later.[3] The resemblance between the Council's authorization of the French presence in Côte d'Ivoire and that of the Coalition in post-conflict Iraq is clear. However, matters then diverged.

While the US sidelining of the Council in 2003 left Member States unwilling to contribute significantly to the multinational force in Iraq, France engaged more positively with the UN than did Washington. Like the United States in Iraq, France was becoming bogged down in a complex and risky security environment in Côte d'Ivoire. With growing anti-French sentiment in his country, Ivorian President Laurent Gbagbo requested that MINUCI be transformed into a full-fledged peacekeeping force (UNOCI). Where the United States had resisted any multilateral military presence in Iraq not under its control, the French agreed to a UN force in Côte d'Ivoire—but secured a guarantee, in February 2004, that its own *Opération Licorne* would remain separate.[4]

The extent to which this diplomatic success by Paris had been able to produce both French freedom of military maneuver and multilateral diplomatic cover became clear in November 2004. On November 6, an Ivorian government bomber struck a French base, killing nine French soldiers and one American. In response, and without consulting UN headquarters, French forces destroyed the entire Ivorian Air Force.[5] SCR 1528 had authorized UNOCI to use 'all necessary means', but extended this right to the French contingent only in

Box 9.1 (cont'd)

'support' of UNOCI and to 'contribute to the general security of the area'. France's actions seemed to go well beyond this mandate (however severe the provocation) but, in a highly unusual move, the Security Council issued a Presidential Statement later that day that 'confirmed' that French and UNOCI forces were 'authorized to use all necessary means' to carry out their mandate.[6] Paris, diplomatically supported by the relevant sub-regional organization, ECOWAS, was thus successful after the fact in gaining acquiescence—even legalization—of its military action.

Like the United States in Iraq, France may be paying the costs in Côte d'Ivoire of a politico-military strategy that did not involve the UN at the outset, as the situation on the ground in Côte d'Ivoire remains highly unstable. But an important difference is that by more successfully multilateralizing the peacekeeping process, France had found a way to share the burden of those costs (financial and other) beyond its own borders, immunizing the former Colonial power against criticism. Both ECOWAS and the AU have become heavily involved in mediation efforts with the AU's special envoy, South African President Thabo Mbeki, achieving some success. At the UN, an arms embargo was imposed, a committee charged with identifying persons to be charged by the ICC appointed, and targeted sanctions repeatedly threatened.[7]

However, the situation deteriorated further during the fall of 2005. The UN assented in a postponement of elections that had been scheduled for October 30, 2005 in the face of intransigence on the part of the Ivorian players. The AU, supported by the UN Security Council, hashed out a compromise plan involving the appointment of a stronger prime minister to act as a counter-weight to Gbagbo and guide the country to elections by October 30, 2006.[8] But violence, the principal tool of the Gbagbo camp, reignited in January 2006, with the President's youth wing marching on several UNOCI camps. UN troops fired on the rioters, killing five, and were forced to evacuate their encampments in Guiglo and Duekoue, in the north.[9] While the situation on the ground risked spiralling out of control, Paris could at least take comfort from UN Security Council support for its strategies.

the dashing diplomacy (or shrill histrionics, depending on one's view) of his then Foreign Minister Dominique de Villepin (later Prime Minister) galvanized public support. So potent was the Iraq drama in French public debate that little notice was taken of France's own impending foreign military quagmire in Côte d'Ivoire.

On Iraq, while the French intelligentsia took quiet delight in the excesses of US anti-French rhetoric (talk in the United States of an 'Axis of Weasels' involving Germany, France, and other false friends), roaring business was done in France and elsewhere in caricaturing not only the Bush Administration but American values and culture as well. It took the nominally left-wing daily *Le Monde* to point this out in a stinging response to lazy anti-Americanism.[7]

The confrontation between France and the United States over Iraq in early 2003 was not inevitable—it required a degree of political mismanagement by both. As we have seen, France did offer Washington an informal 'way out' of a continuing and damaging deadlock in the Council (the Kosovo model), but it was not then an easy one for London or Washington to accept, each for its own reasons. The Canadian 'process' initiative of February 2003 to bridge Council differences was scuttled by both Washington and (less publicly) Paris.[8]

While France triumphed for a period in UN circles for its opposition to the United States, it fared less well in the European Union, where the split between London and Paris soon generated a firefight of its own for approval of EU governments. Here, Chirac seriously overplayed France's hand in dealing dismissively with candidate Member States from Central and Eastern Europe (still grateful and close to Washington). France's pilot role within the EU had still not fully recovered in late 2005—and was further damaged by the defeat of a referendum on the European constitution in France in May 2005. And, while able to aggravate Washington on the margins of its multilateral salvage diplomacy, notably by resisting any meaningful NATO involvement in Iraq, France all in all seemed somewhat diminished on the international stage in late 2005.

RUSSIA: A SHRINKING SPHERE OF INFLUENCE

The Cold War between the United States and USSR had long divided much of the world into rival 'spheres of influence'. With Gorbachev's abandonment of superpower confrontation, the Soviet Union's geostrategic outlook became opaque, particularly after it supported the Western powers in confronting Saddam Hussein in 1990. In the immediate aftermath of the Gulf War, the USSR was wracked by internal political and constitutional upheavals, succeeded at the UN by the smaller although still vast Russian Federation, and had little option but to yield to Washington's sole superpower status.

Moscow seemed prepared to leave Washington a free hand, so long as situations clearly within its own sphere of influence—as in Chechnya—did not find their way onto the Council's agenda, despite the egregiousness of the human rights violations there. The same approach was evident when it convinced the Council to acquiesce in its approach to conflict in Georgia in 1994.[9] The continuing relevance of the concept of spheres of influence became clear over the Kosovo crisis, when the P-3 avoided seeking Council authorization for military action against Serbia, lest Moscow veto it. In the aftermath, Moscow faltered, failing not only to have the Council adopt a draft resolution condemning NATO's unilateralism, but also only months later accepting SCR 1244 that granted NATO the lead military role in peacekeeping in Kosovo. This was reflective of Moscow's diplomacy in the Council under President Yeltsin, generally accommodating Washington, but receiving little in return. Perhaps not surprisingly, as of 1999 under President Putin, Moscow adopted a frequently more assertive stance, not least on Iraq, where it had significant commercial interests at stake (although it seemed relieved to leave the lead role in confronting Washington on Iraq to France in 2002–3).

The decision by the United States following 9/11 to enlarge its footprint in Central Asia might have posed a threat to Russia's historical role there, but Putin handled this smoothly, making common cause with Washington in the fight against terrorism, indirectly equating Chechnya with Afghanistan under the Taliban.[10] At the same time, Russia also began to chart a new course, providing nuclear support to Iran, signing a Friendship Pact with China, and working with the latter and Central Asian states to build a new regional body, the Shanghai Cooperation Organization.[11] Russian and American policy clashed increasingly over democratic reforms in former Soviet states. But given the largely internal nature of these reforms, they were matters dealt with largely outside the Council. Inside, the commonality of American and Russian interests on counter-terrorism was striking.

CHINA: AN EMERGING SUPERPOWER?

In principle strongly opposed to intervention in the internal affairs of states, China during the 1990s quietly acquiesced in a variety of just such initiatives—beginning with SCR 688—often formally abstaining on Security Council votes with statements ritualistically disavowing the relevant interventions. The rarity of China's vetoes made them all the more revealing of its vital interests and its own instrumental approach to Council matters. Most notably, it voted down UN peacekeeping missions in Guatemala (briefly) and Macedonia over their respective dalliances with Taiwan.

Before 9/11, the Bush Administration had adopted a stance toward Beijing more challenging than that of the Clinton Administration, although it managed to avoid escalation of the forced landing of a US spy plane by Chinese forces earlier that year. Thereafter, the United States, requiring support for counter-terrorism and Operation Enduring Freedom (ungrudgingly extended by Beijing), and also needing Beijing for its diplomacy on North Korea, changed tack. An increasingly confident and accomplished cadre of Chinese representatives racked up IOUs from other permanent members throughout the years and crises covered in this volume. When necessary, these IOUs could be deployed to reduce friction over Chinese opposition within the Council, for example, when China refused, in the wake of the Abu Ghraib scandal in 2004, to support a further extension of exemption from ICC jurisdiction of US staff serving in UN peacekeeping operations.

Whether the generally serene relationship of China with the other permanent members will survive the dramatic growth of its economy, with attendant growing energy needs and expansion of political influence, remains to be seen.[12] North Korean pursuit of nuclear weapons may, in particular, prove a flash point, with China likely to oppose the adoption of coercive measures by the Council if the matter is referred to it by the IAEA. The lessons from Iraq for Council handling of North Korean nuclear aspirations are many. Like Iraq, North Korea falls outside the exclusive sphere of influence of any single P-5 member; like Iraq, the North Korean regime poses a threat both to its own people and to regional stability; and like Iraq, North Korea has a history of obstruction and deceit in dealing with the international community that occasions great pessimism about the prospect of regulatory approaches—such as weapons inspections—requiring substantial cooperation from the regulated state. The Council might also learn, from its experiences with Iraq, that economic sanctions are unlikely to be effective if neighboring states conduct covert trade with the embargoed state.

THE US: THE DISENCHANTED MULTILATERALIST

Only ahistorical interpretations of American foreign policy would qualify US policy toward Iraq since 1980 as a radical departure. Exceptionalism, isolationism, unilateralism, and, more recently, multilateralism have all vied for dominance of US foreign policy at various times, and a degree of each are generally reflected in Washington's debates over international relations.[13] All, save comprehensive isolationism, have been present in US policy toward Iraq, and isolationism sometimes rears its head in discussion of US policy toward the UN.[14] Yet the bottom-line US commitment to multilateralism has been clear since it underwrote the establishment of the great global institutions in the last days of the Second World War. Only in Iraq has the depth of US disenchantment with multilateralism finally become clear; and with it, the costs. The United States is in many respects no different from the other P-5 powers in its instrumental approach to the UN and particularly the Security Council; what marks it out is the import of that instrumentalism, the global reach of US policy, the extent of its current rejection of multilateral institutionalism and, arguably the domestic objectives of much US instrumentalism in the Council.

The Iraq case initially shows US foreign policy of the Cold War era addressing the Iran–Iraq war through strategies seeking to contain the protagonists and, perhaps more importantly, the role of the Soviet Union in the Gulf shipping lanes (astutely exploited at the time by Kuwait). Following Saddam Hussein's defeat in Operation Desert Storm, containment through sanctions and inspections was Washington's central goal—and here the UN was given a central role as a framework for multilateral action. However, Washington paid a price in international support for failing to calibrate the inspections-plus-sanctions regime, and, to a degree, for its unilateral military enforcement action such as Operation Desert Fox in 1998. By neglecting the growing opposition of international opinion to policies perceived as taking Iraqi civilians hostage, it creating a growing skepticism—among its allies, no less than in the opinion of the Arab 'street'—as to US motives.

Already chafing at the constraints imposed by the multilateral framework of Security Council decision-making, the events of 9/11 resolved key Washington policymakers to throw off the perceived shackles of multilateral decision-making over the use of force. The extent of the shift became clear in a March 2005 National Defense Strategy, which warned that 'our strength as a nation state will continue to be challenged by those who employ a strategy of the weak using international fora, judicial processes, and terrorism'.[15] In this analysis, discussing a matter in the Security Council or arguing a matter before the World Court is likened to negotiating with terrorists.

The implications for the Council were very clear. Washington had moved beyond the long-term investment strategy of multilateral instrumentalism in its treatment of the Council. It had moved even, perhaps, beyond the short-term realism of the other P-5 members, who saw in the Council a useful resource to multiply the effectiveness of their own foreign policies, wielding their vetoes as necessary to defend their spheres of influence. The US policy no longer reflected unilateral implementation of multilateral mandates, or occasional humanitarian exceptionalism; now, it seemed to aim at a reconfiguration of international security arrangements.[16] The Council was an obstacle to those arrangements, and only rarely an opportunity. The Council was just one potential Coalition among many available to it; and in other Coalitions, there were no vetoes. In the 'hierarchy of decision-making' revealed by the

US's treatment of the Council in 2002 and 2003, the Security Council was not at the apex.[17] The question for the Bush Administration was not whether the Security Council would allow a return to military action in Iraq, but whether military action in Iraq would allow a return to the Security Council. Why accept a world powered by rules when it could have a world ruled by power?

That the United States views the UN instrumentally is only natural. All countries do to a large extent, but the United States does so with more import—not least because it now tends to view the whole globe as its natural 'sphere of influence'. Given that Washington's attention span can be very short, and then only on a few issues at any given time, it is hardly surprising that the UN often recedes from view in the US capital. But, as noted by James Traub, 'the United States can determine the agenda of the Security Council, if it wants to, even if it can not quite dictate outcomes'.[18] France's former ambassador to the UN, in the fall of 2002, described the United States as the 'first among equals' within the Security Council, and there is no doubt that President Bush altered the Council's agenda instantly through his forceful September 2002 address to the General Assembly.[19] Armed with strong arguments and pursuing effective diplomacy, George H. W. Bush, James Baker III, and Thomas Pickering demonstrated in 1990 that the United States can decisively and effectively turn to the UN to pursue its interests. So what went wrong?

Having supported with varying degrees of engagement (not least through supportive resolutions of the Security Council) Operation Enduring Freedom in Afghanistan, many UN members perceived the US case on WMD in Iraq as weak. SCR 1441, with its talk of 'serious consequences' further muddied the waters. It did offer creative ambiguity, but at the expense of clarity on the nature and timing of consequences for Saddam Hussein's sins of commission and omission. In retrospect, had Washington and London built their case on Hussein's overall defiance of the UN or on the grounds of a necessary humanitarian intervention to rescue the Iraqi population from the clutches of one of the twentieth century's worst dictators, they might have proved more successful in convincing the Council, and the broader public.[20] But UNMOVIC chief Hans Blix could not translate suspicions he seemed for a time to share with Washington into facts (the IAEA's Mohammed El Baradei having largely debunked allegations that Iraq was pursuing actively a nuclear weapons program). And so, Washington suffered a defeat in the Council that has cost the UN dearly.

For countries such as Mexico, Chile, and Pakistan to oppose an initiative by the United States (on which each of their capitals greatly depended in the security and economic spheres) is to realize how completely the case failed to convince. An additional factor came into play: several Council members now feared gross abuse of US military power, and did not wish to collude in it. Twisting the term used to denote earlier US strategy on Iran and Iraq, Gelson Fonseca, then Brazilian ambassador to the UN stated: 'You have a situation of dual containment: you have to contain the United States; you have to contain Iraq.'[21]

While domestic politics were relevant for all of the P-5 members in the 2002–3 Iraq crisis, much of the time Council debates do not register on domestic electoral radars; sometimes, domestic debates find their way onto the Council's radar. Washington, like Paris, has at times demonstrated a bipartisan willingness to engage the Council in strategies with dominant domestic subtexts. Fearing electoral backlash for the plight of the Kurds, James Baker and George H. W. Bush engineered SCR 688 providing a (thin) basis for US-led humanitarian intervention. Many speculated that US policy on Iraq at the UN and elsewhere in 1998 was driven in part by Bill Clinton's plight in relation to the Lewinsky scandal.[22] Accounts of senior Bush Administration officials calling for an attack on Iraq in response to 9/11 also point to domestic political considerations influencing US policy on Iraq in that period. While such interpretations doubtless short-change Clinton and both Presidents Bush, the complex interplay between domestic politics and international initiatives has been a constant in our narrative, often confounding the diplomacy of successive UN Secretaries-General.[23]

The appeal for support of its strategies on Iraq in early 2003 based on purportedly airtight intelligence that proved false carries its own costs, not least to US credibility next time it advances an intelligence-based claim. The lasting 'blot' on his record of which Colin Powell candidly spoke in September 2005, further to the 'devastating' realization that his assertions to the Council in February 2003 had been misleading of course extends to the international credibility of the Washington Administration as a whole—and also to that of the UK government, for which Tony Blair has already paid a price in his domestic popularity.[24] Taken together with the Abu Ghraib events, these were serious and unnecessary self-inflicted wounds.

The question by late 2005 was whether the enormous costs of its Iraq venture might trigger a re-evaluation in Washington of the risk-reduction and burden-sharing potential of investment in multilateral relations and institutions. Reflecting on this, Jane Boulden and Thomas G. Weiss note:

> The Security Council is not a road Washington always, or never, takes. Clearly no US administration would ever permit the Council to stand in the way of pursuing perceived national security interests. At the same time, ... the Bush Administration is discovering that 'even imperfectly legitimated power is likely to be much more effective than crude coercion'.[25] The political liability of the contested occupation in Iraq provide[s] an opportunity to find ways to engage Washington and encourage its tactical multilateralism.[26]

While true, this may prove a Panglossian view. Secretary-General Annan's travails over the OFF scandal, which have seriously tarnished his reputation in Washington, stimulated a strong effort by his team to engage with the US Congress, but this did not restore UN credibility in Washington. 'Tough love' from John Bolton, Permanent Representative of the United States to the UN in 2005 and of his successors, if it produces results, might prove more effective on the Potomac.

Results matter. By the end of 2005, the neo-con prescriptions for Iraq policy had burdened US deterrent capacity by tying down such a large proportion of its fighting forces, demonstrating the limitations of use of force in addressing complex societal challenges and eroding President Bush's domestic standing.[27] The costs in US and Iraqi lives were high. The draw on the US Treasury was staggering. When Hurricane Katrina devastated the southern Gulf coast of the United States, most notably New Orleans, it was easy for the pundits to ask whether Bush had sent the National Guard to the 'wrong Gulf'.[28]

These harsh realities suggest that the swing of the Administration toward greater accommodation of its allies initiated by Bush following his re-election in late 2004 could herald a more prudent approach to purely military solutions and a somewhat greater appreciation of multilateral processes and the good company they can yield in dangerous ventures when necessary. President Reagan, often cited by members of the Bush Administration as a model, was visionary but also realistic: after the bombing of US Marine headquarters in Beirut in 1983, he took note. His disposition subsequently on Middle East issues (the Iran Contra follies engineered by Oliver North notwithstanding) was generally cautious.

The shock of 9/11 still reverberated in the United States in late 2005, but the US system of government's checks and balances had started to operate, with courts reining in the more extreme practices of the Administration in pursuit of terrorists, American and foreign. Further, the US Congress (not least some of its leading Republican Senators) was starting to reassert itself on Iraq policy, and the US media was once again exercising its critical faculties. Lessons of the Iraq venture, particularly those relating to the difficulties inherent in foreign occupation, were being registered—although the US military was horribly stuck in Iraq for an indefinite future. Thus, the genius of the US system for self-correction over time seemed at play. Whether this dynamic would produce a more favorable Washington consensus on the UN was, however, far from certain.

9.2 A Security Council Under Pressure: Can It Do Better?

9.2.1 *Legality and Legitimacy, Representation and Democracy*

The UN's institutional culture is much opposed to the use of force except as a very last resort (generally to be delayed as much as possible, and beyond). The progression of diplomatic and coercive measures outlined in Chapters VI and VII of the Charter are adduced by many as a hidebound rule. And yet, the credible threat of force is often required in order to address the 'hard cases' of international security. It took just this to induce the military regime usurping power in Haiti to depart in 1994—sadly, only after UN-mandated sanctions had wrecked an already very weak economy.[29]

One of the most serious implications of the way in which events have played out in Iraq may be that 'the brief era of consensual international intervention is already closing . . . '.[30] While Europe remained in favor of a multilateral system with strong powers of intervention, it—along with much of the rest of the world—continued to fear and resist such intervention conducted by the United States. As Tony Judt has argued, this is good news for no one:

> If the US ceases to be credible as a force for good, the world will not come to a stop. Others will still protest and undertake good works in the hope of American support. But the world will become that much safer for tyrants and crooks—at home and abroad.[31]

The costs of reduced legitimacy will not be borne by the United States alone; they will additionally be borne by the Security Council, and by the UN system as a whole, both through reduced operational flexibility, and through reduction of the perceived impartiality and universality of the UN brand. The Council's handling of Iraq, particularly its initial acquiescence in, later inability to stop, US military enforcement of Council resolutions, has done much to discredit the Council and the UN in the Middle East. There, the forceful approach taken on Iraq is routinely, and unflatteringly, set in contrast to the Council's silence on Israeli non-compliance with Council resolutions, although this emphasis on double standards has been tirelessly promoted by autocratic regimes in the Arab world often seeking to distract public attention from their own misrule. The Iraqi sanctions regime, in particular, eroded public support for Council policies, playing into the hands of revolutionary ideologues—whether Shi'a, Wahabist, or Ba'athist. Revelations of corruption in the OFF Program exacerbated that trend.

Thus, the Council's decisions on Iraq came to seem decreasingly legitimate to much of the UN membership. For many, the root of the Council's 'legitimacy' deficit is its unrepresentative membership, slighting the developing world and thus undermining the Council's authority. As Michael Ignatieff has put it:

> The real problem is that the UN that FDR helped create never worked as he intended. What passes for an 'international community' is run by a Security Council that is a museum piece of 1945 vintage.[32]

Such an analysis spurred attempts to reform the membership of the Council in 2005, predictably sucking oxygen away from other important reform initiatives. Debate on possible models for Council reform became both vexed and heated in the spring of 2005, with anti-Japanese demonstrations in China—ostensibly relating to historical grievances—adding an edge to the proceedings.[33] These discussions were described by the President of the General Assembly, Jean Ping, as 'awakening great passions and fixed attitudes'.[34]

That the Council's composition is today unrepresentative of the many currents in international relations is both widely accepted and true. India, Brazil, and South Africa belong there. That the EU is over-represented is clear, and this was particularly so in 2003 with Germany and Spain swelling its ranks in the Council.[35] But would the outcome on Iraq have been much different had Germany and Spain been absent and Brazil and India present (with or without vetoes)? If anything, the Council's experience in Iraq suggests that Council enlargement will not be a cure-all. It may, in fact, risk aggravating a tendency toward dilatory maneuvers and occasional paralysis. As Simon Chesterman pointed out, a more representative Security Council might be fairer, but not necessarily more effective.[36] This is in part the case because meaningful Committee decision-making is generally more difficult in large groups than in small ones. Further, Ramesh Thakur convincingly identifies the Council's 'performance legitimacy' as a much greater problem than its composition.[37]

Indeed, in some American quarters, the problem of representation in the Council was seen almost in reverse: they suggest that the UN system gives *too many* too much power. Ivo Daalder and James Lindsay argued that that the UN's and NATO's usefulness on key security challenges is essentially over. They advocate instead an 'Alliance of Democracies', in part to eliminate the voice in US affairs of critics essentially hostile to Washington's foreign policies:

> What other members of the alliance would receive in return is more predictability in and influence over America's behaviour. Washington would find it more difficult at home to give the back of its hand to an Alliance of Democracies than to the UN.[38]

The utility of such an approach is highly questionable, on at least three bases. First, it ignores the reality that Washington's principal opponents on Iraq policy had been other democracies such as France and Germany. Second, it suggests that confrontation through exclusion of major powers, such as China, would be a good policy for the United States—a debatable thesis at the very least. (The Alliance of Democracies was, in many ways, largely what was intended for the UN when it was contemplated during World War II—prior to the defeat of the enemy powers, and the realization of the need for their reintegration into the international community.) To abandon the attempt to achieve consultative management of key security challenges through the Security Council (and regional security forums) would essentially mean a return to confrontational geopolitics. Third, the risks and costs of such a return to Great Power confrontation are likely very high. Daalder and Lindsay's scheme might make it easier to reach decisions about what threats need containing and how, but it would also make it less likely that those decisions could effectively and safely be implemented. Thus, a caucus of democracies is best conceived as a useful grouping within the broader community of nations, to press and act for democratic change in support of individual freedoms, economic development, and greater global stability.[39]

Debates over representation within the Council point to an attempt to compare the legitimacy of Council decision-making processes with the international legality of its decisions (or those of States relevant to it). However, this is comparing apples and oranges. Considerations of legitimacy pertaining to Council decisions tend to be (often highly) political as opposed, so believe most international lawyers, to issues of legality. In recent years, debates have proliferated about whether some uses of force taken without explicit Council authorization are 'legitimate', if not 'legal'.

The distinction was first explicitly raised in relation to NATO's action in Kosovo.[40] The debate now pervades much discussion of extra-Council uses of force, whether in 'humanitarian intervention' or counter-terrorist prevention.[41] It was notably central to discussion of the US–UK action against Iraq in 2003.[42]

Events in Iraq reveal the limits of such debates. After the invasion, Anne-Marie Slaughter, having revised her earlier opinion that while illegal the military action might be legitimate, commented that

> [t]he most important lesson of the invasion of Iraq is that the safeguards built into the requirement of the multilateral authorization of the use of force by UN members are both justified and necessary.[43]

Once the problems inherent in the occupation of Iraq were clear, the legitimacy of the enterprise faded for many. With considerable foresight, Jeremy Greenstock remarked before the invasion, '[w]hen fantasy meets reality, reality always wins.'[44]

But legality cannot always trump other factors. As Saddam Hussein's actions have made clear, the structural vulnerabilities of the Council referred to earlier in this chapter allow targets of Council persuasion and coercion to manipulate the Council to its own ends, particularly by playing off members of the P-5. In that context, the threat of extra-Council military action may be needed to keep the players honest. There can be little doubt that only the credible threat of force by the United States opened the path to UNMOVIC's deployment in Iraq. Effective multilateralism often requires teeth, as Kofi Annan himself has repeatedly recognized.

This is not to say that the United States is in any way above the law, or even, as Michael Glennon seemed to argue gleefully, that the Security Council's 'failure' on Iraq represents the end of 'the grand attempt to subject the use of force to the rule of law'.[45] Glennon's arguments on the 'desuetude' of such law were, within months, powerfully repudiated by Thomas Franck—and just as much so by subsequent developments, incurring serious costs to the United States.[46]

These factors and the preponderance of instrumental approaches to the Council's decisions by each of the P-5 suggests that the 'collectively authorized use of force' will remain, as the High Level Panel characterized it, neither rule nor exception.[47]

Perhaps the most challenging implication of events in Iraq for these interlocking debates on legality and legitimacy, representation, and democracy has, however, been largely overlooked. This concerns the limits of the UN system in dealing with violent social and religious movements, particularly in an age of transnational terror. Until now, the UN and its Member States have been able to confront threats through the mechanisms of the state system. The major confrontations which have wracked the UN, notably between global capitalism and global communism, and over decolonization, have played out between states or groups aspiring to statehood, willing to buy into the system of rule by international law. Of all the new actors, the most troubling for the UN must be those actors who reject the very authority of international law and the state system, threatening to undermine the universality of the UN. Al Qaeda stands out as rejecting not only the 'representativeness' of the UN, but also its commitment to peaceful resolution of disputes. The targeting of the UN by al Qaeda (first in 1993 in New York, and more successfully a decade later in Baghdad) highlights the very real risk this poses. As this volume reveals, the growth in support of ideologies or faiths rejecting the UN's basic tenets has been present—if obscured—in the Council's dealings with Iraq for the last twenty-five years, first in Iran's promotion of the primacy of *shari'a* over international humanitarian law during the Iran–Iraq war, and more recently in negotiations over the role of *shari'a* in the new Iraqi constitution.[48] The normative systems the UN has done so much to help develop since 1945 are here truly challenged.

As 9/11 made clear, globalization has made it possible for violent religious and social movements to turn rhetorical attacks on this normative system into armed attacks on its centers of power. This transforms not only the strategic calculus that confronts the Member States of the UN, but the very concept of 'collective security', forcing the Security Council to adopt a more preventive stance.[49] That imperative may induce the Council increasingly to opt for the kinds of solutions it imposed in SCRs 1373 (on counter-terrorism) and 1540 (on the proliferation of WMD), where it obliges Member States to take legislative, administrative, and other regulatory measures to control non-state actors' ability to threaten collective security. The danger with such approaches is that they may appear to play the role of 'legislation', despite the fact that the Security Council is no legislature.[50] Such approaches exacerbate complaints about the 'unrepresentative' nature of the Council. But even more, they bring to the fore the issue raised most squarely by the Volcker Inquiry, of whether the Council—and the UN Organization more generally—is equipped to take on such a legal-regulatory role. It is to that question—and the lessons we may learn from Iraq in answering it—that I now turn.

9.3 Two Modes of Maintaining the Peace

The path of the Council, through twenty-five years' engagement with Iraq, has taken it from the politico-military mode of the Cold War, in which the Council mediated between warring states, to its contemporary legal-regulatory mode, in which, with increasing frequency it lays down binding legal standards of conduct, delegates monitoring to administrative agents, and finally authorizes those same, or other, agents to enforce those standards. This volume has charted that evolution. In this concluding chapter, it falls simply to highlight the lessons from Iraq of this evolution—which are many.

9.3.1 *Learning from Iraq*

To begin, it must be understood that these modes represent ideal types. In the *politico-military* mode, the Council typically authorizes a strategic approach to the resolution of a threat to international peace and security, designating actors (the Secretary-General or particular Member States) with extensive discretion to interpret and implement that mandate. Activities undertaken in this mode can include implementation or enforcement by non-UN forces, peace negotiations, and the observation and monitoring of peace settlements. Examples of the Council taking action in this mode in Iraq include its approach to the Iran–Iraq war, the establishment of UNIIMOG, UNIKOM, and the political aspects of UNAMI.

In the *legal-regulatory* mode, the Council typically establishes detailed rules governing the behavior of States, individuals, or other subject entities. It then delegates powers to implement and monitor those rules to administrative delegates, who may be UN staff, agencies, or programs, other organizations (such as the IAEA or ICC), or specially established Council organs. Activities undertaken in this mode typically involve sanctions implementation, domestic regulation of prohibited transfers of goods, funds and persons, and binding international arbitration. Examples of the Council taking action in this mode in Iraq abound: UNSCOM, UNMOVIC, the sanctions regime, the OFF Program, and the UNCC.

The increasing frequency with which the Council adopts a legal-regulatory approach—as with the CTC, the 1540 Committee, the new mechanism for monitoring the use of child soldiers, and even the creation of multiple investigative commissions (on the OFF Program, Darfur, and the assassination of former Lebanese Prime Minister Hariri)—reveals both a growth in the Council's ambition, and a recognition of the need for cooperative regulation to deal with the new generation of transnational threats. Perhaps the most significant lesson of the Council's rich experience with legal regulation in Iraq has been, though, the need for a concomitant growth in UN capacity. UN Deputy Secretary-General Louise Fréchette recognized the need for transformation following the release of the Volcker Inquiry's September 2005 Report:

> Everyone today agrees that the UN faces very different management challenges than those of the Cold War period. The UN was then mainly a deliberative body. Our major task was to support negotiations. Our administrative systems have not adapted to new mandates and activities. On management, the Secretariat and Member States have failed to adjust.[51]

The transformation of management includes—but is not limited to—improved resourcing. It also signifies an understanding of how this new mode differs from the last, and the different demands it will place on the UN system. Confusion between the two modes generated trouble over Iraq, and not only in 2003. Iraq has shown the limits of US politico-military power—and by extension, the politico-military power of the UN Security Council. This suggests continued and perhaps increasing resort to the legal-regulatory approach. The nature of contemporary threats, from pandemics to terrorism—diffuse, global, and often propagated through non-state actors—further encourages such speculation. The future of the Security Council hinges on its ability to manage the consequences. If the conclusions of the Volcker Inquiry are taken to heart by Member States and the UN Secretariat alike, we can be hopeful. But the Council's brief attention span and tendency to improvise in response to immediate stimuli—its tendency, in the words of former UN Under-Secretary-General Kieran Prendergast, to 'expediency'—do not inspire confidence.[52] Instead, what is needed is a sustained and detailed reflection on how legal-regulatory approaches developed in the context of national rule of law may need to be adapted, in their adoption into the international system of rule by law. In the pages that follow, I offer reflections on four aspects of this process: mandates, discretion, accountability, and expertise.

MANDATES

The formulation and interpretation of mandates by the Security Council through its Resolutions is the key to much else in the Council's practice. In mandating a Coalition of the Willing to enforce its Resolutions, the Council forgoes any significant control; in a legal-regulatory mode the Council more significantly limits the discretion of implementing actors. Resolutions adopted in the politico-military mode can afford to use vague or at least purposive language, essentially setting the broad strategic objectives of the Council. In contrast, Resolutions adopted in the legal-regulatory mode must be much more precise, specifying what rules its delegated agent is to implement, the powers available in implementing them, and the process by which they should be enforced.

SCR 687 provided the basis for an extensive legal-regulatory machinery, ranging from UNSCOM to sanctions machinery; but its incorporation of the contract and treaty-law terminology of 'material breach' left many questions open about what constituted substantial performance by Iraq, who could determine Iraqi compliance, and what powers were available to them. Over time, the Council specified more precise rules for determining Iraqi compliance. But by acquiescing in the creeping unilateralism of the United States, the United Kingdom, and France, it created confusion about interpretation of compliance and enforcement. That became particularly problematic further to SCR 1441 of 2002, with many different actors involved, including individual Member States, the Council as a whole, the Secretary-General, and independent agencies such as UNMOVIC and the IAEA. Above all, the uncertain nature, timing, and trigger of the 'serious consequences' threatened by the Council—while a paradigm of drafting in the politico-military mode—compounded the confusion of a Council attempting to act in legal-regulatory mode.

DISCRETION

In the politico-military mode, Council agents exercise substantial policy discretion; as long as they work toward the objective stated by the Council, they have discretion to choose the route taken. The boundaries of that discretion may be expressly and implicitly limited: for example, the discretion of the Multinational Force (MNF) when authorized in 1991 was limited by its UN Charter obligations, the mandate it was given under Chapter VII, and its obligations to abide by international humanitarian law. But within those parameters, the agent has substantial room to maneuver. The Council's validation in Resolution 1483 (2003) of the Coalition Provisional Authority—within specific limits—provides another example of this approach. The discretion was widely understood to be broad in both cases, with limited reporting requirements.

In the legal-regulatory mode, the Council delegates substantive decision-making power on narrow, and often highly technical, issues to independent agents, such as UNSCOM and the UNCC, or the various UN agencies that were to implement the sanctions regime and OFF Program. These agents have very narrow powers, but their decisions are either binding on the Council (as in the case of the UNCC and later the ICTY, ICTR and arguably, in exceptional cases, the ICC), or at least highly authoritative (because of their technical expertise).

Problems can arise when the Council establishes what it seems to intend as an independent delegate, but then fails to allow that delegate to exercise truly independent discretion. In Iraq, this problem arose with political interference on a number of levels in the administration of the OFF Program, UNSCOM, and during the US–UK contestation of UNMOVIC's work in 2003. The mandate and operations of the 661 Committee proved particularly problematic. Considerable confusion existed at various times over the respective roles of the Committee and of the Secretariat in exercising primary responsibility for contracts under OFF. The discretion exercised by decision-makers in the Committee was also, in some cases, highly politicized: Member States acted at once as advocates of their countries' commercial interests, and as defenders of the integrity of the sanctions regime.

Given the nature of contemporary threats, and the legal-regulatory approach increasingly adopted by the Council to contain and meet them, such conflicts of interest are dangerous, falling short of the kind of impartial, judicious examination of evidence, which is routine in scientific inquiry and the administration of justice—but historically alien to politics, and the decision to go to war. A failure to adopt an impartial decision-making procedure risks producing illegitimacy, as the UN Compensation Commission's refusal to give Iraq standing in its claim process risked aggravating Iraq's victim mentality. In the long-term, that can only hurt the UN.

Such considerations also need to pertain to the decision-making procedures of the Council itself, not least in engagement with relevant stake-holders and in the transparency of its own proceedings. One former German ambassador has described a

> complete loss of transparency and of the right of the concerned parties, e.g. Iraq, to address the Council *in corpore* while it is still in the process of deliberation.[53]

Bardo Fassbender, a respected scholar on Council practice, suggests that in certain cases this may amount to a violation of the 'constitutional equality' provided UN members states by Article 2 of the Charter.[54] (Arguably, there is a similar disdain for due process at play in many of the Council's working methods relating to individualized sanctions.[55])

Resourcing is also a factor crucial to maintaining the capacity to exercise discretion effectively, in the absence of which decision-makers may become dependent on others. The burden placed on Member States to scrutinize contracts in the 661 Committee provided an example. With the exception of the United States, and to a lesser extent the United Kingdom and France, most Council members lacked the expert personnel necessary adequately to perform this task. The result was a dysfunctional Committee dominated by a few Member States. UNSCOM's reliance on Member State personnel ultimately proved similarly problematic.

Intelligence will likely remain a key issue for the Council in years to come. We now know that the conclusions drawn from US and UK intelligence, based largely on satellite imagery and self-interested exile informants, proved wrong. On the other hand, the UN's information, and its cautious approach to drawing conclusions from contradictory indicators (ranging from past Iraqi behavior through Saddam Hussein's presumed ambitions, to hard evidence or the lack thereof on the ground), was right. We were not, as David Kay asserted, all wrong: in exercising prudence in judgement, Mohammed El Baradei and Hans Blix turned out to be right.[56] George A. Lopez and David Cortright comment:

> The crisis of intelligence that pundits and politicians should be considering is not why so many officials overestimated what was wrong in Iraq; it is why they ignored so much readily available evidence of what was right about existing policies. By disregarding the success of inspections and sanctions, Washington discarded an effective system of containment and deterrence and on the basis of faulty intelligence and wrong assumptions, launched a preventive war in its place.[57]

The various inquiries mentioned in earlier chapters have exonerated US and UK intelligence agencies of willful distortion of their conclusions and advice, but it is hard to believe that intelligence officials were not influenced by the fevered atmosphere in Washington and London and the expectations of their political masters. Carne Ross remarks:

> Back in capitals, there is ... an invisible undertow at work on the civil servants who collate and analyse ... information. If Ministers want a particular story to emerge, it has a way of emerging. The facts are made to fit the policy ... and caveats are left out.[58]

These reflections suggest that the UN might, in certain cases, provide a useful source of independent, impartial information gathering and analysis, against which Member States' own assumptions and conclusions can be tested. But such a possibility is anathema to many Member States.

Proposals for a centralized, independent forecasting unit—crucial for serious peace-building efforts—has been scotched in discussion of the High Level Panel report. The proposal by France to retain permanently UNMOVIC as a proven resource has been opposed by the United States, China, and some developing countries, which express concerns about the uses to which such a standing monitoring capacity might be put, in addition to the costs of maintaining such a body.[59] In late 2005, as a shell of its former self, UNMOVIC lingers in bureaucratic limbo, as there is no agreement either to kill it off.

ACCOUNTABILITY

In the politico-military mode, accountability is not always a major issue, because the Council either retains decision-making discretion or grants it to others. But in the legal-regulatory mode, accountability is crucial. If the Council delegates substantial authority for the interpretation and implementation of a regime to an agent, it follows that this agent should be accountable to the Council. All too often accountability systems were lacking on Iraq. The 661 Committee left unclear how the OIP's performance was to be monitored and, perhaps more significantly, how Member State behavior on sanctions (including that of the P-5, who turned a blind eye to significant sanctions-busting by Turkey, Jordan, and Syria) was to be regulated. Reminding us that the OFF Program was largely designed by the Clinton Administration and Major government in London, James Traub writes:

> the compromises that allowed Saddam to exploit the program were baked in from the start.... [In 1995,] with the humanitarian crisis deepening and the sanctions ... threatened, American and British negotiators agreed to let Saddam control the distribution of goods within the country and choose who would buy Iraqi oil. It was plain that the dictator would use the deal to line his own pockets and to try to evade the sanctions. According to Sir Jeremy Greenstock, then an official in the British Foreign Office and later his country's ambassador to the United Nations, 'It was realized that a certain amount of misbehaviour was going to happen on the Iraqi side if they were going to accept this. But the Iraqi government had to agree, or it wouldn't work'.[60]

The failure to ensure that the regulatory systems the Council set up with respect to Iraq contained robust accountability systems came home to roost through the OFF scandal and subsequent Volcker Inquiry. The UN Secretariat has been excoriated for mismanagement and worse but, so far, Security Council members have largely enjoyed a 'free ride'.[61]

EXPERTISE

Students of the Security Council and of other multilateral decision-making forums learn to recognize trends in decision-making, ostensibly based on past experiences generically applied (the 'lessons of Somalia' crippling the possibility of meaningful international response to genocide in Rwanda, for example). Country and region-specific expertise of the depth required to assist in charting a new course for conflict countries is rarely hitched up to national and international decision-making. The International Crisis Group and several other research organizations have bravely and often successfully sought to fill this breach, but an absence of historical, anthropological, sociological, and economic knowledge of societies the UN seeks to help is striking. (Asking one senior UN appointee dispatched to a country foundering in dire distress what he had read on the place by local and foreign writers, I was only mildly surprised to be told 'nothing'.)

No regulation can succeed without adequate expertise. Increasingly, the Security Council delegates fact-finding roles to groups of experts or commissions of inquiry with appropriate technical and contextual knowledge—for example in the Democratic Republic of Congo, Liberia, Lebanon following the assassination of former Prime Minister Hariri, and Darfur to assess evidence of genocide.[62] Yet the Council, particularly the P-5, is much inclined to second-guess these experts. Ultimately, that is exactly what the United States and the United Kingdom did with UNMOVIC in 2003. That experience may point to the limits of the type of fact-finding, which the Council is willing—and able—to delegate.

We should also be realistic about the limits of 'expertise'. This tale provides evidence of 'group think' and tribal loyalties in cities as sophisticated as Washington. The State Department's preliminary planning for post-war Iraq was dismissed out of hand by a Pentagon sure it needed to know nothing more—although Pentagon supporters deride what the State Department had been able to draw together.[63] Experts themselves also sometimes fail to predict what later seems obvious. Pondering why nobody much had seen the Sunni insurgency coming, I asked several respected academic authorities on Iraq whether they had done better than the officials. One responded, with considerable insight:

> Most of the people who dealt with this were thinking of how to ensure that 'the majority' [the Shi'a] had the decisive voice in postwar Iraq. Very different to attitudes in 1991, but in the minds of most of the officials I encountered the Shi'a had by 2003 acquired a collective identity and a kind of collective virtue by being the majority of the population. For understandable reasons, no-one really considered the Sunnis, qua Sunnis, to be a community and saw them more in their

various incarnations: as Saddamists, as Ba'thists, as Communists, as Salafis, as secularists, as tribalists etc etc. The notion of a 'Sunni community' is very recent, after all, and, as events in Iraq have demonstrated, it is doubtful that there is one in any meaningful sense of the term. This is what is making it so difficult to identify and to bring in a group or individuals that would be seen as representative in any way of the Sunni Arabs as a whole.[64]

Making war is risky, with the law of unintended consequences kicking in spectacularly in the case of Iraq. This makes contingency planning involving a wide variety of scenarios (including state collapse) advisable. It is not at all clear that the planners of Operation Iraqi Freedom were drawing on a broad range of expertise or open to the range of possible outcomes on the ground to Saddam Hussein's overthrow.

9.4 Building Peace In and Through States

Few experts—inside or outside government—predicted the extent and nature of state collapse in Iraq following the US–UK invasion. As Toby Dodge has commented:

> The expert view on the socio-political dynamics post Saddam was that Iraqi nationalism was strong, as was a commitment in the non-Kurdish areas of the country to a unified state. The big thing all the policy makers missed was the almost complete collapse of the state. Once that had happened and was not rectified, the traumatised population of Iraq grabbed whatever sub-state identities it could in order to gain some foothold in the chaos that has swept the country.... Once the institutions of the state disappear (for whatever reason) different local, communal or sectarian identities leap up to take their place.[73]

At the time of writing, it remains to be seen whether politics will take hold in Iraq, or whether it will descend, once more, into violence. The questions raised about Iraq's future are increasingly those relevant to domestic politics, particularly the relations between the major ethnic and political factions within the country. Having endured the tyranny of a minority regime for so long, might Iraq now succumb to insensitive, possibly autocratic leaders representing a majority challenged, through terrorist violence, by an insurgency rooted in that very minority?

To answer that question, we must also consider how the collapse of the Iraqi state is connected to regional politics. (The absence of an even mildly effective regional organization in the Middle East is one of the peculiarities of this case, the Arab League having proved severely challenged in responding to Saddam Hussein's serial provocations after 1990, prior to which Arab governments broadly supported his aggression.) A regime as despotic as Saddam Hussein's could only flourish as easily as it did in a region of dysfunctional polities, as Kanan Makiya and many others have pointed out.[74] Whether the regional inclination toward totalitarian and authoritarian government of various stripes will overwhelm budding Iraqi representative government or whether, rather, a new Iraqi model will influence its region, inducing more inclusive government elsewhere—the neo-con vision—also remains to be seen. The influence of events in Iraq, including its recent elections, on the broader Arab scene, restless and yearning for political change, should not be underestimated.[75]

The Security Council itself is implicated in the collapse of the Iraqi state. The costs borne in Iraq of a sanctions regime decreed in New York have doubtless contributed to nascent militancy in Iraq. Many Iraqis—whether Sunni or Shi'a—felt disempowered, disenfranchised, and disillusioned by the Security Council's strategy in the 1990s. Combined with this, the Council's assertive role in supporting the fight against terrorism, through SCR 1373 and subsequent decisions, contributes to a sense among many peaceable Arabs that the UN is an instrument of a self-serving P-5 dealing in double standards and aiming to marginalize the Muslim world.[76] That this analysis leaves out many relevant factors and does not correspond to the intent of the Council takes little away from its currency in the region. A larger role in reconstruction and development in Iraq might help the UN to counter these perceptions.

Writing about future prospects for Iraq in 2002, Charles Tripp suggested:

> Those who are seeking to develop a new narrative for the history of Iraq must recognize the powerful legacies at work in the country if they do not wish to succumb to their logic.... The restricted circle of rulers and the primacy of military force have combined with the massive financial power granted to successive Iraqi governments by oil revenues to create dominant narratives marked by powerful, authoritarian leadership.[77]

It is not clear that the UN holds out much prospect of serving as a circuit breaker in this infernal dynamic, but fortunately, perceptions of a single Shi'a vision for Iraq's future seem grossly oversimplified. Likewise, while the Kurds wish for autonomy, there is little consensus among them on the precise form that this autonomy should take.[78] This space and fluidity provides political actors in Iraq not only with opportunities for negative agendas, but also for positive ones aiming to promote the interests of the Iraqi state and all of its citizens. Whether the privileges of those currently in command of government will simply be entrenched, as Iraq's history suggests could well be the case, or whether a new departure for Iraqi politics, allowing for dissent and dialog is possible remains unknowable.

If the UN is to play a role here, it will be an inherently political one. As Lakhdar Brahimi's role in 2004 showed, the UN can at times play the same skilful mediatory role in internal conflicts, and in the process of 'building peace' between substate factions, that it played between states in the Iran–Iraq war. This requires, however, recognition of the inherently political nature of peace-building, and perhaps a willingness by the Council to return to the politico-military mode that has, in recent times, been eclipsed by the preference for legal-regulatory solutions.

That same preference may be detectable in discussions of 'state-building', which risk characterizing inherently political interventions as technical capacity-building exercises. Such a perspective risks creating an environment where 'humanitarian intervention' and 'preventive counterterrorism' begin to be perceived in some quarters as apolitical exercises in the enforcement of legitimate legal standards. We are not at that point yet. Military intervention on the scale of the interventions in Iraq of the last decade-and-a-half remain fundamentally controversial, highly political ventures. In order to be successful, they require a broad political consensus within the international community—for which Council approval remains perhaps the best measure. Absent such support, they seem likely to fail. As Phebe Marr has commented,

> the best advice to draw ... may be this: if you cannot garner adequate resources—and public opinion at home and abroad—to rebuild a nation, do not start.... In the meantime ... look harder for ways to shore up or bring change to failing states before they warrant intervention at all.[79]

States can be locked into an effective security management apparatus, particularly through the detailed legal-regulatory mechanisms the Council is increasingly turning to. But in order to do so, they must have effective management capacity, and act as the agents of the Council in its defense of all the Charter values: peace, security, development, and human rights. That capacity can only be achieved through the preventive and buttressing action that Marr points to, through peace-building. Peace-building must adopt a multidisciplinary, preventive approach drawing on all the expertise and experience of the international community. The UN remains, because of its universality, the only viable institution for such an enterprise. Marr's advice applies, however, also to peace-building: without adequate resources and the support of public opinion, measured through debate in the Council, perhaps we should not even start.

9.5 Applying the Lessons

9.5.1 *Sanctions*

SCR 687, imposing a starkly intrusive and sweeping internal disarmament regime backed up by comprehensive economic sanctions on Iraq, represents the high-water mark of the Council's ambitions. However, its implementation was often absent-minded, inconsistent, and, over time, increasingly incoherent in terms of shared objectives. It mostly achieved its disarmament goals, although the sanctions regime became very leaky.

Much has been made of the evils of the sanctions regime. Concern over the humanitarian costs of sanctions led to declining public support internationally for the Council's strategy in Iraq, of which several Council members took too little heed. In 1998–9, the United States and the United Kingdom made clear that while they could do without weapons inspections, they would cling to the sanctions regime as the ultimate tool for containing Saddam Hussein. In pursuing this widely disliked policy as single-mindedly as they did, they may have laid the foundations for the lack of support in the Council in 2002–3 for their objective of confronting Saddam Hussein forcibly. Their strategies were increasingly seen as punitive rather than aimed at achieving disarmament.

In part, these heavy costs resulted from a failure to understand how the administrative complexity of the sanctions regime created opportunities for the deliberate or inadvertent corruption of the regime. The movement away from a politico-military approach to a legal-regulatory one proved problematic, not least because the shift was not well understood by those who implemented it. It made the Council dependent on agents—either the staff of the UN, or the Member States themselves—who implemented, monitored, and enforced the rules it laid down. That created the opportunity for those agents to corrupt, in a variety of ways, application of the regulatory regime. The corruption revealed by the Volcker Inquiry is only the most obvious, and perhaps not the most invidious. Other examples included the US intelligence infiltration of UNSCOM, and the willingness of even Council advocates for a tough approach to Baghdad to condone illegal oil-smuggling from Iraq to Turkey, Jordan, and Syria. Former UK delegate Carne Ross writes:

> In the Security Council, any attempt the UK made to propose collective action against smuggling was invariably blocked by France or Russia, on the alleged grounds that there was insufficient proof of smuggling, or that such action might further harm Iraq's people.... The US and UK now claim that this was the reason the sanctions failed (when in doubt, blame the French). Yet, in truth, too little

energy was exerted on enforcing controls. While in New York we argued ourselves hoarse in negotiation, Washington and London rarely lifted a finger to pressure Iraq's neighbours to stem the illegal flows.[65]

Another obstacle to the successful implementation of the regime was the emerging dispute, among Council principals, over its ultimate objective. The goal of 'regime change', so often articulated in Washington (and occasionally London) after 1997, was unpopular among many governments at the UN, who suggested it shifted SCR 687's goalposts. Some were preoccupied with their own regime survival; others were fearful of where such policies might lead for weaker countries. In fact, SCR 687 sought to stigmatize the Iraqi regime and to deter others in the region and beyond from similar behavior. When Washington and London moved to implement regime change in Baghdad in 2002–3, this long-running and sour debate handicapped their arguments. Indirectly and for some, SCR 687 might also have been intended to promote regional stability and societal change in the Middle East. It did undermine Iraq's capacity for aggression against neighboring countries. But the relationship between events in and affecting Iraq, and broader peace in the Israeli–Palestinian theatre of conflict, remains elusive. Yassir Arafat's death in late 2004 may be more relevant. The military presence of the United States in Iraq undoubtedly contributed to the success of SCR 1559 in securing Syrian withdrawal from Lebanon. And, for a number of reasons of which the Iraqi elections of January 2005 was one, the winds of change began to stir—albeit listlessly—in the Arab World. But the eruption in Iraq, the impact on neighboring countries, and the costs for intervening powers all heavily outweigh the regional benefits to date.

The confusion over the goal of the sanctions regime was in part a result of the Council's acquiescence in the creeping unilateralism of the United States and the United Kingdom. But France's defection in 1996 from a passive Western consensus supporting this approach shattered Council complacency. French company (most often French leadership) induced Moscow and Beijing to voice increasingly strident criticism of the United States and the United Kingdom as of that year. That, in turn, created the possibility for developing countries (the overwhelming majority at the UN, and sometimes the majority in the Council) to develop serious and vocal reservations over the stringent sanctions punishing Iraq's population with little apparent effect on Baghdad's leaders. A united Council would have been preferable both tactically and strategically, but this would have required greater flexibility in policy than Washington and London, benefiting from the 'reverse veto', were prepared to contemplate.

What could have been done to address these risks and deficiencies? There is today, in the wake of the Volcker Inquiry and other investigative reports an understanding that greater and more closely monitored accountability, as well as management reforms, are required at the UN. In keeping with (sometimes partisan) Congressional fixation on probity within international organizations, but rooted in the useful Gingrich–Mitchell report of 2005, the United States is in the vanguard of those insisting on such administrative change. But necessary reform of the administrative practices of the Council's agents—particularly the UN Secretariat—obscures the responsibility of the Security Council (in which the United States, of course, sits) for signal failures of oversight of the implementation of many of its own decisions.

A key change would require the Council to recognize that it is engaging in enforcement through regulation and delegated administration. Only then can it consciously improve the design, resourcing, and management of relevant regimes. Clearly, lines of accountability in both the OFF program and UNSCOM were muddied. As the Volcker Inquiry recognized, in the OFF

> [n]either the Security Council nor the Secretariat was clearly in command. That turned out to be a recipe for the dilution of Secretariat authority and evasion of personal responsibility at all levels. When things went awry—and they surely did—when troublesome conflicts arose between political objectives and administrative effectiveness, decisions were delayed, bungled or simply shunned.[66]

Beyond that, good design needs to ensure that regulatory regimes do not become merely 'bureaucratically rational': doing their own jobs well, but working against other parts of the system. The Iraq sanctions regime suffered from exactly this problem: it was successful in degrading not only the Ba'athist military capacity, but also Iraqi welfare, setting the security interests of the UN system against its humanitarian interests. Regulation often requires regulators to balance strategic objectives; increasingly, the Council will have to find ways to balance the non-security purposes and principles of the UN Charter—development, justice, human rights—with its action to maintain collective security.

9.5.2 *Secretary or General?*

The position of the UN Secretary-General is unique, in principle drawing legitimacy largely from his independence.[67] At the same time, the Secretary-

General must work closely with—and often under mandates given by—the Security Council. Understanding the nature of the Secretary-General's discretion, his mandate(s), and his accountability to the Council—and other organs of the UN, and the Member States—is crucial in the proper management of expectations of what the Secretary-General can achieve.

Operating in the politico-military mode, the Secretary-General is given wide discretion, a mandate based on his independence or good offices, and is only weakly accountable to the Council: he is more general than secretary. Operating in the legal-regulatory mode, the Secretary-General is more likely to have a mandate delegated from the Council, a narrow technical discretion, and to be held more closely accountable by the Security Council: he is more secretary than general. What lessons can we learn from Iraq as to the future of this unique role; will future office-bearers be more Secretary, or more General?

Kofi Annan's travails in 2005 will no doubt induce many in the Council to demand that future Secretaries-General be held on a short leash. Yet they would do well to learn the lessons of Iraq on the benefits of an independent—but impartial—mediator in this role. The UN's usefulness could well be seriously compromised unless the United States is prepared to recognize and protect the independence of the office of the Secretary-General, as a resource. The challenge is summed up by David Rieff:

> Even if the UN secretariat begins to behave with less secrecy and more dispatch, and shows more resolve to tackle corruption ... the real challenge is defining the UN's role in the post-cold war, post 9/11 world. Should it be a servicing secretariat, along the lines of the African Union, for Member States—above all, powerful states such as the US and other permanent members of the Security Council? If so, how does it remain faithful to the ideals of the UN charter, for instance in confronting uses of force that may violate the provisions that require a Security Council mandate, while remaining relevant and adequately funded. The pitfalls of that approach have been shown by the orchestrated campaign against Mr. Annan and the UN by US conservatives angered by his description of the invasion of Iraq as illegal.[68]

Two Secretaries-General of the UN in succession have now experienced serious difficulties in managing steady and constructive relations with Washington.[69] While it is perfectly legitimate for Washington to press the incumbent to support American policy, the Secretary-General needs to maintain substantive integrity in order to command respect among the membership as a whole. Standing his ground is all a Secretary-General can do. He cannot be seen to be attacking Member States, particularly powerful ones, too pointedly, even when the facts would back him up. The Secretary-General jousts with Washington (when he does) one hand tied behind his back. Still, as Annan's shift of strategy in early 2005 suggests, there may now be a recognition at the UN that the support of the overwhelming majority of Member States cannot substitute for a constructive working relationship with today's supreme power.

Like his earlier predecessor Kurt Waldheim who addressed the Iran–Iraq war in the early 1980s, Annan's ability to maneuver as of 1997 was constrained by a divided P-5. But where Waldheim was confronted by the challenges of bipolarity, Annan faced a Council rent by a new unipolar dispensation. The combination of responsiveness and independence which the Secretary-General must display is possible only if the Council acts responsibly on the issues of mandate, discretion, accountability, and expertise discussed above. Otherwise, the Secretary-General is left with impossible challenges and often consigned to the function of scapegoat for the failures of others. As the Volcker Inquiry puts it:

> Whatever the founders had in mind, the Secretary-General—any Secretary-General—has not been chosen for his managerial or administrative skills, nor has he been provided with the structure and instruments conducive to strong executive oversight and control.... The reality is that the Secretary-General has come to be viewed as a chief diplomatic and political agent of the UN.... In these turbulent times, those responsibilities tend to be all consuming. The record reflects consequent administrative failings.[70]

It was on this basis that the Volcker Inquiry recommended the creation of a position of Chief Operating Officer (COO)—a proposal that may yet founder on Member State opposition. Yet whether or not such a position is created, the underlying need for a stronger independent executive capacity within the Organization remains the same. The proposal to create a COO in essence suggested the division of the role of Secretary from that of General; what that points to is the need for the UN organization, if it is to improve its effectiveness and maintain its legitimacy, to drastically overhaul its administrative capacity.

As the Inquiry recognized, a key to the development of such a capacity is the need to appoint staff on the basis of merit, not political connection or nationality. The power to appoint is one of the few that the Secretary-General can exercise with a degree of initiative. Kofi Annan has performed impressively in assigning prominent and competent women to senior UN positions. But otherwise, he has often been slow and uninspired in his choices. The appointment of Richard Butler as UNSCOM Chairman, in particular, provides an interesting example of tunnel vision pursued with intelligence and great energy, but little perspective. Butler failed not because of his own qualities, which are impressive, but because of the poor fit between those qualities and the difficult role assigned to him.

The success of persons appointed to key UN positions often depends far more on temperament than on intellect. People who perform well in one capacity do not always distinguish themselves in another. A competent envoy in the Security Council may be out of his or her depth in the field. The belief that private sector management experience, or leadership of a government, qualify one for politically complex, frequently under-resourced, and often chaotic UN management or field positions has been demonstrated to be wrong again and again.

Secretaries-General might legitimately claim that the pool of talent available to them in making appointments is limited. Lakhdar Brahimi has had to pinch-hit for the UN repeatedly in tight spots, particularly since the death of Sergio Vieira de Mello. But how broadly does the Secretary-General cast his net? In 2005, in the wake of the OFF inquiries, he introduced new procedures for high-level appointments that aim to limit Member State lobbying and to preclude cronyism.[71] But this comes very late.

Without progress by the Council in managing its own work, and by the Secretary-General in administering the organization, the UN's credibility will continue to wane, resulting in 'a much more modest UN, not politically aggressive, not making strong statements about what is legal and what is not, a much weaker secretary general after this one is gone'.[72]

Kofi Annan's first term, during which he focused on normative development in fields such as human rights, was the most impressive, overall, of any Secretary-General to date. That Iraq came to bedevil his second term, as we have seen, was not just damaging for the UN but also tragic for this very fine man to whose strengths the Iraq file did not play. While it is much too soon to suggest how history will remember his tenure as a whole, undoubtedly in the realm of ideas, intellectual integrity and personal commitment he stands with Dag Hammarskjöld (who had a much smaller and simpler organization to run for most of his tenure) as a meaningful world leader.

Box 9.2 SYRIA–LEBANON: 'REGIME CHANGE' THROUGH SECURITY COUNCIL PRESSURE?

In contrast to the military intervention in Iraq in 2003, US and French efforts to terminate Syria's military involvement within Lebanon and to address the 2005 assassination of former Lebanese Prime Minister Rafiq Hariri were pursued, very effectively, through concerted pressure from the UN Security Council. By the end of 2005, Syria had withdrawn its troops from Lebanon and was 'on the spot' for Hariri's murder further to an extensive and detailed UN investigation of its circumstances.

Washington had, for many years, been a sharp critic of Syrian patronage of groups it deemed terrorist, for its unrelenting hostility towards Israel, and, more recently, for the transit through Syria of fighters swelling the ranks of the Iraqi insurgency as of 2003. France, the former Colonial power in Lebanon, had long wanted to guarantee that country's sovereignty and effective independence from Syria, which had deployed troops into Lebanon during its lengthy civil war from the mid-1970s until the late 1980s.

An opportunity arose in August 2004, when Lebanon's government declared its intention to extend pro-Syrian President Emile Lahoud's constitutionally-defined six-year mandate by three years. (Prime Minister Hariri who opposed the idea, resigned shortly thereafter in protest.) France and the United States seized onto this provocation, within days persuading the Security Council to adopt SCR 1559 reaffirming Lebanon's independence, calling for the withdrawal of foreign (read: Syrian) forces, and urging the disbandment of Lebanon's fractious militias.[1] SCR 1559 received only the minimum nine affirmative votes for passage—with China, Russia, Pakistan, Algeria, the Philippines and Brazil abstaining, perhaps fearful of engagement in a complex issue involving sovereignty and of consequences for the broader Middle East. Syria effected some cosmetic redeployments of its troops. Lahoud's term was extended.

This apparent stand-off was shattered by Hariri's assassination on February 14, 2005. In spite of threatening rhetoric from some in Washington ('We're going to turn up the heat on Syria, that's for sure'[2]), the Council's response—shaped once again by Paris and Washington working closely together—was measured. In SCR 1595, adopted unanimously, it established an investigative commission to determine the extent of Syrian involvement in the crime.[3] The lead investigator, Germany's Detlev Mehlis, noted the 'unique and unprecedented' nature of this Commission.[4] In essence, the UN had added yet another vocation to its regulatory arsenal: that of police inspector.

With its traditional support in the Arab world undercut by the brazenness of the Hariri affair, Damascus buckled, and Syrian troops withdrew from Lebanon in late April, followed by fresh parliamentary elections and mass demonstrations (and counter-demonstrations) for democracy and Lebanese independence.

Mehlis meant business. A bold August 30, 2005, dawn raid on the homes of four Lebanese Generals yielded fruit, implicating them in the murder. Having engaged in discussions with some leading figures in the Damascus regime, and undoubtedly influenced by the mysterious demise of former Syrian Interior Minister Ghazi Kanaan a week earlier, in October Mehlis reported to the Council that Hariri's assassination 'was carried out by a group with an extensive organization and considerable resources and capabilities' and that 'converging evidence' pointed to 'both Lebanese and Syrian involvement'. The Assad regime was now well and truly under pressure, with support within the Arab world diminishing rapidly and signs of dissent (albeit still timid, in keeping with the government's fearsome reputation) growing.

The case of Lebanon and Syria shows Washington, together with Paris, carefully establishing the foundations for effective international action through the Security Council, specifically its SCR 1559, as it had on Iraq in 1990 with SCR

660. While 'regime change' did not ensue, change in the Syrian regime's behaviour certainly did, as its military withdrawal from Lebanon in 2005 attests.

Syria's withdrawal from Lebanon and the UN's effective follow-up to the Hariri murder in late 2005 risked driving a wedge between Paris and Washington. The former remained narrowly focused on the restoration of Lebanese sovereignty, while the latter seemed eager to wrest from Damascus further concessions relating to Syria's border with Iraq and possibly still extending to regime change. This was to require careful fine-tuning between the two capitals in order to prevent a collapse of the Council's unity on the matter.

But at year's end, their joint strategy still held, with the Council further tightening the screws on the Assad regime in SCR 1644 on December 15, 2005. The UN investigation team pressed to speak directly to the Syrian President.[6] Slowly, Syria was being backed into a corner by a determined, unified, temperate, and innovative Security Council.

9.6 Envoi

In the wake of Operation Iraqi Freedom, the Security Council continues to function, often hyperactively, issuing statements, adopting Resolutions and, on a number of crises serving as the lead deliberative and decision-making forum for the international community. But many of these crises are 'orphan conflicts' (often in Africa), engaging the interests of the Great Powers only marginally.[80] And if the Council resigns itself, or is consigned by the major powers, merely to address often intractable civil wars of a geostrategically secondary character, then the UN, in the security sphere, will recede to little more than it amounted to during the Cold War years, a far cry from the terms and ambitions of the Charter.

Where P-5 interests converge, as in the fight against terrorism, the Council is likely increasingly to make decisions in the legislative mode (strongly disliked by many Member States), setting up elaborate regulatory and monitoring regimes. But, as we have seen, their own commitment—and the UN's capacity—to implement such sweeping decisions effectively and consensually over time remains in doubt.

It would be tragic if it took a nuclear detonation or a devastating chemical attack (possibly engineered by a terrorist group) to galvanize the Council members into a greater willingness to work together. Operation Iraqi Freedom stands as a powerful testament to the risks of going it alone. But the narcissism of essentially small differences—in contrast to the culture of mutual accommodation so prevalent among the P-5 in the 1990s—could frustrate the Council's potential to serve as the key international forum on the hardest security issues.

As matters stand, it is not at all clear that the Council could again agree on demands as unambiguous or as convincingly advanced as those contained in SCR 678 or devise a multilateral strategy of intrusive disarmament as comprehensive as that enshrined in SCR 687. The Council has failed to grapple seriously or effectively with the challenge of North Korea's nuclear program, first referred to it by the IAEA in 1993. It also failed to come together on Iraq, producing nothing but losers at the international level. (Admittedly both countries represent cockpits of geostrategic competition.) What does this presage for a united approach to Iran's budding nuclear program and for future challenges as yet unimagined?

The UN Charter provides a carefully designed role for the Council, as valid and necessary today as in 1945, central in international law, and potentially again central in international politics. The Iraq case shows it used for good and ill over the twenty-five years to 2005 and highlights its unique attributes and value when engaging creatively and meaningfully the key international players. As the Volcker Inquiry into the OFF Program put it:

> In the absence of the United Nations, no other organization or nation, or no grouping of organizations or nations, may be readily available, or available at all, to take on the complex missions cutting across national boundaries and diverse areas of competence. And, singly or together, the Agencies do have skills and experience—and a presumption of legitimacy—difficult or impossible to match.[81]

It would take a global catastrophe to design an alternative and that alternative might not represent an improvement.

The Iraq saga is replete with lessons for actors in and students of international relations, some of which this narrative has attempted to distil. I very much hope that its conclusions may arouse some interest among UN professionals and those in capitals who influence national decisions on international relations. Most of all, I would be delighted if the generation soon to pick up the challenge of managing international relations in dangerous times had found this volume of some use.

Notes

1. This phrase refers to the conclusions of Rosemary Foot, S. Neil MacFarlane, and Michael Mastanduno, *US Hegemony and International Organizations* (Oxford: Oxford University Press, 2003), 265–72. Richard N. Haass, while an official of the George W. Bush Administration, had advocated a US policy of 'multilateralism à

la carte'. See his *The Opportunity: America's Moment to Alter History's Course* (New York: Public Affairs, 2005), 181–2 for his further thinking on this topic.

2. James Cockayne with Cyrus Samii, 'The Iraq Crisis and World Order: Structural and Normative Challenges', August 16–18, 2004 Conference Report, Bangkok; International Peace Academy and United Nations University.
3. Jan Eliasson, interview with the author, June 23, 2005.
4. Tony Judt, 'The New World Order', *New York Review of Books* 52/12, July 14, 2005, 16.
5. On the dilemmas this created for non-permanent members, see Mahbubani, *Beyond the Age of Innocence*, 147–8.
6. Stephen C. Schlesinger, *Act of Creation: The Founding of the United Nations: A Story of Superpowers, Secret Agents, Wartime Allies and Enemies, and their Quest for a Peaceful World* (Boulder, CO: Westview Press, 2003).
7. Patrick Jarreau, 'Crispation américanophobe', *Le Monde*, November 26, 2004, 1.
8. Fred Kaplan, Give Saddam Two MoreWeeks: A good idea from the Canadians', Slate, February 28, 2003, http://slate.msn.com/id/2079497.
9. See UN Security Council resolution 896, January 31, 1994.
10. See for example Steven R. Weisman and C. J. Chivers, 'At NATO Talks, Accord and Discord for U.S. and Russia', *New York Times*, April 22, 2005, 10.
11. For more information on the Shanghai Cooperation Organization, see www.sectsco.org.
12. See for example Toshi Yoshihira and Richard Sokolski, 'The United States and China in the Persian Gulf: Challenges and Opportunities', *Fletcher Forum of World Affairs* 26/1 (2002).
13. See David M. Malone, 'A Decade of U.S. Unilateralism', in Malone and Foong Khong (eds.), *Unilateralism and US Foreign Policy*, 24. See also Arthur M. Schlesinger Jr., 'Unilateralism in Historical Perspective', in Gwyn Prins (ed.), *Understanding Unilateralism in American Foreign Relations* (London: Royal Institute of International Affairs, 2000).
14. This proposition is countered by John R. Bolton, 'Unilateralism is not Isolationism', in Prins (ed.), *Understanding Unilateralism in American Foreign Relations*.
15. United States Department of National Defense, *National Defense Strategy of the United States of America* (March 18, 2005), 5.
16. See Walter Lafeber, 'The Bush Doctrine', *Diplomatic History* 26/4 (2002), 555.
17. The phrase is Mark Danner's: 'The Secret Way to War', 48.
18. James Traub, 'Who needs the UN Security Council?', *New York Times Magazine*, November 17, 2002, 47.
19. Traub, 'Who needs the UN Security Council?', 47.
20. Perhaps under the Responsibility to Protect doctrine. See generally Thomas G. Weiss and Don Hubert, *Responsibility to Protect: Research, Bibliography, and Background*, Supplementary volume of the International Commission on Intervention and State Sovereignty (Ottawa: International Development Research Centre, 2001).

21. Traub, 'Who needs the UN Security Council?', 47.
22. See Christopher Hitchens, 'Weapons of Mass Distraction', *Vanity Fair*, March 1, 1999. In his last weekly 'Letter from America', in early 2004, Alistair Cook reminded his BBC audience that Clinton might well have invaded Iraq but for the Monica Lewinsky affair. 'By the time Clinton was ready to mobilize an American or allied force, he didn't possess the moral authority to invade Long Island.' ('Alistair Cook', *The Economist*, April 3, 2004.) Conversely, 9/11 gave his successor all of the authority he needed.
23. Clinton was also dogged by suggestions that his forceful reaction to the Kosovo crisis of 1999 was politically motivated. See Elaine Sciolino and Ethan Bronner, 'How a President, Distracted by Scandal, Entered Balkan War', *New York Times*, April 18, 1999, 1.
24. Steven R. Weisman, 'Powell Calls His U.N. Speech A Lasting Blot on His Record', *New York Times*, September 9, 2005, 10.
25. Andrew Hurrell, 'International Law and the Changing Constitution of International Society', in Michael Byers (ed.), *The Role of Law in International Politics: Essays in International relations and International Law* (Oxford: OUP, 2000), 344.
26. Jane Boulden and Thomas G. Weiss, 'Tactical Multilateralism: Coaxing America Back to the UN', *Survival* 46/3 (2004), 111.
27. Indeed, the compromised US capacity for deterrence seems to have emboldened both Iran and North Korean in accelerating their nuclear programs.
28. See for example Dennis Kucinich, 'Our Troops Are Stationed in the Wrong Gulf', Address to the US Congress, HCR 7625, September 2, 2005.
29. See Malone, *Decision-Making in the UN Security Council: The Case of Haiti*, 172–3.
30. Judt, 'The New World Order', 18. On the politics of intervention, see Neil S. MacFarlane, *Intervention in Contemporary World Politics*, Adelphi Paper 350 (London: International Institute for Strategic Studies, 2002).
31. Judt, 'The New World Order', 18.
32. Michael Ignatieff, 'Why are we in Iraq? (And Liberia? And Afghanistan?)', *New York Times Magazine*, September 7, 2003, 28.
33. See David M. Malone, 'The High-Level Panel and the Security Council', *Security Dialogue* 36/3 (2005).
34. 'Assembly President Previews Possible Outcome of Summit on UN Reform', *UN News Centre*, June 3, 2005.
35. If Europe is to pursue a common foreign policy—a goal ardently endorsed by this author—defeat of the European constitution in 2005 notwithstanding, why did Germany believe Europe needed three permanent seats? Skepticism was rife in Washington, particularly after 2003. In conversation with the author, a senior Administration official wondered: 'We have to cope with one France in the Council. Why would we want two?'
36. Cited in 'A nasty smell', *The Economist*, August 11, 2005.
37. See Ramesh Thakur, 'Intervention, Sovereignty and the Responsibility to Protect: Experiences from ICISS', *Security Dialogue* 33/3 (2002).

38. Ivo Daalder and James Lindsay, 'Our way or the highway', *Financial Times Weekend*, November 6, 2004, 16.
39. Such a caucus exists, alas lethargically. Originally championed by Secretary of State Albright, over 100 countries—some of them with flawed democratic credentials, to be sure—convened under the banner of the Community of Democracies in 2000 in Poland. This group met most recently for a depressingly rhetorical meeting in Santiago in April 2005. For it to be effective at the UN and elsewhere it would need concrete goals and projects, which it currently lacks. See www.santiago2005.org; see also Tom Farer, *Collectively Defending Democracy in a World of Sovereign States: The Western Hemisphere's Prospect* (Montreal: International Center for Human Rights and Democratic Development, 1993).
40. Independent International Commission on Kosovo, *The Kosovo Report: Conflict, International Response, Lessons Learned* (Oxford: OUP, 2000).
41. Correspondence with James Cockayne.
42. *Proceedings of the 97th Annual Meeting of the American Society of International Law*, 2–5 April 2003, American Society of International Law.
43. Anne-Marie Slaughter, 'The clear, cruel lessons of Iraq', *Financial Times*, April 8, 2004, 19.
44. In conversation with the author, February 2003.
45. Glennon, 'Why the Security Council Failed'. See also his 'How International Rules Die', *Georgetown Law Journal* 93/3 (2005).
46. Franck, 'What Happens Now? The United Nations after Iraq'.
47. *Note [transmitting report of the High-level Panel on Threats, Challenges and Change, entitled 'A more secure world: our shared responsibility']*, 32.
48. Cockayne, 'Islam and International Humanitarian Law', 616–19.
49. Correspondence with James Cockayne.
50. Paul C. Szasz, 'The Security Council Starts Legislating', *American Journal of International Law* 96 (2002).
51. See Louise Fréchette, 'L'ONU doit réformer sa gestion', *Le Figaro*, September 8, 2005. Author's translation from the original French.
52. Conversation with the author, March 3, 2005.
53. Tono Eitel, 'The UN Security Council and its Future Contribution in the Field of International Law', *Max Planck Yearbook of United Nations Law* 4 (2000), 59.
54. See Bardo Fassbender, 'Uncertain Steps Into a Post-Cold War World: The Role and Functioning of the UN Security Council After a Decade of Measures Against Iraq', *European Journal of International Law* 13/1 (2002), 289.
55. E. Alexandra Dosman, 'For the Record: Designating "Listed Entities" for the Purposes of Terrorist Financing Offences at Canadian Law', *University of Toronto Faculty of Law Review* 62/1 (2004), 1.
56. Fareed Zakaria, 'We had good Intel—The UN's', *Newsweek*, February 9, 2004, 39; Jessica Mathews, 'Inspectors had the real WMD clues', *Financial Times*, February 9, 2004, 15.

57. Lopez and Cortright, 'Containing Iraq: Sanctions Worked', Foreign Affairs 83/4 (2004), 103. For their earlier case-specific and cross-cutting work on sanctions, see Cortwright and Lopez, *The Sanctions Decade* and *Sanctions and the Search for Security.*
58. As also pointed out by the Butler Report. Carne Ross, 'War Stories', *Financial Times Weekend,* January 29–30, 2005.
59. Conversations with Security Council delegations, July 2005.
60. James Traub, 'Off target', *The New Republic* 232/6 (2005), 14–17. This situation to a degree parallels that pertaining to the Rwanda genocide in 1994, for which Annan and other international civil servants (including Lt. Gen. Roméo Dallaire, then the UN's Force Commander in Kigali and one of the few who actually did anything to head off and then to contain this catastrophe) have repeatedly apologized, while only President Clinton, among the political figures involved, has made any real attempt to assume responsibility.
61. In one of his last comments on Iraq as Secretary of State, on January 11, 2005, Colin Powell underscored that responsibility for the OFF Program was shared by the Security Council, noting that the Council exercised day-to-day supervision over it. See Kralev, 'Powell urges UN Council to take blame for scandal', *Washington Times,* January 12, 2005, A11. The Volcker-led Independent Inquiry Committee, through leaks and several interim reports, exposed Annan, in the words of *The Economist,* to a form of 'Chinese water torture'. See 'Torturing the United Nations', *The Economist,* April 2, 2005.
62. See Philip Alston, 'The Darfur Commission as a Model for Future Responses to Crisis Situations', *Journal of International Criminal Justice* 3/3 (2005).
63. See Phillips, *Losing Iraq.* See also the review of this book, Reuel Marc Gerecht, 'Now What?', *New York Times Book Review,* July 10, 2005.
64. Charles Tripp in correspondence with the author, June 6, 2005. Questions have since surfaced about Shi'a unity in Iraq in light of the apoplectic constitutional debate and increasing Iranian influence in Baghdad. Groups such as SCIRI, Moqtada al-Sadr's followers, and Fadhila have increasingly defected from a unified core. See Adrian Blomfield, 'British forces are powerless as Basra descends into anarchy', *Daily Telegraph,* September 21, 2005, 11, and Adrian Blomfield, 'Ayatollah urges party to reject draft constitution', *Daily Telegraph,* September 24, 2005, 18.
65. Ross, 'War Stories'.
66. Independent Inquiry Committee into the United Nations Oil-for-Food Programme, *Report on the Management of the Oil-for-Food Program,* I, 3.
67. Only the ICC Prosecutor can claim any similar kind of mandate, and that is much narrower.
68. David Rieff, 'The UN must plot a new course', *Financial Times,* February 21, 2005, 19.
69. For a balanced assessment of Annan's difficulties in maintaining good relations with Washington, see John M. Goshko, 'Iraq Dilemma Erodes Annan's Bond with US', *Washington Post,* February 23, 1999, A13.

70. Independent Inquiry Committee into the United Nations Oil-for-Food Programme, *Report on the Management of the Oil-for-Food Programme*, I, 3.
71. These procedures were used for the selection of Kemal Dervis as the new Administrator of UNDP in April 2005, in succession to Mark Malloch Brown, *en catastrophe* appointed Annan's Chief of Staff that January.
72. A senior UN official, quoted in Warren Hoge, 'U.N. Is Transforming Itself, but Into What Is Unclear', *New York Times*, February 28, 2005, 3.
73. Toby Dodge in correspondence with the author, June 6, 2005. Dodge in mid-2005 published a stimulating analysis of contemporary Iraq and its prospects. See Toby Dodge, *Iraq's future, the aftermath of regime change*, Adelphi Paper 372 (London: International Institute for Strategic Studies, 2005).
74. See Kanan Makiya, *Cruelty and Silence: War, Tyranny, Uprising and the Arab World* (New York: W. W. Norton, 1993).
75. See Marc Lynch, 'Beyond the Arab Street: Iraq and the Arab Public Sphere', *Politics & Society* 31/1 (2003).
76. Such was the nature of the indictment of the UN made by Osama bin Laden in his address broadcast on Al Jazeera on November 3, 2001 in the wake of the invasion of Afghanistan.
77. Tripp, *A History of Iraq*, 295–6 and 312–28.
78. A sophisticated account of Kurdish history and some of its contemporary implications can be found in Michael Gunther, *The Kurdish Predicament in Iraq: A Political Analysis* (New York: St. Martin's Press, 1999).
79. Marr, 'Occupational Hazard', 186.
80. Conversation with Jean-David Levitte. David M. Malone, 'Conclusions', in Malone, *The UN Security Council: From the Cold War to the 21st Century*, 644.
81. Independent Inquiry Committee into the United Nations Oil-for-Food Programme, *Report on the Management of the Oil-for-Food Programme*, I, 2.

Box 9.1 Notes

1. Philippe Leymarie, 'La Côte d'Ivoire à la derive' , *Le Monde Diplomatique*, October 1, 2002, www.monde-diplomatique.fr/dossiers/derive.
2. UN Security Council resolution 1464, February 4, 2003.
3. UN Security Council resolution 1528, February 27, 2004. See also Third progress report of the Secretary-General on the United Nations operation in Côte d'Ivoire' (UN Security Council Document S/2004/962), December 9, 2004, 15.
4. SCR 1528.
5. Third progress report of the Secretary-General on the United Nations operation in Cote d Ivoire , 34. In conversations they did not wish attributed to them by senior officials of the UN Department of Peacekeeping Operations in New York confirmed that they were taken entirely by surprise by these French measures, however understandable in the heat of the moment.

6. 'Statement by the President of the Security Council' (UN Security Council Document S/PRST/2004/42), November 6, 2004.
7. UN Security Council resolution 1572, November 15, 2004; UN Security Council resolution 1584, February 1, 2005. Suspicion has arisen that Chinese commercial interests may have broken the embargo by supplying weapons to the Côte d'Ivoire military.
8. 'Côte d'Ivoire: UN endorses plan to leave president in office beyond mandate', IRINnews.org, October 14, 2005, www.irinnews.org/print.asp?ReportID=49576
9. Jonathan Clayton, 'UN in retreat as rampaging thugs threaten new civil war', *The Times,* January 19, 2006, 41.

Box 9.2 Notes

1. UN Security Council resolution 1559, September 2, 2004.
2. Steven R. Weisman, Warren Hoge, and Richard W. Stevenson, 'U.S. Seems Sure of the Hand Of Syria, Hinting at Penalities', *New York Times*, February 15, 2005, 6.
3. SCR 1595, April 7, 2005.
4. UN Document S/PV.5292, October 25, 2005, 5.
5. UN Document S/2005/662, October 20, 2005, p. 6. An earlier version of this report, made available by error, pointed the finger of suspicion directly at President Assad's brother and brother-in-law. See also Roula Khoulaf and Ferry Biedermann, 'Top Syrian in Hariri inquiry found dead', *FT.com,* October 13, 2005.
6. Hassan M. Fattah, 'Saudis Urge Syrian Leader to Cooperate With U.N.' *New York Times*, January 9, 2006, 6.

Appendix A: UN SCRs Pertaining to Iraq

Resolution No. Date	Resolution	In Favor	Vote Against	Abstain
348 (1974) 28/5/74	Welcomes the determination of Iran and Iraq to de-escalate the prevailing situation and to improve their relations, and their agreement to observe the March 7, 1974 cease-fire, withdraw armed forces along the border, refrain from hostile actions and resume conversation with a view to a comprehensive settlement of all bilateral issues.	14	0	0 (China did not participate)
	Iran-Iraq War			
479 (1980) 28/9/80	After the outbreak of the Iran–Iraq war, calls upon both to refrain from use of force and to settle their dispute by peaceful means, urges them to accept any appropriate offer of mediation or conciliation, and supports the Secretary-General's offer of good offices.	15	0	0
487 (1981) 19/6/81	Condemns the Israeli air attack on Iraqi nuclear installations on June 7, 1981 as a violation of the UN Charter and the norms of international conduct and, *inter alia*, calls upon Israel to stop such attacks, considers that the attack is a threat to the safeguards regime of the IAEA, calls upon Israel to place its nuclear facilities under the regime and considers that Iraq is entitled to redress.	15	0	0
514 (1982) 12/7/82	Calls for a cease-fire between Iran and Iraq and a withdrawal of forces to internationally recognized boundaries, decides to send a team of UN observers to supervise the cease-fire and withdrawal and urges that the mediation efforts be continued through the Secretary-General.	15	0	0
522 (1982) 4/10/82	Reiterates call for Iran/Iraq cease-fire, welcomes the readiness of one of the parties to cooperate in implementing SCR 514 (1982) and calls on the other party to do so.	15	0	0
540 (1983) 31/10/83	Condemns violations of international humanitarian law in the Iran–Iraq conflict, calls for attacks on civilians to stop, affirms the right of free navigation and commerce in international waters, and calls on the belligerents to stop hostilities in the Gulf.	12	0	3 Malta Nicaragua Pakistan
552 (1984) 1/6/84	Condemns attacks on commercial ships en route to and from Saudi Arabia and Kuwait.	13	0	2 Nicaragua Zimbabwe

continued

Resolution No. Date	Resolution	In Favor	Vote Against	Abstain
582 (1986) 24/2/86	Deplores the 'initial acts' which led to the Iran–Iraq conflict and the continuation and escalation of the conflict, calls for a cease-fire and prisoner exchange, and calls upon Iran and Iraq to submit to mediation with the Secretary-General lending his good offices.	15	0	0
588 (1986) 8/10/86	Calls upon Iran and Iraq to implement immediately SCR 582 (1986) and requests the Secretary-General to intensify his efforts to this end.	15	0	0
598 (1987) 20/7/87	Acting under Articles 39 and 40 of the UN Charter, demands that Iran and Iraq observe a cease-fire and requests the Secretary-General to send observers to supervise the cease-fire; calls upon Iran and Iraq to cooperate with the Secretary-General to achieve a settlement of all issues, and requests the Secretary-General 'to explore . . . the question of entrusting an impartial body with inquiring into responsibility for the conflict', and 'to examine measures to enhance the security and stability of the region'.	15	0	0
612 (1988) 9/5/88	Condemns continued use of chemical weapons, as concluded by the Mission dispatched by the Secretary-General to investigate the matter, expects both sides to refrain from the future use of chemical weapons, calls on all States to strictly control exports to both sides of chemical products serving for the production of chemical weapons.	15	0	0
616 (1988) 20/7/88	Expresses deep distress at the downing of Iran Air flight 655 by *USS Vincennes* in the Persian Gulf. Welcomes the ICAO [Int. Civil Aviation Org.] decision to begin a fact-finding investigation.	15	0	0
619 (1988) 9/8/88	With Iran finally accepting a cease-fire, the SC approves Secretary-General's report under SCR 598 (1987) and decides to set up immediately a UN Iran–Iraq Military Observer Group (UNIIMOG). Decides that UNIIMOG shall be established for six months, unless the Council decides otherwise.	15	0	0
620 (1988) 26/8/88	Condemns again use of chemical weapons in Iran/Iraq conflict.	15	0	0
631 (1989) 8/2/89	Extends UNIIMOG to September 30, 1989.	15	0	0
642 (1989) 29/9/89	Extends UNIIMOG to March 31, 1990.	15	0	0
651 (1990) 29/3/90	Extends UNIIMOG to September 30, 1990.	15	0	0
First Gulf War (& Iran–Iraq War cont.)				
660 (1990) 2/8/90	Acting under Articles 39 and 40, determines that there exists a breach of international peace and security, condemns the Iraqi invasion of Kuwait and demands that Iraq withdraw immediately and unconditionally.	14	0	0 (Yemen did not participate)
661 (1990) 6/8/90	Acting under Chapter VII, imposes comprehensive sanctions on Iraq, prohibiting trade with the exception of strictly medical or humanitarian goods. Decides to establish a Committee to oversee the implementation of these measures.	13	0	2 Cuba Yemen

662 (1990) 9/8/90	Declares Iraqi annexation of Kuwait legally invalid; calls on states not to recognize it.	15	0	0
664 (1990) 18/8/90	Acting under Chapter VII, demands that Iraq allow departure of or consular help for foreign nationals in Iraq and Kuwait.	15	0	0
665 (1990) 25/8/90	Calls upon Member States to use such measures as may be necessary to halt all maritime shipping to and from Iraq and Kuwait in order to inspect and verify their cargoes and destinations. States are requested to submit reports on their activities to the Committee established by SCR 661 (1990).	13	0	2 Cuba Yemen
666 (1990) 13/9/90	Acting under Chapter VII decides that the Committee established by SCR 661 (1990) should determine the circumstances in which there is an urgent humanitarian need to supply foodstuffs to Iraq or Kuwait in order to relieve human suffering.	13	2 Cuba Yemen	
667 (1990) 16/9/90	Acting under Chapter VII, condemns Iraqi violation of diplomatic premises in Kuwait. Decides to consult to take concrete measures under Chapter VII.	15	0	0
669 (1990) 24/9/90	Entrusts the Committee established under SCR 661 with the task of examining requests for assistance under Article 50 of the UN Charter.	15	0	0
670 (1990) 25/9/90	Acting under Chapter VII, tightens restrictions on air and sea traffic with Iraq.	14	1 Cuba	0
671 (1990) 27/9/90	Extends UNIIMOG to November 30, 1990.	15	0	0
674 (1990) 29/10/90	Acting under Chapter VII, invites states to collate evidence of human rights breaches by Iraq in Kuwait.	13	2 Cuba Yemen	0
676 (1990) 28/11/90	Extends UNIIMOG to January 31, 1991.	15	0	0
677 (1990) 28/11/90	Acting under Chapter VII, condemns Iraqi attempts to change Kuwait's demography and destroy civil records.	15	0	0
678 (1990) 29/11/90	Acting under Chapter VII, authorizes Member States cooperating with Kuwait to use all necessary means to uphold and implement SCR 660 (1990) and all subsequent relevant resolutions and to restore international peace and security in the area, unless Iraq on or before January 15, 1991 fully implements the foregoing resolutions.	12	2 Cuba Yemen	1 China
685 (1991) 31/1/91	Extends UNIIMOG to February 28, 1991.	15	0	0
686 (1991) 2/3/91	Acting under Chapter VII, demands that Iraq implement its acceptance of all twelve resolutions on Iraq's invasion of Kuwait and further demands that Iraq cease hostile action and release POWs.	11	1 Cuba	3 China India Yemen

continued

Appendix A: (Cont.)

Resolution No. Date	Resolution	In Favor	Vote Against	Abstain
Sanctions, Inspections, Oil-For-Food				
687 (1991) 3/4/91	Following the cease-fire between Coalition and Iraqi forces, and acting under Chapter VII: (a) Demands that Iraq and Kuwait respect the inviolability of the boundary between their states; calls upon the Secretary-General to arrange for its demarcation; (b) Establishes a demilitarized zone on both sides of the boundary; requests the Secretary-General to submit a plan for the immediate deployment of a UN observer unit to monitor that zone; (c) Decides that Iraq shall accept the destruction, removal, or rendering harmless of all its chemical and biological weapons, and ballistic missiles with a range of over 150 km; decides that the Secretary-General shall submit a plan for a special commission to carry this out. Decides that Iraq shall agree not to acquire or develop nuclear weapons and related material, and to render its stocks thereof to the IAEA for removal and destruction. Requests the Director of the IAEA to inspect and report on Iraq's nuclear capabilities so the Council can decide upon the future monitoring of Iraq; (d) Creates a Compensation Fund for Kuwaitis and a Commission to administer it; directs the Secretary-General to organize the modalities of the Fund; (e) Decides to lift the ban on important Iraqi commodities and products and financial transactions related thereto when Iraq meets its obligations under (c) above; (f) Decides that Iraq shall not commit or support any act of international terrorism.	12	1 Cuba	2 Ecuador Yemen
688 (1991) 5/4/91	Condemns Iraqi repression of civilians, particularly Kurds; insists that Iraq allow access to those in need by international humanitarian organizations, requests the Secretary-General to report on the plight of the Kurds. First reference to refugee flows as threats to international peace and security, though without recourse to Chapter VII.	10	3 Cuba Yemen Zimbabwe	2 China India
689 (1991) 9/4/91	Acting under Chapter VII, approves Secretary-General's proposed mandate for UN Iraq-Kuwait Observation Mission (UNIKOM).	15	0	0
692 (1991) 20/5/91	Acting under Chapter VII, decides to establish the UN Compensation Commission (UNCC) referred to in SCR 687, para. 18 (1991) to pay compensation for claims against Iraq resulting from its unlawful invasion and occupation of Kuwait.	14	0	1 Cuba
699 (1991) 17/6/91	Acting under Chapter VII, approves the plan contained in the report of the Secretary-General of May 17, 1991 for the destruction, removal, or rendering	15	0	0

	harmless of all Iraqi chemical and biological weapons, reaffirms that the Special Commission (UNSCOM) and the IAEA, under Section (c) of SCR 687 (1991) are to carry this out, and decides that Iraq is liable for the full costs of them so doing.			
700 (1991) 17/6/91	Acting under Chapter VII, approves guidelines in Secretary-General's report on preventing supply of military material to Iraq.	15	0	0
705 (1991) 15/8/91	Acting under Chapter VII, limits compensation payable by Iraq to 30% of the annual value of exports of petroleum and petroleum products.	15	0	0
706 (1991) 15/8/91	Acting under Chapter VII, authorizes states to import Iraqi oil to finance humanitarian supplies to Iraq, compensation and half the costs of demarcating the Iraq–Kuwait boundary.	13	1 Cuba	1 Yemen
707 (1991) 15/8/91	Acting under Chapter VII, condemns Iraq's serious violations of its obligations under SCR 687 (1991) and demands that Iraq provide full disclosure of all aspects of its programs to develop weapons of mass destruction and all other nuclear programs and that Iraq allow UNSCOM and IAEA immediate and unrestricted access to inspect all facilities.	15	0	0
712 (1991) 19/9/91	Acting under Chapter VII, reaffirms use of escrow account under SCR 706 (1991); authorizes release of funds for humanitarian purposes.	13	1 Cuba	1 Yemen
715 (1991) 11/10/91	Acting under Chapter VII, approves IAEA plans for inspections in Iraq; demands Iraqi cooperation.	15	0	0
773 (1992) 26/8/92	Welcomes work of UN Iraq–Kuwait Boundary Demarcation Commission; calls on parties to continue cooperation.	14	0	1 Ecuador
778 (1992) 2/10/92	Acting under Chapter VII, deploring Iraq's refusal to cooperate in the implementation of SCRs 706 (1991) and 712 (1991), decides that all states shall transfer Iraqi funds to the escrow account. Requests the Secretary-General to transfer a proportion of these funds to the Compensation Fund, and to use the remainder to cover the costs of the UN eliminating Iraq's weapons of mass destruction, sending humanitarian relief to Iraq, and other UN activities specified in SCR 706 (1991).	14	0	1 China
806 (1993) 5/2/93	Acting under Chapter VII, guarantees inviolability of Iraq–Kuwait border; requests Secretary-General to strengthen UNIKOM.	15	0	0
833 (1993) 27/5/93	Acting under Chapter VII, reaffirms that decisions of Iraq–Kuwait boundary demarcation Commission are final.	15	0	0
899 (1994) 4/3/94	Acting under Chapter VII, approves compensation for Iraqi citizens losing assets through border demarcation, notwithstanding SCR 661 (1990).	15	0	0
949 (1994) 15/10/94	Acting under Chapter VII, demands that Iraq immediately withdraw its military units recently deployed to southern Iraq; demands that Iraq not use its military or other forces in a hostile or provocative manner to threaten its neighbors or UN personnel in Iraq; and demands that Iraq cooperate with UNSCOM.	15	0	0

continued

Appendix A: (Cont.)

Resolution No. Date	Resolution	In Favor	Vote Against	Abstain
986 (1995) 14/4/95	Acting under Chapter VII, authorizes States notwithstanding certain paragraphs of SCR 661 (1990), to permit the import of Iraqi oil not exceeding US$1 billion every ninety days subject to approval by the Committee established by SCR 661 (1990), and payment by the purchase of the full amount into an escrow account to be established by the Secretary-General. Decides that the funds in the escrow account shall be used to meet the humanitarian needs of the Iraqi population ('Oil-For-Food') as well as *inter alia* going to the Compensation Fund and the current operating expenses of UNSCOM.	15	0	0
1051 (1996) 27/3/96	Acting under Chapter VII, approves the mechanism developed by the SCR 661 (1991) Committee with UNSCOM and the IAEA for monitoring future sales or supplies to Iraq of items relevant to the implementation of SCR 687 (1991) Section (c), and other SCRs including 715 (1991). Demands that Iraq unconditionally meet all its obligations under the mechanism and to cooperate fully with UNSCOM and the IAEA.	15	0	0
1060 (1996) 12/6/96	Acting under Chapter VII, deplores Iraq's refusal to allow access to sites designated by UNSCOM, which constitutes a clear violation of SCRs 687, 707, and 715 (1991); demands that Iraq allow UNSCOM's inspectors immediate, unconditional, and unrestricted access to any and all areas, facilities, equipment, records, and means of transportation which they wish to inspect.	15	0	0
1111 (1997) 4/6/97	Acting under Chapter VII, extends the provisions of SCR 986 (Oil-For-Food), except those in paragraphs 4, 11, and 12, for another period of 180 days beginning on June 8, 1997. Also requests the Committee established by SCR 661 to report on the implementation of the arrangements in paragraphs 1, 2, 6, 8, 9, and 10 of SCR 986.	15	0	0
1115 (1997) 21/6/97	Acting under Chapter VII, demands that Iraq comply with UNSCOM inspections.	15	0	0
1129 (1997) 12/9/97	Acting under Chapter VII, extends Iraq Oil-For-Food program for 120 days from June 8, 1997. Authorises sale of US$1 billion of Iraqi oil.	14	0	1 Russia
1134 (1997) 23/10/97	Acting under Chapter VII, determines that Iraqi actions to date with respect to UNSCOM constitute a flagrant violation of SCRs 687, 707, 715, and 1060. Demands that Iraq comply with inspections, and threatens travel sanctions on Iraqi officials.	10	0	5 China Egypt France Kenya Russia

1137 (1997) 12/11/97	Acting under Chapter VII, and in the face of serious and repeated obstructions on the part of Iraqi officials with respect to UNSCOM inspectors, imposes travel restrictions on Iraqi officials, threatening further measures if necessary.	15	0	0
1143 (1997) 4/12/97	Acting under Chapter VII, extends Iraq Oil-For-Food program for 180 days from 5 December 1997.	15	0	0
1153 (1998) 20/2/98	Acting under Chapter VII, extends Iraq Oil-For-Food program for 180 days, after receipt of a report by the Security Council of the Secretary-General on a new plan for ensuring equitable distribution of medicinal and humanitarian goods. Authorizes sale of US$5.256 billion of Iraqi oil.	15	0	0
1154 (1998) 02/03/98	Acting under Chapter VII, endorses Memorandum of Understanding between Secretary-General and Iraq on UNSCOM inspections, especially with reference to inspections of Presidential sites.	15	0	0
1158 (1998) 25/3/98	Acting under Chapter VII, extends Iraq Oil-For-Food program for ninety days from March 5, 1998. Authorizes sale of up to US$1.4 billion of Iraqi oil.	15	0	0
1175 (1998) 19/6/98	Acting under Chapter VII, authorizes States to supply Iraq with US$300 million worth of parts to enable Iraq to increase oil exports. Request the Committee established by SCR 661 to approve the contracts for the parts and equipment.	15	0	0
1194 (1998) 9/9/98	Acting under Chapter VII, continues sanctions imposed on Iraq until it co-operates with UNSCOM. Condemns the decision by Iraq of August 5, 1998 to suspend cooperation with UNSCOM and the IAEA, which constitutes a totally unacceptable contravention of its obligations under SCRs 687, 707, 715, 1060, 1115, and 1154 and the Memorandum of Understanding signed by the Deputy Prime Minister of Iraq and the Secretary-General on February 23, 1998.	15	0	0
1205 (1998) 5/11/98	Acting under Chapter VII, demands Iraqi cooperation with UNSCOM and continues sanctions.	15	0	0
1210 (1998) 24/11/98	Acting under Chapter VII, extends Iraq Oil-For-Food program in Iraq for 180 days from November 26, 1998. Requests the Secretary-General to continue to ensure the effective and efficient implementation of this resolution, and to review, by December 31, 1998, the various options to resolve the difficulties encountered in the financial process. Decides to conduct a thorough review of all aspects of the implementation of this resolution.	15	0	0
1242 (1999) 21/5/99	Acting under Chapter VII, extends Iraq Oil-For-Food program for 180 days from May 25, 1999.	15	0	0
1266 (1999) 4/10/99	Acting under amends SCR 1242 (1999) to allows the sale of US$3.04 billion of Iraqi oil.	15	0	0

continued

Appendix A: (Cont.)

Resolution No. Date	Resolution	In Favor	Vote Against	Abstain
1275 (1999) 19/11/99	Acting under Chapter VII, extends Iraq Oil-For-Food program to December 4, 1999.	15	0	0
1280 (1999) 3/12/99	Acting under Chapter VII, extends Iraq Oil-For-Food program to December 11, 1999.	11	0	3 China Malaysia Russia (France did not participate)
1281 (1999) 10/12/99	Acting under Chapter VII, extends Iraq Oil-For-Food program for 180 days from 12 December 1999.	15	0	0
1284 (1999) 17/12/99	Acting under Chapter VII, establishes United Nations Monitoring, Verification and Inspection Commission (UNMOVIC), to replace UNSCOM. Decides that UNMOVIC will establish and operate a reinforced system of ongoing monitoring and verification. Decides that Iraq shall allow UNMOVIC teams immediate, unconditional, and unrestricted access to any and all areas, facilities, equipment, records, and means of transport which they wish to inspect.	11	0	4 China France Malaysia Russia
1293 (2000) 31/1/00	Acting under Chapter VII, decides to permit US$600 million in the Oil-For-Food account to be used to meet any reasonable expenses, other than expenses payable in Iraq, which follow directly from the contracts approved in accordance with SCR 1175 (1998) (machinery parts for oil production).	15	0	0
1302 (2000) 8/6/00	Acting under Chapter VII, extends Iraq Oil-For-Food program for 180 days from June 9, 2000.	15	0	0
1330 (2000) 5/12/00	Acting under Chapter VII, extends Iraq Oil-For-Food program for 180 days from December 6, 2000.	15	0	0
1352 (2001) 1/6/01	Acting under Chapter VII, extends Iraq Oil-For-Food program for 180 days from July 3, 2001. Expresses its intention to consider new arrangements for the sale or supply of commodities and products to Iraq and for the facilitation of civilian trade and economic cooperation with Iraq in civilian sectors.	15	0	0
1360 (2001) 3/7/01	Acting under Chapter VII, extends Iraq Oil-For-Food program for 150 days from July 4, 2001. Requests the Secretary-General to continue to take the actions	15	0	0

	necessary to ensure the effective and efficient implementation of this resolution, and to continue to enhance as necessary the UN observation process in Iraq in such a way as to provide the required assurance to the Council that the goods produced in accordance with this resolution are distributed equitably and that all supplies authorized for procurement, including dual usage items and spare parts, are utilized for the purpose for which they have been authorized, including in the housing sector and related infrastructure development.			
1382 (2001) 29/11/01	Acting under Chapter VII, extends Iraq Oil-For-Food program for 180 days from December 1, 2001.	15	0	0
1409 (2002) 14/5/02	Acting under Chapter VII, extends Iraq Oil-For-Food program for 180 days from May 30, 2002. Decides to adopt the revised Goods Review List and revised procedures for its application as a basis for the humanitarian program in Iraq as referred to in SCR 986 (1995) and other relevant resolutions.	15	0	0
Second Gulf War				
1441 (2002) 8/11/02	Acting under Chapter VII, decides that Iraq has been and remains in material breach of its obligations under relevant resolutions, including SCR 687 (1991). Decides to afford Iraq a final opportunity to comply; and accordingly decides to set up an enhanced inspection regime. Decides that Iraq shall provide to UNMOVIC, the IAEA, and the Council, a currently accurate, full, and complete declaration of all aspects of its programs to develop chemical, biological, and nuclear weapons, ballistic missiles, and other delivery systems. Decides that false statements or omissions in the declarations submitted by Iraq or failure to cooperate fully in the implementation of this resolution shall constitute a further material breach of Iraq's obligations. Decides that Iraq shall provide UNMOVIC and the IAEA immediate, unimpeded, unconditional, and unrestricted access to any facilities and personnel which they wish to inspect. Recalls that the Council has repeatedly warned Iraq that it will face serious consequences as a result of its continued violations of its obligations. Decides to consider the matter further in the event of specified Iraqi non-cooperation reported by UNMOVIC or the IAEA.	15	0	0
1443 (2002) 25/11/02	Acting under Chapter VII, extends Iraq Oil-For-Food program to 4 December 2002.	15	0	0
1447 (2002) 4/12/02	Acting under Chapter VII, extends Iraq Oil-For-Food program for 180 days from 5 December 2002. Decides to consider necessary adjustments to the Goods Review List no later than thirty days from the adoption of this resolution and thereafter to conduct regular, thorough reviews.	15	0	0

continued

Appendix A: (Cont.)

Resolution No. Date	Resolution	In Favor	Vote Against	Abstain
1454 (2002) 30/12/02	Acting under Chapter VII, approves adjustments to the Goods Review List and the procedures for its implementation, as of December 31, 2002.	13	0	2 Russia Syria
Post-War				
1472 (2003) 28/3/03	Acting under Chapter VII, requests all parties concerned to strictly abide by their obligations under international law, particularly in relation to essential civilian needs. Calls on the international community also to provide immediate humanitarian assistance to the people of Iraq. Permits, in view of the exceptional circumstances prevailing in Iraq, technical and temporary adjustments to the Iraq Oil-For-Food program so as to fund humanitarian relief for the people of Iraq.	15	0	0
1476 (2003) 24/4/03	Acting under Chapter VII, extends Iraq Oil-For-Food program to June 3; 2003.	15	0	0
1483 (2003) 22/5/03	Acting under Chapter VII, appeals to Member States to assist the people of Iraq in their efforts to reform their institutions and rebuild their country. Recognizes the Coalition Provisional Authority and its attempts to promote the welfare of the Iraqi people, as well as the formation of an Iraqi interim administration. Requests the Secretary-General to appoint a Special Representative for Iraq. Decides that, with the exception of arms, all sanctions deriving from SCR 661 (1990) and subsequent relevant resolutions shall no longer apply, with the 661 Committee disbanded. Requests also that the Secretary-General, in coordination with the Authority, terminate within six months the ongoing operations of the Iraq Oil-for-Food program. Establishes the International Advisory and Monitoring Board (IAMB) to manage the new Development Fund for Iraq (DFI).	14	0	0 (Syria did not participate)
1490 (2003) 3/7/03	Acting under Chapter VII, decides to continue the mandate of the UN Iraq Kuwait Observer Mission (UNIKOM) for a final period until October 6, 2003. Decides to simultaneously end the demilitarized zone extending 10 km into Iraq and 5 into Kuwait from the Iraq–Kuwait border.	15	0	0
1500 (2003) 14/8/03	Welcomes the establishment of the Governing Council of Iraq on July 13, 2003. Decides to establish the United Nations Assistance Mission for Iraq (UNAMI) to support the Secretary-General in the fulfillment of his mandate under resolution 1483, for an initial period of twelve months.	14	0	1 Syria

1502 (2003) 26/8/03	In response to the August 19, 2003 bombing of the UNAMI headquarters in Baghdad, reaffirms the obligation of parties to comply fully with the rules and principles of international humanitarian law, especially as applicable to United Nations personnel. Calls for Secretary-General to ensure adoption by host countries of the Convention on the Safety of United Nations and Associated Personnel, with attendant clauses concerning the establishment of such attacks as crimes punishable by law and the prosecution or extradition of offenders. Requests Secretary-General to include UN personnel security situation in future country reports.	15	0	0
1511 (2003) 16/10/03	Acting under Chapter VII, invites the Governing Council to outline a timetable and a program for the drafting of a new constitution for Iraq and for the holding of democratic elections under that constitution. Resolves that the UN should strengthen its vital role in Iraq. Authorizes a Multinational Force (MNF) under unified command to take all necessary measures to contribute to the maintenance of security and stability in Iraq, and urges states to contribute militarily to this force. Mandate of the force to expire upon the completion of the political process (elections and the promulgation of a constitution), with potential for extension. Calls upon Member States to rebuild the Iraqi economy and give generously to the October Madrid Donors Conference.	15	0	0
1518 (2003) 24/11/03	Acting under Chapter VII, decides to establish a Committee of the Security Council to continue to identify, pursuant to paragraph 19 of resolution 1483 (2003), individuals and entities of the former regime with financial assets outside of Iraq.	15	0	0
1538 (2004) 21/4/04	Welcomes the appointment of the independent high-level inquiry into the administration and management of the Iraq Oil-For-Food program, including allegations of fraud and corruption.	15	0	0
1546 (2004) 8/6/04	Acting under Chapter VII, endorses the formation of a sovereign Interim Government of Iraq, as presented on June 1, 2004, to assume full responsibility and authority by June 30, 2004 for governing Iraq from the Coalition Provisional Authority. Calls for the election of a Transitional National Assembly no later than January 31, 2005 and of a constitutionally elected government by December 31, 2005. Welcomes ongoing efforts by the incoming Interim Government of Iraq to develop Iraqi security forces while reaffirming the authorization for the multinational force established under resolution 1511 (2003).	15	0	0
1557 (2004) 12/8/04	Decides to extend the mandate of UNAMI for a period of twelve months.	15	0	0

continued

Appendix A: (Cont.)

Resolution No. Date	Resolution	In Favor	Vote Against	Abstain
1618 (2005) 4/8/05	Condemns terrorist violence in Iraq and reaffirms the obligations of Member States under SCR 1373 (2001) and related counter-terrorism resolutions.	15	0	0
1619 (2005) 11/8/05	Decides to extend the mandate of UNAMI for a period of twelve months.	15	0	0
1637 (2005) 11/11/05	Acting under chapter VII, extends the mandate of the multinational force until December 31, 2006, with termination at any time if requested by the Iraqui government, and subject to review no later than June 15, 2006.	15	0	0

Sources: United Kingdom, Foreign and Commonwealth Office, 'Research Analysts Memorandum: Summary of UN Security Council Resolutions, 1946–1998, Part A', September 1999; United Kingdom, Foreign and Commonwealth Office, 'Research Analysts Memorandum: Summary of UN Security Council Resolutions, 1946–1998, Part B', September 1999; United Kingdom, Foreign and Commonwealth Office, 'Iraq-related resolutions in the UN Security Council: May 1999–July 2003 (DRAFT)', July 2003. UN Website: http://www.un.org/Docs/sc/index.html

Appendix B: Iraq and the Security Council—A Chronology

1920
November 11: 'State of Iraq' declared under British mandate.

1932
October 3: Iraq achieves independence. Britain continues to wield extensive influence in Iraq, commercially as well as politically.

1941
May 2: Britain invades Iraq after the establishment of a pro-Axis government, and re-installs a pro-British government under King Faisal II.

1945
March 22: Iraq becomes a charter member of the Arab League.
December 21: Iraq becomes a charter member of the United Nations.

1948
May 15: Iraq and other Arab countries launch an unsuccessful war against Israel.

1958
July 14: General Abd al-Qasim leads a coup, which kills Faisal II and many other top officials, declaring Iraq a republic.

1961
September: General al-Qasim rejects an autonomy plan proposed by the Kurds; fighting erupts.

A narrative development of most of this chronology can be found in David Malone and James Cockayne, 'Lines in the Sand: The United Nations in Iraq, 1980–2001', ch. 2, and 'Quicksand: The United Nations and Iraq, 2001–2005', ch. 22, in Ramesh Thakur and Waheguru Pal Singh Sidhu (eds.), *The Iraq Crisis and World Order: Structural, Institutional and Normative Challenges* (Tokyo: United Nations University Press, forthcoming).

1968

July 17: Ahmad Hasan al-Bakr overthrows the erstwhile regime in a bloodless coup. The Ba'ath party, which advocates pan-Arabism, secularism, and socialism, comes to power.

1975

March 6: In light of Iranian military strength, Iraq and Iran sign the Algiers Accord, agreeing to share the Shat al-Arab waterway.

1979

January 16: The Shah is forced to flee Iran, precipitating the Iranian Revolution.
July 16: Saddam Hussein becomes President of Iraq.
November 4: Sixty-six diplomats and citizens at the US embassy in Tehran are taken hostage. The ordeal lasts 444 days and sours Iranian–American relations.
December 24: The USSR invades Afghanistan.

1980

September 17: Iraq proclaims sovereignty over the Shat al-Arab waterway.
September 23: The Iran–Iraq war begins with an Iraqi ground offensive.
September 28: Security Council Resolution (SCR) 479 deplores the commencement of hostilities and calls upon both sides to refrain from use of force.
November 20–24: Olaf Palme makes his first peace shuttle between Tehran and Baghdad.

1981

January 20: Ronald Reagan becomes President of the United States.
May 21: François Mitterrand becomes president of the French Republic.
June 7: Israel bombs the Osiraq nuclear reactor, claiming Iraq plans to use it to supply materials for nuclear weapons.
November 29: Iran launches a major offensive on the central front with Iraq.

1982

January 1: Javier Pérez de Cuéllar becomes UN Secretary General.
June 10: Iraq declares a unilateral cease-fire in its war with Iran.

1983

July 26: The United States warns of intent to preserve navigation in the Persian Gulf.
November 26: US National Security Directive 114 states that US will do 'whatever is necessary and legal' to ensure that Iraq does not lose its war with Iran.
December 20: Donald Rumsfeld meets with Saddam Hussein to assure him of US support.

1984

March 5: US accuses Iraq of using chemical weapons against Iran, though mustard gas may have been used as early as August 1983.

March 27: 'Tanker war' begins with Iraqi attacks on shipping near the Iranian coast.

July: CIA begins passing military intelligence to Iraq.

1985

March 11: Mikhail Gorbachev becomes Soviet leader.

May–June: 'Battle of the Cities', with both Iran and Iraq bombing urban centers.

1986

February 9: Iran crosses the Shat al-Arab and captures the southern Faw peninsula. Saddam Hussein vows to repulse Iran 'at all costs'.

March: Security Council discussions of Iraqi chemical weapons end in deadlock.

August 2: In an open letter to Iran, Saddam Hussein offers peace.

1987

February 26: Tower Commission reports on Iran-Contra affair.

May 17: Iraqi missile hits the *USS Stark*, killing 37 sailors. Hussein officially apologizes. US begins 'reflagging' Kuwaiti tankers as American, with American crews.

July 7: SCR 598 calls for a cease-fire, withdrawal of troops to the internationally recognized border, and a commission to decide responsibility for the Iran–Iraq war. Iraq accepts the provisions.

September 22: US attacks Iranian vessel laying mines in the Persian Gulf, and later destroys Iran's Rostam oil platform.

1988

February: *Anfal* (plunder) campaign against northern Kurds, killing 100,000.

April 29: The United States announces protection for all shipping in the Persian Gulf.

April–August: Iraq achieves series of victories over Iran, recapturing Faw peninsula and Majnoon islands.

May 15: Red Army begins its withdrawal from Afghanistan, signaling the terminal phase of that conflict.

July 18: Iran accepts SCR 598.

August 10: Initial deployment of UNIIMOG.

August: Iraq and Iran declare a cease-fire. Iraq begins renewed chemical attacks against the Kurds.
September–October: De Cuéllar hosts Iran–Iraq negotiations in Geneva.
November 8: George H.W. Bush is elected US President.

1989

June 4: Tiananmen Square massacre in Beijing; *Solidarity* wins government in Poland.
November 9: Berlin Wall falls.

1990

February 7: Central Committee of the Soviet Communist Party cedes power.
February 11: In South Africa, Nelson Mandela is released from prison.
March 21: Namibian independence achieved under UN supervision.
July 16: Iraq accuses Kuwait of 'stealing' $2.4 million worth of Iraqi oil and demands reimbursement.
July 23: Iraq masses 30,000 troops on Kuwait border; US Gulf fleet placed on alert.
July 25: Meeting with Hussein, US Ambassador April Glaspie reportedly states that the United States has 'no opinion on the Arab–Arab conflicts, like the border conflict with Kuwait'. President Bush later writes to Saddam, advising against military action.
August 2: Iraqi forces invade Kuwait. The Security Council adopts Resolution 660, condemning the invasion and demanding withdrawal. Iraqi and Kuwaiti overseas assets frozen by US, UK, and France. USSR stops arms deliveries to Iraq.
August 6: SCR 661 adopted imposing sanctions on Iraq and establishing the '661' Sanctions Committee to implement the Resolution. 'Operation Desert Shield' launched.
August 8: Iraq annexes Kuwait as its nineteenth province. Washington calls for a 'multinational' force in Saudi Arabia. USSR indicates it will only join a UN force.
August 9: SCR 662 unanimously adopted, declares annexation illegal.
August 15: Hussein indicates he will accept all Iranian conditions to formally end the Iran–Iraq war.
August 17: Iraq detains Western and Japanese nationals for use as 'human shields'. Western navies begin blockade of Iraq, later specifically mandated and broadened in SCR 665.
August 31: Pérez de Cuéllar and Iraqi Foreign Minister Tariq Aziz hold talks, without success.
September 13: SCR 666 sets procedures for determining extent of humanitarian need for food supplies among the civilian population in Iraq and Kuwait.

September 25: SCR 670 imposes air blockade, with humanitarian exceptions.
September 26: Shevardnadze tells the General Assembly that the USSR may support the use of force if Iraq's occupation continues.
October 5: Soviet Envoy Yevgeny Primakov meets Hussein, says a political solution is possible. Almost 200,000 US and 100,000 other foreign troops assemble in the Gulf.
October 15: Gorbachev awarded the Nobel Peace Prize.
October 26: CIA Director William Webster says Gulf cannot be secured as long as Saddam Hussein rules Iraq and that destruction of Iraq's arsenal may be necessary.
October 29: SCR 674 holds Iraq responsible for breaches of Geneva Convention on prisoners of war and Vienna Convention on Diplomatic Relations.
November 28: Security Council unanimously condemns Iraq's efforts to alter the demographic composition of Kuwait.
November 29: SCR 678 authorizes 'all necessary means' from January 15, 1991, to secure Iraqi compliance with resolutions. China abstains, Cuba and Yemen vote no.
November 30: Iraqi government calls SCR 678 illegal and invalid, rejects UN's January 15 ultimatum. Bush suggests talks, which later break down.
December 23: US Secretary of Defense, Richard Cheney, reports that Iraq has 500,000 troops in Kuwait.

1991

January 7: Hussein predicts the 'Mother of all Battles' in the event of war.
January 9: Latest US–Iraq talks fail. Bush characterizes the Iraqi position as 'a total stiff-arm'.
January 11: The United States pressures Israel not to respond if attacked by Iraq.
January 12: US Congress votes war powers to President Bush, pursuant to SCR 678.
January 13: Pérez de Cuéllar travels to Baghdad, but fails to persuade Hussein to withdraw from Kuwait.
January 16: 'Operation Desert Storm' begins Coalition air war after expiry of UN deadline.
January 17: Iraq fires eight to ten SCUD missiles at Israel, wounding roughly twenty civilians.
January 29: US and USSR issue a joint statement that the attack on Iraq could end 'if Iraq would make an unequivocal commitment' to withdraw from Kuwait and makes immediate moves to comply with UN Resolutions.

February 13: Yevgeny Primakov visits Baghdad to tell Hussein he must comply with UN SCRs.
February 15: Iraq offers a conditional withdrawal from Kuwait. Bush rejects it as a 'cruel hoax' and calls on the Iraqi people to force Hussein to 'step aside'.
February 23: After talks with Baghdad, President Gorbachev requests delay in ground offensive, but the United States says Soviet peace initiative falls 'well short of what would be required'.
February 24: Coalition ground offensive begins. In the Security Council, Cuba, India, and Yemen deplore the allied action.
February 27: After military rout, Iraq accepts SCRs 660, 662, and 674. Security Council permanent members demand unconditional acceptance of all resolutions relevant to the crisis. Bush declares end to hostilities with cease-fire to take effect on February 28.
March 2: Security Council adopts SCR 686, laying down framework for permanent cease-fire. Cuba votes against the Resolution, China, India, and Yemen abstain. Shi'a uprising begins in southern Iraq, with Kurdish uprising in the North beginning on March 4.
March 10: The United States states its determination not to get involved in 'Iraqi internal affairs'.
March 20: A UN report warns of imminent catastrophe in Iraq if massive assistance is not provided.
April 1: Kurdish leaders call on Coalition to protect Kurds against genocide; remind them of their encouragement of the uprising.
April 3: SCR 687 sets terms for a cease-fire, establishes foundation for weapons inspection regime, UNSCOM. Cuba opposes the resolution, Ecuador and Yemen abstain.
April 5: SCR 688: characterizes Iraqi repression of Kurds as threat to international peace and security (though does not invoke Chapter VII). Cuba, Yemen, and Zimbabwe oppose the Resolution; China and India abstain.
April 6: Iraqi parliament accepts SCR 687.
April 8: James Baker visits Kurdish refugee camp on Turkish border, calls for quick and effective international response. 'Operation Provide Comfort', to begin April 17, endorsed by UK Prime Minister Major and EC. Claim that SCR 688 provides the basis to send troops to northern Iraq.
April 18: Iraq provides initial declaration required under SCR 687, declares some chemical weapons and materials and a missile program, but declares it has no biological weapons. It revises this statement in August in light of UNSCOM inspections.

April 20: James Baker meets with Fatah leaders in bid to convene an Arab–Israeli peace conference.
April 24: Patriotic Union of Kurdistan and Baghdad reach provisional agreement on Kurdish autonomy.
May: UN program is established to meet immediate needs of vulnerable Iraqis. Funding totals $964 million from 1991 to 1996.
May 20: Security Council establishes a fund to be financed by Iraqi oil revenue to pay for war damage.
June 9: UNSCOM commences its first chemical weapons inspection.
June 17: SCR 699 unanimously confirms that UNSCOM and the IAEA have continuing authority to conduct activities in Iraq, and makes Iraq liable for the costs.
June 23–28: UNSCOM/IAEA inspectors try to intercept Iraqi vehicles carrying nuclear related equipment (calutrons). Iraqi personnel fire warning shots. The equipment is later seized and destroyed.
July 1: Warsaw Pact officially dissolved.
July 14: Bush and Mitterand threaten to order new air attacks if Hussein persecutes the Kurds or Shi'i.
July 18–20: Iraqi ballistic missile concealment revealed. Missiles and launch support equipment destroyed.
August 15: SCR 706 offers oil-for-food arrangements.
August 18–21: Failed coup against Gorbachev leads to collapse of Communism in USSR.
September 21–30: UNSCOM and IAEA discover documents relating to Iraqi nuclear weapons programs.
October 11: SCR 715 approves plan for Ongoing Monitoring and Verification (OMV) of Iraqi weapons capacities. Iraq rejects it as unlawful.

1992

January: Boutros Boutros-Ghali new UN Secretary-General.
January 31: First ever UN Security Council Summit. Robust statement rooted in success of Council's approach to Iraq.
March 8: Deteriorating situations in Yugoslavia and Somalia compel the UN to deploy peacekeepers, first in Croatia and then in Somalia (September). The two conflagrations will tax the UN's resources and momentum.
May–June: Iraq provides its first Full, Final, and Complete Disclosure in relation to its chemical, biological, and missile programs.
June 17: Secretary-General Boutros Boutros-Ghali issues 'An Agenda for Peace' on preventive diplomacy, peacemaking, peacekeeping, and peacebuilding.

July: UNSCOM begins the destruction of large quantities of Iraq's chemical weapons and production facilities.
July 6–29: Crisis over Iraqi refusal of UNSCOM access to the Ministry of Agriculture.
August 26: US, UK, and France announce establishment of a southern Iraqi 'no-fly zone'.

1993

January: Iraq refuses to allow UNSCOM the use of its own aircraft to fly into Iraq. Iraqi incursions into the demilitarized zone between Iraq and Kuwait.
January 7–19: The United States alleges Iraq has moved surface-to-air missiles into the southern no-fly zone. Security Council warns Iraqi prohibition of UNSCOM use of aircraft is an 'unacceptable and material breach' of SCR 687 and warns of 'serious consequences'. Allied warplanes attack Iraq missile and nuclear sites.
January 20: William Jefferson Clinton becomes President of the United States.
April 13: The United States uncovers plot to assassinate former President George H. W. Bush during visit to Kuwait. Coalition responds with air strikes against Iraq.
August 20: Oslo Accord reached granting Palestinians interim self-government.
October 3–4: Eighteen US soldiers killed in Mogadishu, leading to US and then UN military withdrawal from Somalia, with knock-on effects for the UN in Haiti and elsewhere.
November 26: Iraq accepts SCR 715 and OMV.

1994

February 10: UNSCOM and the Iraq authorities indicate progress in weapons inspection. Rwandan genocide commences.
June: UNSCOM destroys large quantities of chemical weapons agents and production equipment.
September: Iraq deploys troops towards Kuwaiti border. The United States responds with its own troop buildup in Kuwait.
October 15: SCR 949 demands that Iraq 'cooperate fully' with UNSCOM and withdraw its troops. Further to Russian diplomacy, Iraq withdraws its troops.

1995

April 14: SCR 986 refines Oil-for-Food Program.
May 17: Jacques Chirac assumes the French Presidency.
July: Iraq threatens to end all cooperation with weapons inspectors if there is no progress toward the lifting of economic sanctions by August 31, 1995.
July 1: For the first time, Iraq admits the existence of an offensive biological weapons program, but denies weaponization.

July 6–16: UN strategies in Bosnia collapse following the Srebrenica massacre in July. NATO air strikes and a Croatian ground offensive follow. The Dayton Accord, largely imposed by the United States, ends active hostilities, and establishes international authority over Bosnia.
August 8: Iraq's weapons program chief, General Hussein Kamel al-Majid, defects to Jordan. Iraq claims that he had hidden important information on the prohibited weapons programs. Iraq admits an extensive biological warfare program, including weaponization.

1996
May–June: UNSCOM supervises the destruction of Al-Hakam, Iraq's main facility for the production of biological warfare agents.
June 12: Following continued denial of access for UNSCOM teams, SCR 1060 terms Iraq's actions a clear violation of SCRs. It demands immediate and unrestricted access to all sites designated for inspection by UNSCOM.
June 19–22: UNSCOM and Iraq establish modalities for inspection of so-called 'sensitive sites', taking account of Iraq's concerns.
June: A US-backed coup involving Iraqi and Kurdish agents is foiled by Hussein.
August 31: Iraq military forces push into Kurdistan, capturing Irbil.
September 2: The United States retaliates against Iraqi military action with cruise missile attacks and by extending the southern no-fly zone. France refuses to patrol the extended zone.
November: Iraq blocks UNSCOM from removing remnants of missile engines for in-depth analysis outside Iraq.
November 17: Despite Russian and French entreaties, a Chinese company is the first to develop an oil field in Iraq since the war, at al-Ahdab.
December 10: Oil-for-Food program finally gets under way.
December 17: Kofi Annan elected UN Secretary-General.

1997
January 19: PLO leader Arafat returns to Hebron after more than thirty years.
March 22: Iraqi Oil Minister Amer Rashid announces the establishment of a new Iraq–Russian oil company, worth perhaps $80 billion according to a later report.
May 1: Tony Blair becomes UK Prime Minister.
June: Iraqi interference with UNSCOM helicopter patrols. The Security Council responds.
June 21: Following further Iraqi non-cooperation, the Security Council suspends the periodic sanctions review process.

July: Richard Butler succeeds Rolf Ekéus as Executive Chairman of UNSCOM.
October 15: The Secretary-General establishes the Office of the Iraq Program (OIP), to consolidate and manage the activities of the Secretariat in implementing the Oil-for-Food program. Benon Sevan is appointed Executive Director.
October 23: SCR 1134 continues the suspension of the periodic sanctions review. Five countries abstain.
November 12: SCR 1137 imposes travel restrictions on Iraqi officials involved in non-compliance with UNSCOM.
November 13: Iraq forces US UNSCOM personnel out of Iraq.
November 20: In agreement brokered by Russia, weapons inspections resume.
December 17: UNSCOM barred from 'Presidential and Sovereign' sites.

1998

January 13: Iraq withdraws its cooperation with the inspections team because it has too many US and UK members.
February 18: Security Council approves a visit to Baghdad by Annan to negotiate a solution to the Presidential sites crisis.
February 20: SCR 1153 more than doubles the amount of oil Iraq can export under the Oil-for-Food program.
February 20–23: Annan travels to Baghdad, signs a Memorandum of Understanding (MOU) allowing for UNSCOM inspection of Presidential sites.
March 2: SCR 1154 unanimously endorses the Baghdad MOU. Violations will result in the 'severest consequences'.
May 8: Security Council lifts the travel bans on Iraqi government officials.
May 11–13: India conducts a series of nuclear tests in the Rajasthan Desert. Pakistan follows suit on May 28. The United States and Japan impose sanctions on both.
August 5: Iraq halts cooperation with UNSCOM and the IAEA pending Security Council agreement to lift the oil embargo. In the interim, Iraq would, on its own terms, permit monitoring under SCR 715.
August 7: US embassies in Nairobi and Dar es Salaam bombed, killing 224.
August 20: Iraq and Syria sign an agreement to reopen a shared oil pipeline. The United States launches cruise missiles against Al Qaeda camps in Afghanistan and a chemical factory in Sudan, in response to the embassy bombings.
August 26: UNSCOM inspector Scott Ritter resigns, highly critical of UNSCOM and the Clinton Administration.
September 9: SCR 1194 condemns Iraq's suspension of cooperation with UNSCOM.

September 29: US Congress passes the *Iraq Liberation Act*, making regime change an explicit goal of US policy in Iraq.
October 31: Iraq ceases all interaction with UNSCOM.
November 14: President Clinton orders, then aborts, air-strikes against Iraq after Baghdad pledges unconditional cooperation with UNSCOM.
December 16–19: After UNSCOM is forced to withdraw, US and UK conduct Operation Desert Fox, bombing targets in Baghdad. Iraq announces that UNSCOM's 'mission is over'.
December 21: France, Germany, and Russia call for the end of sanctions against Iraq, and for UNSCOM to be recast.

1999
January 30: Security Council establishes 'Amorim' panels on UN policy in Iraq, looking for new approaches.
March 24: NATO, bypassing the Security Council where Russia threatens a veto, launches air-strikes against Serb forces in Kosovo. In June, SCR 1244 establishes UN-supervised international Transitional Administration in Kosovo. Later, after violence against the local population, Security Council also establishes a UN Transitional Administration in East Timor.
June 30: Butler's term as Executive Chairman of UNSCOM ends. He is not replaced.
September 23: P-5 pledge to continue to work towards a consensus on a new policy for Iraq.
October 22: Secretary-General expresses concern to the Security Council over the growing number of holds placed on draft contracts under the Oil-for-Food program by the 661 Committee.
December 31: Boris Yeltsin unexpectedly resigns as President of Russia, to be replaced by Vladimir Putin.

2000
January 27: Hans Blix becomes Chairman of UNMOVIC (UNSCOM's successor organization responsible for weapons inspections).
March 29: Security Council expands the 'fast track' approval procedure.
June 8: SCR 1302 grants extension to the Oil-for-Food program, but invites the Secretary-General to appoint independent experts to prepare a comprehensive report of the humanitarian situation in Iraq.
August 24: Iraq asserts it will not cooperate with UNMOVIC.

2001
January 20: George W. Bush sworn in as President of the United States.

February: US and UK forces carry out bombing raids against Iraq's air defense network.
June 1: UNMOVIC submits a revised list of dual-use goods to the Security Council. SCR 1352 extends the Oil-for-Food Program, but only for thirty days.
June: Iraq suspends its oil exports in rejection of SCR 1352.
July 3: SCR 1360 extends the Oil-for-Food Program for 150 days.
July 11: After a draft US–UK sanctions reform resolution does not come to vote, Iraq resumes oil exports.
August 10: US and UK reject a proposal by Secretary-General Kofi Annan to permit the Iraqi government to use $1 billion per year to fund infrastructure improvements and to increase oil production capacity.
September 11: Al Qaeda terrorist attacks against the World Trade Center and Pentagon in the United States, killing roughly 3,000.
November 27: Iraq rejects a call by President Bush to let weapons inspectors back into the country to determine whether it is building weapons of mass destruction.
November 29: SCR 1382 announces intention to adopt the Goods Review List approach.

2002

January 29: President Bush identifies Iraq, Iran, and North Korea, as an 'axis of evil.'
February 13: Iraq says that it will not allow UN weapons inspectors to return to Iraq.
May 14: SCR 1409 establishes the Goods Review List.
September 12: President Bush addresses the General Assembly, stating that 'The Security Council resolutions will be enforced ... or action will be unavoidable.'
September 16: Iraq allows the return of weapons inspectors.
October 2: US Congress passes a joint resolution explicitly authorizing the President to use force as he determines to be necessary in relation to Iraq.
October 12: Terrorist bombing of a night club in Bali kills 202 and injures 300.
November 8: Security Council unanimously adopts SCR 1441, giving UN inspectors the unconditional right to search anywhere in Iraq for prohibited weapons. The Resolution indicates that violations will lead to 'serious consequences'.
November 13: Iraq accepts SCR 1441, 'despite its bad contents'.
November 27: UNMOVIC commences weapons inspections in Iraq.
December 7: Iraq provides a weapons declaration as required by SCR 1441. It runs to 12,000 pages.

December 19: Blix provides an initial briefing to the Security Council on Iraq's declaration. US Secretary of State Colin Powell declares Iraq to be in 'material breach' of previous Resolutions, declaring the Iraqi declaration 'anything but currently accurate, full or complete.'

2003

January 17: Iraq awards a contract to Russian company Stroitransgaz for a small oil field in western Iraq and sets aside two others for Russian companies.

January 20: French Foreign Minister Dominique de Villepin states that France views military intervention as 'the worst possible solution'.

January 30: Leaders from the UK, Spain, Italy, Portugal, Hungary, Poland, Denmark, and the Czech Republic issue a statement supporting the US position on Iraq.

February 5: US Secretary of State Colin Powell presents evidence of Iraqi noncompliance to the Security Council.

February 28: Russian Foreign Minister Igor Ivanov threatens to veto any Security Council Resolution authorizing war in Iraq.

March 1: At an Arab League summit, UAE publicly proposes that Saddam Hussein step down.

March 7: US, UK, and Spain propose an ultimatum resolution requiring Hussein to give up banned weapons by March 17 or face war. Vocal opposition by others, France in the lead. Chirac later states, 'Whatever happens, France will vote "no".'

March 17: US and UK abandon efforts to pass a 'second' Security Council Resolution. President Bush issues an ultimatum requiring Hussein to leave Iraq.

March 18: Iraq rejects Bush's ultimatum.

March 19: The United States begins war on Iraq with a failed 'decapitation' strike on Dora Farms, a target south of Baghdad where Saddam Hussein and his sons were thought to be.

March 22: US and UK begin a campaign of 'shock and awe' with massive air-strikes on Baghdad.

March 28: Security Council unanimously adopts SCR 1472 adjusting the Oil-for-Food program to deal with the consequences of the war.

April 9: US troops take control of Baghdad. They are met by jubilant crowds, then turn to looting.

April 21: Retired US General Jay Garner becomes Interim Civil Administrator of Iraq.

April 30: President Bush releases the 'Road Map' for an Israeli–Palestinian peace process.

May 1: President Bush announces the end of 'major combat operations in Iraq'. The first US combat death in the post-war period is caused by a sniper's bullet on May 8.
May 6: Garner is replaced by former State Department counter-terrorism chief Paul Bremer. One of Bremer's first decisions is to dissolve the Iraqi army.
May 11: Ba'ath Party formally dissolved.
May 22: SCR 1483 recognizes the Coalition Provisional Authority as the occupying force in Iraq, lifts sanctions, and gives authority over remaining aspects of the Oil-for-Food program to the CPA.
July 13: Creation of the Iraqi Governing Council (IGC), comprising Shiites, Sunnis, Kurds, Christians, and Turkmen. IGC has the power to name ministers and approve a budget, but the United States maintains overall control.
July 22: Hussein's sons, Qusay and Uday killed in a gun battle with US troops.
August 19: Terrorist attack on UNAMI Headquarters in Baghdad kills Sergio Vieira de Mello and twenty-one other UN staff.
August 29: A car bomb kills at least eighty-three Iraqis, including top Shi'ite leader Ayatollah Mohammed Baqer al-Hakim at the Imam Ali mosque in Najaf.
September 23: Another terrorist attack at UN headquarters, killing one. A month later, terrorists bomb the headquarters of the Red Crescent (Islamic Red Cross) in Baghdad.
November 21: The Oil-for-Food program is officially terminated.
December 9: Countries that opposed the war, such as France and Germany, are barred from US reconstruction contracts.
December 13: Saddam Hussein captured, hiding in a special 'spider hole'.
December 20: Libya admits and renounces its nuclear weapons program.

2004

January 28: Hutton Inquiry in the United Kingdom refutes allegations by the BBC that the Government had 'sexed up' WMD information dossier, and criticizes the BBC's role in the suicide of scientist David Kelly. In the US, David Kay, former head of the US weapons inspections team in Iraq, says that pre-war intelligence was 'almost all wrong' about the extent of Iraq's WMD arsenal.
February 1: One hundred people killed in a double suicide bombing of offices of the two main Kurdish factions in Irbil.
February 16: Former British cabinet minister Clare Short reveals that UK intelligence bugged Secretary-General Annan and other UN officials in the lead up to the invasion of Iraq.

March 1: US-backed IGC agrees an interim constitution, including a bill of rights and recognition of Islam as a source of legislation.
March 2: More than 180 people are killed in Karbala and Baghdad during a Shia holy day.
March 11: Terrorist attacks on Madrid train system kill over 190 people.
March 31: Four American civilian contractors are killed and their bodies mutilated in Fallujah.
April 20: A tribunal charged with prosecuting Saddam Hussein and other Ba'ath regime leaders is set up.
April 21: Kofi Annan appoints an independent panel, chaired by Paul Volcker, to conduct an inquiry into the Oil-for-Food Program.
April 23: Bremer signals a shift in American policy by stating that former Ba'athists may hold positions in the new government.
April 29: The first photos of abuse in the Abu Ghraib prison are released to the public.
May 11: Terrorists release a video of the beheading of US citizen Nick Berg.
May 17: The President of the IGC, Ezzedine Salim, is assassinated, beginning a wave of murders of leading Iraqi officials.
May 28: Iyad Allawi, a Shi'a, is named prime minister. The IGC is officially dissolved two days later.
June 8: SCR 1546 approves the formal end of the occupation and recognizes the transfer of sovereignty to the Iraqi interim administration. The resolution reaffirms authorization of the Coalition under SCRs 1483 and 1511.
July 1: Saddam Hussein in court on charges of war crimes and genocide.
October 24: Forty recruits for the new Iraqi army are killed in a roadside ambush. Attacks on Iraqi army and police recruits soon multiply.
November 15: Fallujah is retaken from insurgents in a large-scale American operation. Over 1,500 people are believed to have been killed.

2005
January 12: The last members of the Iraq Survey Group return to the United States, declaring that no weapons of mass destruction have been found.
January 30: Millions of Iraqis vote in the first election in Iraq in over fifty years.
February 3: Volcker releases his interim OFF report, which terms the program 'tainted.'
February 13: Election results: 58 percent turnout; a broad Shi'ite alliance and Kurdish groups are the main winners.
February 28: A suicide bomber kills 122 people in Hilla in the single deadliest bombing since March 2003. The State Department deplores documented cases of torture by the Iraqi security forces.

February 28: Facing mass protests denouncing the murder of former Prime Minister Rafik Hariri, Lebanon's pro-Syrian prime minister, Omar Karami, resigns.

March 30: The Volcker Commission voices reservations with respect to Annan's role in OFF, as well as that of some his closest advisors.

April 6: Jalal Talabani, a Kurd, is named first president of the new Iraqi administration.

April 7: Iraqi Shia leader Ibrahim al-Ja'afari is named prime minister of Iraq.

April 11: Senior American officers say the number of Iraqi insurgents has dwindled to perhaps 12,000–20,000 hard-core fighters. The number of attacks and deaths declines.

May 1: The leaked British 'Downing Street Memo' of July 23, 2002 acknowledges the 'thin' case for war, but asserts that 'Bush had made up his mind to take military action.' The US wanted the war 'justified by the conjunction of terrorism and WMD. But the intelligence and facts were being fixed around the policy.' The controversy simmers.

May 5: Tony Blair re-elected in the UK.

May 10: A fifty-five-member committee is announced to draft Iraq's constitution, due on August 15.

June 6: Iraq's PM and President declare official support for the Badr Organization, a Shi'ite militia, raising the specter of a splintering of Iraqi security forces and increased sectarianism.

June 16: Sunnis agree to accept fifteen seats on the constitutional council, raising their levels from two.

June 30: UN Claims Commission completes its main body of work after twelve years of processing claims. Total awards of damages figured about $52.5 billion, out of 2.68 million claims seeking approximately $354 billion in compensation since 1993.

July 7: During the G-8 Summit in Scotland, four bombs detonate in London, killing over fifty and wounding 700. In Iraq, terrorists kill Egypt's ambassador-to-be after kidnapping him and staging attacks on Pakistani and Bahraini officials.

July 16: 11 US soldiers are charged with abuse of prisoners in Iraq.

August 28: Three deadlines pass under dubious legal circumstances, but Iraq's leaders adopt a new constitution. Sunni leaders oppose the federalist structure outlined in the document, vowing to vote against it.

August 31: Almost 1,000 people at a religious festival die in a stampede in northern Baghdad, spurred by rumours of a suicide bomber. Two weeks later a suicide bomber kills 114 in a single attack.

September 8: The Volcker Inquiry documents the corruption of OFF, and failures in oversight by the UN Secretariat and by Security Council members. It calls for widespread administrative and management reforms.
September 14–16: The much-trumpeted UN World Summit produces a lacklustre Outcome Document, dimming prospects for UN reform.
September 20: Afghani President Hamid Karzai declares his country is no longer a haven for terrorists and asks the US military to stop air strikes and invasive searches.
September 27: NATO begins its officer training mission in Iraq.
October 7: Mohamed El Baradei and the IAEA win the Nobel Peace Prize.
October 15: Iraqis vote on the constitution after an agreement is reached to charge the incoming parliament with finalizing a number of important issues. Two Sunni provinces reject the constitution by the required two-thirds majority, but only 55% of voters in Nineveh vote 'no'.
October 19: Saddam Hussein and seven former lieutenants go on trial for the 1982 massacre of 148 Shi'ites from the town of Dujail
October 25: The American post-invasion death toll in Iraq reaches 2,000.
October 27: The final Volcker report reveals that $1.8 billion in surcharges and kickbacks were paid to Iraq by about 2,400 companies in at least 66 countries
November 5: The IECI announces that 228 coalitions and political entities are registered to participate in Iraqi parliamentary elections scheduled for 15 December. Unlike in the January vote, Sunni leaders pledge their full participation.
November 8: SCR 1637 extends the term of multinational forces in Iraq for one year, allowing for 'a review of that mandate at any time, no later than mid-June 2006, or for its termination, at the request of the Iraqi Government'.
November 13: 173 detainees are found by US troops in an interior ministry building in Baghdad, many bearing signs of malnutrition and mistreatment. Many of the prisoners are Sunni, precipitaing accusations of torture against the Shi'ite-led government.
November 18: France's former Ambassador to the UN (and Special UN Envoy) Jean-Bernard Mérimée admits having accepted kickbacks from Iraq.
December 14: President Bush announces that the State Department, under Condoleezza Rice, will assume the lead for Iraqi reconstruction, displacing the Pentagon.
December 15: Despite threats of violence, Iraqis of all stripes vote *en masse* in parliamentary elections. Sunni parties cry foul five days later after initial results show nearly 59 percent of the vote going to the Shiite United Iraqi Alliance. Violence dips during the electoral and immediate post-electroal period but picks up with a vengeance in early 2006.

Bibliography

BOOKS AND PUBLISHED REPORTS

Abdulghani, J. M. (1984). *Iraq and Iran: The Years of Crisis*. Baltimore, MD: Johns Hopkins University Press.

Abiew, F. K. (1999). *The Evolution of the Doctrine and Practice of Humanitarian Intervention*. The Hague: Kluwer.

Aburish, S. K. (2000). *Saddam Hussein: The Politics of Revenge*. New York: Bloomsbury.

Académie du Droit International (1993). *Colloque 1992: Le développement du rôle du Conseil de Sécurité*. Dordrecht: Martinus Nijhoff.

Advisory Council on International Affairs and Advisory Committee on Issues of Public International Law (2000). *Humanitarian Intervention*. The Hague: AIV and CAVV.

al-Khalil, S. (1989). *Republic of Fear: The Politics of Modern Iraq*. Berkeley, CA: University of California Press.

Allin, D. H. (2002). *NATO's Balkan Interventions*, Adelphi Paper 347. London: International Institute for Strategic Studies.

Alnasrawi, A. (2002). *Iraq's Burdens: Oil, Sanctions and Underdevelopment*. Westport, CT: Greenwood.

Anderson, S., Bennis, P., and Cavanagh, J. *Coalition of the Willing or Coalition of the Coerced?* Institute for Policy Studies, February 26, 2003 www.ips-dc.org/COERCED.pdf

Annan, K. A. (1999). *The Question of Intervention*. New York: United Nations.

Arend, A. C. and Beck, R. J. (1993). *International Law and the Use of Force: Beyond the UN Charter Paradigm*. London: Routledge.

Atkinson, R. (1993). *Crusade: The Untold Story of the Persian Gulf War*. Boston, MA: Houghton Mifflin.

Axelgard, F. W. (ed.) (1986). *Iraq in Transition: A Political, Economic and Strategic Perspective*. Boulder, CO: Westview.

—— (1988). *A New Iraq?* New York: Praeger.

Baehr, P. R. and Gordenker, L. (1994). *The United Nations in the 1990s*, 2nd edn. Basingstoke: Macmillan.

Bailey, S. D. (1994). *The UN Security Council and Human Rights*. New York: St. Martin's Press.

—— and Daws, S. (1995). *The United Nations: A Concise Political Guide*, 3rd edn. London: Macmillan.

—— —— (1998). *The Procedure of the Security Council*, 3rd edn. Oxford: Clarendon.

Baker, J. A. (1995). *The Politics of Diplomacy: Revolution, War and Peace, 1989–1992*. New York: G.P. Putnam's Sons.

Barnaby, F. (1989). *The Invisible Bomb: The Nuclear Arms Race in the Middle East*. London: I. B. Tauris.

Bassiouni, M. C. (2001). *International Terrorism: Multilateral Conventions, 1937–2001*. Ardsley, NY: Transnational Publishers.

Batatu, H. (1978). *The Old Social Classes and the Revolutionary Movements of Iraq: A Study of Iraq's Old Landed and Commercial Classes and of Its Communists, Ba'thists, and Free Officers*. Princeton, NJ: Princeton University Press.

Bedjaoui, M. (1994). *The New World Order and the Security Council: Testing the Legality of Its Acts*. Boston: Martinus Nijhoff.

Bennis, P. and Moushabeck, M. (eds.) (1991). *Beyond the Storm: A Gulf Crisis Reader*. Brooklyn, NY: Olive Branch.

Berdal, M. and Malone, D. M. (eds.) (2000). *Greed and Grievance: Economic Agendas in Civil Wars*. Boulder, CO: Lynne Rienner.

—— Economides, S., and Mayall, J. (eds.) *The New Interventionism, 1991–2004* (Cambridge: Cambridge University Press, 2006 (forthcoming)).

Bettati, M. (1996). *Le droit d'ingérence: Mutation de l'ordre international*. Paris: Odile Jacob.

—— and Kouchner, B. (1987). *Le devoir d'ingérence*. Paris: Denoël.

Blix, H. (2004). *Disarming Iraq: The Search for Weapons of Mass Destruction*. New York: Pantheon.

Boone, P., et al. (1997). *Sanctions Against Iraq: Costs of Failure*. Brooklyn, NY: Center for Economic and Social Rights.

Boudreau, T. E. (1991). *Sheathing the Sword: The U.N. Secretary-General and the Prevention of International Conflict*. New York: Greenwood.

Boulden, J. and Weiss, T. (eds.) (2004) Terrorism and the UN: Before and After September 11 (Bloomington: Indiana University Press.)

Bourantonis, D. and Wiener, J. (1995). *The United Nations in the New World Order: The World Organization at Fifty*. Basingstoke: Macmillan.

Boutros-Ghali, B. (ed.) (1996). *The United Nations and the Iraq-Kuwait Conflict, 1990–1996*. New York: United Nations.

—— (1999). *Unvanquished: A US-UN Saga*. New York: Random House.

Boyd, A. (1971). *Fifteen Men on a Powder Keg: A History of the UN Security Council*. New York: Stein and Day.

Brilliant, F., Cuny, F. C. and Tanner, V. (1995). *Humanitarian Intervention: A Study of Operation Provide Comfort*. Dallas, TX: INTERTECT.

Bremer, L. P. (2006). *My year in Iraq: The Struggle to Build a Future of Hope*. New York: Simon & Schuster.

Bull, H. (2002). *The Anarchical Society: A Study of Order in World Politics*, 3rd edn. New York: Columbia University Press.

Bulloch, J. and Morris, H. (1991). *The Gulf War: Its Origins, History and Consequences*. London: Methuen.

—— (1991). *Saddam's War: The Origins of the Kuwait Conflict and the International Response*. London: Faber.

Bush, G. and Scowcroft, B. (1998). *A World Transformed*. New York: Alfred A. Knopf.

Bustelo, M. R. and Alston, P. (eds.) (1991). *Whose New World Order: What Role for the United Nations?* Annandale: Federation.

Butler, R. (2000). *The Greatest Threat: Iraq, Weapons of Mass Destruction, and the Crisis of Global Security*. New York: Public Affairs.

Byers, M. (ed.) (2000). *The Role of Law in International Politics: Essays in International Relations and International Law*. Oxford: Oxford University Press.

Cain, K., Postlewait, H., and Thomson, A. (2004). *Emergency Sex and Other Desperate Measures*. New York: Hyperion.

Caplan, R. (2005). *International Governance of War-Torn Territories: Rule and Reconstruction*. Oxford: Oxford University Press.

Center for Economic and Social Rights (1996). *Unsanctioned Suffering: A Human Rights Assessment of the United Nations Sanctions on Iraq*.

Chesterman, S. (2001). *Just War or Just Peace? Humanitarian Intervention and International Law*. Oxford: Oxford University Press.

—— Ignatieff, M., and Thakur, R. (eds.) (2005). *Making States Work: State Failure and the Crisis of Governance*. Tokyo: United Nations University Press.

—— and Pouligny, B. *The Politics of Sanctions*, IPA-CERI-RIIA Policy Brief, May 1, 2002, www.ipacademy.org/PDF_Reports/POLITICS_OF_SANCTIONS.pdf.

Christopher, W., et al. (1985). *American Hostages in Iran: The Conduct of a Crisis*. New Haven, CT: Yale University Press.

Chubin, S. and Tripp, C. (1988). *Iran and Iraq at War*. London: I.B. Tauris.

Clancy, T., Zinni, T. and Koltz, T. (2004). *Battle Ready*. New York: G.P. Putnam's Sons.

Clark, I. (2005). *Legitimacy in International Society*. Oxford: Oxford University Press.

Clarke, R. A. (2004). *Against All Enemies: Inside America's War on Terror*. New York: Free Press.

Claude, I. L. (1964). *Swords into Plowshares: The Problems and Progress of International Organization*, 3rd edn. New York: Random House.

—— (1988). *States and the Global System: Politics, Law, and Organization*. New York: St. Martin's Press.

Clements, K. and Wilson, C. (1994). *UN Peacekeeping at the Crossroads*. Canberra: Australian National University Press.

Coalition for International Justice. *Sources of Revenue For Saddam & Sons: A Primer on the Financial Underpinnings of the Regime in Baghdad*, September 18, 2002, www.cij.org/pdf/CIJ_Saddam.pdf

Cockayne, J. and Samii, C. *'The Iraq Crisis and World Order: Structural and Normative Changes'*, August 16–18, 2004 Conference Report, Bangkok, www.ipacademy.org.

Coicaud, J. M. and Heiskanen, V. (eds.) (2001). *The Legitimacy of International Organizations*. Tokyo: United Nations University Press.

Committee Against Repression and for Democratic Rights in Iraq (CADRI) (1986). *Saddam's Iraq: Revolution or Reaction?* London: Zed.

Conlon, P. (2000). *United Nations Sanctions Management: A Case Study of the Iraq Sanctions Committee, 1990–1994*. Ardsley, NY: Transnational Publishers.

Cook, R. (2004). *The Point of Departure*. New York: Simon & Schuster.

Cordesman, A. H. (1999). *Iraq and the War of Sanctions: Conventional Threats and Weapons of Mass Destruction*. Westport, CT: Praeger.

—— *Proliferation in Iran and Iraq, Is There an Answer?* CSIS Strategic Assessment, March 28, 2000.

—— and Hashim, A. S. (1987). *Iraq: Sanctions and Beyond*. Boulder, CO: Westview Press.

Cornish, P. (ed.) (2004). *The Conflict in Iraq 2003*. London: Palgrave/Macmillan.

Cortright, D. and Lopez, G. A. (2000). *The Sanctions Decade: Assessing UN Strategies in the 1990s*. Boulder, CO: Lynne Rienner.

—— —— (2002). *Sanctions and the Search for Security: Challenges to UN Action*. Boulder, CO: Lynne Rienner.

Cortright, D., et al. (1997). *Political Gain and Civilian Pain: Humanitarian Impacts of Economic Sanctions*. Lanham, MD: Rowman and Littlefield Publishers, Inc.

Cot, J. -P. and Pellet, A. (eds.) (1991). *La Charte des Nations Unies: Commentaire article par article*, 2nd edn. Paris: Éditions Economica.

Council on Foreign Relations (2003). *Iraq: The Day After: Report of an Independent Task Force Sponsored by the Council on Foreign Relations; Thomas R. Pickering and James R. Schlesinger, co-chairs, Eric P. Schwartz, project director*. New York: Council on Foreign Relations.

Crocker, C. A. (1992). *High Noon in Southern Africa: Making Peace in a Rough Neighborhood*. New York: W.W. Norton.

Crocker, C., Hampson, F. O., and Aall, P. (eds.) (1999). *Herding Cats: Multiparty Mediation in a Complex World*. Washington, DC: USIP.

—— —— —— (eds.) (2001). *Turbulent Peace: The Challenges of Managing International Conflict*. Washington, DC: USIP.

Damrosch, L. (1993). *Enforcing Restraint: Collective Intervention in Internal Conflicts*. New York: Council of Foreign Relations.

Davies, C. (ed.) (1990). *After the War: Iran, Iraq, and the Arab Gulf*. Chichester: Carden Publications.

Davis, M. J. (ed.) (1996). *Security Issues in the Post-Cold War World*. Cheltenham: Edward Elgar.

Deaver, M. V. (2001). *Disarming Iraq: Monitoring Power and Resistance*. Westport, CT: Praeger.

Deldique, P. -E. (1994). *Le mythe des Nations Unies: L'ONU après la Guerre Froide*. Paris: Hachètte.

Deng, F. M., et al. (1996). *Sovereignty as Responsibility*. Washington, DC: Brookings Institution.

Dershowitz, A. M. (2002). *Why Terrorism Works: Understanding the Threat, Responding to the Challenge*. New Haven, CT: Yale University Press.

Dodge, T. (2003). *Inventing Iraq: The Failure of Nation Building and a History Denied*. New York: Columbia University Press.

—— (2005). *Iraq's Future, the Aftermath of Regime Change*, Adelphi Paper 372. London: International Institute for Strategic Studies.

—— and Simon, S. (eds.) (2003). *Iraq at the Crossroads: State and Society in the Shadow of Regime Change*. Oxford: Oxford University Press.

Donini, A., Niland, N., and Wermester, K. (eds.) (2004). *Nation-Building Unraveled? Aid, Peace and Justice in Afghanistan*. Bloomfield, CT: Kumarian Press.

Doyle, M., Johnstone, I., and Orr, R. (eds.) (1997). *Keeping the Peace: Multidimensional UN Operations in Cambodia and El Salvador.* Cambridge: Cambridge University Press.

Drezner, D. W. (1999). *The Sanctions Paradox: Economic Statecraft and International Relations*. Cambridge: Cambridge University Press.

Dupuy, R. -J. (ed.) (1993). *The Development of the Role of the Security Council: Peace-Keeping and Peace-Building.* Boston: Martinus Nijhoff.

Durch, W. J. (1993). *The Evolution of UN Peacekeeping: Case Studies and Comparative Analysis*. London: St. Martin's Press.

—— (ed.) (1996). *UN Peacekeeping, American Politics, and the Uncivil Wars of the 1990s*. New York: St. Martin's Press.

El Azhary, M. S. (ed.) (1984). *The Iran-Iraq War: An Historical, Economic and Political Analysis*. London: Croom Helm.

Evans, G. J. (1993). *Cooperating for Peace: The Global Agenda for the 1990's and Beyond*. St. Leonards: Allen & Unwin.

FAFO. *Iraq Multiple Indicator Rapid Assessment*, May 12, 2005, www.fafo.no/ais/middeast/iraq/imira/index.htm.

Falk, R. A., Kim, S. S., and Mendlovitz, S. H. (eds.) (1991). *The United Nations and a Just World Order.* Boulder, CO: Westview.

Farer, T. (1993). *Collectively Defending Democracy in a World of Sovereign States: The Western Hemisphere's Prospect.* Montreal: International Center for Human Rights and Democratic Development.

Fassbender, B. (1998). *UN Security Council Reform and the Right of Veto: A Constitutional Perspective*. The Hague: Kluwer.

Ferencz, B. B. (1994). *New Legal Foundations for Global Survival: Security Through the Security Council.* Dobbs Ferry, NY: Oceana.

Findlay, T. (2005). *A Standing United Nations WMD Verification Body: Necessary and Feasible*. Stockholm: VERTIC.

Foot, R., MacFarlane, S. N., and Mastanduno, M. (2003). *US Hegemony and International Organizations*. Oxford: Oxford University Press.

Forsythe, D. P. (1993). *Human Rights and Peace: International and National Dimensions*. Lincoln: University of Nebraska Press.

Fox, G. H. and Roth, B. R. (eds.) (2000). *Democratic Governance and International Law.* Cambridge: Cambridge University Press.

Franck, T. M. (1985). *Nation Against Nation: What Happened to the UN Dream and What the U.S. Can Do About It*. New York: Oxford University Press.

—— (1990). *The Power of Legitimacy Among Nations*. New York: Oxford University Press.

—— (2002). *Recourse to Force: State Action Against Threats and Armed Attacks*. Cambridge: Cambridge University Press.

Fukuyama, F. (2004). *State Building: Governance and World Order in the 21st Century*. Ithaca, NY: Cornell University Press.

Galbraith, P. W. 'Operation Save Face', *American Prospect Online*, November 21, 2004, www.prospect.org/web/page.ww?section=root&name=ViewPrint&articleId=888.

Garrett, S. A. (1999). *Doing Good and Doing Well: An Examination of Humanitarian Intervention*. Westport, CT: Praeger.

Global Issues Research Group, Foreign and Commonwealth Office (1999). *Research Analysts Memorandum: Table of Vetoed Draft Resolutions in the United Nations Security Council, 1946–1998*. London: Global Issues Research Group.

Global Policy Forum. *'Sanctions'*, www.globalpolicy.org/security/sanction/theindex.htm.

Goldstein, G. M. (1998). *Leadership, Multilateral Security, and Coercive Cooperation: The Role of the UN Security Council in the Persian Gulf War*. New York: G. M. Goldstein.

Goodrich, L. M. and Simons, A. P. (1955). *The United Nations and the Maintenance of International Peace and Security*. Washington, DC: Brookings Institution.

—— Hambro, E., and Simons, A. P. (1969). *Charter of the United Nations: Commentary and Documents*, 3rd edn. New York: Columbia University Press.

Gordon, P. H. and Shapiro, J. (2004). *Allies at War: America, Europe and the Crisis over Iraq*. New York: McGraw Hill.

Goulding, M. (2003). *Peacemonger*. Baltimore, MD: Johns Hopkins University Press.

Gow, J. (ed.) (1993). *Iraq, The Gulf Conflict and the World Community*. London: Brassey.

Gowing, N. (1994). 'Real-Time Television Coverage of Armed Conflicts and Diplomatic Crises: Does it Pressure or Distort Foreign Policy Decisions?' Joan Shorenstein Barone Center, John F. Kennedy School of Government, Harvard University, Working Paper.

Gowlland Debbas, V. (2001). *United Nations Sanctions and International Law*. The Hague: Kluwer Law International.

Graham-Brown, S. (1999). *Sanctioning Saddam: The Politics of Intervention in Iraq*. London: I.B. Tauris.

—— 'No-Fly Zones: Rhetoric and Real Intentions', *MERIP Press Information Note 49*, February 20, 2001, www.merip.org/mero/mero022001.html

Gray, C. (2000). *International Law and the Use of Force*. Oxford: Oxford University Press.

Greenberg, K. J. and Dratel, J. L. (eds.) (2005). *The Torture Papers: The Road to Abu Ghraib*. New York: Cambridge University Press.

Greenberg, M., Barton, J. and McGuiness, M. (2000). *Words over War: Mediation and Arbitration to Prevent Deadly Conflict*. Lanham, MD: Rowman & Littlefield.

Greenwood, C. (2001). *Humanitarian Intervention: Law and Policy*. Oxford: Oxford University Press.

Gregg, R. W. (1993). *About Face? The United States and the United Nations*. Boulder, CO: Lynne Rienner.

Grummon, S. R. (1982). *The Iran-Iraq War: Islam Embattled.* New York: Praeger.

Gunter, M. (1992). *The Kurds of Iraq: Tragedy and Hope.* New York: St. Martin's Press.

—— (1999). *The Kurdish Predicament in Iraq: A Political Analysis.* New York: St. Martin's Press.

Haass, R. N. (2005). *The Opportunity: America's Moment to Alter History's Course.* New York: Public Affairs.

Hazelton, F. (ed.) (1994). *Iraq Since the Gulf War: Prospects for Democracy.* London: Zed.

Heininger, J. E. (1994). *Peacekeeping in Transition: The United Nations in Cambodia.* New York: Twentieth Century Fund Press.

Henderson, A. E. (2005). *The Coalition Provisional Authority's Experience with Economic Reconstruction in Iraq: Lessons Identified,* United States Institute for Peace, Special Report 138.

Henderson, S. (1991). *Instant Empire: Saddam Hussein's Ambition for Iraq.* San Francisco, CA: Mercury House.

Higgins, R. (1963). *The Development of International Law Through the Political Organs of the United Nations.* Oxford: Oxford University Press.

Hill, S. M. (1996). *Peacekeeping and the United Nations.* Aldershot: Dartmouth.

Hiro, D. (1990). *The Longest War: The Iran-Iraq Military Conflict.* New York: Paladin.

—— (1992). *Desert Shield to Desert Storm: The Second Gulf War.* London: HarperCollins.

—— (2001). *Neighbours Not Friends: Iraq and Iran After the Gulf Wars.* London: Routledge.

—— (2002). *Iraq: In the Eye of the Storm.* New York: Thunder's Mouth Press/Nation Books.

Hirsch, J. L. (2001). *Sierra Leone: Diamonds and the Struggle for Democracy.* Boulder, CO: Lynne Rienner.

Hiscocks, R. (1973). *The Security Council: A Study in Adolescence.* London: Longman.

Holzgrefe, J. L. and Keohane, R. O. (eds.) (2003). *Humanitarian Intervention: Ethical, Legal, and Political Dilemmas.* Cambridge: Cambridge University Press.

Hopwood, D., Ishow, H. and Koszinowski, T. (eds.) (1993). *Iraq: Power and Society.* Reading: Ithaca.

Human Rights Watch. '*Whatever Happened To The Iraqi Kurds?*' March 11, 1991, www.hrw.org/reports/1991/IRAQ913.htm

—— (1993). *Genocide in Iraq, the Anfal Campaign Against the Kurds.* New York: Human Rights Watch.

—— (1993). *The Lost Agenda: Human Rights and UN Field Operations.* New York: Human Rights Watch.

—— (2003). 'The Iraqi Government Assault on the Marsh Arabs'. Briefing Paper.

Humanitarian Intervention: Legal and Political Aspects (1999). Copenhagen: Danish Institute of International Affairs.

Hume, C. R. (1994). *The United Nations, Iran and Iraq: How Peacemaking Changed.* Bloomington, IN: Indian University Press.

Huntington, S. (1991). *The Third Wave: Democratization in the Late Twentieth Century*. Norman, OK: University of Oklahoma Press.

Hussein, S. (1983). *Thus We Should Fight Persians*. Baghdad: Dar al-Ma'mun.

Iklé, F. C. (1965). *How Nations Negotiate*. New York: Harper Row.

Independent International Commission on Kosovo (2000). *The Kosovo Report: Conflict, International Response, Lessons Learned*. Oxford: Oxford University Press.

Independent Working Group on the Future of the United Nations (1995). *The United Nations in Its Second Half-Century*. New Haven, CT: Yale University Press.

Indyk, M. 'The Clinton Administration's Approach to the Middle East', Keynote Address to the Soref Symposium on 'Challenges to US Interests in the Middle East: Obstacles and Opportunities', *Proceedings of the Washington Institute for Near East Policy*, May 18–19, 1993.

International Crisis Group. *Iraq Policy Briefing: Is There An Alternative To War? Middle East Report No. 9*, February 24, 2003.

—— 'Iraq's Kurds: Towards An Historic Compromise?' *Middle East Report No. 26*, April 8, 2004.

—— 'Iraq's Transition: On a Knife Edge'. *Middle East Report No. 27*, April 27, 2004.

International Peace Academy. 'The Future of UN State-Building: Strategic and Operational Challenges and the Legacy of Iraq'. International Peace Academy, New York, December 2003.

—— 'The Future of UN State-Building: Strategic and Operational Challenges and the Legacy of Iraq'. Kirsti Samuels and Sebastien von Einsiedel, Rapporteurs, June 2004.

International Study Team. 'Our Common Responsibility: The Impact of a New War on Iraqi Children'. January 26, 2003.

Ismael, T. Y. (1982). *Iraq and Iran: Roots of Conflict*. Syracuse, NY: Syracuse University Press.

Jackson, R. (2000). *The Global Covenant: Human Conduct in a World of States*. Oxford: Oxford University Press.

Jentleson, B. W. (ed.) (2000). *Opportunities Missed, Opportunities Seized: Preventive Diplomacy in the Post-Cold War World*. Lanham, MD: Rowman & Littlefield.

Johnstone, I. (1994). *Aftermath of the Gulf War: An Assessment of UN Action*. Boulder, CO: Lynne Rienner.

Joyner, C. C. (ed.) (1990). *The Persian Gulf War: Lessons for Strategy, Law, and Diplomacy*. New York: Greenwood.

Karaosmanoglu, A. L. (1970). *Les actions militaires coercitives et non coercitives des Nations Unies*. Geneva: Librairie Droz.

Karns, M. P. and Mingst, K. (eds.) (1990). *The United States and Multilateral Institutions: Patterns of Changing Instrumentality and Influence*. Boston, MA: Unwin Hyman.

Karp, C. (2001). *US Policy Towards Jerusalem and the Occupied Arab Territories, 1948 and 1967*. Jerusalem: PASSIA.

Karsh, E. (ed.) (1989). *The Iran-Iraq War: Impact and Implications*. New York: St. Martin's Press.

Karsh, E. and Rautsi, I. (eds.) (1991). *Saddam Hussein: A Political Biography.* New York: Free Press.

Katzmann, K. 'Iraq: Oil-For-Food Program, International Sanctions, and Illicit Trade', *Congressional Research Service* (April 16, 2003).

—— 'Iraq: U.S. Regime Change Efforts and Post-Saddam Governance'. *Congressional Research Service* (May 16, 2005).

Kaufmann, J., Leurdijk, D., and Schrijver, N. (1991). *The World in Turmoil: Testing the UN's Capacity.* Hanover, NH: Academic Council on the United Nations System.

Khadduri, M. (1960). *Independent Iraq, 1932–58: A Study in Iraqi Politics*, 2nd edn. Oxford: Oxford University Press.

—— (1978). *Socialist Iraq: A Study in Iraqi Politics Since 1968.* Washington, DC: Middle East Institute.

—— (1988). *The Gulf War: The Origins and Implications of the Iraq-Iran Conflict.* New York: Oxford University Press.

Kirsch, P. (1990). *The Changing Role of the Security Council.* New York: Ralph Bunche Institute on the United Nations.

Kissinger, H. (2001). *Does America Need a Foreign Policy?: Toward a Diplomacy for the 21st Century.* New York: Simon & Schuster.

Klare, M. and Chandrani, Y. (eds.) (1998). *World Security: Challenges for a New Century*, 3rd edn. New York: St. Martin's Press.

Krasner, S. D. (1999). *Sovereignty: Organized Hypocrisy.* Princeton, NJ: Princeton University Press.

Krasno, J. E. and Sutterlin, J. S. (2003). *The United Nations and Iraq: Defanging the Viper.* London: Praeger.

Kühne, W. (ed.) (1996). *Winning the Peace: Concept and Lessons Learned of Post-Conflict Peacebuilding.* Ebenhausen: Stiftung Wissenschaft und Politik.

Kumar, K. (ed.) (1998). *Postconflict Elections, Democratization, and International Assistance.* Boulder, CO: Lynne Rienner.

Kuperman, A. J. (2001). *The Limits of Humanitarian Intervention: Genocide in Rwanda.* Washington, DC: Brookings Institution.

Lambeth, B. S. (1992). *Desert Storm and Its Meaning: The View from Moscow.* Santa Monica, CA: RAND.

Lauterpacht, E., et al. (eds.) (1991). *The Kuwait Crisis—Basic Documents.* Cambridge: Grotius.

Lee, J. M., von Pagenhardt, R., and Stanley, T. W. (1992). *To Unite Our Strength: Enhancing the United Nations Peace and Security System.* Lanham, MD: University Press of America.

Legault, A., Murphy, C. N., and Ofuatey-Kodjoe, W. B. (1992). *The State of the United Nations, 1992.* Providence, RI: Academic Council on the United Nations System.

Livingston, S. (1997). *Clarifying the CNN Effect: An Examination of Media Effects According to Type of Military Intervention*, Joan Shorenstein Center, John F. Kennedy School of Government, Harvard University, Research Paper R-18, June 1997.

Liu, F. T. (1992). *United Nations Peacekeeping and the Non-Use of Force*. Boulder, CO: Lynne Rienner.

Longrigg, S. H. and Stoakes, F. (1958). *Iraq*. London: Ernest Benn Ltd.

Lopez, G. A. 'Toward Smart Sanctions on Iraq'. *Kroc Policy Brief #5*, April 2001, www.nd.edu/~krocinst/polbriefs/pbrief5.html.

Luck, E. C. (1999). *Mixed Messages: American Politics and International Organization, 1919–1999*. Washington, DC: Brookings Institution.

—— (2006) *The Life and Times of the UN Security Council*. London: Routledge.

Lukitz, L. (1995). *Iraq, the Search for National Identity*. London: Frank Cass.

Lynch, M. 'Smart Sanctions: Rebuilding Consensus or Maintaining Conflict?' *MERIP Online*, June 28, 2001, www.merip.org/mero/mero062801.html

MacFarlane, N. S. *Intervention in Contemporary World Politics*, Adelphi Paper 350. London: International Institute for Strategic Studies, 2002.

Mackey, S. (2002). *The Reckoning: Iraq and the Legacy of Saddam Hussein*. New York: Norton.

MacKinnon, M. G. (2000). *The Evolution of U.S. Peacekeeping Policy Under Clinton: A Fairweather Friend?* London: Frank Cass.

Mahbubani, K. (2005). *Beyond the Age of Innocence*. New York: Public Affairs.

Makiya, K. (1993). *Cruelty and Silence: War, Tyranny, Uprising and the Arab World*. New York: W. W. Norton.

Malone, D. M. (1998). *Decision-Making in the Security Council: The Case of Haiti, 1990–1997*. Oxford: Clarendon Press.

—— (2001). 'The Security Council in the 1990s', in: *Proceedings of the 28th Annual Conference of the Canadian Council on International Law*. The Hague and London: Kluwer, p. 42.

—— (ed.) (2004). *The UN Security Council: From the Cold War to the 21st Century*. Boulder, CO: Lynne Rienner.

—— and Khong, Y. F. (eds.) (2003). *Unilateralism and US Foreign Policy: International Perspectives. Boulder, CO: Lynne Rienner.*

Marr, P. (2004). *The Modern History of Iraq*, 2nd edn. Boulder, CO: Westview.

Matar, F. (1981). *Saddam Hussein: The Man, The Cause and the Future*. London: Third World Centre.

Mathews, J. T. (ed.) (2002). *Iraq: A New Approach*. New York: Carnegie Endowment.

Matthews, K. (1993). *The Gulf Conflict and International Relations*. London: Routledge.

Maull, H. W. and Pick, O. (eds.) (1989). *The Gulf War: Regional and International Dimensions*. New York: St. Martin's Press.

Mayall, J. (ed.) (1996). *The New Interventionism, 1991–1994: United Nations Experience in Cambodia, Former Yugoslavia, and Somalia*. New York: Cambridge University Press.

McRae, R. and Hubert, D. (eds.) (2001). *Human Security and the New Diplomacy*. Montreal: McGill-Queen's University Press.

Melville, A. and Lapidus, G. W. (eds.) (1990). *The Glasnost Papers: Voices on Reform from Moscow*. Boulder, CO: Westview.

Meyer, C. (2005). *DC Confidential: The Controversial Memoirs of Britain's Ambassador to the U.S. at the Time of 9/11 and the Iraq War*. London: Weidenfeld & Nicolson.

Miller, J. and Mylroie, L. (1990). *Saddam Hussein and the Crisis in the Gulf.* New York: Times Books.

Mills, N. and Brunner, K. (eds.) (2002). *The New Killing Fields: Massacre and the Politics of Intervention.* New York: Basic Books.

Minear, L. (2002). *The Humanitarian Enterprise: Dilemmas and Discoveries.* Bloomfield, CT: Kumarian.

—— et al. (1992). *United Nations Coordination of the International Humanitarian Response to the Gulf Crisis, 1990–1992,* Occasional Paper No. 13. Providence, RI: Watson Institute.

Mingst, K. and Karns, M. P. (2000). *The United Nations in the Post-Cold War Era,* 2nd edn. Boulder, CO: Westview.

Moore, J. (ed.) (1998). *Hard Choices: Moral Dilemmas in Humanitarian Intervention.* Lanham, MD: Rowman & Littlefield.

Mostyn, T. (1991). *Major Political Events in Iran, Iraq and the Arabian Peninsula 1945–1990.* New York: Facts on File.

Mohamedou, M. -M. (1998). *Iraq and the Second Gulf War: State Building and Regime Security.* San Francisco, CA: Austin & Winfield.

Muldoon, J. P. (ed.) (1999). *Multilateral Diplomacy and the United Nations Today.* Boulder, CO: Westview.

Murphy, S. D. (1996). *Humanitarian Intervention: The United Nations in an Evolving World Order.* Philadelphia, PA: University of Pennsylvania Press.

Musallam, M. A. (1996). *The Iraqi Invasion of Kuwait: Saddam Hussein, His State and International Power Politics.* London: British Academic Press.

Nakash, Y. (1994). *The Shi'is of Iraq.* Princeton, NJ: Princeton University Press.

Nonneman, G. (1986). *Iraq, the Gulf States, & the War: A Changing Relationship 1980–1986 and Beyond.* London: Ithaca.

Nye, J. S., Jr. (2002). *The Paradox of American Power: Why the World's Only Superpower Can't Go It Alone.* Oxford: Oxford University Press.

O'Ballance, E. (1988). *The Gulf War.* London: Brassey's Defence Publishers.

Obeidi, M. and Pitzer, K. (2004). *The Bomb in My Garden: The Secret of Saddam's Nuclear Mastermind.* Hoboken, NJ: John Wiley and Sons.

Ogata, S. N. (2005). *The Turbulent Decade: Confronting the Refugee Crises of the 1990s.* New York: W. W. Norton.

Oil-For-Food Facts. 'Oil-For-Food: FAQ', www.oilforfoodfacts.com/faq.aspx

Olsson, L. (1999). *Gendering UN Peacekeeping: Mainstreaming a Gender Perspective in Multidimensional Peacekeeping.* Uppsala University, Department of Peace and Conflict Research.

Ottaway, M. (2005). 'Iraq: Without Consensus, Democracy Is Not the Answer', *Policy Brief 36,* Carnegie Endowment for International Peace, March 2005.

Otunnu, O. and Doyle, M. (eds.) (1998). *Peacemaking and Peacekeeping for the New Century.* Lanham, MD: Rowman & Littlefield.

Parsons, A. (1994). *The Security Council: An Uncertain Future.* London: David Davies Memorial Institute.

Parsons, A. (1995). *From Cold War to Hot Peace: UN Interventions 1946–1994.* London: Michael Joseph.

Patil, A. V. (2001). *The Veto: A Historical Necessity, 1946–2001: A Comprehensive Record of the Use of the Veto in the UN Security Council.* New York: A. V. Patil.

Patrick, S. and Forman, S. (eds.) (2002). *Multilateralism and U.S. Foreign Policy: Ambivalent Engagement.* Boulder, CO: Lynne Rienner.

Pearson, G. S. (1999). *The UNSCOM Saga: Chemical and Biological Weapons Non-Proliferation.* New York: St. Martin's Press.

Peck, C. (1996). *The United Nations as a Dispute Settlement System: Improving Mechanisms for the Prevention and Resolution of Conflict.* The Hague: Kluwer.

Pelletiere, S. C. (1992). *The Iran-Iraq War: Chaos in a Vacuum.* New York: Praeger.

Pérez de Cuéllar, J. (1997). *Pilgrimage for Peace: A Secretary-General's Memoir.* New York: St. Martin's Press.

Phillips, D. L. (2005). *Losing Iraq: Inside the Postwar Reconstruction Fiasco.* New York: Westview.

Phythian, M. (1997). *Arming Iraq.* Boston: Northeastern University.

Picco, G. (1999). *Man Without a Gun: One Diplomat's Secret Struggle to Free the Hostages, Fight Terrorism, and End a War.* New York: Random House.

Pitt, W. R. (2002). *War on Iraq.* New York: Context Books.

Pollack, K. M. (2002). *Arabs at War: Military Effectiveness, 1948–1991.* Lincoln, NE: University of Nebraska Press.

—— (2002). *The Threatening Storm: The Case for Invading Iraq.* New York: Random House.

Potter, L. G. and Sick, G. (eds.) (2005). *Iran, Iraq, and the Legacies of War.* Basingstoke: Palgrave.

Prins, G. (1996). *The Applicability of the NATO Model to UN Peace Support Operations Under the Security Council.* New York: UNA-USA.

—— (ed.) (2000). *Understanding Unilateralism in American Foreign Relations.* London: Royal Institute for International Affairs.

Proceedings of the 97th Annual Meeting of the American Society of International Law, April 2–5, 2003, American Society of International Law.

Project for the New American Century. 'Welcome to the Project for the New American Century', www.newamericancentury.org.

Pugh, M. (ed.) (1997). *The UN, Peace, and Force.* London: Frank Cass.

Rajaee, F. (ed.) (1993). *The Iran-Iraq War: The Politics of Aggression.* Gainesville, FL: University Press of Florida.

—— (ed.) (1997). *Iranian Perspectives on the Iran-Iraq War.* Gainesville, FL: University Press of Florida.

Ramsbotham, O. and Woodhouse, T. (1999). *Encyclopedia of International Peacekeeping Operations.* Santa Barbara, CA: ABC-CLIO.

'Report of the International Committee of the Red Cross (ICRC) on the Treatment by the Coalition Forces of Prisoners of War and Other Protected Persons by the

Geneva Conventions in Iraq During Arrest, Internment and Interrogation'. International Committee of the Red Cross, February 2004.

Reuters (2003). *Saddam's Iraq: Face-off in the Gulf.* Upper Saddle River, NJ: Prentice Hall.

Rieff, D. (2002). *A Bed for the Night: Humanitarianism in Crisis.* New York: Simon & Schuster.

Righter, R. (1995). *Utopia Lost: The United Nations and World Order.* New York: Twentieth Century Fund.

Rikhye, I. J. (1992). *The United Nations and the Aftermath of the Gulf Crisis.* Toronto: Editions du GREF.

Risen, J. (2006). *State of War: The Secret History of the CIA and the Bush Administration.* New York: Free Press.

Risse, T., Ropp, S. C. and Sikkink, K. (eds.) (1999). *The Power of Human Rights: International Norms and Domestic Change.* New York: Cambridge University Press.

Ritter, S. (1999). *Endgame: Solving the Iraq Problem—Once and for All.* New York: Simon and Schuster.

Rivlin, B. and Gordenker, L. (eds.) (1993). *The Challenging Role of the UN Secretary-General: Making 'the Most Impossible Job in the World' Possible.* Westport, CT: Praeger.

Roberts, A. and Kingsbury, B. (eds.) (1993). *United Nations, Divided World: The UN's Roles in International Relations*, 2nd edn. Oxford: Clarendon.

Rodley, N. S. (ed.) (1992). *To Loose the Bands of Wickedness: International Intervention in Defence of Human Rights.* London: Brassey.

Roper, J., et al. (eds.) (1993). *Keeping the Peace in the Post-Cold War Era: Strengthening Multilateral Peacekeeping: A Report to the Trilateral Commission.* New York: Trilateral Commission.

Ruggie, J. G. (1996). *Winning the Peace: America and World Order in the New Era.* New York: Columbia University Press.

Russett, B. M. (ed.) (1997). *The Once and Future Security Council.* New York: St. Martin's Press.

Saksena, K. P. (1974). *The United Nations and Collective Security, 1945–1964: A Historical Analysis.* Delhi: D. K. Publishing House.

—— (1993). *Reforming the United Nations: The Challenge of Relevance.* Newbury Park, CA: Sage.

Sarooshi, D. (1999). *The United Nations and the Development of Collective Security: The Delegation by the UN Security Council of Its Chapter VII Powers.* Oxford: Clarendon.

Scales, R. H. (1993). *Certain Victory.* Washington, DC: Office of the Chief of Staff, US Army.

Schachter, O. and Joyner, C. C. (eds.) (1995). *United Nations Legal Order*, 2 vols. Cambridge: Cambridge University Press.

Schenker, D. K. (2003). *Dancing with Saddam: The Dangerous Tango of Jordanian-Iraq Relations.* Lanham, MA: Lexington Books.

Schlesinger, S. C. (2003). *Act of Creation: The Founding of the United Nations: A Story of Superpowers, Secret Agents, Wartime Allies and Enemies, and Their Quest for a Peaceful World.* Boulder, CO: Westview Press.

Schwarzkopf, H. N. and Petre, P. (1992). *It Doesn't Take a Hero*. New York: Bantam Books.

Schweigman, D. (2001). *The Authority of the Security Council Under Chapter VII of the UN Charter: Legal Limits and the Role of the International Court of Justice*. Boston: Kluwer.

Sciolino, E. (1991). *The Outlaw State: Saddam Hussein's Quest for Power and the Gulf Crisis*. New York: John Wiley & Sons.

Seiple, C. (1996). *The U.S. Military/NGO Relationship in Humanitarian Interventions*. Carlisle Barracks, PA: U.S. Army College.

Shadid, A. (2005). *Night Draws Near: Iraq's People in the Shadow of America's War*. New York: Henry Holt & Co.

Shlaim, A. (1995). *War and Peace in the Middle East: A Concise History*. London: Penguin Books.

Sifri, M. L. and Cerf, C. (eds.) (1991). *The Gulf War Reader: History, Documents, Opinions*. New York: Times Books.

Simma, B., et al. (eds.) (2002). *The Charter of the United Nations: A Commentary*, 2nd edn., 2 vols. Oxford: Oxford University Press.

SIPRI (1988). *SIPRI Yearbook 1988*. Stockholm: Almquist & Wiksell.

Smolansky, O. M. (1991). *The USSR and Iraq: The Soviet Quest for Influence*. Durham, NC: Duke University Press.

Snow, D. M. (1993). *Peacekeeping, Peacemaking, and Peace-Enforcement: The U.S. Role in the New International Order*. Carlisle Barracks, PA: U.S. Army War College.

Sriram, C. (2005). *Globalising Justice for Mass Atrocities: Revolution in Accountability*. New York: Routledge.

—— and Wermester, K. (eds.) (2003). *From Promise to Practice: Strengthening UN Capacities for the Prevention of Violent Conflict*. Boulder, CO: Lynne Rienner.

Suleiman, E. (2003). *Dismantling Democratic States*. Princeton, NJ: Princeton University Press.

Sutterlin, J. S. (1995). *The United Nations and the Maintenance of International Security: A Challenge to Be Met*. Westport, CT: Praeger.

Tahir-Kheli, S. and Ayubi, S. (eds.) (1983). *The Iran-Iraq War: New Weapons, Old Conflicts*. New York: Praeger.

Tarock, A. (1998). *The Superpowers' Involvement in the Iran-Iraq War*. Commack, NY: Nova Science Publishers.

Taylor, P., Daws, S. and Adamczick-Gerteis, U. (eds.) (1997). *Documents on Reform of the United Nations*. Aldershot: Dartmouth.

Teixeira da Silva, P. (2002). *Le Conseil de Sécurité à l'aube du XXIème siècle*. Geneva: UNIDIR.

Teng, C. G. (ed.) (1968). *Synopses of United Nations Cases in the Field of Peace and Security, 1946–1967*. New York: CEIP.

Tesón, F. R. (1997). *Humanitarian Intervention: An Inquiry into Law and Morality*, 2nd edn. Irvington-On-Hudson, NY: Transnational.

Thakur, R. and Schnabel, A. (eds.) (2001). *United Nations Peacekeeping Operations: Ad Hoc Missions, Permanent Engagement*. Tokyo: United Nations University Press.

Thakur, R. and Sidhu, W. P. S. (eds.) (forthcoming). *The Iraq Crisis and World Order: Structural, Institutional and Normative Challenges*. Tokyo: United Nations University Press.

—— and and Thayer, C. A. (eds.) (1995). *A Crisis of Expectations: UN Peacekeeping in the 1990s*. Boulder, CO: Westview.

Thatcher, M. (1993). *The Downing Street Years*. New York: HarperCollins.

Traub, J. (2006). *The UN in the Era of Kofi Annan*. New York: Farra Straus and Giroux (forthcoming).

Trevan, T. (1999). *Saddam's Secrets: The Hunt for Iraq's Hidden Weapons*. London: HarperCollins.

Tripp, C. (2002). *A History of Iraq*, 2nd edn. Cambridge: Cambridge University Press.

UNICEF (2001). *The State of the World's Children*. New York: UNICEF.

United Nations. 'Iran-Iraq—UNIIMOG Background', www.un.org/Depts/dpko/dpko/co_mission/uniimogbackgr.html.

Urquhart, B. (1987). *A Life in Peace and War*. New York: Harper & Row.

United States Institute of Peace (2005). *American Interests and UN Reform: Report of the Task Force on the United Nations*. Washington, DC: USIP.

van Genugten, W. J. M. and de Groot, G. A. (eds.) (1999). *United Nations Sanctions: Effectiveness and Effects, Especially in the Field of Human Rights: A Multi-Disciplinary Approach*. Antwerp: Intersentia.

Védrine, H. (2001). *France in an Age of Globalization*, Philip H. Gordon, trans. Washington, DC: Brookings Institution Press.

Vernet, H. and Cantaloube, T. (2004). *Chirac contre Bush: l'autre guerre*. Paris: JC Lattès.

Wallensteen, P. (2002). *Understanding Conflict Resolution: War, Peace, and the Global System*. London: Sage.

Wallensteen, P., Staibono, C. and Eriksson, M. (eds.) (2003). *Making Targeted Sanctions Effective: Guidelines for the Implementation of UN Policy Options: Results from the Stockholm Process on the Implementation of Targeted Sanctions*. Uppsala: Uppsala University Department of Peace and Conflict Research.

Weiss, T. G. (ed.) (1998). *Beyond UN Subcontracting: Task-Sharing with Regional Security Arrangements and Service-Providing NGOs*. London: Macmillan.

—— (1999). *Military-Civilian Interactions: Intervening in Humanitarian Crises*. Oxford: Rowman & Littlefield.

—— Forsythe, D. P. and Coate, R. A. (1994). *The United Nations and Changing World Politics*. Boulder, CO: Westview.

—— and Hubert, D. (2001). *The Responsibility to Protect: Research, Bibliography, and Background*, Supplementary volume of the International Commission on Intervention and State Sovereignty. Ottawa: International Development Research Center, www.iciss-ciise.gc.ca

Wheeler, N. J. (2000). *Saving Strangers: Humanitarian Intervention in International Society*. Oxford, Oxford University Press.

White, N. D. (1997). *Keeping the Peace: The United Nations and the Maintenance of International Peace and Security*, 2nd edn. Manchester: Manchester University Press.

Wilkinson, M. J. and O'Sullivan, C. D. 'The UN Security Council and Iraq: Why it Succeeded in 1990, Why it Didn't in 2003, and Why the United States Should Redeem it', AmericanDiplomacy.org, February 6, 2004, www.unc.edu/depts /diplomat/archives_roll/2004_01-03/wilkinosull_unsec/wilkinosull_unsec.html.

Williamson, R. (2001). *Seeking Firm Footing: America in the New Century.* Chicago: Prairie Institute.

Wolfrum, R. (1995). *United Nations: Law, Policies, and Practice.* Dordrecht: Martinus Nijhoff.

Wood, A., Apthorpe, R., and Borton, J. (eds.) (2001). *Evaluating International Humanitarian Action: Reflection from Practitioners.* London: Zed Books.

Woodward, B. (2004). *Plan of Attack.* New York: Simon & Schuster.

Zacarias, A. (1996). *The United Nations and International Peacekeeping.* London: I. B. Tauris.

Zieck, M. (1997). *UNHCR and Voluntary Repatriation of Refugees: A Legal Analysis.* The Hague: Martinus Nijhoff.

SCHOLARLY ARTICLES

Alston, P. (2005). 'The Darfur Commission as a Model for Future Responses to Crisis Situations', *Journal of International Criminal Justice*, 3(3): 600–7.

Berdal, M. (2004). 'The UN After Iraq', *Survival*, 46(3): 83–101.

Bisharat, G. E. (2001). 'Sanctions as Genocide', *Transnational Law & Contemporary Problems*, 11(2): 379–426.

Bluth, C. (2004). 'The British Road to War: Blair, Bush and the Decision to Invade Iraq', *International Affairs*, 80(5): 871–92.

Boileau, A. E. (1997). 'To The Suburbs of Baghdad: Clinton's Extension of the Southern Iraqi No-Fly Zone', *ILSA Journal of International and Comparative Law*, 3: 875.

Boulden, J. and Weiss, T. G. (2004). 'Tactical Multilateralism: Coaxing America Back to the UN', *Survival*, 46(3): 103–14.

Brzezinski, Z., Scowcroft, B. and Murphy, R. (1997). 'Differentiated Containment', *Foreign Affairs*, 76(3): 20–30.

Byers, M. (2002). 'The Shifting Foundations of International Law: A Decade of Forceful Measures Against Iraq', *European Journal of International Law*, 13(1): 21–41.

Byman, D. and Waxman, M. (2000). 'Kosovo and the Great Air Power Debate', *International Security*, 24(4): 5–38.

Caron, D. D. (1993). 'The Legitimacy of the Collective Authority of the Security Council', *American Journal of International Law*, 87(4): 552–88.

—— and Morris, B. (2002). 'The UN Compensation Commission: Practical Justice, Not Retribution', *European Journal of International Law*, 13(1): 183–99.

Carver, N. (2002). 'Is Iraq/Kurdistan a State Such that it Can Be Said to Operate State Systems and Thereby Offer Protection to Its "Citizens"?', *International Journal of Refugee Law*, 14(1): 57–84.

Cockayne, J. (2002). 'Islam and International Humanitarian Law: From a Clash to a Conversation Between Civilizations', *International Review of the Red Cross*, 847: 597–626.

Cortright, D. and Lopez, G. A. (1999). 'Are Sanctions Just? The Problematic Case of Iraq', *Journal of International Affairs*, 52(2): 735–56.

Craven, M. (2002). 'Humanitarianism and the Quest for Smarter Sanctions', *European Journal of International Law*, 13(1): 43–61.

Dalgaard-Nielsen, A. (2003). 'Gulf War: The German Resistance', *Survival*, 45(1): 99–116.

D'Amato, A. (1996). 'Israel's Air Strike Against the Osiraq Reactor: A Retrospective', *Temple International and Comparative Law Journal*, 10(1): 259–64.

de Jonge Oudraat, C. (2002). 'UNSCOM: Between Iraq and a Hard Place', *European Journal of International Law*, 13(1): 139–52.

Donaher, W. F. and DeBlois, R. B. (2001). 'Is the Current UN and US Policy Toward Iraq Effective?', *Parameters*, 31(4): 112–25.

Dosman, E. A. (2004). 'For the Record: Designating "Listed Entities" for the Purposes of Terrorist Financing Offences at Canadian Law', *University of Toronto Faculty of Law Review*, 62(1): 1.

Eitel, T. (2000). 'The UN Security Council and Its Future Contribution in the Field of International Law', *Max Planck Yearbook of United Nations Law*, 4: 5.

Farer, T. (2005). 'The UN Reports: Addressing the Gnarled Issues of Our Time', *International Spectator*, 40(2): 7–17.

Fassbender, B. (2002). 'Uncertain Steps Into a Post-Cold War World: The Role and Functioning of the UN Security Council After a Decade of Measures Against Iraq', *European Journal of International Law*, 13(1): 273–303.

Fine, J. (2003). 'The Iraq Sanctions Catastrophe', *Middle East Report*, 174: 36, 39.

Franck, T. (2003). 'What Happens Now? The United Nations After Iraq', *American Journal of International Law*, 97(3): 607–20.

Freedman, L. (2004). 'War in Iraq: Selling the Threat', *Survival*, 46(2): 7–49.

Freeman, C. W., Jr. (1989). 'The Angola-Namibia Accords', *Foreign Affairs*, 68(3): 126–41.

Gaddis, J. L. (2005). 'Grand Strategy in the Second Term', *Foreign Affairs*, 84(1): 2–15.

Gattini, A. (2002). 'The UN Compensation Commission: Old Rules, New Procedures on War Reparations', *European Journal of International Law*, 13(1): 161–81.

Garfield, R. (2001). 'Health and Well-Being in Iraq: Sanctions and the Impact of the Oil-for-Food Program', *Transnational Law & Contemporary Problems*, 11(2): 277–98.

Gause, F. G., III, (1999). 'Getting It backward on Iraq', *Foreign Affairs*, 78(3): 54.

Glennon, M. (2005). 'How International Rules Die', *Georgetown Law Journal*, 93(3): 939–92.

—— (2003). 'Why the Security Council Failed', *Foreign Affairs*, 82(3): 16–35.

Gordon, J. (2002). 'When Intent Makes All the Difference in the World: Economic Sanctions on Iraq and the Accusation of Genocide', *Yale Human Rights and Development Law Journal*, 5: 57–84.

Gordon, P. H. (2003). 'Bush's Middle East Vision', *Survival*, 45(1): 155–65.

Gordon, R. (1994). 'United Nations Intervention in Internal Conflicts: Iraq, Somalia and Beyond', *Michigan Journal of International Law*, 15: 519.

Grant, T. D. (2003). 'The Security Council and Iraq: An Incremental Practice', *American Journal of International Law*, 97(4): 823–42.

Greenwood, C. (2000). 'International Law and the NATO Intervention in Kosovo, Memorandum Submitted to the Foreign Affairs Committee of the House of Commons', reprinted in *International & Comparative Law Quarterly*, 49(4): 926–34.

Haass, R. (2005). 'Regime Change and Its Limits', *Foreign Affairs*, 84(4): 66–78.

Hurrell, A. (2004). 'America and the World: Issues in the Teaching of U.S. Foreign Policy', *Perspectives on Politics*, 2(1): 101–11.

—— (2005). 'Pax Americana or the empire of insecurity?', *International Relations of the Asia-Pacific*, 5(2): 153–76.

Joyner, C. C. (2003). 'United Nations Sanctions After Iraq: Looking Back to See Ahead', *Chicago Journal of International Law*, 4(2): 329–54.

Lafeber, W. (2002). 'The Bush Doctrine', *Diplomatic History*, 26(4): 543–58.

Lim, C. L. (2000). 'On the Law, Procedures and Politics of United Nations Gulf War Reparations', *Singapore Journal of International and Comparative Law*, 4(2): 435–78.

Lopez, G. A. and Cortright, D. (2004). 'Containing Iraq: Sanctions Worked', *Foreign Affairs*, 83(4): 90–103.

Luttwak, E. N. (2005). 'Iraq: The Logic of Disengagement', *Foreign Affairs*, 84(1): 26–36.

Lynch, M. (2003). 'Beyond the Arab Street: Iraq and the Arab Public Sphere', *Politics & Society*, 31(1): 55–91.

Malone, D. M. (1997). 'The UN Security Council in the Post-Cold War World: 1987–97', *Security Dialogue*, 28(4): 393–408.

—— (1999). 'Goodbye UNSCOM: A Sad Tale in US-UN Relations', *Global Governance*, 30(4): 393–411.

—— (2005). 'The High-Level Panel and the Security Council', *Security Dialogue*, 36(3): 370–2.

Marr, P. (2005). 'Occupational Hazards: Washington's Record in Iraq', *Foreign Affairs*, 84(4): 180–6.

Mayall, J. (1991). 'Non-Intervention, Self-Determination and the "New World Order" ', *International Affairs*, 67(3): 421–9.

McIlmail, T. P. (1994). 'No-Fly Zones: The Imposition and Enforcement of Air Exclusion Regimes Over Bosnia and Iraq', *Loyola of Los Angeles International and Comparative Law Review*, 17: 35.

Mearsheimer, J. J. and Walt, S. (2003). 'An unnecessary war', *Foreign Policy*, 134: 50–9.

Meek, P. A., Col., (1994). 'Operation Provide Comfort: A Case Study in Humanitarian Relief and Foreign Assistance', *Air Force Law Review*, 37: 225–38.

Oette, L. (2002). 'A Decade of Sanctions Against Iraq: Never Again! The End of Unlimited Sanctions in the Recent Practice of the UN Security Council', *European Journal of International Law*, 13(1): 93–103.

Pollack, K. (2002). 'Next Stop Baghdad?' *Foreign Affairs*, 81(2): 32–47.

Prantl, J. (2005). 'Informal Groups of States and the UN Security Council,' *International Organization*, 59(3): 559–92.

Rice, C. (2000). 'Campaign 2000: Promoting the National Interest', *Foreign Affairs*, 79(1): 45–62.

Ruiz Fabri, H. (2002). 'The UNSCOM Experience: Lessons from an Experiment', *European Journal of International Law*, 13(1): 153–9.

Saikal, A. (1999). 'Iraq, UNSCOM and the US: A UN Debacle?' *Australian Journal of International Affairs*, 53(3): 283–94.

Scheffer, D. (2003). 'Beyond Occupation Law', *American Journal of International Law*, 97(4): 842–60.

—— (2005). 'Article 98(2) of the Rome Statute: America's Original Intent', *Journal of International Criminal Justice*, 3(2): 333–53.

Schorr, D. (1991). 'Ten Days That Shook the White House', *Columbia Journalism Review*, 30(4): 21–3.

Shehabaldin, A. and Laughlin, W. M. (1999). 'Economic Sanctions against Iraq: Human and Economic Costs', *International Journal of Human Rights*, 3(4): 1–18.

Sick, G. (1998). 'Rethinking Dual Containment', *Survival*, 40(1): 5–32.

Sieminski, G. C. (1995). 'The Art of Naming Operation', *Parameters*, 25(3): 81–98.

Silliman, S. L. (2002). 'The Iraqi Quagmire: Enforcing the No-Fly Zones', *New England Law Review*, 36(4): 767–73.

Sponeck, H. C. G. (2002). 'Sanctions and Humanitarian Exemptions: A Practitioner's Commentary', *European Journal of International Law*, 13(1): 81–7.

Stopford, M. (1993). 'Humanitarian Assistance in the Wake of the Persian Gulf War', *Virginia Journal of International Law*, 33: 491–502.

Surchin, A. D. (1995). 'Terror and the Law: The Unilateral Use of Force and the June 1993 Bombing of Baghdad', *Duke Journal of Comparative & International Law*, 5: 457–98.

Symes, G. A. (1998). 'Force Without Law: Seeking A Legal Justification for the September 1996 U.S. Military Intervention in Iraq', *Michigan Journal of International Law*, 19: 581–622.

Szasz, P. C. (2002). 'The Security Council Starts Legislating', *American Journal of International Law*, 96: 901–4.

Thakur, R. (2002). 'Intervention, Sovereignty and the Responsibility to Protect: Experiences from ICISS', *Security Dialogue*, 33(3): 323–40.

Traub, J. (2005). 'Off target', *The New Republic*, 232(6): 14–17.

Yoshihira, T. and Sokolski, R. (2002). 'The United States and China in the Persian Gulf: Challenges and Opportunities', *Fletcher Forum of World Affairs*, 26(1): 63–77.

NEWS MEDIA

Atlantic Monthly

Fallows, J. (2004). 'Blind into Baghdad', *Atlantic Monthly*, 293(1): 74.

Mylroie, L. (1992). 'Kurdistan: After Saddam Hussein', *Atlantic Monthly*, 270(6): 36, 38, 49, 52.

Pollack, K. (2004). 'Spies, Lies, and Weapons: What Went Wrong', *Atlantic Monthly*, 293(1): 79–92.

Secor, L. (2004). 'The Pragmatist', *Atlantic Monthly*, 294(1): 44–8.

The Economist

'A European Superpower', *The Economist*, November 13, 2004, 58.

'A gentle glow: How much credit should President Bush get for recent changes in the Middle East?', *The Economist*, March 12, 2005, 32–3.

'Alistair Cook', *The Economist*, April 3, 2004, 89.

'A Nasty Smell', *The Economist*, August 13, 2005, 26–7.

Annan, K. A., 'Courage to Fulfil our Responsibilities', *The Economist*, December 4, 2004, 23–5.

'Blaming Annan: Calls for the secretary-general to resign over the oil-for-food scandal are premature', *The Economist*, December 11, 2004, 11.

'The damage Iraq has done him', *The Economist*, October 2, 2004, 55.

'Fumbling the Moment', *The Economist*, May 29, 2004, 21–4.

Greenstock, J., 'What must be done now', *The Economist*, May 8, 2004, 24–6.

Haass, R., 'The World on His Desk', *The Economist*, November 6, 2004, 36–7.

'Something Stirs', *The Economist*, March 5, 2005, 24–6.

'Torturing the United Nations', *The Economist*, April 2, 2005, 12–13.

New York Review of Books

Danner, M., 'Iraq: The Real Election', *New York Review of Books* 52(7), April 28, 2005, 41–4.

—— 'The Secret Way to War', *New York Review of Books* 52(10), June 9, 2005.

—— 'Torture and Truth', *New York Review of Books* 51(10), June 10, 2004.

Galbraith, P. W., 'How to Get Out of Iraq', *New York Review of Books* 51(8), May 13, 2004.

—— 'Iraq: The Bungled Transition', *New York Review of Books* 51(14), September 23, 2004.

—— 'Iraq: Bush's Islamic Republic', *New York Review of Books* 52(13), August 11, 2005.
Judt, T., 'The New World Order', *New York Review of Books* 52(12), July 14, 2005.
Lewis, A., 'Bush and the Lesser Evil', *New York Review of Books* 51(9), May 27, 2004.
Massing, M., 'Iraq, the Press & the Election', *New York Review of Books* 51(20), December 16, 2004.
—— 'Unfit to Print?', *New York Review of Books* 51(11), June 24, 2004.
Powers, T., 'How Bush Got it Wrong', *New York Review of Books* 51(14), September 23, 2004.
—— 'The Failure', *New York Review of Books* 51(7), April 29, 2004.
Urquhart, B., 'A Cautionary Tale', *New York Review of Books* 51(10), June 10, 2004.
—— 'How not to Fight a Dictator', *The New York Review of Books* 46(8), May 6, 1999, 25–9.

New York Times Book Review

Foer, F., 'Once Again America First', *New York Times Book Review*, October 10, 2004, 22.
Gerecht, R. M., 'Now What?', *New York Times Book Review*, July 10, 2005, 8.

New York Times Magazine

Ignatieff, M., 'The Uncommitted', *New York Times Magazine*, January 30, 2005, 15.
—— 'Why are we in Iraq? (And Liberia? And Afghanistan?)', *New York Times Magazine*, September 7, 2003, 28.
Rieff, D., 'Blueprint For A Mess', *New York Times Magazine*, November 2, 2003, 28.
Traub, J., 'Kofi Annan's Next Test', *New York Times Magazine*, March 29, 1998, 44.
—— 'Who needs the UN Security Council?', *New York Times Magazine*, November 17, 2002, 47.

New Yorker

Anderson, J. L., 'A Man of the Shadows', *New Yorker*, January 24/31, 2005.
Gourevitch, P., 'Power Plays', *New Yorker* 80/39, December 13, 2004.
Hersh, S. M., 'Chain of Command', *New Yorker* 80/12, May 17, 2004.
—— 'Saddam's Best Friend', *New Yorker* 75/6, April 5, 1999, 32–41.
—— 'The Spoils of the Gulf War', *New Yorker*, September 6, 1993, 70–81.
—— 'Torture at Abu Ghraib', *New Yorker* 80/11, May 10, 2004.
—— 'Get Out the Vote', *New Yorker*, July 25, 2005, 52–7.
Hertzberg, H., 'Landmarks', *New Yorker*, February, 14/21 2005.
Mayer, J., 'Outsourcing Torture', *New Yorker*, February 14, 2005.
—— 'The Manipulator', *New Yorker* 80/15, June 7, 2004.
McGrath, B., 'Just Whistle; the Diplomats', *New Yorker* 80/40–1, December 20/27, 2004.
Remnick, D., 'The Masochism Campaign', *New Yorker* 81/11, May 2, 2005.

Newsweek

Barry, J., et al., 'The Roots of Torture', *Newsweek*, May 24, 2004, 26–34.

Glain, S., 'Yet Another Great Game: Beijing's aggressive petrodiplomacy in Africa has put it on a collision course with Washington', *Newsweek*, December 20, 2004, 24.

Hirsh, M., 'The Hyde Factor', *Newsweek Online*, June 1, 2005.

McGuire, S., 'Tony's Second Chance: The Crisis in Sudan gives Britain's Prime Minister a Shot at Redemption', *Newsweek*, August 9, 2004, 22.

Moravcsik, A., 'How the World Sees It', *Newsweek Online*, November 15, 2004.

Zakaria, F., 'We had good Intel—The UN's', *Newsweek*, February 9, 2004, 39.

—— 'Why Kerry is Right on Iraq', *Newsweek*, August 23, 2004, 35.

OTHER

Agence France-Presse, Al Hayat, Al-Jazeera, Arms Control Today, Associated Press, The Australian, BBC News, The Boston Globe, CBS (*60 Minutes*), *Christian Science Monitor, CNN.com, The Daily Star* (Beirut), *Financial Times* (and *FT.com*), *Financial Times Weekend, The Globe and Mail, The Guardian* (UK), *Hindustan Times, The Independent* (UK), *International Herald Tribune, Japan Times, Jeune Afrique l'Intelligent, Knight Ridder/Tribune News Service, Le Monde, Le Monde Diplomatique, Los Angeles Times, Melbourne Age, Middle East Report, The Nation (Islamabad), National Journal* (US), NBC (*News* and *Today*), *The New Republic, The New York Sun, The New York Times* (and *New York Times Online*), *The Observer* (UK), *Reuters, Seattle Post-Intelligencer, Slate, Sunday Gazette-Mail* (Charleston), *Sydney Morning Herald, Talk, Time, he Daily Telegraph* (and *Sunday Telegraph*), *The Times* (UK), *UN News Service, US Newswire, USA Today, USIA Wireless File, Vanity Fair, Voice of America* Press Releases and Documents, *Wall Street Journal, Wall Street Journal Europe, The Washington Post, The Washington Times, Xinhua News Agency.*

OFFICIAL AND RELATED GOVERNMENT DOCUMENTS

Aust, A. (Legal Counsellor, FCO) (1992). Statement before HC Foreign Affairs Committee, 2 December 1992, Parliamentary Papers, 1992–1993, HC, Paper 235-iii, 85. (Reprinted in) *British Yearbook of International Law* 53: 827.

'A Decade of Deception and Defiance', White House Office of the Press Secretary, September 12, 2002, www.whitehouse.gov/news/releases/2002/09/20020912. html

Albright, M. K. 'A Humanitarian Exception to the Iraqi Sanctions', US Department of State Dispatch 6/17, April 24, 1995.

—— 'Preserving Principle and Safeguarding Stability: United States Policy Toward Iraq', March 26, 1997, http://secretary.state.gov/www/statements/970326.html

Article 15–6 Investigation of the 800th Military Police Brigade (The Taguba Report), May 5, 2004, www.publicintegrity.org/docs/AbuGhraib/Taguba_Report.pdf

Bush, G. H. W. (1990–1993). 'Remarks on Assistance for Iraqi Refugees and a News Conference', April 16, 1991, in *Public Papers of the Presidents of the United States: George Bush*, 4 vols. Washington, DC: US Govt Printing Office.

—— (1990–1993). 'Remarks to the American Association for the Advancement of Science', February 15, 1991, in *Public Papers of the Presidents of the United States: George Bush*, 4 vols. Washington, DC: US Govt Printing Office.

—— 'Address Before the 45th Session of the United Nations General Assembly in New York, New York', October 1, 1990, http://bushlibrary.tamu.edu/research/papers/1990/90100100.html.

Clinton, W. 'Statement on Iraq', November 14, 1997, www.fas.org/news/iraq/1997/11/97111407_tpo.html.

—— Text of President Clinton's address to Joint Chiefs of Staff and Pentagon staff, February 17, 1998, www.cnn.com/ALLPOLITICS/1998/02/17/transcripts/clinton.iraq.

Commission on Presidential Debates. '2000 Debate Transcript: The Second Gore-Bush Presidential Debate', October 11, 2000, www.debates.org/pages/trans2000b.html.

Commission on the Intelligence Capabilities of the United States regarding Weapons of Mass Destruction. Report to the President of the United States, March 31, 2005, www.wmd.gov/report/index.html.

Defense Contract Audit Agency and the Defense Contract Management Agency. Report on the Pricing Evaluation of Contracts Awarded under the Iraq Oil for Food Program (Washington, DC: September 12, 2003).

Defense Department news briefing, April 11, 2003, www.defenselink.mil/transcripts/2003/tr20030411-secdef0090.html.

Defense Department news briefing, August 21, 2003, www.defenselink.mil/transcripts/2003/tr20030821-secdef0604.html.

Deputy Secretary of Defense Paul Wolfowitz testimony before the Senate Foreign Relations Committee, May 22, 2003, www.defenselink.mil/speeches/2003/sp20030522-depsecdef0223.html.

Deputy Secretary of Defense Paul Wolfowitz testimony before the Senate Foreign Relations Committee, July 29, 2003, www.defenselink.mil/speeches/2003/sp20030729-depsecdef0385.html.

Deputy Secretary Wolfowitz interview with Sam Tannenhaus, *Vanity Fair*, May 9, 2003, www.defenselink.mil/transcripts/2003/tr20030509-depsecdef0223.html.

'Douglas Hurd: Parliamentary Papers 1992–93' (1992). *British Yearbook of International Law* 53: 824.

Duelfer, C. Comprehensive Report of the Special Advisor to the DCI on Iraq's WMD (Washington, DC: Central Intelligence Agency, September 30, 2004), www.cia.gov/cia/reports/iraq_wmd_2004.

Final Report to Congress. Conduct of the Persian Gulf War (Washington, DC: Department of Defense, 1992), www.globalsecurity.org/military/library/report/1992/cpgw.pdf.

'Iraq Liberation Act of 1998', H.R. 4655, October 31, 1998.

Iraq's Transitional Law, (Document GAO-04-746R), May 25, 2004.

Iraq's weapons of mass destruction: the assessment of the British government (London: The Stationery Office, September 24, 2002), www.fco.gov.uk/Files/kfile/iraqdossier.pdf.

Kucinich, D. 'Our Troops Are Stationed in the Wrong Gulf', Address to the US Congress, HCR 7625, September 2, 2005, www.kucinich.us/floor_speeches/iq_wrong_gulf2sep.php.

'Letter to Congressional Leaders reporting on Iraq's Compliance with UN SCRs', Weekly Compilation of Presidential Documents 29 (January 19, 1993).

Lt. Gen. (Ret.) Jay Garner testimony before the House Committee on Government Reform, Subcommittee on National Security, May 13, 2003.

National Commission on Terrorist Attacks upon the United States (2004). The 9/11 Commission report: final report of the National Commission on Terrorist Attacks upon the United States. New York: Norton.

Operation Provide Comfort After Action Report (U), Headquarters United States European Command/ECJ3, January 29, 1992.

Persian Gulf Crisis: Humanitarian Relief Provided to Evacuees from Kuwait and Iraq, (Document GAO/NSIAD-91-160), March 12, 1991.

'President Addresses United Nations High-Level Plenary Meeting', White House Office of the Press Secretary, September 14, 2005, www.whitehouse.gov/news/releases/2005/09/20050914.html.

'President Bush Delivers Graduation Speech at West Point', White House Office of the Press Secretary, June 1, 2002, www.whitehouse.gov/news/releases/2002/06/20020601-3.html.

'President Bush Outlines Iraqi Threat', White House Office of the Press Secretary, October 7, 2002, www.whitehouse.gov/news/releases/2002/10/20021007-8.html.

'President Congratulates Iraqis on Election', White House Office of the Press Secretary, January 30, 2005, www.whitehouse.gov/news/releases/2005/01/20050130-2.html.

'President Discusses War on Terror', White House Office of the Press Secretary, March 8, 2005, www.whitehouse.gov/news/releases/2005/03/20050308-3.html.

'President Delivers State of the Union Address', White House Office of the Press Secretary, January 29, 2002, www.whitehouse.gov/news/releases/2002/01/20020129-11.html.

'President Says Saddam Hussein Must Leave Iraq Within 48 Hours', White House Office of the Press Secretary, March 17, 2003, www.whitehouse.gov/news/releases/2003/03/iraq/20030317-7.html.

'President sworn in to Second Term', White House Office of the Press Secretary, January 20, 2005, www.whitehouse.gov/news/releases/2005/01/20050120-1.html.

'The President's News Conference', Weekly Compilation of Presidential Documents 27 (April 16, 1991).

'President's Remarks on Intelligence Reform', White House Office of the Press Secretary, August 2, 2004, www.whitehouse.gov/news/releases/2004/08/20040802-2.html.

Proliferation: Threat and Response, Office of the Secretary of Defense, January 10, 2001, www.defenselink.mil/pubs/ptr20010110.pdf.

'Report on the US Intelligence Community's Prewar Intelligence Assessments on Iraq', Senate Select Committee on Intelligence, July 7, 2004.

Ruggie, J. G. 'Hearing on The United Nations Oil-for-Food Program: Issues of Accountability and Transparency', United States House of Representatives Committee on International Relations, April 28, 2004.

Statement by Ambassador Patrick F. Kennedy, United States Representative for UN Management and Reform on the UN Oil-For-Food Program, before the House Committee on Government Reform Subcommittee on National Security, Emerging Threats, and International Relations (April 21, 2004).

Statement for the Record of Ambassador John Negroponte, Permanent Representative US Mission to the UN, Before the Committee on Foreign Relations, United States Senate, on Oil-for-Food Program, Second Session, 108th Congress (April 7, 2004).

Statement of Edward C. Luck to the Subcommittee on National Security, Emerging Threats and International Relations Committee on Government Reform of the United States House of Representatives (April 21, 2004).

Statement of Joseph A. Christoff before the Committee on Foreign Relations, (Document GAO-04-651T), April 7, 2004, 6–8.

Statement of Joseph A. Christoff before the Committee on Foreign Relations, (Document GAO-04-953T), July 8, 2004, 11–12.

Transcript of Press Conference given by Prime Minister John Major in Luxembourg (April 8, 1991) (1993). (Reprinted in M. Weller, ed.), *Iraq and Kuwait: The Hostilities and their Aftermath*. Cambridge: Grotius Publications.

United Kingdom, Attorney General, 'Iraq: Resolution 1441', March 7, 2003, www.number-10.gov.uk/files/pdf/Iraq%20Resolution%201441.pdf.

United Kingdom, Review of Intelligence on Weapons of Mass Destruction: Implementation of Its Conclusions (London: The Stationery Office, 14 July 2004).

United States Congress, Authorization for the Use of Military Force Against Iraq, Public Law 107-243, 116 Stat. 1498, H. J. Res. 114, October 16, 2002.

United States Department of National Defense, National Defense Strategy of the United States of America (March 18, 2005), www.defenselink.mil/news/Mar2005/d20050318nds1.pdf.

United States Department of State, 'Daily Press Briefing', April 19, 1999.

United States Department of State, 'Iraq: U.S./U.K./Spain Draft Resolution', February 24, 2003, www.state.gov/p/io/rls/othr/17937.htm.

United States, President of the United States (2002). The National Security Strategy of the United States of America, Washington, DC: The White House.

'U.S. Secretary of State Colin Powell Addresses the U.N. Security Council', White House Office of the Press Secretary, February 5, 2003, www.whitehouse.gov/news/releases/2003/02/20030205-1.html.

'Vice President Honors Veterans of Korean War', White House Office of the Press Secretary, August 29, 2002, www.whitehouse.gov/news/releases/2002/08/20020829-5.html.

Weapons Of Mass Destruction: U.N. Confronts Significant Challenges in Implementing Sanctions against Iraq (Document GAO-02-625), May 17, 2002.

William J. Perry and Gen. Joseph Ralston, News Briefing and Question and Answer Session, September 3, 1996, www.defenselink.mil/speeches/1996/r19960903-ralston.html.

OFFICIAL AND RELATED UN DOCUMENTS

2005 World Summit Outcome: draft resolution referred to the High-level Plenary Meeting of the General Assembly by the General Assembly at its 59th session (UN General Assembly Document A/60/L.1), September 15, 2005.

Adverse consequences of economic sanctions on the enjoyment of human rights, (UN Document E/CN.4/Sub.2/RES/1997/35), August 28, 1997.

An Agenda for Peace, Preventive diplomacy, peacemaking and peace-keeping (UN Doc. A/47/277 -S/24111), June 17, 1992.

Arab Human Development Report 2003. New York: United Nations Development Programme, www.undp.org/rbas/ahdr/english2003.html.

El Baradei, M. 'The Status of Nuclear Inspections in Iraq: An Update', March 7, 2003, www.iaea.org/NewsCenter/Statements/2003/ebsp2003n006.shtml.

Further report of the Secretary-General on the implementation of Security Council resolution 598 (1987), (UN Secretariat Document S/23273), December 9, 1991.

General Assembly official records, 57th session: 2nd plenary meeting (UN General Assembly Document A/57/PV.2), September 12, 2002.

General Assembly official records, 57th session: 3rd plenary meeting (UN General Assembly Document A/57/PV.3), September 12, 2002.

General Assembly official records, 58th session: 7th plenary meeting (UN General Assembly Document A/58/PV.7), September 23, 2003.

General Assembly official records, 59th session: 4th plenary meeting (UN General Assembly Document A/59/PV.4), September 21, 2004.

'Goal In Iraq Is Early End To Occupation, Formation Of Representative Government, Secretary-General Tells Security Council' (UN Press Release SC/7821), July 23, 2003.

'Guidelines for The Application of Paragraphs 19 and 23 of Resolution 1483 (2003)', www.un.org/Docs/sc/committees/1518/1483guide.pdf.

Identical letters dated 2000/08/21 from the Secretary-General to the President of the General Assembly and the President of the Security Council [Report of the Panel on United Nations Peace Operations] [Brahimi Report] (UN

General Assembly-Security Council Document A/55/305-S/2000/809), August 21, 2000.

Independent Inquiry Committee into the United Nations Oil-for-Food Programme, Briefing Paper (October 21, 2004), www.iic-offp.org/documents/Briefing%20Paper21October04.pdf.

Independent Inquiry Committee into the United Nations Oil-for-Food Programme, Briefing Paper (January 9, 2005), www.iic-offp.org/documents/IAD%20Briefing%20Paper.pdf.

Independent Inquiry Committee into the United Nations Oil-for-Food Programme, 'Hussein Received Billions of Dollars More In Illicit Money Through Illegal Trades Than The Oil-For-Food Program', www.oilforfoodfacts.org/smuggling.aspx.

Independent Inquiry Committee into the United Nations Oil-for-Food Programme, The Impact of the Oil-for-Food Programme on the Iraqi People: Report of an independent Working Group established by the Independent Inquiry Committee (September 7, 2005), www.iic-offp.org/documents/Sept05/WG_Impact.pdf.

Independent Inquiry Committee into the United Nations Oil-for-Food Programme, Report on the Manipulation of the Oil-for-Food Programme (October 27, 2005) http://www.iic/offp.org/documents./IIC%20Final%Report%2027Oct2005.pdf.

Independent Inquiry Committee into the United Nations Oil-for-Food Programme, 'Independent Inquiry Committee', www.iic-offp.org.

Independent Inquiry Committee into the United Nations Oil-for-Food Programme, Interim Report (February 3, 2005), www.iic-offp.org/documents/InterimReport-Feb2005.pdf.

Independent Inquiry Committee into the United Nations Oil-for-Food Programme, Report on the Management of the Oil-for-Food Programme (September 7, 2005), www.iic-offp.org/Mgmt_Report.htm.

Independent Inquiry Committee into the United Nations Oil-for-Food Programme, Second Interim Report (March 29, 2005), www.iic-offp.org/documents/InterimReportMar2005.pdf.

Independent Inquiry Committee into the United Nations Oil-for-Food Programme, Third Interim Report (August 8, 2005), www.iic-offp.org/documents/Third%20Interim%20Report.pdf.

Interim report of the Secretary-General on the United Nations Iran-Iraq Military Observer Group (UN Secretariat Document S/20242), October 25, 1988.

In larger freedom: towards development, security and human rights for all: report of the Secretary-General (UN General Assembly Document A/59/2005), March 21, 2005.

Letter dated 22 September 1980 from the Charge d'affaires a.i. of the Permanent Mission of Iraq to the United Nations addressed to the Secretary-General (UN Security Council Document S/14191), September 22, 1980.

Letter dated 87/08/11 from the Permanent Representative of the Islamic Republic of Iran to the United Nations addressed to the Secretary-General (UN Document S/19031), August 11, 1987.

Letter dated 87/09/18 from the deputy head of the delegation of the Union of Soviet Socialist Republics to the 42nd session addressed to the Secretary-General (UN General Assembly-Security Council Document A/42/574-S/19143), September 18, 1987.

Letter dated 90/08/17 from the Permanent Representative of the Islamic Republic of Iran to the United Nations addressed to the Secretary-General (UN Document S/21556), August 17, 1990.

Letter dated 91/04/02 from the Permanent Representative of Turkey to the United Nations addressed to the President of the Security Council (UN Document S/22435), April 3, 1991.

Letter dated 91/04/04 from the Permanent Representative of the Islamic Republic of Iran to the United Nations addressed to the Secretary-General (UN Document S/22447), April 4, 1991.

Letter dated 91/05/30 from the Secretary-General addressed to the President of the Security Council (UN Document S/22663), May 31, 1991.

Letter dated 91/07/15 from the Secretary-General addressed to the President of the Security Council (Annex) (UN Secretariat Document S/22799), July 17, 1991.

Letter dated 96/09/03 from the Chargé d'affaires a.i. of the Permanent Mission of the United States of America to the United Nations addressed to the President of the Security Council (UN Security Council Document S/1996/711), September 3, 1996.

Letter dated 98/02/25 from the Secretary-General addressed to the President of the Security Council (UN Security Council Document S/1998/166), February 27, 1998.

Letter dated 98/03/27 from the Executive Chairman of the Special Commission established by the Secretary-General pursuant to paragraph 9 (b) (i) of Security Council resolution 687 (1991) addressed to the President of the Security Council (UN Security Council Document S/1998/278), March 27, 1998.

Letter dated 98/08/05 from the Executive Chairman of the Special Commission established by the Secretary-General pursuant to paragraph 9 (b) (i) of Security Council resolution 687 (1991) addressed to the President of the Security Council (UN Security Council Document S/1998/719), August 5, 1998.

Letter dated 98/12/15 from the Secretary-General addressed to the President of the Security Council (UN Security Council Document S/1998/1172), December 15, 1998.

Letter dated 99/03/27 from the Chairman of the panels established pursuant to the note by the President of the Security Council of 30 January 1999 (S/1999/100) addressed to the President of the Security Council (UN Security Council Document S/1999/356), March 30, 1999.

Letter dated 99/12/15 from the Secretary-General addressed to the President of the Security Council [Report of the Independent Inquiry into the Actions of the United Nations During the 1994 Genocide in Rwanda] (UN Security Council Document S/1999/1257), December 16, 1999.

Letter dated 2002/05/03 from the Deputy Permanent Representative of the United States of America to the United Nations addressed to the President of the Security Council (UN Security Council Document S/2002/515), May 3, 2002.

Letter dated 2002/11/13 from the Secretary-General addressed to the President of the Security Council (UN Security Council Document S/2002/1242), November 13, 2002.

Letter dated 2004/02/19 from the Chairman of the Security Council Committee established pursuant to resolution 1373 (2001) concerning counter-terrorism addressed to the President of the Security Council (UN Security Council Document S/2004/124), February 19, 2004.

Letter dated 2004/02/23 from the Secretary-General to the President of the Security Council (UN Security Council Document S/2004/140), February 23, 2004.

Letter dated 2004/03/18 from the Secretary-General addressed to the President of the Security Council (UN Security Council Document S/2004/225), March 19, 2004.

Letter dated 2004/10/25 from the Secretary-General addressed to the President of the Security Council (UN Security Council Document S/2004/831), October 25, 2004.

Note [on the establishment of an informal working group on improving the effectiveness of United Nations sanctions] (UN Security Council Document S/2000/319), April 17, 2000.

Note [on the Summit Meeting of the Security Council to be held on 31 January 1992] (UN Security Council Document S/23500), January 31, 1992.

Note [transmitting report of the High-level Panel on Threats, Challenges and Change, entitled 'A more secure world: our shared responsibility'] (UN General Assembly Document A/59/565), December 2, 2004.

Note [transmitting report on the status of the implementation of the Special Commission's plan for the ongoing monitoring and verification of Iraq's compliance with relevant parts of section C of Security Council resolution 687 (1991)] (UN Security Council Document S/1995/864), October 11, 1995.

Note [transmitting the 21st quarterly report on the activities of the UN Monitoring, Verification and Inspection Commission, in accordance with para. 12 of Security Council resolution 1284 (1999)] (UN Security Document S/2005/351), May 27, 2005.

Note [transmitting the organizational plan for the UN Monitoring, Verification and Inspection Commission (UNMOVIC) prepared by the Executive Chairman] (UN Secretariat Document S/2000/292), April 6, 2000.

Presidential Statement, 'The situation between Iraq and Kuwait' UN Doc. S/PRST/1998/1, January 14, 1998.

Press Statement by Security Council President on Iraq Elections (UN Secretariat Document SC/8303-IK/477), February 1, 2005.

Provisional verbatim record of the 2902nd meeting (UN Security Council Document S/PV.2902), December 23, 1989.

Provisional verbatim record of the 2982nd meeting (UN Security Council Document S/PV.2982), April 5, 1991.

Provisional verbatim record of the 3046th meeting (UN Security Council Document S/PV.3046), January 31, 1992.

Provisional verbatim record of the 3105th meeting (UN Security Council Document S/PV.3105), August 11, 1992.

Report and recommendations made by the Panel of Commissioners concerning the fifth instalment of 'F4' claims (UN Security Council Document S/AC.26/2005/10), June 30, 2005.

'Report of the Independent Panel on the Safety and Security of UN Personnel in Iraq', Independent Panel on the Safety and Security of the United Nations Personnel in Iraq, October 20, 2003.

'Report of the International Advisory and Monitoring Board of the Development Fund for Iraq', IAMB, December 14, 2004, www.iamb.info/pdf/IAMBreport.pdf.

Report of the Secretary-General on the implementation of operative paragraph 2 of Security Council resolution 598 (1987) (UN Secretariat Document S/20093), August 7, 1988.

Report of the Secretary-General on the United Nations Interim Administration Mission in Kosovo (UN Security Council Document S/1999/779), July 12, 1999.

Report of the Secretary-General on the United Nations Iran-Iraq Military Observer Group (UN Secretariat Document S/20442), February 2, 1989.

Report of the Secretary-General pursuant to General Assembly resolution 53/35: the fall of Srebrenica (UN General Assembly Document A/54/549), November 15, 1999.

Report of the Secretary-General pursuant to paragraph 5 of the Security Council resolution 706 (1991) (UN Secretariat Document S/23006), September 4, 1991.

Report of the Secretary-General Pursuant to Paragraph 6 of Security Council Resolution 1210 (1998) (Introductory Statement) (UN Secretariat Document S/1999/187), February 22, 1999.

Report of the Secretary-General pursuant to paragraph 19 of Security Council resolution 687 (1991) (UN Secretariat Document S/22559), May 2, 1991.

Report of the Secretary-General pursuant to paragraph 24 of Security Council resolution 1483 (2003) (UN Security Council Document S/2003/715), July 17, 2003.

'Report of the Security in Iraq Accountability Panel (SIAP)', Security in Iraq Accountability Panel, March 3, 2004.

Report of the specialists appointed by the Secretary-General to investigate allegations by the Islamic Republic of Iran concerning the use of chemical weapons (UN Security Council Document S/16433), March 26, 1984.

Report on humanitarian needs in Iraq in the immediate post-crisis environment by a mission to the area led by the Under-Secretary-General for Administration and Management, 10–17 March 1991 (UN Document S/22366), March 20, 1991.

Report on the situation of human rights in Iraq (UN Document E/CN.4/1992/31), February 18, 1992.

Secretary-General's press encounter with his Special Representative for Iraq, Ashraf Qazi, July 22, 2004, www.un.org/apps/sg/offthecuff.asp?nid=619.

Security Council, 54th year: 4084th meeting (UN Security Council Document S/PV.4084), December 17, 1999.

Security Council, 55th year: 4128th meeting (UN Security Council Document S/PV.4128), April 17, 2000.

Security Council, 57th year: 4644th meeting (UN Security Council Document S/PV.4644), November 8, 2002.

Security Council, 58th year: 4707th meeting (UN Security Council Document S/PV.4707), February 14, 2003.

Security Council, 58th year: 4721st meeting (UN Security Council Document S/PV.4721), March 19, 2003.

Sevan, Benon V., Letter of resignation, August 7, 2005.

Situation of human rights in Iraq: note (UN Document A/47/367), August 10, 1992, November 13, 1992 (Addendum).

Statement by the President of the Security Council (UN Security Council Document S/PRST/2004/42), November 6, 2004.

Statement [on the item entitled 'The situation between Iraq and Kuwait'] (UN Security Council Document S/PRST/1998/1), January 14, 1998.

Statement from the Secretary-General on the Iraqi Elections, 30 January 2005, www.un.org/apps/sg/sgstats.asp?nid=1284.

'Third progress report of the Secretary-General on the United Nations operation in Côte d'Ivoire' (UN Security Council Document S/2004/962), December 9, 2004.

Transcript of Press Conference by Secretary-General Javier Pérez de Cuéllar at Headquarters (UN Secretariat Document SG/SM/3956), January 13, 1987.

Transcript of press conference by Secretary-General Kofi Annan at United Nations Headquarters (UN Secretariat Document SG/SM/9281), April 28, 2004.

Transcript of Press Conference by Secretary-General Kofi Annan at United Nations Headquarters (UN Secretariat Document SG/SM/9664), January 3, 2005.

CASELAW

Aerial Incident of July 3, 1988 (Islamic Republic of Iran v. United States of America), International Court of Justice, February 22, 1996.

Case Concerning Oil Platforms (Islamic Republic of Iran v. United States of America), International Court of Justice, November 6, 2003.

Hamdi et al. v. Rumsfeld, Secretary of Defense, et al., US Supreme Court, No. 03-6696, June 28, 2004.

Rasul et al. v. Bush, President of the United States, et al., US Supreme Court, No. 03-334, June 28, 2004.

Rumsfeld, Secretary of Defense v. Padilla et al., US Supreme Court, No. 03-1027, June 28, 2004.

Territorial Dispute (Libyan Arab Jamahiriya v. Republic of Chad), International Court of Justice, February 13, 1994.

Index